THE GENERAL ASSEMBLY OF THE UNITED NATIONS

SYDNEY D. BAILEY

BOOKS (Author)

A Short Political Guide to the United Nations. London: Pall Mall. New York: Praeger, 1963.

The Secretariat of the United Nations. London: Pall Mall. New York: Praeger, second edition, 1964. Arabic edition in preparation.

British Parliamentary Democracy. London: Harrap. Boston: Houghton Mifflin, 2nd edition, 1962. Arabic edition in preparation.

Naissance de Nouvelles Démocraties. Paris: Armand Colin, 1953.

Parliamentary Government in Southern Asia. London: Hansard Society. New York: Institute of Pacific Relations, 1953.

Ceylon. London: Hutchinson's University Library, 1952.

BOOKS (Edited)

Aspects of American Government. London: Hansard Society, 1950.

Parliamentary Government in the Commonwealth. London: Hansard Society. New York: Philosophical Library, 1951.

The British Party System. London: Hansard Society. New York: Praeger, second edition, 1953.

Problems of Parliamentary Government in Colonies. London: Hansard Society, 1953.

The Future of the House of Lords. London: Hansard Society. New York: Praeger, 1954.

PAMPHLETS

United Europe. London: National News-letter, second edition, 1948.

The Palace of Westminster. London: Hansard Society, 1949.

Constitutions of British Colonies. London: Hansard Society, 1950.

The Korean Crisis. London: National Peace Council, 1950.

Lords and Commons. London: H.M. Stationery Office, 1951.

Parliamentary Government. London: British Council, second edition, 1958.

The Troika and the Future of the U.N. New York: Carnegie Endowment for International Peace, 1962.

Sydney D. Bailey

THE GENERAL
ASSEMBLY OF THE
UNITED NATIONS

A Study of Procedure and Practice

Revised Edition

*Published under the auspices of the
Carnegie Endowment for International Peace*

FREDERICK A. PRAEGER, *Publishers*
New York • Washington • London

FREDERICK A. PRAEGER, *Publishers*
111 Fourth Avenue, New York 3, N.Y., U.S.A.
77-79 Charlotte Street, London W.1, England

First published in the United States of America in 1960
by Frederick A. Praeger, Inc., Publishers

Revised edition published in 1964

Library of Congress Catalog Card Number: 64-22485

Printed in the United States of America

CONTENTS

APPENDICES

TABLES

PREFACE

TO THE READER—I have undertaken a subject that I am very sensible requires one of more sufficiency than I am master of to treat it as, in truth, it deserves . . . but since bunglers may stumble upon the game as well as masters, though it belongs to the skilful to hunt and catch it, I hope this essay . . . may provoke abler pens to improve and perform the design with better judgment and success.*

WILLIAM PENN

WHENEVER a new institution of social and political co-operation is born, there are those who are sceptical. I have no doubt that some medieval Englishmen complained that Parliament was the fad of a few muddle-headed idealists. It had no real power to enforce its decisions; members talked too much; it wasted the tax-payers' money; it interfered in matters which were essentially within the jurisdiction of the counties; it was hamstrung by the royal veto.

I expect there were also a few enthusiastic supporters of Parliament, who would have killed it with kindness. They had infinite faith in its ability to solve problems, and when it was by-passed, they did the medieval equivalent of writing to the newspapers.

Parliament was able to survive the scorn of the doubters and the zeal of the supporters because it was a necessary institution, in the sense that if it had not evolved fortuitously, it would have been necessary to invent it. It also had the capacity to change.

The United Nations is a necessary institution, and it has managed to survive in our tumultuous world because it has been able to

* This quotation and those at the head of each Chapter are taken from *An Essay Towards the Present and Future Peace of Europe by the Establishment of an European Diet, Parliament, or Estates*, by William Penn, first published in 1693.

change. Its usefulness depends to a considerable extent on its capacity to change still further.

In this book I examine the working of the only principal organ of the United Nations of which all Member States are permanent members. This organ—the General Assembly—has been growing in importance and changing in function. Many of the merits of contemporary diplomatic processes, and also some of the disadvantages, can be seen in the General Assembly.

I am concerned primarily with procedure rather than with politics. Although good results cannot be guaranteed by good procedure, they can certainly be prevented by bad procedure. Good procedure is a lubricant rather than a fuel; it does not drive the machine, but its absence soon brings the machine to a halt, and in extreme cases can cause irreparable damage.

Procedure should be a servant and not a master. One of the requirements of a good presiding officer is that he has one blind eye, and knows when not to see. In any living organization, the formal procedure should occasionally be forgotten.

In order to forget the formal procedure, however, one must first know what it is. In the case of the General Assembly of the United Nations, the formal procedure is derived from three main sources. There is, first, the United Nations Charter itself, which cannot easily be amended. Certain provisions of the Charter, such as Article 9 concerning the composition of the Assembly and Article 18 concerning voting, determine part of the procedure of the Assembly.

I have not, in this book, examined the possibility of improving procedure by amending the Charter. Considerable flexibility of practice has been and will be possible within the present Charter.

Secondly, there are the Rules of Procedure, with the annexes; these Rules correspond to the standing orders or rules of order of parliamentary bodies.* The first annex to the Rules of Procedure consists of 'Recommendations and Suggestions' of a committee on

* The Rules of Procedure now in force are based on a draft prepared by the Executive Committee of the Preparatory Commission of the United Nations in 1945. This draft was revised by the Preparatory Commission and approved by the Assembly during the first part of the first session on a provisional basis. The Provisional Rules were amended by General Assembly resolutions 2, 15, 17, 73, 77, 87, and 88 of the first session. They were amended during the second session by resolutions 116 and 173, and the word 'Provisional' was dropped from the title. The Rules have been amended since the second session by resolutions 262 (III), 362 (IV), 377A (V), 475 (V), 689B (VII), 791 (VIII), 844 (IX), 1104 (XI), 1192 (XII), 1659 (XVI), and 1990 (XVIII).

procedure; these were approved by the General Assembly in 1949. The second annex consists of 'Recommendations' of the Assembly (1952) on certain legal and drafting questions, together with excerpts from the report of a special committee of the Assembly. The third annex consists of six Special Rules, approved by the Assembly in 1954, on the procedure for the examination of reports and petitions relating to the territory of South West Africa. These Special Rules have a particular importance since Special Rule F represents an explicit determination by the Assembly that a particular category of question is 'important', within the meaning of Article 18 (2) of the Charter, and should therefore be among the matters decided by a two-thirds majority of the Members present and voting.

Certain resolutions of the Assembly itself form a third source of procedure. Resolution 264 (III), for example, determined the conditions under which a State which is a party to the Statute of the International Court but is not a Member of the United Nations may participate in the election of judges of the Court. Resolution 1990 (XVIII) decided that in the election of the President of the General Assembly, regard should be had for equitable geographical rotation of the office among regions specified in the resolution.

Supplementing the formal and written procedures are the accepted precedents and practices. These may be usages which are now generally observed in intergovernmental assemblies, or which have been implicitly accepted by the General Assembly, or which have become established as a result of express decision or presidential ruling. Examples of usages which are now accepted in the General Assembly are:

Representatives of States which are permanent members of the Security Council are not elected to the presidency of the General Assembly.

At the beginning of each session of the Assembly, there takes place in a series of plenary meetings a General Debate in which the heads of delegations express the views of their countries.

Representatives in plenary meetings of the Assembly speak from the rostrum, while in committees they speak from their places.

Delegations sit in the English alphabetical order of the names of Member States.

The Main Committee of the Assembly concerned with

administrative and budgetary matters considers the budget estimates by means of consecutive 'readings'.

Sometimes the Assembly codifies practices and incorporates them in the Rules of Procedure. During the second session, for example, the following practices were formally codified:

> The phrase 'members present and voting', which is used in Article 18 of the Charter, means Members casting an affirmative or negative vote; Members abstaining are considered as not voting (now Rules 88 and 127).
>
> During the course of a debate, the presiding officer may announce the list of speakers and, with the consent of the Assembly or committee, declare the list closed (now part of Rules 75 and 116).
>
> If a Vice-President of the Assembly finds it necessary to be absent during a meeting of the General Committee, he may designate a member of his delegation as his substitute; a Chairman of a Main Committee shall, in case of absence, designate the Vice-Chairman of the Committee as his substitute (now part of Rule 39).

The relation of procedure to practice is analogous to that between statute law and common law. However, since reports of procedural discussions are often not included in the official records of the Assembly, knowledge of what really are the precedents or what really is the practice depends to a considerable extent on oral tradition. It is here that the role of the Secretariat is important. Sir Alfred Zimmern, writing of the League, commented that a major source of the power of the League Secretariat was in the domain of procedure.*[1]

* The references, which are numbered consecutively, are given on pages 351–368.

ACKNOWLEDGMENTS

A book of this kind is a collective effort, though I am responsible for its present form. Most of the cost of the study was met by a grant from the Rockefeller Foundation. Dean Rusk, at that time President of the Foundation, and Kenneth W. Thompson, at that time Director of the Social Sciences Division and now Vice-President of the Foundation, took a personal as well as an official interest in the study. To them, and to the trustees of the Foundation, I express my gratitude.

The research and writing was done under the auspices of the Carnegie Endowment for International Peace, and the Endowment also made a financial contribution to the project. I can think of no institution which would have provided a more congenial setting for the study. To the trustees and officers of the Endowment, and to my colleagues on the staff, I express my appreciation.

Many of the matters of procedure and practice with which this book deals are discussed and decided in private conversations outside the formal United Nations meetings. These discussions do not form part of the public record, but some knowledge of them is essential to an understanding of the way the General Assembly works. I could not have completed this study had I not been the recipient of much information and advice. I record my thanks to those who helped me in this way, and I trust that my discretion has matched their candour.

SYDNEY D. BAILEY

London,
  February 1964

I

CONTEMPORARY DIPLOMACY AND THE UNITED NATIONS

The advantage that justice has upon war is seen by the success of embassies, that so often prevent war by hearing the pleas and memorials of justice in the hands and mouths of the wronged party. . . . [But] men seek their wills by war rather than peace. . . . Though I must needs say the remedy is almost ever worse than the disease : the aggressors seldom getting what they seek, or performing, if they prevail, what they promised. . . . For that which prevents a civil war in a nation is that which may prevent it abroad, viz., justice. . . . Now if the sovereign princes . . . would . . . agree to meet by their stated deputies in a . . . parliament, and there establish rules of justice for sovereign princes to observe one to another ; and thus to meet yearly. . . . For it saves the great expense that frequent and splendid embassies require, and all their appendages of spies and intelligence, which in the most prudent governments have devoured mighty sums of money ; and that not without some immoral practices also ; such as corrupting of servants to betray their masters, by revealing their secrets. . . . I am come now to the . . . objection, that sovereign princes and states will hereby become not sovereign : a thing they will never endure. But this also, under correction, is a mistake. . . . If this be called a lessening of their power, it must be only because the great fish can no longer eat up the little ones.

WILLIAM PENN

THE United Nations is an instrument to help in building a world order based on the principles of justice and international law, but it differs greatly from the traditional diplomacy it supplements and to some extent replaces. Traditional diplomacy, during the three centuries ending in 1919, was predicated on the assumption that everything important happened in Europe or was done by Europeans; it was based on the inequality of States; diplomats and politicians agreed that problems of foreign policy were beyond the comprehension of the man-in-the-street and his wife; it was taken for granted that relations among States should be governed by power rather than law, and war was regarded as a natural extension of diplomacy; it was assumed that all negotiation, whether about the matrimonial affairs of sovereigns or the annexation of territory, should be conducted in private.

This has largely changed.

Europe's long-standing claim to centricity has been challenged. The Bolshevik Revolution in 1917, and the extension of the Communist system during and since the second world war, brought to power men with a revolutionary ideology sharply opposed to the aristocratic Europe of yesterday. The peoples of the newly-independent and still-emerging countries of Asia, Africa, and the Caribbean are determined to eliminate European colonialism. The United States was largely peopled by refugees from European oppression. Europe is not now the political centre of the world.

The two colossi of the modern age have been in rebellion against the wickedness of old-fashioned diplomacy. Wilson and Lenin, with equal fervour, denounced secret covenants, appealed to the peoples of Europe over the heads of governments, and asserted the principle of self-determination.

Nationalism has, in parts of the world, come to be regarded as more important than democracy; many people would rather have national independence than political freedom. The application of the principle of self-determination has brought into existence since the second world war some fifty new States, and Membership in the United Nations is a mark of their sovereign equality.

Each State has one vote in the General Assembly.* If two States are created where one existed before, as happened in the case of India and Pakistan, the successor States have one vote each. If two States merge, as when Egypt and Syria joined to form the United Arab Republic, the new State has one vote.

But the principle of the juridical equality of States is not consistently applied. The rule of unanimity among the permanent

---

* The Soviet Union is in an exceptional situation in that the Byelorussian and Ukrainian Soviet Socialist Republics have separate Membership in the United Nations.

members of the Security Council is clearly discriminatory; if States were really equal, all or none would have the veto.

The contraction of the world and the rise of democracy during the past century and a half has meant that every crisis is now everybody's crisis. It is not simply that foreign offices know and respond to each development in the international situation; public opinion, too, is aware of much that is happening. There may be millions who do not know the precise difference between ECOSOC and UNESCO, between the United Arab Republic and the League of Arab States; and yet these same millions may have strong, if vague, opinions about such questions as the status of Berlin, the exact location of the border between India and China, or whether the people of some colonial territory are or are not ready for independence.

Moreover, parliaments in the democratic countries now participate in the formulation of foreign policy. Wilson's experience in connection with the League of Nations, the opposition in Britain to the Hoare-Laval Pact, and (to come to a recent question) the widespread anxiety which was expressed in the parliaments of many countries about the effects of testing nuclear weapons, are examples of the influence of public and parliamentary opinion on the emphasis or direction of foreign policy.

Public opinion is not easily evaluated. Those who are most vociferous are not necessarily most wise or most representative. Foreign policy (including its military aspects) is the one subject on which governments reach decisions on the basis of information that may not be available to the general public. Because the public does not have information which a government may regard as decisive, and because laymen are necessarily given to over-simplification, public opinion may sometimes be little more than a collection of slogans.

Alexis de Tocqueville, in an oft-quoted passage, maintained that it was 'especially in the conduct of foreign relations' that democracies were 'decidely inferior' to other forms of government.

> Foreign politics demand scarcely any of those qualities which are peculiar to a democracy; they require, on the contrary, the perfect use of almost all those in which it is deficient . . . [A] democracy can only with great difficulty regulate the details of an important undertaking, persevere in a fixed design, and work out its execution in spite of serious obstacles. It cannot combine its measures with secrecy or await their consequences with patience.[2]

3

These reflections have surely been echoed by many foreign ministers.

Public opinion tends to reduce international problems to the simplest terms: to be for or against appeasement, unconditional surrender, general and complete disarmament, or the liberation of colonial peoples. And the public in the democratic West often seems to prefer the known hazards of the status quo to the unknown hazards of change. It is easy to demonstrate that to change a policy is dangerous; what is often forgotten is that it may be more dangerous not to change a policy. In an imperfect world, there is no policy that has no risks.

Ideology has intruded into modern diplomacy, so that our age is comparable to the period of the Crusades or the religious struggles of Europe. We are constantly asked to take sides, to declare ourselves for or against communism, colonialism, or constitutional democracy. These are important questions, but in international affairs they often cloak the real issues. George Bernard Shaw, writing when Russia was still governed by Tsar Nicholas II, based his plea for an international organization to maintain peace on the assumption (which at the time was regarded as slightly subversive) that international problems after the first world war would not differ essentially from those that had existed before, and indeed had caused, that war.

> Russia will still burn to protect the Balkans ... to cling to Poland like a big brother, and to pick up more of the White Man's Burden in Asia than the other Powers may think healthy for her, or than India, for instance, may be disposed to cast on any shoulders but her own.[3]

Although ideological differences may aggravate political conflicts, most of the conflicts would have been there anyway. The strategic interests of Russia, India, or China are affected but little by the ideology of their rulers.

The strongly ideological character of the contemporary world has, however, retarded progress towards greater reliance on the rule of law in international relations. Secretary-General Hammarskjold drew attention to this on many occasions, especially in the introductions to his annual reports. He pointed out that nations have been slow to submit their juridical disputes to the International Court of Justice and that fewer than half of the parties to the Statute of the

4

Court have accepted the Court's compulsory jurisdiction. Hammarskjold repeatedly pleaded for the greatest possible restriction of the sphere where sheer strength is an argument and for the extension of the area ruled by considerations of law and justice.[4]

But although international law has not played as significant a role as the founders of the League of Nations and the United Nations had hoped, there has been a remarkable proliferation of agencies for international co-operation, particularly to help the less privileged people of the world; slaves, refugees, victims of war or natural disaster, the homeless and the hungry, the ignorant and the diseased. Such humanitarian action is not wholly disinterested; governments may act from moral principles, but they are rarely moved by compassion. It is realized, however, that bad economic and social conditions breed the instability and discontent which so often lead to international tension and trouble. The urge to save succeeding generations from the scourge of war requires not only the concept of the fire brigade, by which the flames of conflict are extinguished; it requires also vigilant efforts to remove the causes of fire.

The rapid development of science and technology has had important effects on diplomacy. The ease of communication in the modern world has enabled governments to learn almost instantly of troublesome incidents abroad which, in former times, would have cleared themselves up before all but a few could do anything about it. 'So much becomes unimportant', Dean Acheson has written, 'if one does not know about it for months or years.'[5] Moreover, it is not only information that can be transmitted rapidly to any part of the globe; foreign ministers and heads of government can travel almost as fast. The ease and speed of communication, which make possible the summit diplomacy of political leaders, have affected the role of professional diplomats.

There is another and more important respect in which scientific and technological development has affected contemporary diplomacy. Every generation considers that the problems it faces are uniquely grave; ours is no exception. No doubt there have been other times in history when wise men thought that civilization was at stake, but the undeniable fact about the contemporary international situation is that mistakes are more costly than they have ever been before. Since the dawn of history, men have fought for the things they valued and have progressively become more efficient at fighting, but as weapons have become more destructive, to threaten their use

5

has become more risky. Until our day, it was possible to assume that if the diplomats failed, the generals could take over; today war is anachronistic and self-defeating. Some of today's difficulties, to be sure, are the consequence of yesterday's mistakes; others are the consequence of today's successes.

The desert, which could blossom as the rose, has been a place for testing weapons which civilized men should shrink from using. 'We prepare for war like precocious giants', said Lester B. Pearson in his Nobel Peace Prize lecture, 'and for peace like retarded pygmies.'[6]

Foreign policy partakes of the imperfections of all politics. Though a government may willingly affirm its support for certain general principles of international conduct, its foreign policy consists in large measure of improvised responses to external events which in some degree are thought to affect the national interest. These responses may be based in part on consistent standards, but perhaps the outstanding fact about them is that they are always compromises; compromises between conflicting principles, compromises between different political and social pressures within a country, compromises between various departmental interests within a government, compromises between the need to avoid injuring too severely the interests of hostile or potentially hostile States on the one hand and the need to placate friendly or potentially friendly States on the other. In this sense, foreign policies tend to be impure, questions are rarely decided on their intrinsic merits, and few public statements of foreign policy can be taken entirely at face value.

Diplomacy has been described as the process of seeking international compromises out of national compromises. A communiqué from a diplomatic conference may often seem vague, platitudinous, and evasive, but this is inevitable. What is left out is often more important than what is put in. Moreover, the words that are public may represent only the visible part of an iceberg, of which the larger and more significant part is hidden from view. A resolution of the General Assembly may be much less important than the fact that an issue has been publicly debated; and the public debate may have been much less important than the fact that the issue was privately discussed.

It was never intended that the United Nations should disavow the principle of privacy, nor that its own procedures for public debate should be a substitute for negotiation. The lure of public debate, with the temptation to establish before the world the guilt of others, with the tendency to dramatization and exaggeration, is not wholly harmful. It may, on occasion, release tension by enabling leaders of States to verbalize their anxieties. But public debate is no substitute for negotiation and is sometimes a bad prelude to it. Lester B. Pearson has put the matter this way:

> The United Nations is a place where we can meet either to settle problems or to make settlement more difficult. It is a place where we can try to find collective solutions, or one which we can use to get support and publicity for purely national solutions. It is a place where we can talk to each other with a view to securing general agreement, or to television and radio audiences in order to explain that disagreement is the fault of somebody else. . . .
>
> But the United Nations has, or it should have, a private as well as a public face. There should be opportunities here for other than public appearances. . . .
>
> It is, of course, essential that all free peoples should know and understand the great issues of policy which may mean life or death to them. But it is not essential, as I see it—indeed it is often harmful—for the negotiation of policy always to be conducted in glass houses. . . .[7]

'Parliamentary Diplomacy'

There was no moment in time when traditional diplomacy was dramatically cast aside and something new put in its place. Many of the methods of traditional diplomacy are still used. But within the past fifty years new institutional methods have been developed to help in managing the relations among States. The League of Nations and the United Nations, and the related technical agencies, have performed mainly new tasks in mainly new ways.

In point of time, the first important change in diplomatic method was the wide acceptance of the idea of public debate of diplomatic questions.

> The real underlying conception of the assembly . . . is that it is the forum of opinion. . . . It is the debating body; it is the body where the thought of the little nation along with the thought of the big nation is brought to bear upon . . . those matters which affect the good understanding between nations upon which the peace of the world depends; where the stifled voice of humanity

is at last to be heard, where nations that have borne the unspeakable sufferings of the ages that must have seemed to them like aeons will find voice and expression, where the moral judgment of mankind can sway the opinion of the world.

The assembly was created in order that anybody that purposed anything wrong should be subjected to the awkward circumstance that everybody could talk about it.[8]

This was how Woodrow Wilson described the Assembly of the League of Nations.

It is relatively easy to pass from the idea of public debate to the idea that the debate should be terminated by a vote. The principle of the sovereign equality of the Members of the United Nations is the basis for giving equal voting rights to the Members, irrespective of size or power. Indeed, it is theoretically possible for States paying less than six per cent of the regular budget of the United Nations to secure a two-thirds vote in the General Assembly.* The five permanent members of the Security Council, together with the Byelorussian and Ukrainian Republics, pay more than two-thirds of the regular budget.

The principle of 'one Member, one vote' may occasionally produce anomalous results, but so can any system of voting. The only alternative to equality of voting is inequality of voting, which would require that each State should be given a number of votes determined by such factors as population, area, and financial contribution to the budget of the United Nations. It is not difficult to devise systems of voting to give extra weight to powerful, rich, or large countries (such systems are, in fact, used in some intergovernmental organizations), but at least it should be said that a sense of international responsibility is not a monopoly of powerful, rich, or large countries.[9] Time and again in the affairs of the United Nations, medium and small powers have played a decisive role in efforts to preserve or restore peace.

> I do not believe [said Dag Hammarskjold] that the small nations have less of an understanding of central political problems of concern to the whole world than those who are more closely related to them and who traditionally wield greater power in the international councils. For that reason, I cannot . . . share the view of those who regard the possible influence of smaller Powers as a danger. . . .[10]

* The basis of assessment is explained on pages 207–8.

It is the practice of public debate, followed by voting, which has given to so much of contemporary multilateral diplomacy its 'parliamentary' character, yet the General Assembly is not a parliament. In the parliaments of those countries where the democratic tradition is firmly entrenched, sharp differences of opinion can safely be revealed and even exaggerated because the parties tacitly accept that politics is a game which should be played according to certain rules: the issues may be important, but disagreement is unlikely to lead to mortal danger. The situation is different in international politics: the rules themselves are often in question, and disagreement can be disastrous. Most national legislatures operate within precisely defined limits, geographical and constitutional; the limits within which the General Assembly operates are blurred and constantly changing. Most national legislatures function in relation to a known political executive which exercises leadership; the leadership in the General Assembly changes from issue to issue, and there is no political executive comparable to a national cabinet. When national legislatures resort to voting, it is normally to resolve a difference of opinion; a vote in the General Assembly on a contentious political question often expresses and emphasizes, rather than resolves, differences of opinion.

Sir Harold Nicolson has suggested that the new methods of diplomacy, which are symbolized by public debate and voting, developed from the belief that what had worked well in internal affairs ought to work well in external affairs.

> It was not the telephone that, from 1919 onwards, brought about the transition from the old diplomacy to the new. It was the belief that it was possible to apply to the conduct of *external* affairs, the ideas and practices which, in the conduct of *internal* affairs, had for generations been regarded as the essentials of liberal democracy.[11]

Whether or not one agrees that this is the sole explanation of a complex development, it is surely significant that increasingly there have come into use in international affairs a number of expressions derived from domestic politics: 'democratic foreign policy', 'the legislative power of the General Assembly', 'parliamentary diplomacy'.*

* Tickets for admission to United Nations, meetings bear the following note: 'In accordance with parliamentary procedure, visitors are requested to refrain from applause. . . .'

9

The term 'parliamentary diplomacy' was coined by Dean Rusk to describe a form of multilateral negotiation involving the following factors:

> First, a continuing organization with interest and responsibilities which are broader than the specific items that happen to appear upon the agenda at any particular time—in other words, more than a traditional international conference called to cover specific agenda. Second, regular public debate exposed to the media of mass communication and in touch, therefore, with public opinions around the globe. Third, rules of procedure which govern the process of debate and which are themselves subject to tactical manipulation to advance or oppose a point of view. And lastly, formal conclusions, ordinarily expressed in resolution, which are reached by majority votes of some description, on a simple or two-thirds majority or based upon a financial contribution or economic stake—some with and some without a veto. Typically, we are talking about the United Nations and its related organizations, although not exclusively so, because the same type of organization is growing up in other parts of the international scene.[12]

The process described by Mr Rusk is in some respects akin to the procedures of a democratic legislature of the Western type. In its original form, derived from the French *parler* and retained in the English 'parley', the word 'parliamentary' conveys the idea of discussion and negotiation, but more should not be read into the expression than Mr Rusk intended.

The practice of 'parliamentary diplomacy' brings with it the danger of 'diplomatic oratory'. It has been said that speeches may change opinions, but they never change votes. The fact is that in many cases nowadays, speeches are not meant primarily for the ears of the diplomats who hear them.

> We addressed our speeches [wrote Trotsky of the Brest-Litovsk negotiations] to the war-weary workers of all countries. . . . When speaking to Kühlmann and Czernin, we all the time had in our mind's eye our friends and comrades, Karl Liebknecht and Fritz Adler.
> We made it the task of our diplomacy to enlighten the masses of the people, to open their eyes to the real meaning of the policy of their governments, in order to weld them together in a common struggle.[13]

Fifty years later, this is a commonplace of the diplomatic process. Speeches and votes are directed not only to other delegations and governments, but to the unseen millions.

There is another factor that encourages diplomatic oratory. A study of the United Nations prepared in Canada makes this comment:

> The delegates of the Member States are appointed by their governments, and whether or not they wish to be reappointed, many of them aspire to a public career of some kind which may well be furthered by their performance at the Assembly. A politician or official . . . , presented with a chance to appear on a world stage, naturally strives to make the most of it in the interest of increasing his reputation in his own country. . . . Opportunities for such indulgence are all too plentiful.[14]

It was an outstanding contribution of Dag Hammarskjold to insist that 'parliamentary diplomacy' should not exclude quiet diplomacy.

> The [United Nations] Organization should be more than an instrument of what may be described as conference diplomacy. . . . We find introduced in conference diplomacy an aspect of propaganda and an element of rigidity which may be harmful to sound negotiation. . . . This new diplomacy . . . is not . . . sufficient for the efforts towards understanding and reconciliation which are of such importance now. . . . The legislative process in the United Nations . . . serves its purpose only when it helps diplomacy to arrive at agreements. . . . It is diplomacy, not speeches and votes, that continues to have last the word in the process of peace-making.[15]

Public diplomacy has its uses, provided it is carried on in the right way and at the right time. Debate can sometimes play a role in promoting conciliation; in the last resort, however, the reconciliation of differences which leads to a meeting of minds, or at least an accommodation of interests, usually takes place in an atmosphere of quiet, where there is no gallery to play to. The drama of public discussion, the clashes of temperament and tradition, the cut and thrust of debate—these may provide exciting copy for the journalists, but they sometimes frustrate the adjustments of view and the compromises which are, after all, the final purposes of diplomacy.

Elements of Continuity in 'Parliamentary Diplomacy'

Mr Rusk gives as the first essential feature of 'parliamentary diplomacy' the idea of a continuing organization with broader interests and responsibilities than the specific items of the agenda at any particular time. This continuity is facilitated by two new diplomatic institutions: permanent diplomatic missions accredited to intergovernmental agencies, and international secretariats to service those agencies.

The Secretariat of the League of Nations was concerned that there should be orderly means for communicating with governments, and members of the League were encouraged to establish special sections on League affairs within their foreign ministries. This system, while useful, did not entirely meet the need, and in consequence governments began the practice of designating diplomatic representatives stationed in or near Geneva to act in a liaison capacity with the League. Poland was the first member of the League to establish a permanent liaison office in Geneva. By 1922, ten League members had established offices in Geneva, and fifteen others had designated diplomatic representatives in other cities to maintain contact with League affairs. States which were not members of the League, such as Germany (before 1926) and the United States, often designated the Consul or Consul-General in Geneva as having special duties regarding liaison with the League. Delegations to maintain contact with the League were occasionally maintained in Geneva or Paris by governments in exile (for example, Armenia and the Ukraine).

There was no uniformity of title or method of appointment of these 'permanent delegations', as they were usually termed. Some were accredited to the Secretary-General and some to the Secretariat, while others were not 'accredited' to the League in any formal sense. The Secretary-General was often, but not invariably, informed of their appointment, either by the government or by the person appointed. Those diplomatic representatives who were stationed permanently in Geneva enjoyed diplomatic privileges and immunities. They were often referred to as the *corps diplomatique*, but it was not until the early 1930s that they were constituted as a formal *corps diplomatique*, with a *doyen*, and were received as a corporate body by the Secretary-General

The most important function of the permanent delegations was to act as a channel of communication between the League Secretariat and the governments. In a few cases, they also acted as national representatives to organs of the League. Some of the permanent delegates acquired considerable expertise regarding the inner workings of the League. They maintained close contact with officials of the Secretariat, but Francis P. Walters comments in his history of the League that 'the system of Permanent Delegations was of no serious significance in League history'.[16] This judgment could not be applied to the permanent diplomatic missions attached to the United Nations.

The Charter of the United Nations made no provision for permanent diplomatic representation of Member States, but the fact that the Security Council 'shall be so organized as to be able to function continuously' meant that at least eleven of the original fifty-one Member States had to maintain continuous representation at the seat of the Organization. Members of the other two Councils and of various subsidiary organs soon established similar forms of permanent representation. By May 1948, forty-one out of fifty-eight Member States had submitted to the Secretary-General lists of persons who were members of permanent delegations.

At the time of the most recent report of the Secretary-General (11 December 1963), all Member States had set up permanent missions at the seat of the United Nations, and all except Argentina, Honduras, Mauritania, Saudi Arabia, Spain, and Togo had transmitted credentials of their Permanent Representatives to the Secretary-General. In sixteen cases the Permanent Representative also acted as ambassador in Washington. The Byelorussian and Ukrainian Soviet Socialist Republics have a joint office in New York with the Soviet Union. The Federal Republic of Germany, the Republic of Korea, Monaco, Switzerland, and the Republic of Viet-Nam, though not Members of the United Nations, maintain permanent observers in New York to keep in touch with United Nations affairs. The status of these representatives is imprecise, but they are granted facilities to carry on their function of observation.

It is a normal diplomatic practice for a State to obtain the *agréation*, or prior agreement, that any diplomatic agent to be appointed is acceptable to the State to which he will be accredited. In the case of the United Nations, no such practice is followed. In 1949 the Secretary-General suggested a standard form of credentials, but there is no question of the Secretary-General granting or withholding recognition to the Permanent Representative of a Member

13

State. Questions relating to the credentials of representatives are decided by United Nations organs, on the basis of a report from a credentials committee in the case of the Assembly, the President and Vice-Presidents in the case of the Economic and Social Council, and the Secretary-General in the case of the Security Council and the Trusteeship Council.

After assuming his post, a Permanent Representative presents his credentials to the Secretary-General; there is a brief ceremony of presentation. The practice of leaving calling cards on members of the United Nations diplomatic corps and senior officials of the Secretariat has been discontinued, but it is customary for a newly-appointed Permanent Representative to call on the President of any principal organ which is in session when he assumes his duties. In addition, a Permanent Representative informs other Permanent Representatives in writing when he has presented his credentials and assumed his duties. Permanent Representatives and other members of permanent missions are entitled to diplomatic privileges and immunities.[17]

A regular nomenclature has been established. Diplomatic missions of Member States attached to the United Nations are known as 'Permanent Missions',* and the head of each Mission is known as 'Permanent Representative to the United Nations'. The 'Permanent Representative' usually has the rank of Ambassador Extraordinary and Plenipotentiary. The representatives of a Member State to the General Assembly comprise its delegation. A General Assembly delegation normally includes the staff of the Permanent Mission, together with a number of foreign service officers and other officials. More than half of the delegations to the General Assembly are lead by heads of government or foreign ministers during the first month or so of the session. Some Member States, such as Canada, Sweden, and the United States, include members of the legislature as delegates or observers.

There has taken place a steady development of the functions of the Permanent Missions. Some of the newer nations, which do not yet have fully developed diplomatic services and are perhaps represented in a dozen or even fewer foreign capitals, can keep in touch

* I am told that there has occasionally been confusion between Permanent Missions and Visiting Missions of the Trusteeship Council, and a Trusteeship Council Visiting Mission has reported that in one Trust Territory 'the name "Visiting Mission" is often confused with religious missions'.[18]

with more than one hundred governments through their Permanent Missions at United Nations headquarters. In cases where diplomatic relations have been severed, representatives in New York can engage in informal contacts and discussions. The Secretary-General can readily communicate, either formally or informally, with Member States through their Permanent Representatives. National representatives at United Nations headquarters are often able to find out from members of the Secretariat the trend of thinking on international questions. There are permanently in New York more than eight hundred members of the diplomatic corps, constituting what Hammarskjold called 'a standing diplomatic conference'. Personal intimacy and understanding often develop among the staffs of these Permanent Missions, even across the most substantial political barriers. 'Perhaps the most important result of conducting diplomacy by conference', wrote Lord Hankey, 'is the knowledge responsible statesmen acquire of one another.'[19]

The existence of Permanent Missions at United Nations headquarters makes possible continuous discussion and negotiation on a variety of questions and can facilitate the preparation for meetings of the General Assembly and other United Nations bodies. Informal discussions can take place between delegations, within groups of delegations, and between delegations and the Secretariat, on such matters as the choice of officers and the planning of the agenda. The presence at headquarters of the Permanent Missions of Member States has facilitated the development of regional and ideological groups. Proposals for United Nations action are often given 'trial runs' in the groups, and are later presented to an official organ of the United Nations in an amended and more widely acceptable form.

The advantages of having Permanent Missions attached to the United Nations are obvious, but two potential difficulties should be mentioned. When expert or technical bodies are created by one of the principal organs, it is desirable that the members should have a special competence regarding the work to be done. Since almost all governments have too few officials chasing too much work, it is tempting to designate as a representative on a United Nations technical body a diplomatic officer who happens to be stationed wherever the body will meet. Thus a member of a Permanent Mission in New York may find himself an expert on colonialism in February, international commodity trade in April, and outer space in June. All matters dealt with by the United Nations bear some

Security Council to situations which are likely to endanger international peace and security; and it may make recommendations.[26]

In spite of limitations on its authority to take binding decisions, the Assembly has assumed a leading position in the United Nations system and has interpreted broadly its powers under the Charter. It has on four occasions met in emergency special session to take up matters regarding which the Security Council was unable to act because of the veto, and in the Suez case it created an important precedent by authorizing the establishment of a United Nations Force to secure the cessation of hostilities.

Although the Assembly is often thought of as a parliamentary body, it lacks one of the attributes of an ordinary parliament: a continuing centre of leadership and authority. There is no cabinet, no leader of the house; there is not even a majority party. The President of the Assembly may initiate proposals of a procedural kind and help move things along behind the scenes, but he normally cannot acquire the prestige or authority of the speaker of a national parliament who holds office for many years. The General Committee of the Assembly might have provided a focus of authority, but its utility has declined as its size has increased. There has, however, emerged a group of countries reputed for their prudence and moderation, somewhat detached from the more pressing exigencies of the various ideological and power struggles. Some of these countries are influential primarily because they contribute men and money to United Nations operations, some primarily because they are recognized as spokesmen of geographical or ideological groups, some primarily because of the wisdom and integrity of those men and women who have represented them in United Nations organs. The nucleus has varied from issue to issue and from period to period, but it has included countries like Australia, Brazil, Canada, India, Ireland, Mexico, Nigeria, Norway, Pakistan, Sweden, Tunisia, the United Arab Republic, and Yugoslavia.

The Assembly has other difficulties, some of which cannot be avoided. It is a large and heterogeneous body, sometimes slow-moving and clumsy, sometimes volatile and impetuous. Excessive preoccupation with the more public manifestations of parliamentary diplomacy can divert attention from the real possibilities for using the Assembly as a centre for harmonizing the actions of nations. Moreover, some Member States have had reservations about the legal propriety or political expediency of those decisions of the Assembly which, in substance even if not in form, sought to go beyond the making of recommendations.

In emergency situations in which it has seemed unlikely that a sufficient majority can be found in either the Security Council or the General Assembly in favour of a precise course of action, there has sometimes been general agreement that the Secretary-General should be entrusted with diplomatic or operational responsibilities expressed in general terms, leaving to him the details of interpretation and implementation. This, in itself, would have added considerably to the importance of the Office, but parallel to this trend, and related to it, was the growing exercise by the Secretary-General of independent initiatives in diplomatic and related matters under the powers inherent in his Office.[27] Whether the Secretary-General acts as the agent of a policy-making body, or in response to a specific request of a government, or himself takes the initiative, he remains the servant of the Charter and must adhere to the principle that the activities of the United Nations 'are wholly dependent on decisions of the Governments'.[28] The Secretary-General and his senior colleagues should, therefore, be in constant and close touch with the representatives of Member States, both at headquarters and in the various capitals, so that relations of mutual confidence may be taken for granted.

In a number of cases it has been found helpful to create advisory committees of States to work with the Secretary-General regarding matters entrusted to him. These committees meet in private under his chairmanship, and no vote is taken. The Secretary-General sums up his conclusions, and any member of the committee is free to place on record any objection to the summary.

I have suggested elsewhere that when broad responsibilities are committed to the Secretary-General by a policy-making organ and unforeseen questions of interpretation are possible, it might be useful to have some procedure analogous to that used in a number of national political systems for the scrutiny of delegated legislation. In the United Kingdom, a representative committee of the House of Commons examines each exercise of delegated legislation with a view to determining whether the attention of the House should be drawn to it on any one of a number of grounds. These include:

1 that there appears to have been an unjustifiable delay in publishing the relevant documents;

2 that it appears to make some unusual or unexpected use of the powers conferred;

3 that for any special reason the form or purport calls for elucidation.

Such a scrutinizing procedure does not require that the merits of the original decision should be reviewed, but only that the body conferring the mandate should be informed if the authority appears to have been exercised in an unusual or unexpected way.[29]

It is also important that there should be adequate provision for top-level consultation and sharing of responsibility in the Secretariat. After U Thant had been appointed, he stated that he would designate a number of principal advisers from among his senior Secretariat colleagues and would consult them—individually, collectively, or otherwise, as occasion demanded—on important questions pertaining to the performance of functions entrusted to the Secretary-General by the Charter.[30]

No patterns of relationships and responsibilities among the different organs of the United Nations can be fixed for all time. The importance and power of the Assembly will wax and wane, but it will remain the only principal organ of the United Nations to which all Member States permanently belong, and there are some essential functions which it only can perform.

2

COALITIONS AND GROUPS IN THE GENERAL ASSEMBLY

Nor is it said the lamb shall lie down with the lion, but the lion shall lie down with the lamb.

WILLIAM PENN

ONE REASON WHY the General Assembly of the United Nations is sometimes said to resemble a parliamentary body is that there operates within it an embryonic party system. And just as political parties were once regarded as disreputable instruments for the suppression of individual liberty, so the activities of groups of States at the United Nations are occasionally condemned on the ground that moral principle is cynically sacrificed for some selfish sectional interest.

Many of the complaints about the embyronic party system at the United Nations seem to me exaggerated. It is part of the political process, national or international, governmental or non-governmental, that few disputed questions can be settled solely on what are thought to be their intrinsic merits. Indeed, it has long been a recognized diplomatic practice to link a number of questions together in order to achieve an overall settlement based on mutual compromise, and one of the problems of public diplomacy by conference is that questions have to be placed on an agenda and dealt with seriatim and seemingly in isolation.

Ordinarily, issues in diplomacy may be joined together, and in resolving problems with your friends you can give a little on one and take a little on the other. Perhaps, since many of them involve disagreeable choices, you can put a bundle of them

21

together and get a result where you will like one part and your friends will like another part, but you find some basis on which to work it out.[31]

What Mr Rusk says about resolving problems 'with your friends' applies equally to discussion and negotiation with unfriendly States.

It is a normal part of diplomacy for States to consult each other on matters of common interest, and one of the reasons why this happens rather often at United Nations headquarters is that it is rather easy. Representatives of Member States constantly meet each other, not necessarily by careful prearrangement but simply because they so often have business to discharge in the same building, eat in the same dining room, use the same elevators, patronize the same barber. There is a continual process of consultation, arranged and casual, both among friends and across barriers. Much of this consultation is not directly related to immediate and current problems of world politics. It is a normal diplomatic attempt to increase mutual understanding, to win friends and influence people, to acquire or give information.

The critics say that the crystallization of coalitions, groups, and blocs tends to deprive the Assembly of the possibility of reaching an objective and unbiased judgment. To a certain extent, this charge is true—though the situation could hardly be otherwise. The Assembly is not a body of scientists or philosophers engaged in an academic search for ultimate truth; it is not even a judicial body, pursuing justice; it is a political body, searching for the relative solutions and compromises which have merit only because the alternatives are more disagreeable.

States associate with each other to achieve the common ends which seem to them desirable. In this complex process of association, each may sacrifice something, not through cynical disregard of principle, but because they know that the national interest can be promoted only by taking account of the national interests of others. This recognition of an international interest which transcends the interests of each nation is at the basis of the United Nations Charter.

Bargaining in the lobbies of the Assembly and the capitals is, perhaps, most obvious in connection with elections. Most Assembly elections are based, explicitly or implicitly, on the representative principle. It is, of course, impossible to constitute every United

Nations organ so that it is an exact representation in miniature of the whole; the whole is too variegated. Since it would be impracticable to have every organ composed of all Member States, bodies of limited membership are set up, usually in such a way as to be broadly representative of the whole.

It has been the general experience in many realms of social and political organization that once the membership of an executive or deliberative organ exceeds about fifteen, the character of the organ begins to change. Intimacy and cohesion fade; there is a temptation to establish sub-committees; instead of discussing the business in hand, members read prepared speeches. If the effective operation of organs of limited membership were the sole factor of which account should be taken, such organs would no doubt usually be kept small. There is, however, another factor that is often of equal if not greater importance. An organ of limited membership can be successful only if it enjoys a high degree of confidence of the whole, and in practice this usually, though not invariably, means that it should contain within itself representatives of the main streams of thought of the larger body.

In the political life of democratic societies this is facilitated, albeit crudely, by the party system. In an organization of States based on the principle of sovereign equality, in which the interests of the members change and the relations among them fluctuate, a party system in the conventional sense has not evolved. Indeed, the outstanding fact about the way States associate in the General Assembly is their tendency to affiliate differently for different purposes.

Improvised or organized methods of consultation are an integral part of the ordinary processes of diplomacy. In many cases, the consultation takes place at United Nations headquarters or wherever an organ is meeting, but consultation also takes place by conventional diplomatic methods. Indeed, whenever a delegate receives changed instructions from home, he is likely to wonder whether someone has been 'getting at' his foreign ministry.

The forms of organized association which have developed at the United Nations are informal. Some of the groups, though unofficial, meet with the help of facilities provided by the Secretary-General at UN headquarters.[32] The existence of the groups is recognized in statements made on their behalf or with their authority.[33] Even the schedule of meetings may be adjusted to meet the desires or convenience of a group.[34] Informal or formal agreements about the allocation of elective places are often based in part on a regional distribution, though the regions may not correspond exactly to organized groups or blocs.

One type of association among States at the United Nations is the *ad hoc* coalition which is improvised to deal with a particular problem, whether of a long-term or short-term character, and which disappears when the problem passes or changes in character. The Spanish-speaking delegations have on a number of occasions combined to press the claims of the Spanish language in United Nations affairs. The sixteen States which contributed forces to the United Nations Command in Korea co-operated on Korean questions. States administering trust or non-self-governing territories consult each other on matters of common interest, as do the anti-colonial States. During the eleventh session (1956–57), Canada, Japan and Norway acted jointly in connexion with various disarmament matters—giving rise to good-humoured comments about 'the new Northern bloc'.

Another type of association arises when States are organized to meet in caucus, either regularly or sporadically, to exchange ideas on issues of common concern, though without any commitment to act in unison. The Latin American States, the Afro-Asian group (including the Arab and African sub-groups), and the Commonwealth, are associations of this kind. These groups have certain common organizational features. They meet roughly once every few weeks during sessions of the General Assembly, less frequently at other times of the year. They have systems for rotating the chairmanship. They discuss any matter which any member wishes to raise, and all attempt to reach the maximum of agreement without resort to voting.

The Communist States of Eastern Europe have sometimes referred to themselves as a bloc rather than a group. Too much should not be made of this distinction, but I assume that it is meant to suggest that States in a bloc not only consult each other on a systematic basis, but almost always act in unison. Thomas Hovet defines a bloc as 'a group of states which meets regularly in caucus and the members of which are bound in their votes in the General Assembly by the caucus decision. Using this definition, there is at present [1960] only one true *bloc*—the Soviet bloc. . . .'[35]

Two resolutions of the Assembly concerning the distribution of elective places have gone beyond simply endorsing the representative principle and have established patterns to govern future elections.[36] These resolutions mention four categories of States, as follows:

Latin American States
African and Asian States
Eastern European States
Western European and other States

The first three categories are regional; the reference to 'other States' in the fourth category introduces an element of imprecision. The categories do not all correspond to groups used for other United Nations purposes. For geographical distribution of the staff of the Secretariat, for example, the Secretary-General uses seven regional groups:

Latin America
Asia and the Far East
Middle East
Africa
Eastern Europe
Western Europe
North America and the Carribbean

Whatever system of grouping is used, it should be emphasized that regional groups do not necessarily comprise only States which, from a political or ideological point of view, are like-minded. I have, throughout this book, tried to use a consistent and I hope intelligible system of regional classification which is based, to the extent possible, on resolutions of the General Assembly concerning the representative character of the General Committee. Unfortunately, the system I have used, like all such systems, differs in some respects from all other such systems.

Latin America

Twenty Latin American republics are Members of the United Nations, its Economic Commission for Latin America, and the Organization of American States.* The Latin American countries

---

* The Government of Fidel Castro in Cuba is not recognized by the Organization of American States. The Assembly, by Resolution 253 (III), invited the Secretary-General of the Organization of American States to be present as an observer at sessions of the Assembly.

differ in size, in social and political organization, and in degree of economic development, and there are rivalries and antagonisms among them. However, the Latin American republics have inherited a common tradition of thought and religion, and (except for Brazil and Haiti) they use the Spanish language.

TABLE I

Latin American Member States

Argentina	Guatemala
Bolivia	Haiti
Brazil	Honduras
Chile	Mexico
Colombia	Nicaragua
Costa Rica	Panama
Cuba	Paraguay
Dominican Republic	Peru
Ecuador	Uruguay
El Salvador	Venezuela

Even before the San Francisco Conference, the Latin American States had given evidence of their intention of co-operating on United Nations affairs. A resolution on the establishment of an international organization, adopted at the Inter-American Conference held at Chapultepec in 1945, emphasized 'the desirability of giving an adequate representation to Latin America in the Security Council'.[37] The Latin American States worked closely together at the founding conference in San Francisco.

During the first session of the General Assembly in London, the Latin American States, acutely aware of their relative impotence individually, met together informally in an effort to capitalize on their joint voting strength. Initially their attention was directed to ensuring the election of as many Latin Americans as possible to key positions, by agreeing among themselves on a roster of candidates. As time passed, the 'Group' extended its activities to cover all issues of major concern. . . .

The Latin Americans are proud of their 'Group' and not without justification. It provides an opportunity for discussion and clarification of important issues and for the adoption of reasoned positions whether or not a consensus is reached.[38]

The Latin Americans elected as Vice-Presidents of the Assembly (or President and Vice-Presidents) share the chairmanship of the Latin American group. Meetings are held about once a week during the General Assembly, and about once a month at other times of the year; the group met at United Nations headquarters twenty-three times in 1962.[39] Cuba has not participated in the activities of the group since 1962.

Proceedings at meetings are relatively informal. There is free discussion, but the group does not vote or take binding decisions on important matters of substance. The one matter on which every effort is made to achieve a consensus is the nomination of persons or States from Latin America for election to United Nations organs. It has not always been possible to reach total agreement on such nominations, but lack of agreement is regarded by the group as very regrettable.

The number of Latin American Members of the United Nations has not changed since the Organization was founded, so that the relative voting strength of Latin America has declined and will continue to decline as additional States are admitted to the Organization.

In the Secretary-General's report on geographical distribution in the Secretariat in 1963, Jamaica and Trinidad and Tobago were included in the region 'North America and the Caribbean'. During the 1963 Assembly, it was suggested that in allocating the places on the General Committee, the Caribbean and Latin American States should form one category. The Latin American and Caribbean States themselves opposed this, and Jamaica and Trinidad and Tobago presumably come within the grouping 'Western European and other States'.

Africa and Asia

The Afro-Asian group at the United Nations (which includes the Arab States) drew much of its original inspiration from the Bandung Conference of 1955. Fifty-eight Member States, including Cyprus and Turkey, are associated with it, and it is the largest single organized group of Members. Three Member States of the United Nations which fall within the Afro-Asian region are not members of the group: Nationalist China, Israel, and South Africa.

The Afro-Asian group came into existence in 1950, but from the beginning there had been close consultation among Arab Member States on Middle Eastern and related questions. There were five Arab founder Members of the United Nations: Egypt, Iraq, Lebanon, Saudi Arabia, and Syria. Yemen was admitted to Membership in 1947; Jordan and Libya in 1955; Morocco, Sudan and Tunisia in 1956; Algeria in 1962; and Kuwait in 1963.

All of the Arab States which are Members of the United Nations are associated with the League of Arab States. A Palestinian representative also participates in meetings of the Council of the League, and a representative of Oman has attended recent sessions of the General Assembly and participated in the work of the Arab group when matters relating to Oman and neighbouring territories have been under consideration. The Arab League maintains an office in New York which services and co-ordinates the activities of the Arab group.* Some decisions affecting Arab States at the United Nations are taken by the Council of the Arab League. The Council has, from time to time, approved the nomination of Arab persons or States to United Nations bodies.

The Arab group normally meets about once a month, though meetings are held more frequently during the General Assembly. No votes are taken, and every effort is made to reach a consensus. The Arab group has maintained a high degree of solidarity on Middle Eastern and related questions, even during periods when the Arab States have been at odds with one another. Egypt has exercised marked leadership within the group.

Six Arab States (Algeria, Libya, Morocco, Sudan, Tunisia, and the United Arab Republic), together with twenty-eight States from Africa south of the Sahara, but excluding South Africa, form an African group. Prior to the Addis Ababa conference of May 1963, there were several different African groupings. The Brazzaville powers, which had met at Brazzaville in December 1960, comprised twelve French-speaking States closely linked with France and with associate membership of the European Common Market: Cameroon, Central African Republic, Chad, Congo (Brazzaville), Dahomey, Gabon, Ivory Coast, Madagascar, Mauritania, Niger, Senegal, and Upper Volta. The Brazzaville powers, together with Ethiopia, Liberia, Libya, Nigeria, Sierra Leone, Somalia, Togo, and Tunisia, met in Monrovia in May 1961 and established the African and Malagasy States Organization. A more radical grouping, comprising Algeria, Ghana, Guinea, Mali, Morocco, and the United Arab Republic, had met in Casablanca in January 1961.

An attempt to end the rivalries which these groupings represented was made at the Addis Ababa conference. An Organization

* The General Assembly, by Resolution 477 (V), invited the Secretary-General of the League of Arab States to attend sessions of the Assembly as an observer.

of African Unity, with its own Secretariat, was established. The members affirmed their dedication to the principles of the United Nations, asked that their members should receive larger representation in United Nations organs, and decided on means to secure better co-ordination in matters of common concern at the United Nations.

The African group meets nearly every week at United Nations headquarters. The militant anti-colonialism of some of the African States has caused some strains within the larger Afro-Asian group, and it is possible that a separate Asian sub-group will eventually emerge.

China, India, Iran, and the Philippines were the original Asian Members of the United Nations. Afghanistan and Thailand were admitted in 1946; Pakistan in 1947; Burma in 1948; Indonesia in 1950; Cambodia, Ceylon, Laos, and Nepal in 1955; Japan in 1956; Malaya in 1957; and Mongolia in 1961.

The Arab and African groups are sub-groups within the larger Afro-Asian group. The latter began on an improvised basis as an Arab-Asian group of twelve members in 1950, during the early stages of the Korean War. Those attending meetings were Afghanistan, Burma, Egypt, India, Indonesia, Iran, Iraq, Lebanon, Pakistan, Saudi Arabia, Syria, and Yemen. The Philippines and all of these countries except Syria and Lebanon consulted together on the Tunisian question in 1951. Syria and Lebanon returned to the group in 1952, and Thailand joined in 1954.

It was the Bandung Conference in 1955 that gave the group a sense of identity and purpose. Ethiopia, Liberia, and Turkey joined the same year, and the forty States of Asia and Africa (forty-one if Cyprus is included) which have been admitted to United Nations Membership since the Bandung Conference have become associated with the group.

Ten members of the Afro-Asian group were founder members of the United Nations, but the group is now the largest of the caucuses. More than half the Members of the United Nations are associated with it, and its size will increase as new States achieve independence and are admitted to the United Nations. The group met no fewer than seventy-eight times at United Nations headquarters in 1962.[40] The chairmanship rotates among the members on a monthly basis. Meetings of the group are conducted in English and French, with interpretation as necessary.

TABLE 2
African and Asian Member States

Asia	Africa south of the Sahara
Afghanistan	Burundi
Burma	Cameroon
Cambodia	Central African Republic
Ceylon	Chad
India	Congo (Brazzaville)
Indonesia	Congo (Leopoldville)
Iran	Dahomey
Japan	Ethiopia
Laos	Gabon
Malaysia	Ghana
Mongolia	Guinea
Nepal	Ivory Coast
Pakistan	Kenya
Philippines	Liberia
Thailand	Madagascar
	Mali
Arab	Mauritania
Algeria	Niger
Iraq	Nigeria
Jordan	Rwanda
Kuwait	Senegal
Lebanon	Sierra Leone
Libya	Somalia
Morocco	Tanganyika
Saudi Arabia	Togo
Sudan	Uganda
Syria	Upper Volta
Tunisia	Zanzibar
United Arab Republic	
Yemen	

not members of the Afro-Asian group

China	Israel	South Africa

One question for the future is whether the Afro-Asian group can maintain sufficient cohesion and solidarity. It now faces some of the problems with which the United Nations itself is confronted: difficulties arising from diversity of outlook, sheer size, and the fact that the pace tends to be set by the newer and more militant members.

Even if the group continues to meet on a regular basis, it is possible that an increasing amount of essential business will have to be done through regional or ideological sub-groups.

TABLE 3

*Increase in United Nations Membership in Asia and Africa**

Founder Members,

1945	1950	1958	1961
Egypt†	Indonesia	Guinea	Mauritania
Ethiopia			Mongolia
India			Sierra Leone
Iran	1955		Tanganyika
Iraq	Cambodia	1960	1962
Lebanon	Ceylon	Cameroon	Algeria
Liberia	Jordan	Central African Republic	Burundi
Philippines	Laos	Chad	Rwanda
Saudi Arabia	Libya	Congo (Brazzaville)	Uganda
Syria†	Nepal	Congo (Leopoldville)	
		Dahomey	1963
1946	1956	Gabon	Kenya
Afghanistan	Japan	Ivory Coast	Kuwait
Thailand	Morocco	Madagascar	Zanzibar
	Sudan	Mali	
1947	Tunisia	Niger	
Pakistan		Nigeria	
Yemen	1957	Senegal	
	Ghana	Somalia	
1948	Malaya	Togo	
Burma		Upper Volta	

* Excluding China, Cyprus, Israel, South Africa, and Turkey.

† Egypt and Syria joined to form the United Arab Republic in 1958; Syria resumed separate Membership in 1961.

Eastern Europe

As there has been confusion about which Members of the United Nations are in the East European region, let me say at once that I have regarded Eastern Europe as comprising the Soviet Union, including the Byelorussian and Ukrainian Soviet Socialist Republics, those East European States which are or have been members of the Warsaw Pact and the Council for Mutual Economic Assistance (COMECON), and Yugoslavia. This is to follow the practice of the Secretary-General in 1962 and 1963 when reporting to the Assembly on geographical distribution in the Secretariat.*

* During the period 1959–61, the Secretary-General included Yugoslavia in the West European region in his reports on geographical distribution in the Secretariat; when electing the Chairmen of Main Committees in 1960, the Assembly seems to have regarded Yugoslavia as one of the 'Western European and other States'.

United Nations Member States from Eastern Europe were originally six in number: the Soviet Union, the Byelorussian and Ukrainian Republics, Czechoslovakia, Poland, and Yugoslavia. Czechoslovakia became part of the Communist camp in 1948, but Yugoslavia broke with the Cominform States later that year.

The admission to the United Nations of Albania, Bulgaria, Hungary, and Romania in December 1955 increased the number of Member States associated with the Soviet Union to nine.

TABLE 4

Eastern European Member States

Albania
Byelorussian SSR
Bulgaria
Czechoslovakia
Hungary
Poland
Romania
Ukrainian SSR
USSR
Yugoslavia

While Eastern Europe as a regional group comprises the States referred to above and listed in Table 4, this is not the same as the Communist bloc—or the socialist States, as they would call themselves. Cuba and Mongolia now form part of the Communist bloc; Yugoslavia does not. Albania, though still formally part of the Warsaw Pact, left Comecon in October 1961.

The States of the Communist bloc share the Marxist ideology, but during the past decade there have been centrifugal tendencies and increasing emphasis on the right of each country to choose its own road to socialism. The dispute between the Soviet and Chinese Communist parties has affected inter-State relations, but Albania is the only Communist Member State to have publicly identified itself with Peking's point of view.

Little is known about the procedures by which the States of the Communist bloc consult each other, but whether they reach binding decisions after consultation or whether they reach a common view by other means is immaterial. The fact is that these States have the same policy on major questions. Divergencies in voting rarely occur on matters of major importance; deviations on matters of lesser importance happen from time to time, though these may be caused by a misunderstanding either as to what the position of the bloc is or what exactly was being voted on. If deviations because of misunder-standing occur, members of the bloc usually try to change their votes subsequently so as to present a united front.[41]

Western Europe

The fourth category of States referred to in the Assembly's resolu-tions on the composition of the General Committee is called 'Western Europe and other States', but this is not a regularly organized group nor even a precise geographical expression. Western Europe, in this context, is an elastic term, extending from Iceland to Finland in the

TABLE 5

Western European Member States

Austria	Italy
Belgium	Luxembourg
Cyprus*	Netherlands
Denmark	Norway
Finland	Portugal
France	Spain
Greece*	Sweden
Iceland	Turkey*
Ireland	United Kingdom

* Cyprus and Turkey both meet with the Afro-Asian caucus. Cyprus has been regarded as West European for some purposes; in his 1963 report on geographical distribution in the Secretariat, the Secretary-General placed Cyprus in the Middle East region; Cyprus was elected to one of the Assembly's Vice-Presi-dencies for the Afro-Asian category in both 1961 and 1963.

Turkey, geographically situated in the eastern Mediterranean, is a member of the North Atlantic Treaty Organization and of such European bodies as the United Nations Economic Commission for Europe and the Council of Europe. Turkey has sometimes been regarded as part of Western Europe; sometimes, for such purposes as Security Council elections, as part of Eastern Europe. To con-fuse the picture still further, when Turkey was a candidate for one of the Assembly's Vice-Presidencies in 1959, it was uncertain until the last moment for which category she was a candidate. Turkey was, in fact, elected for the Afro-Asian category in 1959; she was a candidate for the same category in 1961, but in 1963 was elected a Vice-President for the category 'Western European and other States'.

Greece is usually regarded as part of Western Europe but for some purposes, such as Security Council elections, has also been regarded as part of Eastern Europe. Indeed, in 1960 Greece received votes for one of the Assembly's Vice-Presidencies for both the East European and West European categories.

Since it would be confusing to regard Cyprus, Turkey, and Greece as belong-ing to more than one region, I have throughout this book (unless there are specific indications to the contrary) regarded them as within the region 'Western Europe'.

north and from Spain to Greece in the south. It would be more exact to refer to these States as Western, Northern, and Southern Europe, but for the sake of brevity I have used the term 'Western Europe'.

There were nine founder Members of the United Nations from Western Europe: Belgium, Denmark, France, Greece, Luxembourg, the Netherlands, Norway, Turkey, and the United Kingdom. Iceland and Sweden were admitted to Membership in 1946; Austria, Finland, Ireland, Italy, Portugal, and Spain in 1955; Cyprus in 1960.

Within the region are a number of associations for political or economic co-operation, but for United Nations purposes, it may be convenient to sub-divide the States of this region into:

(*a*) the European members of NATO which belong to the United Nations, together with Spain;

(*b*) the neutrals (Austria, Cyprus, Finland, Ireland, and Sweden).

The Western European group meets four or five times a year, under the joint chairmanship of France and the United Kingdom.

'Other States'

Four of the five permanent members of the Security Council, which form a separate category in the Assembly's resolutions on the composition of the General Committee, fall within regions referred to in the resolutions, although China (Taiwan) does not meet with the Afro-Asian caucus. The United States does not come within any of the regional categories mentioned in the Assembly's resolutions.

The resolutions refer to 'Western European and other States'. From the elections held since the first resolution was adopted, one may deduce that 'other States' includes Australia (elected to a Vice-Presidency in 1962), Canada (elected to a Vice-Presidency in 1960 and a Chairmanship in 1963), New Zealand (received votes for a Vice-Presidency in 1958), and South Africa (elected to a Vice-Presidency in 1959). Israel, although part of the Asian and African region, received votes for a Vice-Presidency in the category 'Western European and other States' in 1963. Presumably also included among 'Western European and other States' are two countries admitted to the United Nations in 1962: Jamaica, and Trinidad and Tobago.

The Commonwealth

The Commonwealth was once described to me in the following way: 'The Commonwealth cannot be defined, but it undoubtedly exists. We meet from time to time to exchange ideas on matters on which we are agreed. We always vote for each other, unless we happen to prefer some other candidate. It is a very superior form of co-operation, but it cannot be copied.' This is doubtless a caricature, but like all real caricatures it contains an element of truth. The Commonwealth possesses neither ideological nor geographical unity, but representatives of Commonwealth States usually understand one another rather readily; they have, in varying degrees, been influenced by British political traditions; and their representatives are generally at home in the English language. Australia, Canada, and New Zealand are referred to in this book by the admittedly clumsy expression 'older Commonwealth States'.

TABLE 6

United Nations Member States of the Commonwealth

Australia	Jamaica	Sierra Leone
Canada	Kenya	Tanganyika
Ceylon	Malaysia	Trinidad and Tobago
Cyprus	New Zealand	Uganda
Ghana	Nigeria	United Kingdom
India	Pakistan	Zanzibar

The Commonwealth group meets about once a fortnight while the Assembly is in session, and irregularly at other times of the year. Until 1963 the meeting was chaired by the senior British representative, but the chairmanship now rotates. The agenda consists of those matters whose inclusion has been requested by any Commonwealth member. Representatives are free, if they wish, to express the views of their governments on matters as they arise, but there is no obligation to reach a consensus. Although every effort is made to reach agreement on nominations for Commonwealth vacancies on United Nations organs, this is usually dealt with by discussion and consultation outside Commonwealth group meetings.* An

---

* During the first session of the Assembly, both Australia and Canada were candidates for the Commonwealth seat on the Security Council. Australia withdrew after the third ballot and Canada was elected. This unhappy situation was avoided on future occasions by reaching prior, informal agreement on a single Commonwealth candidate.

important feature of the Commonwealth group is that it overlaps other groups and regions.

The resolution on the composition of the General Committee adopted in 1957 provided that at least one member of the Assembly's General Committee, in addition to the United Kingdom, should be from a Commonwealth country, though without altering the over-all geographical distribution. A similar provision was proposed by the older Commonwealth States when the question of enlarging the General Committee was considered in 1963, but was not pressed to a vote.

Changes in relative strength of regions and groups

As the Membership of the United Nations has increased, so the relative strength of the regions has changed. Western European Membership has declined from 18 per cent in 1945 to 16 per cent on 1 January 1964, Eastern Europe from 12 per cent to 9 per cent. The most substantial change, however, has been that Latin America's proportion of seats has more than halved, while the Afro-Asian area's has more than doubled. There has been a small increase in the proportion of Commonwealth Members.

TABLE 7

Changes in relative strength of regions and groups in the Assembly, 1945 and 1964

| | 1945 | | 1 January 1964 | |
	no. of Members	percentage of seats	no. of Members	percentage of seats
Latin America	20	39	20	18
Asia and Africa (including China and South Africa)	12	24	59	52
Eastern Europe	6	12	10	9
Western Europe	9	18	18	16
Commonwealth	6	12	18	16

Distribution or Rotation of Elective Places

In addition to the regional distribution of members of the General Committee established by Resolution 1990 (XVIII), certain other elective places are distributed or rotated on a regional basis, either because this is required by the Charter or the Rules of Procedure or because of some unwritten but generally accepted understanding.

TABLE 8

Factors to be taken into account in electing individuals

Office or organ	Factors to be taken into account	References
1. President of the General Assembly	Regard shall be had for equitable geographical rotation among the following regions: Africa and Asia, Eastern Europe, Latin America, Western Europe and other States.	Resolution 1990 (XVIII)
2. Chairmen, Vice-Chairmen, and Rapporteurs of Main Committees	Equitable geographical distribution, experience, and personal competence. Resolution 1990 (XVIII) established the following pattern for the distribution of Chairmanships: Latin America 1 Asia and Africa 3 Eastern Europe 1 Western Europe and other States 1 The seventh Chairmanship rotates every alternate year among representatives of Latin American States and Western European and other States.	Rule 105, Resolution 1990 (XVIII)
3. International Court of Justice	The Court shall be composed of independent judges, elected regardless of their nationality from among persons of high moral character, who possess the qualifications required in their respective countries for appointment to the highest judicial offices, or are jurisconsults of recognized competence in international law. The electors shall bear in mind not only that the persons to be elected should individually possess the qualifications required, but also that in the body as a whole the representation of the main forms of civilization and of the principal legal systems of the world should be assured.	Articles 2 and 9 of the Statute
4. Advisory Committee on Administrative and Budgetary Questions	Broad geographical representation, personal qualifications, and experience	Rule 157
5. Committee on Contributions		Rule 160
6. International Law Commission	Persons of recognized competence in international law and representing as a whole the chief forms of civilization and the basic legal systems of the world	Resolution 174 (III)

TABLE 9

Factors to be taken into account in electing States

Office or organ	*Factors to be taken into account*	*References*
1. Vice-Presidents of the General Assembly	On the basis of ensuring the representative character of the General Committee. The pattern specified in the annex to Resolution 1990 (XVIII) is as follows: Latin America 3 Asia and Africa 7 Eastern Europe 1 Western Europe and other States 2 Permanent members of the Security Council 5 The region from which the President of the Assembly is elected has one Vice-President less than is indicated above.	Rules 31 and 38 Resolution 1990 (XVIII)
2. Credentials Committee	None specified	—
3. Elected members of the Security Council	In the first instance to the contribution of Members to the maintenance of international peace and security and to the other purposes of the Organization, and also to equitable geographical distribution	Article 23 Rule 144
4. Economic and Social Council	None specified	
5. Elected members of the Trusteeship Council	States which do not administer trust territories	Article 86 (I) (c)

It is inevitable that systems for the rotation or distribution of elective places should often take priority over personal competence (in the case of individuals) or the contribution made to the purposes of the United Nations (in the case of States). It would be impossible for governments to agree on criteria for evaluating the personal competence of individuals or the contribution of States to the purposes of the United Nations, whereas anyone who can count can set down on paper a scheme for the rotation or distribution of elective places which—on the surface, at any rate—looks fair. However, the mechanical application of such systems has drawbacks. It can, and often does, result in the election of less than the best. It tends to crystallize and even exaggerate regional differences. Its chief merit is that justice seems to be done.

There has developed a practice by which groups of States conduct what are, in effect, primary elections in the hope or expectation that the Assembly will give a formal endorsement to the candidates thus nominated. The Soviet Union, in particular, has held that this should be the normal practice. When, during the fourth session, Yugoslavia defeated Czechoslovakia for the seat on the Security Council vacated by the Ukraine, the Soviet representative protested in most vigorous terms:

> There had . . . been a violation of the firmly established tradition that candidates were always nominated by the States belonging to the geographical areas concerned. . . . Yugoslavia's entry into the Security Council was not based on a free election held in conformity with the principles of the Charter and established tradition; it was the result of a lobby conspiracy, . . . a bargain struck behind the scenes by Yugoslavia, the United States and various delegations which thus hoped to consolidate their position in the Security Council so as better to transform that Council into an obedient tool of the Anglo-American bloc.
>
> The delegation of the Soviet Union wished to state most emphatically that Yugoslavia did not represent the countries of Eastern Europe. . . .[42]

It has been suggested that, as a purely practical matter, the automatic election of States nominated by groups or regions has the merit of excluding from the public meetings of the Assembly controversy regarding elections. This argument should not be pressed too far, however; the differences concerning the presidency of the

Assembly in 1958 and 1961 show that no arrangement, whether nominations are permitted or prohibited, and whether the election is by secret or public ballot, can guarantee that controversy will be excluded from the public meetings. Moreover, the practice of nominations by groups works to the disadvantage of a State which happens to be at odds with its neighbours in the same region.

From a strictly constitutional point of view, the nomination of States by groups or regions is not binding; representatives are free to vote for any eligible candidate. In nine cases out of ten, it may be in the general interest that the nominations of regional groups should be endorsed, but this should not interfere with the right to vote for any eligible candidate.

3

THE BEGINNING OF THE SESSION

The place of their first session should be central, as much as is possible, afterwards as they agree. To avoid quarrel for precedency, the room may be round, and have divers doors to come in and go out at. . . . They may preside by turns, to whom all speeches should be addressed, and who should collect the sense of the debates, and state the question for a vote. . . . I should think it extremely necessary that every sovereignty should be present under great penalties, and that none leave the session without leave, till all be finished. . . . I will say little of the language in which the session . . . should be held, but to be sure it must be in Latin or French; the first would be very well for civilians, but the last most easily for men of quality.

WILLIAM PENN

EVERY YEAR there take place at United Nations headquarters in New York more than 2,000 meetings of United Nations organs, most of them in public; the meetings of the General Assembly are of special importance. The Assembly normally convenes in New York on the third Tuesday of September.

There has been discussion from time to time about the possibility of changing the opening date of regular sessions or of spreading the activities of the General Assembly over the whole year. Several proposals to change the opening date have involved minor variations in the present practice. Mr. Mongi Slim, President of the sixteenth session, suggested that regular sessions should begin on the first rather than the third Tuesday in September.[43] Iraq suggested in 1953 that the Assembly should convene on the fourth Tuesday in September, and the Advisory Committee on Administrative and

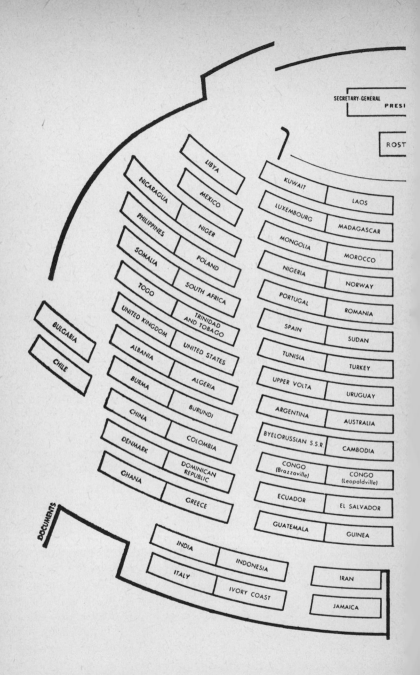

SECRETARY-GENERAL

PRESI

ROST

LIBYA

NICARAGUA
MEXICO

KUWAIT
LAOS

PHILIPPINES
NIGER

LUXEMBOURG
MADAGASCAR

SOMALIA
POLAND

MONGOLIA
MOROCCO

TOGO
SOUTH AFRICA

NIGERIA
NORWAY

UNITED KINGDOM
TRINIDAD AND TOBAGO

PORTUGAL
ROMANIA

BULGARIA

ALBANIA
UNITED STATES

SPAIN
SUDAN

CHILE

BURMA
ALGERIA

TUNISIA
TURKEY

CHINA
BURUNDI

UPPER VOLTA
URUGUAY

DENMARK
COLOMBIA

ARGENTINA
AUSTRALIA

GHANA
DOMINICAN REPUBLIC

BYELORUSSIAN S.S.R.
CAMBODIA

GREECE

CONGO (Brazzaville)
CONGO (Leopoldville)

DOCUMENTS

ECUADOR
EL SALVADOR

GUATEMALA
GUINEA

INDIA
INDONESIA

ITALY
IVORY COAST

IRAN

JAMAICA

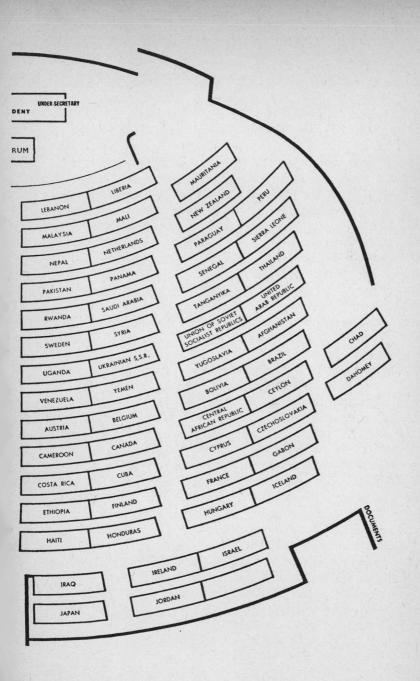

Budgetary Questions suggested, 'though without making a firm recommendation', deferring the opening date until the first Tuesday in October.[44]

A more radical change would involve convening the Assembly some time between mid-March and mid-April. The Secretary-General reported in 1953 that 'an opening date during the first half of the year would reduce the risk of postponements . . . and would allow the Assembly to complete a session of normal length by the beginning of the summer'.[45] A similar proposal was considered by the 1963 Committee on procedure.*[46] A change of this kind would probably require that the financial year of the United Nations run from 1 July to 30 June rather than for a calendar year as at present. Such a change would provide an incentive to complete the work of the session in only one part before the summer holidays, and there would be an indirect advantage in that a greater proportion of financial contributions would be received at the beginning of a financial year running from 1 July. The main disadvantages would be that it would disrupt the present pattern of conferences for the United Nations and the specialized agencies, and that it would be more difficult for some foreign ministers to be absent from their parliamentary duties during the April and May period than in September and October.

Plenary meetings of the Assembly are held in the large blue and gold hall, which is situated at the north end of the cluster of buildings of the United Nations on the east side of Manhattan. A few days before the Assembly is due to open, there will be a bustle of activity at United Nations headquarters as the staff completes the preparations for the session. Heads of State, head of government, foreign ministers, diplomats, and members of parliament will be gathering from all parts of the globe. The opening day is characterized by a sense of drama much like that of the State Opening of Parliament in the countries of the Commonwealth. As three o'clock approaches, sleek black cars draw up at the delegates entrance behind the flags of the United Nations and its Member States. Members of the general public wait in the lobby at the north end of the Assembly building for admission to the meeting.

* There have been four committees of the Assembly to review procedure (see 'A Note on Further Reading', p. 246). Extracts from the reports of these committees will be found in Appendices 7–10, pp. 305–348. In this book I have identified the Committees by the years during which they worked rather than by their precise titles.

Representatives of Member States will have been gathering on the delegates' floor. Old friends greet each other; old opponents exchange pleasantries; new delegates are shown the ropes by the veterans. In the galleries wait a multilingual group of journalists, officials of the Secretariat, representatives of non-governmental organizations, and members of the public. Soon after 3.0 p.m., the Temporary President (the Chairman of the delegation from which the President of the previous session was elected) enters the General Assembly hall, accompanied by the Secretary-General (U Thant) and the Under-Secretary for General Assembly Affairs and Chef de Cabinet (Mr. C. V. Narasimhan). They take their seats on the dais at the front.

For five minutes the hubbub continues, and then the Temporary President raps the gavel and declares the session open. His words are immediately interpreted into the five official languages used by the General Assembly—Chinese, English, French, Russian, and Spanish—and each person present is able to switch the earphones by his seat to the language of his choice.*

The Temporary President then invites representatives to stand and observe one minute of silence dedicated to prayer or meditation (Rule 64). This practice was initiated in 1950 after the receipt by Secretary-General Trygve Lie of hundreds of letters from individuals and organizations urging that the General Assembly should devote a few moments of its time to prayer. It would hardly be possible to devise a public prayer which would be acceptable to all the faiths of which there are adherents among citizens of the Member States of the United Nations, but a short time of silence is a solemn act which gives offence to none.

When the representatives have sat down, the Temporary President speaks briefly of the tasks that lie ahead.

Credentials

The next item of business is the appointment of a Committee to examine the credentials of representatives and report its findings to

---

* A U.N. delegate is allowed to speak in a language other than the five official languages, but if he does so he must himself make arrangements for the interpretation of his remarks. The choice of language can be significant. Victor Andrés Belaúnde of Peru, the President of the fourteenth session, used French when he wished to be precise, English when he wished to understate, and Spanish when he wished to exaggerate.

the full Assembly (Rule 28). This is to ensure that all representatives have been properly appointed and issued with credentials by the head of state or the head of government or the minister for foreign affairs concerned (Rule 27). The Credentials Committee is appointed during the first meeting of the session and is asked to 'report without delay' (Rule 28). Any representative to whose admission objection has been made is seated provisionally with the same rights as other representatives until the Credentials Committee has reported and the General Assembly has given its decision (Rule 29).

There has never been overt controversy about the composition of the Credentials Committee, which consists of nine members 'appointed by the General Assembly on the proposal of the President' (Rule 28); the United States and the Soviet Union are usually included among the members. When the time comes to appoint the Committee, the President refers to the relevant Rule of Procedure, names the nine States which he proposes for membership, and says that if there is no objection he will consider that his proposal has been approved.

The task of the Committee is to see that all representatives are properly accredited. The names of representatives and their credentials should be submitted to the Secretary-General 'if possible not less than one week before the date fixed for the opening of the session' (Rule 27). The Secretariat examines these credentials and makes a report to the Credentials Committee. In 1961 the Secretary-General reported that the credentials of some representatives had not conformed to Rule 27 in that they had not been issued by the proper authority; in other cases the credentials had emanated from the proper authority but had been submitted in the form of a cable rather than in a written document bearing the signature of the issuing authority. Following a recommendation of the Credentials Committee, the Assembly drew the attention of Member States to the necessity of complying with the requirements of Rule 27.[47] In 1963 the Secretary-General again reported that some credentials had not been in order, in that they had been submitted in the form of a cable. The Credentials Committee, in its report, stressed the need for all Member States to comply with Rule 27; in particular, credentials should, if possible, be submitted not less than one week before the date of the opening of the session.[48]

During the first five sessions of the Assembly (1946–50), the Credentials Committee made a first report to the Assembly within a day or so of its appointment, but since the sixth session (1951), the Committee has been asked to consider not only whether representatives have been issued with credentials in proper form, but also whether the issuing authority was entitled to act on behalf of the Member State concerned. This question may arise if rival governments claim to be the only legitimate authority in a Member State, or if a government has been overthrown in circumstances which create doubts as to the legitimacy of its successor, or if questions have been raised as to the representative character of the government of a Member State.

During the period 1956–62, for example, the General Assembly took no decision concerning the credentials submitted on behalf of the representatives of Hungary. In the absence of decisions on their credentials, Hungarian representatives enjoyed the same rights as other representatives.

In 1960, the Assembly had to decide between rival delegations from the Republic of the Congo (Léopoldville), one representing Mr Joseph Kasavubu and the other representing Mr Patrice Lumumba. After sharp debate, the Assembly voted to accept the credentials issued by Kasavubu as Head of the State.[49]

The most difficult case of this kind has concerned China.* The Republic of China is a founding Member of the United Nations and is named in Article 23 of the Charter as a permanent member of the Security Council. The expulsion of the Nationalist Government from the Chinese mainland and the formal establishment in Peking in October 1949 of the Chinese People's Republic posed an awkward constitutional problem for the General Assembly and other organs of the United Nations, a problem which was aggravated a year later by Chinese intervention in Korea. The political and moral arguments for seating Chinese Communist representatives in organs of the United Nations, as well as those in favour of maintaining the representation of the Chinese Nationalists, are well known and there is no need to repeat them.[50]

---

* In documents of the United Nations, the Government of China at present means the Nationalist (Kuomintang) Government headed by President Chiang Kai-shek, based on Taiwan (Formosa); to avoid confusion, I have sometimes referred to this Government by some such phrase as 'Nationalist China' or 'the Kuomintang Government'. The Communist Government established in Peking in 1949 is officially known as the Central People's Government of the People's Republic of China; in referring to this Government, I have used such phrases as 'Communist China' or 'the Peking Government'.

On four occasions the question of the representation of China was raised as a point of order during the opening meeting of the Assembly, in 1950 before the appointment of the Credentials Committee, in 1954 and 1955 during the process of appointing the Credentials Committee, and in 1953 during the process of electing the President. The question of the representation of China was proposed for inclusion in the Assembly's agenda, by India during the period 1956–1959, by the Soviet Union in 1960, by both the Soviet Union and New Zealand in 1961, by the Soviet Union in 1962, and by Albania in 1963. The decisions of the Assembly were as follows:

1950: Special Committee established to consider the question of Chinese representation; pending a decision on the matter, representatives of the Nationalist Government of China were seated with the same rights as other representatives. The Special Committee submitted a report which contained no recommendations, and the Assembly merely took note of the report.

1951–53: Decided to postpone consideration of proposals to exclude representatives of the Nationalist Government of China or to seat representatives of the People's Republic of China.

1954–60: Decided 'not to consider' proposals to exclude representatives of Nationalist China or to seat representatives of the People's Republic of China.

1961: Decided to include the question of Chinese representation in the agenda. Decided also that any proposal to change the representation of China was an important question, decisions on which require a two-thirds majority of the Members present and voting. Rejected a proposal 'to remove immediately . . . representatives of the Chiang Kai-shek clique . . .' and to invite representatives of the People's Republic of China to participate in the work of the United Nations and its organs.

1962 and 1963: Rejected proposals to remove the representatives of Chiang Kai-shek from the United Nations and to invite representatives of the People's Republic of China to occupy China's place.

The Assembly may properly decide to postpone consideration

48

of a question (as it in effect did in relation to Chinese representation in 1950, and as it did explicitly in 1951 to 1953) or it may refuse to consider a question (as it did from 1954 to 1960). It may be doubted, however, whether the Assembly conformed to its own Rules of Procedure from 1954 to 1960, because the resolutions on Chinese representation which it adopted at the beginning of each session had the effect not only of rejecting the request to discuss Chinese representation (which is not open to objection on legal grounds), but also of excluding the credentials of Chinese representatives from scrutiny by the Credentials Committee. Indeed, when the question of Chinese credentials arose in the Credential Committee, the Chairman ruled that the question had already been decided.

As a result of differences regarding credentials, the Credentials Committee now usually meets late in the session; this practice does not conform to the requirement of the Rules of Procedure that it 'report without delay' (Rule 28). Indeed, it is somewhat anomalous that the appointment of the Credentials Committee should be a matter of such urgency that it precedes the election of the President for the session, though it is known that the Committee will probably not meet until twelve weeks later.

The Election of the President

Until the Assembly has elected a President for the session, the Chairman of the delegation from which the President of the previous session was elected acts as Temporary President. When a Credentials Committee has been appointed, the Temporary President invites the Assembly to choose a new President which, according to Article 21 of the Charter, shall be by election. Two matters arise in this connexion: (a) the factors taken into account in the choice of the President; and (b) the method of election. The question of the powers of the President is considered in Chapter 5.

It has been the general experience of assemblies of many kinds that the chief criterion to be borne in mind in the selection of officers should be personal competence, while in the establishment of organs of limited membership the main requirements should be that the organs should be sufficiently expert to fulfil the tasks assigned to them and sufficiently representative so as to enjoy the greatest possible degree of confidence of the whole. The more heterogeneous the membership of an assembly, the more the criterion of personal competence in the selection of officers tends to give way to some system of rotation or equitable distribution. This tendency is clearly apparent in the General Assembly of the United Nations.

The League of Nations was less preoccupied than the United Nations has been with systems for the rotation of offices. Paul Hymans of Belgium was President of the first session of the League Assembly in 1920, and in 1932–33 he presided over the extraordinary session on the Manchurian conflict; Paul van Zeeland, also of Belgium, presided over the resumed sixteenth session of the Assembly in the summer of 1936 on the Italian invasion of Ethiopia. On the two latter occasions, personal competence outweighed the fact that a Belgian had already been President. Similarly, Nicolas Titulesco of Romania presided over the eleventh session of the League Assembly in 1930, and was elected to the same office the following year.

As far as the United Nations General Assembly is concerned, there has been a general understanding that it would be undesirable to elect as President a representative of any of the five States which are permanent members of the Security Council. The Presidents elected by the Assembly are shown in Table 10.

The presidency has rotated from region to region with reasonable equity, except that there has not yet been a President from one of the Communist States. The countries of the Soviet bloc have maintained that this is an injustice, and during the fourteenth session (1959) they proposed that the Presidents for the succeeding four sessions should be elected from the regions as follows:

1960 Eastern Europe
1961 Asia and Africa
1962 Western Europe and other States
1963 Latin America

In an explanatory memorandum submitted by Czechoslovakia, it was stated that the principle of equitable geographical representation, which was one of the fundamental general principles of the United Nations, had not been consistently applied in the elections of the President of the Assembly. Representatives of all geographical areas except Eastern Europe had several times held in turn the office of President. The attainment of an agreement on the correct application of the 'principle of equitable geographical representation in the election of the President' would remove the existing shortcomings and would contribute to a further development of co-operation and the strengthening of mutual confidence among Member States.[51]

TABLE 10

Presidents of the General Assembly, 1946-63

Session	Date	President	State
I	10 Jan.–15 Dec., 46	Paul-Henri Spaak	Belgium
1st Spec. Sess.	28 Apr.–15 May, 47 }	Oswaldo Aranha	Brazil
2	16 Sept.–29 Nov, 47 }		
2nd Spec. Sess.	16 Apr.–14 May, 48	José Arce	Argentina
3	21 Sept., 48–18 May, 49	Herbert V. Evatt	Australia
4	20 Sept.–10 Dec., 49	Carlos P. Romulo	Philippines
5	19 Sept., 50–5 Nov., 51	Nasrollah Entezam	Iran
6	6 Nov., 51–5 Feb., 52	Luis Padilla Nervo	Mexico
7	14 Oct., 52–28 Aug., 53	Lester B. Pearson	Canada
8	15 Sept.–9 Dec., 53	Mrs. Vijaya Lakshmi Pandit	India
9	21 Sept.–17 Dec., 54	Eelco van Kleffens	Netherlands
10	20 Sept.–20 Dec., 55	José Maza	Chile
1st Emergency Special Sess.	1 Nov.–10 Nov., 56 }	Rudecindo Ortega	Chile
2nd Emergency Special Sess.	4 Nov.–Nov. 56 }		
11	12 Nov., 56–8 Mar., 57	Prince Wan Waithayakon	Thailand
12	17 Sept.–14 Dec., 57 }	Sir Leslie Munro	New Zealand
3rd Emergency Special Sess.	8 Aug.–21 Aug., 58 }		
13	16 Sept., 58–13 Mar., 59	Charles Mâlik	Lebanon
14	15 Sept.–13 Dec., 59 }	Victor Andrés Belaúnde	Peru
4th Emergency Special Sess.	17 Sept.–19, 60 }		
15	20 Sept., 60–21 Apr., 61 }	Frederick H. Boland	Ireland
3rd Special Sess.	21 Aug.–25, 61 }		
16	19 Sept., 61–28 June, 62	Mongi Slim	Tunisia
17	18 Sept.–20 Dec., 62 }	Sir Muhammad Zafrulla Khan	Pakistan
4th Special Sess.	14 May–27 June, 63 }		
18	17 Sept.–17 Dec., 63	Carlos Sosa-Rodriguez	Venezuela

The proposal of Czechoslovakia was considered by the Special Political Committee in December 1959. The Soviet bloc countries insisted that there had been discrimination against Eastern Europe, and that this should be ended by the adoption of a precise formula for the rotation of the presidency; moreover, the presidency should always be filled by a candidate nominated by the countries of the region whose turn it was.

There were some objections to the formula proposed on the grounds that it would remedy one injustice by creating others. It was pointed out, for example, that the presidency had gone to the

Afro-Asian area in 1949, 1950, 1953, 1956-57, and 1958-59; it was, in the view of some representatives, the turn of 'Western Europe and other States' before it was the turn of Africa and Asia. Other speakers held that, because the Afro-Asian region had more members than any other region, it was entitled to the presidency more than once in each four-year period.

But the real objection was not so much to the terms of the proposed formula as to having a formula at all. The opponents of the proposal of the Communist States considered that the adoption of any formula would tend to give a lesser importance to personal competence and experience. This led to an interesting discussion of the relationship of genius to geography. Some representatives insisted that genius knew no frontiers and was as likely to appear in Eastern Europe as in other regions, to which it was retorted that genius might appear twice in one country before visiting the rest of the world.

One element of confusion entered the debate. The question before the Assembly was 'the consistent application of the principle of equitable geographical representation', but several speakers insisted that the real issue was whether it would be appropriate to choose a President from a Communist State. The ideological and geographical aspects were obviously closely linked, but to treat them as the same was bound to cause misunderstanding.

The Special Political Committee approved a draft resolution as follows:

> *The General Assembly,*
> *In view* of the spirit of the United Nations Charter and of the provisions of the rules of procedure of the General Assembly pertaining to the President of the General Assembly,
> *Recognizing* the importance of ensuring that the President of the General Assembly possesses the highest personal qualifications for the performance of his duties, and of taking into account in his election the principle of equitable geographical representation,
> *Recommends* that in the election of the President of the General Assembly due regard be specially paid to the qualifications that the President of the General Assembly must possess in order to perform the important duties of his office and to the principle of equitable geographical representation.[52]

This draft might seem unexceptionable though it was, in the

event, rejected in plenary meeting, 36 votes being cast in favour, 40 against, with 6 abstentions.[53]

In 1963 the question was raised again when Czechoslovakia and Poland proposed that the Presidency should rotate among the following six regions: Africa, Asia, Eastern Europe, Latin America and Caribbean States, Middle East, Western Europe and other States. There was little debate of the question, and the proposal of Czechoslovakia and Poland was not pressed to a vote on the understanding that the annex to a draft resolution on the composition of the General Committee should include the following paragraph:

> In the election of the President of the General Assembly, regard shall be had for equitable geographical rotation of this office among the regions mentioned in paragraph 4 below [that is to say, African and Asian States, Eastern European States. Latin American States, Western European and other States.]

The draft resolution was unanimously approved by the plenary.[54]

There is now a certain artificiality about the prohibition of nominations in connection with the election of the President. The Provisional Rules of Procedure did not prohibit nominations, and it was the uneasiness regarding the election of the first President that led to the change in the Rules. Trygve Lie relates how, on Christmas Day of 1945, he received a message that had originated with Adlai Stevenson, who was then acting as head of the United States delegation to the Preparatory Commission of the United Nations. Stevenson had inquired whether Lie 'would be willing to accept election as President' of the first Assembly, which was to open in London a fortnight later. Lie replied in the affirmative, being under the impression that Britain and the Soviet Union also favoured his election. When he arrived in London a couple of days before the opening of the Assembly, Lie learned that Britain 'for the last two months had been vigorously supporting Paul-Henri Spaak, the Foreign Minister of Belgium'. The next day, Lie was informed that the United States 'now regarded Mr Spaak's election as certain' and would therefore 'refrain from trying to influence the Latin American delegations, who . . . were in many instances strongly inclined to vote for Mr Spaak.'[55] On the morning of the day the Assembly was to convene, Lie was told by a Soviet representative that the Soviet Union intended to nominate him.

When the time came to elect the President, the Soviet representative stated that his delegation intended to vote for Trygve Lie of Norway. He referred to the heroic role of Norway during the war, and praised Lie's personal qualities. The Ukrainian, Polish, and Danish representatives then stated that they also would vote for Lie. Although there was no other nomination, the result of the ballot was that Spaak received twenty-eight votes and Lie twenty-three. Spaak was therefore elected on the first ballot. Lie comments that this decision left him 'both relieved and discontented'.[56] Three weeks later he was appointed the first Secretary-General of the Organization, by a vote of forty-five to three in the Assembly.

The direct result of the election of the first President was the adoption of an amendment to the Provisional Rules of Procedure prohibiting nominations in plenary meetings.[57] This did not, of course, get rid of the nominating process: it transferred it from the floor of the Assembly to the corridors. Moreover, it has been impossible to avoid nominations in disguise.

In 1957 Charles Mâlik of Lebanon was the nominee of the Afro-Asian group for the presidency. It was not, however, the turn of the Afro-Asian area since the retiring President, Prince Wan of Thailand, was an Asian. When the time came to elect the President, a former President took the floor and urged Mâlik to withdraw. Mâlik then stated that in the interest of concord, he would yield to his good friend Sir Leslie Munro of New Zealand. Several representatives accordingly announced that they would support Mâlik's candidature on some future occasion. The ballot gave seventy-seven votes to Sir Leslie Munro and one to Charles Mâlik.

An unusual situation thus existed the following year. A large number of delegations had agreed privately, and a few publicly, to vote for Charles Mâlik. It was, however, regarded as virtually certain that within a week of the opening of the Assembly, Mâlik would cease being Foreign Minister of Lebanon. Moreover, the majority of Arab delegations had stated that they had switched support from Charles Mâlik to M. A. Mahgoub, who was at that time the Sudanese Foreign Minister. To complicate the picture further, the countries of the Soviet bloc had let it be known that Jiří Nosek of Czechoslovakia was also a candidate. When the time came to elect the President, the representative of Czechoslovakia stated that 'By agreement with the other east European countries, the Czechoslovak delegation withdraws the candidature of Ambassador Jiří Nosek . . .

in favour of the candidate of the overwhelming majority of the Arab countries' (that is to say, Mahgoub).[58] In the event, Mâlik was elected by forty-five votes to thirty-one for Mahgoub, with four abstentions.

In 1961, there was again a public withdrawal of one candidate in favour of another. Ali Sastroamidjojo of Indonesia said he was grateful to those who had supported his candidacy, but that he was withdrawing in the confident hope that the Assembly would elect Mongi Slim of Tunisia.[59]

The public withdrawal of one candidature in favour of another is, of course, equivalent to a nomination; Carlos P. Romulo, President of the fourth session of the Assembly (1949) had ruled, and had not been challenged, that such a procedure is out of order.[60] Nevertheless, there is something unreal about the prohibition of nominations. Delegations openly lobby for themselves or their friends. Unofficial papers are circulated stating that a particular person is a candidate for a particular post. The groups inform the Press of their choices. Perhaps the chief merit of the ban on nominations is not that it prevents nominations but that it discourages nomination *speeches*.

Election of Committee Officers

After the newly-elected President has addressed the Assembly, the Chairmen of the seven Main Committees are elected. Much of the basic work of the Assembly is done in these Committees, each of which consists of all Member States. Each Main Committee elects its own Chairman, Vice-Chairman, and Rapporteur (Rule 105). Officers of Main Committees are elected in their individual capacities.

The procedure for the election of Chairmen is as follows. The President of the Assembly calls to order, one by one, the Main Committees. Nominations are permitted in committees of the Assembly. A representative, often the Chairman of the Committee the previous year, mounts the rostrum and nominates a person as Chairman. The nomination is seconded by another representative, although this is not required under the Rules of Procedure. If, as is generally the case, there is only one nomination, the President declares the nominee elected by acclamation; if there is more than one nomination, an election is held by secret ballot. The procedure lasts about ten minutes in each Committee. Arrangements for brief speeches of nomination and support are prepared in advance by the Secretariat, in agreement with delegations, in such a way as to distribute the honours and responsibilities as equitably and acceptably as possible.

The Rules state that the Chairmen, Vice-Chairmen, and Rapporteurs of Committees shall be elected on the basis of equitable geographical distribution, experience, and personal competence (Rule 105). Representatives of States which are permanent members of the Security Council have not been elected as Chairmen of Main Committees, with the single exception that T. F. Tsiang of China was elected Chairman of the First Committee by secret ballot during the second special session (1948).

The practice, until it was revised in 1963, was to allocate two chairmanships to Latin America, two to Asia and Africa, one to Eastern Europe, and two to Western Europe and other States. This pattern had been confirmed during the twelfth session (1957).[61]

The question of the composition of the General Committee, including the pattern for election of Chairmen of Main Committees, was considered by the Assembly in 1963, and it was decided to reallocate the chairmanships as follows:[62]

	Practice confirmed during the twelfth session (res. 1192)	Pattern established during the eighteenth session (res. 1990)
Latin America	2	$1\frac{1}{2}$*
Asia and Africa	2	3
Eastern Europe	1	1
Western European and other States	2	$1\frac{1}{2}$*

As the Chairmen are elected at meetings of Main Committees held consecutively, it is theoretically possible that seven separate elections by secret ballot should not produce the specified pattern.

The fact that candidatures are in many cases endorsed by groups of States does not mean that the elections are necessarily mere formalities. An aspirant for a chairmanship who fails to obtain the support of his group may persist with his candidacy and force a ballot. Such a potentially awkward situation existed immediately before the opening of the fourteenth session (1959). The informal

* One chairmanship rotates every alternate year between two groups of States.

slate of candidates for chairmanships corresponded to the Chairmen subsequently elected, except that a representative of the Philippines was an additional candidate for the chairmanship of the Third Committee. Intensive consultations were necessary, and in the end the matter was resolved without the disagreeable necessity of a contested election. Four days before the session was due to open, the Permanent Missions of Japan and the Philippines issued the following carefully-worded joint Press release:

> The Japanese Permanent Representative proposes to withdraw their candidacy for the Vice-Presidency of the United Nations General Assembly in favour of the Philippines in view of the fact that the Philippines has withdrawn its candidacy for the Chairmanship of the Third Committee.
>
> The Philippine Permanent Representative expressed appreciation for the kind gesture of the Japanese Permanent Representative and stated that the announcement of the withdrawal of the Philippine candidacy for the Chairmanship of the Third Committee was released last night.[63]

The electoral process in the election of Vice-Chairmen and Rapporteurs of Main Committees is the same as in the election of Chairmen. If there is only one candidate for a vacancy, as is usually the case, election is by acclamation; if there are two or more candidates, an election is held by secret ballot (Rule 105). In 1959, for example, it was necessary to elect the Vice-Chairman of the Fourth Committee by secret ballot. In 1962, there were two candidates for the Vice-Chairmanship of the Second Committee, and a decision had to be postponed for several days. When the Committee resumed, the votes were equally divided between the two candidates, and a second ballot was held. The Rules provided that if, in a second ballot, the votes are equally divided, the presiding officer shall decide between the candidates by drawing lots (Rule 133).

A chairmanship or other committee office can be a rung on a ladder, bringing honour to the person and his country. If a representative has ambitions for himself or his country and aspires to a committee office, he will let it be known that he is 'available' and will seek the support of any groups to which his country belongs. As he mounts the ladder, he learns the tricks of the trade, the arts of good chairmanship. He learns how to look as if he is enjoying boring speeches; he learns how to smooth the ruffled feelings of aggrieved representatives; he learns when to consult members of the Secretariat and when to act on his own initiative; he learns how to rule on a point of order which he has not fully heard or has not properly understood.

Election of Vice-Presidents

After the Main Committees have elected their Chairmen at consecutive meetings, the plenary meeting of the General Assembly is convened for the election of Vice-Presidents, thus completing the formation of the General Committee.

The President of the Assembly and the Chairmen of Main Committees are elected in their personal capacities; the Vice-Presidents are elected as States, in such a way as to ensure the representative character of the General Committee (Rules 31 and 38). If the President finds it necessary to be absent during all or part of a meeting of the Assembly, he asks one of the Vice-Presidents to take his place (Rule 32); a Vice-President acting as President has the same powers and duties as the President himself (Rule 33).

The five permanent members of the Security Council are included among the Vice-Presidents, since representatives of these States are not normally elected to the presidency or one of the chairmanships. The single exception to this practice occurred during the second special session (1948), when a member of the Chinese delegation was elected Chairman of the First Committee. Since no two members of the General Committee may be members of the same delegation (Rule 38), China was not included among the seven Vice-Presidents elected for that special session.

The importance of limiting the size of the General Committee was generally recognized during the first decade of the life of the United Nations, but following the admission of sixteen new Members in December 1955, pressure to increase the size of the Committee began to mount. During the eleventh session (1956-57), the size of the General Committee was increased to sixteen by the addition of an eighth Vice-President. At the twelfth session (1957) it was decided to include in the agenda a proposal to establish a ninth vice-presidency on an *ad hoc* basis for the session. After a confused debate in the plenary, the Assembly proceeded to elect a ninth Vice-President before it had taken a decision on whether or not to increase the number of Vice-Presidents. The Assembly later decided to confirm what was already the practice regarding the distribution of the chairmanships of the seven Main Committees, to increase the number of vice-presidencies to thirteen, and to establish a regional pattern of distribution of the vice-presidencies.

There was wide agreement at the time this decision was taken that some increase in the size of the General Committee was necessary, but there were differences of view on the extent of the increase, and there was even more disagreement on the proposal that the representative character of the Committee should be ensured by bringing about a fixed pattern of election. Hesitation about the change came mainly from Western Europe, the United States, the older Commonwealth countries, and a few other countries which do not fit easily into any regional group. It was argued by them, in the first place, that a General Committee of sixteen or seventeen members was large enough; to increase its size would reduce its utility. Secondly, some delegations took the view that it was premature to take a decision on the matter. They maintained that the question of the composition of the General Committee should not be separated from the question of the composition of other United Nations organs; in any case, this was a matter on which unanimity was desirable, and it would be unfortunate to force a decision through the Assembly so long as an influential body of Member States remained unconvinced of the merits of the proposed changes.

A third group of objections related to the proposed pattern of regional representation. It was pointed out that most of the advocates of change belonged to organized regional groups, whereas the opponents were being lumped together in a meaningless category of 'Western European and other States'. It was argued that a decision of the Assembly along the lines proposed would crystallize and perpetuate divisions in the world. It was also objected that the Commonwealth was ignored in the proposal in its original form, though this was remedied in the final resolution.

Support for the change came from the Afro-Asian and Communist countries, and some of the countries of Latin America. It was argued by them that the increase in the membership of the Assembly made an increase in the size of the General Committee appropriate, and that opportunity should be taken to guarantee that the Committee would in the future have a more representative character than previously. Czechoslovakia urged that a pattern of representation should be enshrined in a written text, as a previous 'gentlemen's agreement' had not been respected.* To the argument that a Committee with twenty-one members would be unwieldy, India replied that the argument was irrelevant as the Committee was only procedural; while Poland asserted that the efficiency of a committee depends on the quality of its members rather than on its size.

In 1963 it was suggested that a further increase in the number of Vice-Presidencies was necessary, but on this occasion the emphasis was exclusively on the urgent need to give proper representation to the Asian and African States; virtually no attention was given to the effect of increasing the number of Vice-Presidencies on the working of the General Committee. The Assembly decided unanimously to create four additional Vice-Presidencies, thus enlarging the General Committee to twenty-five members. The number of Vice-Presidencies from the Afro-Asian area was increased from four to seven, and the number from Latin America from two to three. This gave a General Committee constituted as follows:

	President and Vice-Presidents elected according to specified pattern	Permanent members of Security Council elected as Vice-Presidents	Chairmen of seven Main Committees	Total
Asia and Africa	7	1	3	11
Eastern Europe	1	1	1	3
Latin America	3	–	$1\frac{1}{2}$†	$4\frac{1}{2}$
Western Europe and other States	2	3	$1\frac{1}{2}$†	$6\frac{1}{2}$

The 1957 and 1963 decisions regarding the composition of the General Committee had three important procedural consequences. First, it undoubtedly made it easier than formerly to constitute the General Committee on a widely representative basis. Secondly, the increase in the Committee's size has meant that it cannot as easily perform the 'steering' functions specified in the Rules of Procedure. A third consequence has been to complicate the procedure for the election of Vice-Presidents. This is by secret ballot, and there are no nominations (Rules 31 and 94).

In the election of Vice-Presidents during the thirteenth session

* This was presumably a reference to an agreement on the composition of the Security Council which was concluded in London in 1946.

† One chairmanship rotates every alternate year between the two groups of States.

in 1958, eighty Members returned ballot papers, and thus a total of 1,040 votes could have been cast. In fact, only 973 valid votes were recorded, distributed among no less than forty-one States, as shown in Table 11.

TABLE 11

Election of Vice-Presidents, 1958

United States of America	78		
Ecuador	77	Canada	4
		Ethiopia	4
United Kingdom	76		
		Iraq	3
France	75		
		India	2
Pakistan	73	Jordan	2
Uruguay	73	New Zealand	2
	elected	Thailand	2
Australia	71	Tunisia	2
Indonesia	71	Turkey	2
Soviet Union	71	United Arab Republic	2
Nepal	65	Argentina	1
		Brazil	1
Czechoslovakia	57	Bulgaria	1
Netherlands	57	Burma	1
		Cambodia	1
China	56	Haiti	1
		Iran	1
Liberia	13	Morocco	1
		Norway	1
Poland	9	Peru	1
		Philippines	1
Austria	7	Ukrainian SSR	1
		Venezuela	1
Ghana	5	Yemen	1

It was theoretically possible for twenty-five Member States to receive a simple majority, though there were only thirteen places to be filled. This, no doubt, is carrying theoretical possibilities to excess; all the same, if the sixty-seven votes not cast or not valid, or the seventy-three votes dispersed among the bottom twenty-eight States, had been concentrated on one State, the pattern of representation specified in the Assembly's resolution could have been upset. In spite of the informal understanding among delegations about the election, and in spite of the fact that the annex to Resolution 1192 (XII) specified that the permanent members of the Security Council should be members of the General Committee, more than one-quarter of the Members did not vote for China.

BALLOT*   BULLETIN DE VOTE   CEDULA DE VOTACION

ELECTION OF THE VICE-PRESIDENTS OF THE GENERAL ASSEMBLY
ELECTION DES VICE-PRESIDENTS DE L'ASSEMBLEE GENERALE
ELECCION DE LOS VICEPRESIDENTES DE LA ASAMBLEA GENERAL

1. The annex to resolution 1192 (XII) of the General Assembly (see rules of procedure, note 4) establishes the following distribution of posts for Vice-Presidents:

L'annexe à la résolution 1192 (XII) de l'Assemblée générale (voir règlement interieur, note 4) établit la répartition suivante pour les sièges des vice-présidents:

El anexo a la resolución 1192 (XII) de la Asamblea General (véase reglamento, nota 4) establece la siguiente distribución para los puestos de Vicepresidentes:

A. Asian and African States – 4 Vice-Presidents
   Etats d'Asie et d'Afrique – 4 vice-présidents
   Estados de Asia y Africa – 4 Vicepresidentes
   1.
   2.
   3.
   4.

B. Eastern European States – 1 Vice-President
   Etats d'Europe orientale – 1 vice-président
   Estados de la Europa oriental – Vicepresidente
   1.

C. Latin American States – 2 Vice-Presidents
   Etats d'Amérique latine – 2 vice-présidents
   Estados de la América Latina – 2 Vicepresidents
   1.
   2.

D. Western European and other States – 2 Vice-Presidents
   Etats d'Europe occidentale et autres Etats – 2 vice-présidents
   Estados de la Europe occidental y otros Estados – 2 Vicepresidents
   1.
   2.

E. Permanent members of the Security Council – 5 Vice-Presidents
   Membres permanents du Conseil de sécurité – 5 vice-présidents
   Miembros permanentes del Consejo de Seguridad – 5 Vicepresidents
   1.
   2.
   3.
   4.
   5.

* This ballot paper is based on Resolution 1192 (XII). In 1964 and thereafter, it will be necessary to use a ballot paper showing the distribution of Vice-Presidencies specified in the annex to Resolution 1990 (XVIII).

2. The number of vice-presidencies allocated to the region from which the Presi-dent is elected will, however, be reduced by one.

Toutefois, une vice-présidence de moins sera attribuée à la région à laquelle appartient le Président.

No obstante, la región a la cual pertenezca el Presidente elegido tendrá un Vicepresidente menos de los asignados a la misma.

3. The number of candidates that may be elected from each group is established by the pattern set forth above. If the number of names for any one group in the ballot paper is greater than the number prescribed for that group, the vote on that group will be considered as invalid.

Le nombre de candidats éligibles de chaque groupe est établi d'après le critère visé plus haut. Si un bulletin de vote renferme plus de noms qu'il n'est prévu, le vote pour ce groupe sera considéré comme nul.

El número de los candidatos que se pueden elegir de cada grupo queda determinado por la distribución arriba expuesta. Si en una cédula el número de candidatos para un grupo cualquiera es mayor que el número asignado a dicho grupo, se considerará nulo el voto correspondiente a ese grupo.

In an attempt to avoid a dispersal of votes to the extent that took place in 1958, the Secretariat now circulates a ballot paper show-ing the distribution of Vice-Presidencies. Before calling on the Assem-bly to proceed with the election, the President reminds the Assembly that the regional distribution of Vice-Presidencies is specified in the Assembly's resolution, and he refers to the sample ballot paper circulated with the Journal. He points out that the number of Vice-Presidencies allocated to the region from which he had been elected should be reduced by one. He then informs the Assembly that if the number of names for any one group in a ballot paper is greater than the number prescribed for that group, the votes as regards that particular group will be considered invalid.

The use of a more elaborate ballot paper led to a significant reduction in the number of States obtaining votes (see Table 12), but it cannot prevent dispersal of votes within each group. More-over, there is no procedure or form of ballot paper which can compel Member States to vote for candidates if they do not wish to do so. In spite of the provisions of Resolution 1192 (XII), 24 Members did not vote for China in 1958; in 1961 the number of Members not voting for China was 38, in 1962 it was 39, and in 1963 it was 35. Moreover, no form of ballot paper can prevent a State from receiv-ing votes in more than one group, as was the case with Greece in 1960.

The 1957 and 1963 decisions regarding the composition of the General Committee did nothing to clear up an existing anomaly, which is that more States can receive a simple (absolute) majority of

TABLE 12

Dispersal of votes in elections of Vice-Presidents, 1958–1963

	Asia and Africa		Latin America		Eastern Europe		Western Europe and other States		Total No. of States obtaining votes (excluding Permanent Members of Security Council)
	No. of vacancies	No. of states obtaining votes	No. of vacancies	No. of states obtaining votes	No. of vacancies	No. of states obtaining votes	No. of vacancies	No. of states obtaining votes	
1958	3	19	2	7	1	4	2	6	36
1959	4	8	1	2	1	2	2	8	20
1960	4	12	2	5	1	3	1	2	22
1961	3	11	2	3	1	3	2	3	20
1962	3	9	2	5	1	2	2	6	22
1963	4	12	1	4	1	2	2	9	27

votes than there are places to be filled. This possibility was commented on by the delegation of Panama during the second session,[64] and on three occasions (1952, 1953, and 1957) in connection with the election of Vice-Presidents more States received a simple majority of votes than there were places. On each occasion, the Assembly has regarded as elected those States, equal in number to the places to be filled, obtaining the greatest number of votes. Nor was any provision made in 1957 or 1963 for the possibility that fewer States might receive the required majority than there are vacancies. This possibility had always existed, but under the previous procedure, balloting continued until all places had been filled. It is not clear what procedure would be followed if, for example, one of the permanent members of the Security Council should fail to obtain a simple majority of votes in repeated ballots. Further, the 1957 and 1963 decisions did not provide for the possibility that the number of States obtaining the required majority might equal the number of vacancies, but that the pattern of election might not conform to that prescribed. No form of ballot paper can entirely eliminate this possibility.

The Question of Nominations

The prohibition of nominations in plenary meetings has been more of a fiction than a fact; and in relation to the presidency, even the fiction has not always been maintained.* If the present system should, in time, prove unsatisfactory, consideration might again be given to the possibility of having a nominations committee, an expedient to which the Assembly of the League of Nations was driven by an incident which occurred during its sixteenth session.

Until 1937 the League of Nations used essentially the same method of electing the President and Vice-Presidents of the Assembly and Chairmen of Committees as is now used by the United Nations Assembly. The abandonment of this method by the League was due to two developments which, on first glance, might appear to have been in conflict. On the one hand, it was often alleged by some of the medium and smaller powers that the General Committee of

---

* Rule 94, which prohibits nominations in plenary meetings, does not apply in connection with the election of judges of the International Court of Justice.

the League Assembly (which was constituted in much the same way as is the General Committee of the United Nations Assembly) was not representative in character, and in particular that the great powers exercised a disproportionate influence. If that had been all there was to the problem, the League might well have adopted the same course as has the United Nations and merely enlarged the General Committee. However, when it came to the election of Vice-Presidents by secret ballot in 1935, it was found that seven States had received an absolute majority of votes, though there were only six places to be filled. The President (Eduard Beneš of Czechoslovakia) announced that the six States which had received the largest num-of votes had been elected as Vice-Presidents. The trouble was that the seventh State, the Soviet Union, newly admitted into the League, had received only one vote less than the fifth and sixth States in the list; more important, it was a firmly established custom of the League (as it has been of the United Nations) that the great powers should always be on the General Committee. The difficulty in 1935 was eliminated when the General Committee proposed, and the Assembly agreed, that the Soviet Union should be elected as an additional Vice-President. This was possible under the League Assembly's Rules of Procedure.

Inevitably there was considerable discussion of how a repetition of the unfortunate 1935 incident could be avoided in the future, and the delegation of Norway suggested the procedure which was approved in 1936 and put into operation in 1937 on a trial basis. By this procedure, the provisional President of the Assembly submitted proposals regarding the composition of an eleven-member committee whose duty it was to nominate candidates for the General Committee. This did not interfere with the right to vote for persons or States other than those proposed by the Committee on Nominations. It was hoped that this procedure would put an end to lobbying for elections, or at least reduce the extent of it, and would also save the Secretary-General from the situation, which he had found embarrassing, of being the recipient of requests for favours which it was not in his power to grant.

The Executive Committee of the Preparatory Commission of the United Nations considered the possibility of recommending for the General Assembly a procedure similar to that which the League had approved in 1936. There was wide support for the idea that there should be a nominations committee, that it should be composed of States rather than individuals, and that its members should be appointed on the proposal of the President of the Assembly. The suggestion was made that such a nominations committee might also make recommendations regarding elections to the three Councils, but the general sentiment did not favour this and it was agreed that these elections should be a matter for informal consultations. However, when the proposal for a nominations committee was finally put to the vote in the Executive Committee, it received a simple, but not the necessary two-thirds, majority; accordingly, no recommendation was made.[65]

During the first session of the General Assembly (1946) there was considerable discussion of the whole question of nominations, and reference was made to the consideration that had been given in the Preparatory Commission to the possibility of creating a special committee on nominations. The General Assembly did not pursue the question, however, but simply adopted an amendment to the Rules to the effect that in plenary meetings 'There shall be no nominations'.[66] This provision remains in Rule 94.

During the consideration of the Provisional Rules of Procedure in the course of the second session, the Swedish delegation reintroduced the proposal for a nominations committee. This proposal, after minor amendment, read as follows:

> A Nominating Committee consisting of representatives of delegations of which the President, Vice-Presidents and the Chairman [sic] of Main Committees of the previous session of the General Assembly were members, shall meet three days before the opening of each session of the General Assembly for the purpose of suggesting one or more candidates for Chairmen, Vice-Chairmen and Rapporteurs of the Main Committees. The Committee shall present a first report to the President of the General Assembly at the opening of the session and such further reports as may be required. The President shall communicate to each Main Committee the suggestions of the Nominating Committee which concern that Committee. These provisions do not affect the right of Members to make nominations in the Main Committees or to cast votes for any eligible person.[67]

This text was approved by a sub-committee of the Sixth Committee by five votes to two, with the United Kingdom abstaining.

In the Sixth Committee itself, the Soviet Union proposed the deletion of the draft rule. The Soviet representative stated that to establish a nominations committee would lead to back-door intrigues; the persons nominated would be those who were best known to members of the nominations committee and not necessarily those who were most capable. The British representative supported the Soviet point of view. The right of nomination belonged to all delegations, he said, and the matter should be dealt with by 'the heads of delegations . . . and not persons who merely happened to be at United Nations headquarters before the Assembly was opened'. The Indian representative considered that the result of having a nominations committee would be that small countries would be subjected to great pressure. The Scandinavian delegations and Canada spoke in favour of the draft rule, but the Soviet proposal was carried by twenty-seven votes to four.[68]

In 1949 a further attempt was made to persuade the Assembly to establish a nominations committee. Among a number of recommendations submitted to the Committee on procedure, the Canadian delegation urged that, in order to ensure the selection at all times of competent and experienced Chairmen of Main Committees, and to maintain the principle of equitable geographical distribution, there be created a nominations committee; that nominations should be submitted in writing to the President and should be announced by him; but that there should be no oral nominations or nomination speeches. If the number of nominations should exceed the number of places to be filled, elections would take place by secret ballot. If the number of candidates should not exceed the number of places to be filled, the President should declare the candidates elected.[69] The Committee on procedure examined the Canadian proposal but decided not to make a recommendation.[70] The matter has not been formally raised since 1949.

The present system of election undoubtedly has many merits, in particular in allowing negotiations which inevitably involve some discussion of personalities to be conducted informally and privately. This, however, is not an argument in favour of the present or any other system, since informal and private negotiations will take place whatever method is used, and whether the method facilitates or forbids formal nominations.

There are three main disadvantages to the present system. First, some Member States have virtually no opportunity of influencing the informal negotiations and may even encounter difficulty in discovering what proposals are being considered. For obvious reasons, this difficulty is most acute for States which are not members of any organized group or bloc.

The second complaint that is made about the present system is that time is wasted because several sets of negotiations on the same question may take place simultaneously, but without apparent connection. This happens most frequently during the early stages of negotiation, but it is by no means confined to the early stages.

The third complaint is that the system encourages log-rolling, a practice which, when carried to excess, becomes an abuse of the electoral system.

None of the tendencies complained of in the present system would be eliminated entirely by having a nominations committee, but their intensity might be lessened. Should the present system eventually prove unsatisfactory, as it did in the League Assembly, the case for establishing a nominations committee might again be examined. Such a committee would need to be small. Perhaps it would be sufficiently representative if it comprised members of the delegations from which the presiding officers of the two procedural committees (the General Committee and the Credentials Committee) and the seven Main Committees of the previous session were elected.

The Swedish proposal of 1947 would have entrusted a nominations committee with the task of suggesting candidates for the Chairmen, Vice-Chairmen, and Rapporteurs of Main Committees. To limit the tasks of a nominations committee to proposing the officers of Main Committees was doubtless due to the fact that, when the Swedish proposal was made, the Provisional Rules of Procedure already prohibited nominations in plenary meetings. If, however, the idea of a nominations committee were revived, it might be desirable for it to be concerned not only with the officers of Main Committees, but also with the President and Vice-Presidents of the Assembly, the members of the Credentials Committee, and possibly also the elected members of the three Councils.

A nominations committee might occasionally perform useful ancillary functions. When dissension arises about the composition of a select committee of the General Assembly, a nominations committee might be entrusted with the task of exploring privately the possibility of agreement. There is no guarantee that in any particular case such an arrangement would be more successful than the present practice, but it could hardly have a positively damaging effect.

The General Debate

In many deliberative assemblies there is an annual debate of a general character which enables representatives to examine the wood as well as the trees. In the British House of Commons, for example, such a debate centres around 'an humble address' in reply to the Gracious Speech from the Throne. During the first part of the first session of the General Assembly, there was a general discussion, in plenary meeting, of the report of the Preparatory Commission. At the beginning of the second part of the same session, there took place a general discussion. At the beginning of the second and all subsequent regular sessions of the Assembly, there has taken place in plenary meeting a General Debate.

There is no provision in the Rules of Procedure for a General Debate. The 1963 Committee on procedure described the General Debate as 'a series of statements made by most Chairmen of delegations on world problems and the role of the United Nations, in the light of the annual report of the Secretary-General on the work of the Organization and reports of other United Nations organs'.[71] The Debate concludes when all Members who wish to participate have done so.

The General Debate in the Assembly is an important diplomatic occasion, an annual gathering at the summit open to all Members of the United Nations. More than fifty heads of state, heads of government, foreign ministers, or other ministers of cabinet rank now participate each year. The Debate itself has certain intrinsic values: it is a barometer, which indicates changes in the international climate, and it has also been compared to a safety valve because it enables governments to let off steam on contentious issues without causing undue damage. Members are able to discuss issues they consider important without the necessity of proposing them as separate items for the agenda. For several years, for example, the Assembly decided not to consider the question of Chinese representation, yet Members freely expressed their views on the matter during the General Debate.

The General Debate also provides the occasion for a less formal kind of diplomatic activity. In addition to the public speeches, which are incorporated in the official records of the Assembly, there is a great deal of informal activity; personal contacts, private meetings, casual discussions, exchanges of view, exploratory soundings; the carefully arranged chance meetings in corridors, elevators, lounges, or dining rooms; the cocktail parties, receptions, lunches, and dinners; even the breakfasts. Dean Rusk has stated that he conferred with fifty-four heads of government or foreign ministers during an eleven-day period in 1963. Such events are not recorded in the official documents of the United Nations, but this plane of activity is potentially more important than the public debate of formal occasions.

The first speech in the General Debate is, by custom, usually made by the representative of Brazil, and the representatives of the United States and the Soviet Union normally speak early in the session. France and Nicaragua do not now take part in the General Debate; other States which do not often participate include Chad, Dahomey, Finland, Iceland, Ivory Coast, and Luxembourg.

TABLE 13

Number of speakers in the General Debate, 10th to 18th regular sessions

Session	Number of Members	Number of speakers	Number of meetings	Dates
10	60	45	13	22 September–4 October 1955
11	79	66	14	16 November–6 December 1956
12	82	71	21	19 September–8 October 1957
13	81	72	23	18 September–7 October 1958
14	82	79	24	17 September–7 October 1959
15	99	79	30	22 September–17 October 1960
16	101	80	29	22 September–18 October 1961
17	109	91	29	20 September–18 October 1962
18	111	96	31	19 September–14 October 1963

As the membership of the Organization has increased, so more time has been needed for the General Debate. During the first six sessions (1946–51), the General Debate occupied all or part of approximately ten plenary meetings each session; during recent sessions about thirty plenary meetings have been required. It is reasonable to assume that the number of plenary meetings required for the General

Debate will increase still further. If allowance is made for the time required to elect the officers of the Assembly, for meetings of the General Committee, and for plenary meetings to consider the recommendations of the General Committee, then almost a month will normally elapse between the opening of the session and the conclusion of the General Debate.

The Secretary-General sends a communication to Permanent Missions before the session opens, asking when they would like to speak in the General Debate. On the basis of their replies, a provisional list of speakers is prepared and submitted to the President. Some delegations like to defer their speeches until they have heard what others have to say, but only one representative can speak last.

The President of the Assembly and officials of the Secretariat do their best to keep the Debate moving along without unnecessary delays. In accordance with Rule 75, the list of speakers is closed as soon as possible, and from that point on the Debate usually proceeds without interruption.

A little time might be saved by a stricter application of Rule 70. This states, *inter alia*, that the President shall call upon speakers in the order in which they signify their desire to speak. It would be consistent with this Rule that, should a representative not be ready to speak when called upon, the President should call upon another speaker. Too often a meeting has to be cancelled, or closed before the usual time, because the next speaker on the list is not ready to speak or is otherwise occupied. It would also save time if delegations would exercise the right of reply in writing.[72]

Proposals have been made from time to time to limit the length of speeches in the General Debate. The most drastic proposal, made by Canada in 1946, was that 'Each speaker in the opening debate in plenary session . . . might be limited to ten minutes with the right to have his remarks extended in the verbatim record.'[73]

4

THE AGENDA

*Before which sovereign assembly should be brought all differ-
ences depending between one sovereign and another that cannot
be made up by private embassies before the sessions begin. . . .*

WILLIAM PENN

WHEN I HEAR complaints that sessions of the General Assembly are needlessly prolonged, I take courage by recalling that
the formal opening of the Congress of Westphalia was delayed three
years while questions of procedure and ceremonial were being
resolved. The Congress was due to open on 25 March 1642, but the
French delegates did not put in an appearance until two years later.
Disputes about the admission of members, credentials, forms of
address, and precedence occupied another year. The Congress
finally opened on 10 April 1645.[74]
Sessions of the General Assembly are lengthy simply because
there is a great deal of complicated business to discharge. Governments and peoples place great hopes in the capacity of the Assembly
to resolve problems, and the agenda tends to increase year by year.
The 1949 and 1953 Committees of the Assembly on procedure both
concluded that lengthy Assembly sessions were not primarily caused
by faulty procedure.[75]
Every deliberative body needs a standard procedure for deciding which of the matters submitted to it shall be discussed. Such a
procedure normally takes account of three considerations: (a) any
constitutional limits on the powers of the body concerned; (b) the
need, as a purely practical matter, to confine the number of matters
to be discussed to what can reasonably be attempted in the time
available; and (c) a judgment on the wisdom of taking up a particular

question at a particular time. The usual practice is for a provisional agenda to be drawn up by officials in accordance with certain rules or customs, and for the deliberative body to decide, sometimes on the basis of recommendations from an organ of limited membership, whether or not to place on the definitive agenda the items included in the provisional agenda.*

The question of the legal competence of the Assembly must be considered from two points of view: the power to *discuss*, and the power to *make recommendations*. The Charter grants to the Assembly virtually unlimited power of discussion.

> The General Assembly may discuss any questions or any matters within the scope of the present Charter or relating to the powers and functions of any organs provided for in the present Charter.[76]

The power to discuss does not automatically carry with it the power to recommend. The Assembly may discuss a dispute or situation in respect of which the Security Council is exercising the functions assigned to it in the Charter, but it may not make recommendations. In a matter with which the Security Council is not concerned, a Member State may favour, or at least acquiesce in, discussion by the Assembly, though opposing the making of recommendations, either because it considers that the question of competence can be decided only after the matter has been discussed or, regarding matters which are essentially within the domestic jurisdiction of a State, because it considers that discussion does not constitute intervention but that the making of recommendations (or certain kinds of recommendations) would constitute intervention and therefore be contrary to the Charter. The Assembly has not, in practice, been inclined to reject proposals for the inclusion of items in the agenda on constitutional grounds. In the few cases in which items proposed for the agenda have been rejected or postponed, practical or political considerations have usually carried more weight than legal arguments.

The agenda of the Assembly has grown year by year. This happens in the case of most continuing organizations; once an item has appeared on the agenda, it is likely to reappear. But two addi-

* Strictly speaking, *agenda* is plural, meaning 'things to be done'; one item of an *agenda* is an *agendum*. In practice, *agenda* is usually treated as singular. The French equivalent is *ordre du jour*. It would, perhaps, be useful to revive the word *agendum* when 'an item of the agenda' is meant.

tional factors have been at work in the case of the Assembly. First, the increase in the number of sovereign States since the war, as well as the interests of the new States, has added to the number and complexity of international problems and to the time required to deal with them. Secondly, the General Assembly and its subsidiary organs have increasingly overshadowed the three Councils; in certain fields the Assembly duplicates debates which have already taken place in the Councils, and in other fields it has assumed responsibilities that could be more effectively discharged by technical organs of limited membership.

Whatever the number of questions submitted to the Assembly, and regardless of their gravity or complexity, there are practical limits to what the Assembly can do effectively within the present general organizational framework. For purely practical reasons relating to the administration of the United Nations and the schedule of meetings, the Assembly should in normal circumstances conclude the main part of its regular session by the third week in December. This, in effect, establishes a duration of thirteen or fourteen weeks, depending on the date of 'the third Tuesday in September' on which the regular sessions commence (Rule 1).* Within that three-month period, only a limited amount of business can receive adequate consideration. If the agenda is overloaded, some matters will receive insufficient attention.

The 1949 Committee on procedure, at a time when the Assembly's agenda was not as heavy as it is now, emphasized the need for discrimination in connection with the agenda. The Committee urged that, in order to maintain the length of sessions within normal limits, proposals for the inclusion of items in the agenda should be scrutinized with greater care. All requests for the inclusion of items should be examined not only with special attention to the importance of the questions in relation to the purposes of the United Nations, but also in relation to the agenda as a whole and the time available for the session. The Committee reaffirmed the right of the Assembly to exclude certain questions from the agenda, as well as to delete questions previously included.[78]

---

* It was thought by the Secretariat in 1947 that regular session of the Assembly would last five to seven weeks, of which three weeks would be taken up with meetings of Main Committees; the 1949 Committee on procedure recorded the opinion that sessions should not exceed eight weeks; the Assembly decided in 1963 that 'save in quite exceptional cases, the duration of regular sessions should not exceed thirteen weeks'.[77]

Matters proposed for inclusion in the agenda are of three kinds, depending on the date of their submission. Most items are included by the Secretary-General in the Provisional Agenda, which is communicated to Member States at least sixty days before the opening of the session (Rule 12); that is to say, approximately the middle of July. An unofficial draft of the provisional agenda is usually available in May.

The Provisional Agenda of a regular session should include (Rule 13):

(a) Report of the Secretary-General on the work of the Organization;

(b) Reports from the Security Council,
>   the Economic and Social Council,
>   the Trusteeship Council,
>   the International Court of Justice,
>   the subsidiary organs of the General Assembly,
>   specialized agencies (where such reports are called for under agreements entered into);

(c) All items the inclusion of which has been ordered by the General Assembly at a previous session;

(d) All items proposed by the other principal organs of the United Nations;

(e) All items proposed by any Member of the United Nations;

(f) All items pertaining to the budget for the next financial year and the report on the accounts for the last financial year;

(g) All items which the Secretary-General deems it necessary to put before the General Assembly; and

(h) All items proposed under Article 35, paragraph 2, of the Charter by States not Members of the United Nations.

In spite of the terms of Rule 13, the International Court of Justice does not submit a report to the Assembly, and the Provisional Agenda includes no reference to such a report. Practice in this matter does not conform to the Rules, and there seems no reason why the reference to a report from the Court should not be deleted when the Rules of Procedure are next revised.

The stipulation in Rule 13 that 'the provisional agenda of a regular session shall include . . . reports from . . . the subsidiary organs of the General Assembly' does not mean that every subsidiary organ reports every session. Reports of a subsidiary organ are included in the Provisional Agenda only if this has been specifically requested or ordered by the Assembly at a previous session or if the subsidiary organ itself considers that a report is necessary.

Resolutions of the Assembly requesting that reports be prepared have not always indicated clearly what procedure should be followed regarding the inclusion of such reports in the Provisional Agenda of a future session. The 1953 Committee on procedure commented:

> The situation would be clarified if the practice were adopted of stating in the resolution whether it is intended that the report should be submitted to the General Assembly for consideration or to Members for their information. . . . As regards, in particular, resolutions calling for the submission of annual reports, it is especially desirable to avoid any possible uncertainty as to whether or not the Secretary-General should include such reports each year in the provisional agenda.[79]

Matters submitted too late for inclusion in the Provisional Agenda, but at least thirty days before the opening of the session, are known as Supplementary Items and are placed on a Supplementary List (Rule 14). The Rules of Procedure provide that any Member or principal organ or the Secretary-General may request the inclusion of items in the Supplementary List. States not Members of the United Nations (which may, under certain circumstances, bring to the attention of the Assembly disputes to which they are parties) and also subsidiary organs of the Assembly, are not specifically given the right to propose items for the Supplementary List.*

Matters which are proposed for inclusion in the agenda after the Supplementary List has been closed (that is to say, matters submitted less than thirty days before the opening of the session or during the session) are known as Additional Items (Rule 15). Such Additional Items, by the very fact of having been submitted late, are presumed to be both important and urgent. The Rules provide that, unless the Assembly decides otherwise by a two-thirds majority of Members present and voting, an Additional Item may not be considered until seven days have elapsed since it was placed on the

* If it were thought desirable to make specific provision for the submission of Supplementary Items by States not Members or by subsidiary organs of the Assembly, it would be necessary to revise Rule 14 of the Rules of Procedure.

agenda; the Rules also provide that no Additional Item may be considered until a committee has reported on the matter.

Rule 15 regarding Additional Items, which is based on a similar rule of the League Assembly, does not specify by whom Additional Items may be submitted. The provision that no Additional Item may be considered until it has been on the agenda for a week, unless a decision to the contrary is taken by a two-thirds majority vote, is intended to prevent the Assembly from taking up a new matter before delegations have received instructions. The difficulty is that if the matter is 'important and urgent', the sponsor or sponsors may well take the view that it should be considered immediately.

The Rules of Procedure state that each item proposed for the agenda 'shall be accompanied by an explanatory memorandum and if possible, by basic documents or by a draft resolution' (Rule 20). In practice it is not always possible or wise to circulate a draft resolution until the debate is well under way.

It would be a useful practice, in the case of disputes or situations which are in the nature of disputes, if Member States proposing items for inclusion in the agenda would state in the explanatory memorandum which of the 'peaceful means' which, under Article 33 of the Charter, shall be resorted to 'first of all', have been tried. This would help the Assembly to judge the gravity of the situation and the extent to which the parties had already made efforts to reach agreement.

The General Committee: Composition

All proposals for the inclusion of items in the agenda are examined by the General Committee (*le Bureau*), which makes recommendations to the plenary Assembly. The General Committee consists of the officers of the Assembly, that is to say, the President, Vice-Presidents, and Chairmen of the seven Main Committees (Rule 38). It has been the experience of most deliberative bodies with more than about twenty members that a small 'steering' group or committee is needed if business is to be handled in an orderly and expeditious manner. Such a 'steering' group should be quite small in size, so that a degree of intimacy and cohesion may develop. It should proceed with its work without undue hurry and, as necessary, in private. It need not have the power to act on its own responsibility; its primary function should be advisory.

The Executive Committee of the Preparatory Commission of the United Nations recommended that the General Committee should consist of fifteen members:

    (a) the President of the Assembly;
    (b) seven Vice-Presidents;
    (c) the Chairmen of the six Main Committees;
    (d) the Chairman of the Credentials Committee.

The Executive Committee also recommended that the Assembly should have the right to add to the General Committee 'the Chairmen of the other Committees of the General Assembly and, in exceptional cases, other members'.[80]

The Preparatory Committee itself considered that the General Committee should have 'a small membership' and reduced the size to fourteen members by omitting the Chairman of the Credentials Committee. The Preparatory Committee also stipulated that:

    (a) no two members of the General Committee should be nationals of the same State;
    (b) the Vice-Presidents should be chosen on the basis of ensuring the representative character of the Committee;
    (c) the Chairmen should be chosen on the basis of equitable geographical distribution, experience, and personal competence.[81]

These recommendations were approved during the first part of the first session of the Assembly.

During the fourth session, it was agreed that the Chairman of any sessional committee of the whole membership should be entitled to attend meetings of the General Committee and participate without vote in the discussions.[82] As an *Ad Hoc* Political Committee was created for the third and subsequent sessions, this change in the Rules in effect increased the number of members of the General Committee to fifteen. The Chairman of the *Ad Hoc* Political Committee was made a voting member of the General Committee during the eighth session.[83] During the eleventh session, the *Ad Hoc* Political Committee was made permanent and its name was changed to 'Special Political Committee'; and the number of Vice-Presidents was increased from seven to eight.[84] During the twelfth session, the number of Vice-Presidents was increased to thirteen, giving the

General Committee a total membership of twenty-one.[85] During the eighteenth session, the number of Vice-Presidents was increased to seventeen, thus making the total membership of the General Committee twenty-five.[86]

The Assembly's eight presiding officers are elected in their individual capacities; if the Chairman of a Main Committee is unable to attend a meeting of the General Committee, he designates the Vice-Chairman rather than a member of his delegation as his substitute. A Vice-Chairman acting as substitute for a Chairman is not entitled to vote in the General Committee if he is of the same delegation as another member of the Committee. In the case of resumed sessions and sessions in two or more parts, it has sometimes happened that neither the Chairman nor the Vice-Chairman of a Committee has been able to function. In these circumstances, the head of the delegation to which the chairman belonged has replaced him.[87]

Vice-Presidents, as in the League of Nations, are States rather than persons. During the election of Vice-Presidents during the first session, the President stated: 'I should like to remind the delegations that they should vote for countries and not for individual representatives'.[88] If a Vice-President finds it necessary to be absent during a meeting of the General Committee, he may designate a member of his own delegation as his substitute (Rule 39).

During the first session, it was agreed that a Member of the Assembly which did not have a representative on the General Committee, but which had requested the inclusion of an Additional Item in the agenda, should be entitled to attend any meetings of the General Committee at which its request was being discussed, and might participate, without vote, in the discussion of that item.[89] The word 'Additional' was eliminated during the 1947 revision of the Rules.[90]

There have been two problems connected with the participation of non-members of the General Committee. First, when a large number of governments propose that an item should be included in the agenda, it is undesirable that all of them should participate in the work of the General Committee when the request is discussed. The League of Nations eventually fixed a limit to the number of States which might propose a new item or sponsor a proposal. The matter was raised by Norway in the following terms:

It is ... conceivable that proposals might be submitted by so considerable a number of signatories that the other Members of the League would find themselves exposed to moral pressure and would hesitate to express their misgivings or doubts. . . . A proposal signed by more than half the Members of the League would more or less settle the question in advance. . . .

It seems desirable to remedy in good time the drawbacks . . . by stipulating that no proposal for the placing of a new question on the Assembly's agenda and no draft resolution, amendment or motion should be signed by more than a small number of Members. . . .

The Norwegian Government ventures to suggest that the figure should be fixed at ten. . . .[91]

Several States urged that the number might be increased from ten to fifteen, and Norway agreed.[92] The rules of procedure of the League Assembly were revised accordingly.

In the General Assembly of the United Nations there is no limitation on the number of Member States which may propose an item for inclusion in the agenda, and in the early days there was a tendency for all the sponsors to participate in the discussion in the General Committee. During the first special session, for example, the delegations of Iraq, Lebanon, Saudi Arabia, and Syria took an active part in the work of the General Committee during consideration of the proposal to include the Palestine question in the agenda: in addition, Egypt was a member of the Committee.[93] There has developed over the years a commendable tradition by which all the sponsors of an item do not insist on participating in the work of the General Committee when the request is under discussion; indeed, in the majority of cases there is now little or no discussion in the General Committee.

The second problem in connection with the participation of non-members in General Committee discussions has been that Rule 43 limits participation to those States which have 'requested the inclusion of an item'; a Member State which is opposed to the inclusion of an item, or is in some other way directly concerned in the matter, has no specific right of participation. This matter arose during the first part of the third session during consideration of the Indian proposal to include in the agenda the item 'Treatment of Indians in the Union of South Africa.' The South African representative made a formal request to participate in the discussion. The Chairman pointed out that there was no Rule of Procedure which covered this contingency, but he considered that it was only fair to hear the views of the South African representative. He therefore put his proposal to the vote, and it was adopted without opposition.[94]

During the second part of the same session, a similar question arose when India and Australia requested that the Indonesian question should be included in the agenda. The Netherlands was not represented on the General Committee, and Indonesia was not yet a Member of the United Nations. The Chairman suggested that, following the practice of the first part of the session, it would only be fair to allow the representative of the Netherlands to speak. The Soviet and Polish representatives objected to this, but did not press the matter to a vote. Following the statement of the representative of the Netherlands, the Chairman said that a representative of the Republic of Indonesia had 'expressed the wish to state his views'. It is not clear from the summary in the official records whether there was any objection to this request; the records merely state: 'the Chairman invited him to make a statement'.[95]

During the tenth session, both the Netherlands and Australia requested permission to take part in the discussion in the General Committee on the proposal to include the question of West Irian (West New Guinea) in the agenda, but the Egyptian delegate opposed granting the Australian request. The matter was pressed to a vote, and the Committee decided to invite the Australian representative to take part in the discussion.[96]

During the seventeenth session, Portugal asked to speak in the General Committee on a proposal to include in the agenda an item relating to colonialism. After some discussion, the Committee voted eight in favour, eight against, with five abstentions, on Portugal's request. The Chairman of the Committee 'considered it preferable in the circumstances that Portugal should not be heard. . . .' Later in the same meeting, the Committee agreed by eleven votes to five, with five abstentions, that Portugal should be heard on a proposal to include in the agenda an item on the situation in Angola.[97]

During the eighteenth session, a somewhat different question arose. An item on the violation of human rights in South Viet-Nam was proposed for inclusion in the agenda. The Republic of Viet-Nam was not a Member of the United Nations but maintained a Permanent Observer at UN headquarters. The Permanent Observer asked to participate in the discussion in the General Committee, but the consensus of the General Committee was that he should not be heard.[98]

General Committee : Functions

One of the main responsibilities of the General Committee is to examine all proposals for the inclusion of items in the agenda and to make recommendations to the plenary Assembly. The five permanent members of the Security Council are, by well-established tradition, always elected to the General Committee, but the medium and smaller powers have from the beginning feared lest the General Committee should become an instrument of the great powers for dominating the Assembly. This apprehension was voiced in the Preparatory Commission, when Belgium proposed to add to the Provisional Rules of Procedure the sentence: 'The General Committee cannot decide any political question'. This proposal received twenty-four affirmative and seventeen negative votes, but as a two-thirds majority was not received, it failed of adoption.

In view of the anxiety which lay behind the Belgian proposal, several delegations made statements regarding their conception of the role of the General Committee. The United States emphasized that the plenary Assembly would have complete control over policy and would be the 'supreme authority'; the functions of the General Committee would be mainly those of 'administrative management'. The United Kingdom denied that the General Committee would be a secret caucus; it would be concerned with procedure, and the plenary must and would stop any political manipulations under the cloak of procedure. The Soviet Union said that the General Committee would not take decisions of political importance, and in any case its recommendations would be subject to approval by the full Assembly.[99]

During the first part of the first session, a sentence substantially the same as that proposed by Belgium in the Preparatory Commission was added to the Provisional Rules of Procedure, in spite of the opposition of China, the Soviet Union, the United Kingdom, and the United States.[100] The main problem in practice, however, has not been to prevent the General Committee from deciding political questions; it has been to prevent it from engaging in lengthy political debate prior to making procedural recommendations.

During the second part of the first session, Canada urged that the General Committee, in discussing matters related to the agenda, should not debate the substance of a question but should confine itself to discussing whether or not it should recommend that an item be included in the agenda.[101] Nothing came of this proposal when it was first put forward, but the idea was revived by Canada when the 1949 Committee on procedure invited Member States to submit proposals. The Canadian delegation pointed out that Presidents of the Assembly had found it difficult to restrict the discussions in the General Committee to matters within the Committee's jurisdiction. The Committee was precluded from *deciding* any political question, but nothing was said about the extent to which the Committee might *discuss* the substance of items proposed for the agenda. Canada proposed that the Rules should state explicitly that the General Committee should not discuss the substance of an item except in so far as this might bear on the Committee's recommendations. This proposal was approved by the Committee and an addition was made to the relevant Rule.[102]

Until 1949, the General Committee was merely asked to consider the matters proposed for inclusion in the agenda and to 'report thereon to the General Assembly'. Acting on a suggestion of the British delegation, the 1949 Committee on procedure proposed that the General Committee should be specifically required to make one of three recommendations with regard to each item proposed: inclusion in the agenda, rejection of the request for inclusion, or inclusion in the provisional agenda of a future session (which is tantamount to postponement).[103] This proposal was approved.

The 1949 Committee on procedure emphasized that the Assembly has the power 'to decide, at the beginning of or during the session, to refer certain items, without preliminary debate, to other organs of the United Nations . . . such as one of the existing subsidiary organs of the General Assembly, an *ad hoc* committee, one of the Councils, a specialized agency or the Secretary-General'.[104] It is within the competence of the General Committee, should it recommend such action to the plenary, to recommend also that any such items be included in the provisional agenda of a future session.

Like other organs of the United Nations, the General Committee did not immediately settle into an established routine. During the first three sessions it met relatively frequently (see Table 16, page 106), easily became involved in substantive debate, and discussed a variety of matters which in later sessions were dealt with by other and usually more informal means. During the first session, for example, the Committee considered such matters as a request from the

World Federation of Trade Unions for representation in the General Assembly, the procedure for dealing with communications from non-governmental organizations, seating arrangements in committees of the Assembly, a reply to a congratulatory communication from the Italian Government, arrangements for the installation of the first Secretary-General, the translation of speeches, and arrangements for heads of principal organs, specialized agencies, and other international organizations to attend the General Assembly.

During the first flush of enthusiasm for the United Nations, there was a tendency to submit for inclusion in the Assembly's agenda idealistic proposals of marginal importance. This had been true of the League Assembly, which had been asked to take up such matters as how the teaching of Esperanto could become more general. Among the items submitted for inclusion in the agenda of the first session of the United Nations Assembly were the following:

> Proposal that the Assembly should express 'its keen sympathy with the impending start of the construction of the Columbus Lighthouse Memorial. . . .'[105]

> Proposal regarding 'the translation and publication of the classics into the languages of Members of the United Nations'.[106]

> Proposal for the 'creation of a world university alliance'.[107]

Member States soon realized that the Assembly could not perform its essential functions if it took up too many matters of secondary importance.

The General Committee no longer exercises to the full the functions specified in the Rules. It now makes recommendations to the plenary concerning:

(1) The inclusion, exclusion, or postponement of items proposed for the agenda;

(2) The rewording of items, and the amalgamation or grouping of related items;

(3) The allocation of items to the plenary and to Main Committees;

(4) The closing date of the session.

The General Committee has the authority to revise resolutions adopted by the Assembly, changing their form but not their substance; any such changes must be reported to the Assembly for its consideration (Rule 44). The Committee meets at such times as the President deems necessary, or upon the request of any other of its members (Rule 42).

There are two groups of functions which the Rules state are the responsibility of the General Committee but which in practice have not been exercised. First, the Committee should assist the President and the General Assembly in drawing up the agenda for each plenary meeting, in determining the priority of its items, and in the co-ordination of the proceedings of all committees of the Assembly, and should also assist the President in the general conduct of the work of the Assembly which falls within his competence (Rule 41). The wording is an adaptation of paragraph 2 of Rule 8 of the rules of procedure of the League Assembly.

Secondly, the General Committee should meet periodically throughout each session to review the progress of the Assembly and its committees, and to make recommendations for furthering such progress (Rule 42). This wording is based on a British revision of a proposal of the 1949 Committee on procedure.[108]

The above functions, which formally belong to the General Committee, have in practice been discharged by informal means, and in particular by a weekly lunch held throughout the session attended by the presiding officers of the Assembly and officials of the Secretariat specially concerned with the business of the Assembly.[109] The General Assembly decided in 1963 that the General Committee ought to fulfil its functions under the Rules of Procedure 'and, in particular, make appropriate recommendations for furthering the progress of the Assembly and its Committees, in such a way as to facilitate the closing of the session by the date fixed; to this end, the General Committee should meet at least once every three weeks.'[110]

Governments and the Agenda

There are, broadly speaking, two main views concerning proposals to include items in the agenda. There is, first, the view which one may term 'unselective' and which seems to be the view of most Member States. Those holding this view would say that the Assembly should reject a request to include an item in the agenda only in the most exceptional circumstances; that the Charter implies the right of Member States to have their grievances and problems aired in the Assembly; that the Assembly is strengthened rather than weakened by having a great deal of work to do; and that the effect of Assembly debate is almost always beneficial. Such a view may not be held with complete consistency; a government may take this general position and yet at the same time oppose a request that some particularly controversial item be included in the agenda (as, indeed, many governments did for several years on the question of Chinese representation).

I can best illustrate this point of view by letting some delegates speak for themselves.

Ceylon: 'his delegation . . . attached great importance to the principle that items proposed by Member States should be included in the agenda. . . .'[111]

Ecuador: 'his delegation had unreservedly supported the principle that the General Assembly should not refuse to discuss any item which a Member State had requested for inclusion in the agenda. . . .'[112]

Ghana: 'It is the view of my delegation that any Member of the United Nations has a right to place on the agenda . . . any item that it wishes to propose for discussion.'[113]

Guatemala: 'he would vote in favour of inclusion of the item . . . in accordance with his delegation's policy of agreeing to the inclusion of all items requested.'[114]

India: 'An item could not be deleted . . . without a serious infringement of the Assembly's prerogatives.'[115]

Iraq: 'Member States should have the right to secure the inclusion in the agenda of problems they considered to be of importance.'[116]

United States: 'the United States delegation would not vote against the inclusion of the proposal item in the agenda, because it believed that a Member of the United Nations was entitled to express any views it desired . . .'[117]

The general approach which these statements express is in contrast to the view which one may term 'restrictive'. Those holding the latter view ask that every proposal for the inclusion of items in the agenda should be examined with regard to the Assembly's competence, as well as the political wisdom and practical consequences of taking up a question at a particular time. As a British Foreign Secretary has put it:

> We also think . . . that the inscription of items should be approached not just from the legalistic point of view; there also should be a practical political attitude towards the agenda. . . . I cannot accept the conception, although I know it is held by many, that inscription should be automatic.[118]

This is not the place to examine in detail the question of the Assembly's competence. It is, however, significant that several of the delegations which have been most insistent that the Charter provisions on competence be strictly applied have taken the view that the issue of competence cannot be settled until after substantive debate. These delegations have not regarded doubts about the Assembly's competence as a reason for opposing the inclusion of an item in the agenda—though they may consider that there are political or practical reasons in particular cases for opposing inclusion. Again I let the delegates speak for themselves.

> *Belgium:* 'The Assembly . . . could not determine whether the Organization was competent to deal with a matter unless that matter was first included in the agenda.'[119]

> *Egypt:* '. . . the inclusion of a question in the Assembly agenda did not prejudge the question of competence'.[120]

> *India:* 'before we can discuss the question of competence, it is essential first to place the item on the agenda'.[121]

> *Mexico:* 'Whether or not the General Assembly was competent to deal with the proposed item . . . could be decided only by the General Assembly itself, after discussion.'[122]

> *U.S.S.R.:* 'Only when the time comes to discuss the substance of any given item can the question of the General Assembly's competence be raised. . . . It is absolutely unprecedented to consider the question of whether an item should be included in the agenda or not from the the point of view of the Assembly's competence.'[123]

> *United Kingdom:* 'reserved the right to speak on the question of competence in the General Assembly; a recommendation by the General Committee to include an item in the agenda in no way prejudged that issue'.[124]

> *Mr F. M. Urquia* (El Salvador, Chairman of the *Ad Hoc*

Political Committee, 1953): 'The Chairman explained that, when the General Assembly included an item in its agenda, it did not prejudge the question of its competence. . . . It had always been agreed that the question of competence was considered by the committee concerned or by the Assembly itself.'[125]

The problem of the Assembly's competence has usually centred around Articles 2 (7) or 12 (1) of the Charter. Article 2 (7) states that the Assembly (or, indeed, any organ of the United Nations) is not authorized to intervene in matters which are essentially within the domestic jurisdiction of any State, except in relation to the application of enforcement measures under Chapter VII of the Charter. The following are among the questions raised in connection with this provision:

What is meant by 'matters which are essentially within the domestic jurisdiction of any state'?

Does the inclusion of an item in the agenda, and consequently the discussion of it, constitute intervention?

Does a recommendation, whether of a general nature or addressed to a particular State or group of States, constitute intervention?

Does the creation of a subsidiary organ to study and report constitute intervention?

These questions are not solely legal in character; they have important political implications. Moreover, the interpretation of the Charter changes as new concepts develop regarding the nature of sovereignty and the purposes of intergovernmental organizations. The Permanent Court of International Justice declared: 'The question whether a certain matter is or is not solely within the jurisdiction of a State is an essentially relative question; it depends upon the development of international relations.'[126]

The other Article of the Charter which has given rise to discussion regarding the Assembly's competence states that 'While the Security Council is exercising in respect of any dispute or situation the functions assigned to it in the present Charter, the General Assembly shall not make any recommendations with regard to that dispute or situation unless the Security Council so requests.' The purpose of this provision was to prevent the General Assembly and the Security Council from acting concurrently in the same question, a problem which had troubled the League. Differences concerning the interpretation of Article 12 (1) have, in the main, centred around two questions:

> What is the meaning of the phrase 'while the Security Council is exercising . . . the functions assigned to it . . .'?
> What is the scope of the term 'recommendation'?

The practice of the Assembly regarding competence has been neither clear nor uniform. Article 12 (1) does not appear to impose any limitation on the Assembly's right of discussion; Article 2 (7) has generally been interpreted as not imposing any limitation on the right of discussion. It has been widely, though not universally, held that in cases where the question of competence is unclear, the matter cannot be decided until after substantive debate.

If governments believe, before substantive debate has taken place, that the Assembly is not competent even to discuss some question submitted to it, the legal objections are usually stated before a vote is taken on whether to include, postpone, or reject the item. As a practical matter, however, such legal objections rarely carry weight in influencing the General Committee or the Assembly. At this stage it seems more effective to use a political argument, such as that to include the matter in the agenda will provoke unnecessary discord, or will prejudice negotiations that are taking place or contemplated elsewhere, or will interfere with other efforts to deal with a question.*

Practical considerations are often as important as legal or political ones. The practical question in relation to the agenda, though the one mentioned least often by representatives, is the relative importance of different questions. In a limited period of time, only a limited amount of business can receive adequate attention. All proposals for the agenda, whether new items or hardy perennials, should be examined with reference to the important practical consideration that if the Assembly deals with one matter, it almost certainly deals less effectively with some other matter. The question is not whether a particular matter is urgent or important; the question is how urgent and important it is in relation to all the other matters that have been or may be proposed.

* The head of one delegation is said to have told his subordinates: 'Whenever possible, use good political arguments. If there are no good political arguments, use bad political arguments. If there are no bad political arguments, use legal arguments.'

Proposals for an Agenda Committee

I have indicated above some of the reasons why the General Committee has not exercised a great deal of discrimination regarding proposals for the agenda. There is an additional reason of a practical nature that may be stressed here: the General Committee inevitably works under a sense of pressure because it meets at a time when its members are preoccupied with other matters. Various procedures to circumvent this difficulty have been suggested, including the idea that a small agenda committee might scrutinize proposals for the agenda before the session begins.[127]

The League of Nations had an agenda committee as well as a general committee, the function of the former being to consider applications for the inclusion of *new* questions in the agenda and to report to the Assembly thereon. The Executive Committee of the Preparatory Commission of the United Nations considered a proposal for the establishment of both a general committee and an agenda committee; the latter would have performed the functions now given to the General Committee by Rule 40. Those who favoured the establishment of an agenda committee argued that it would lighten the task of the General Committee. The majority of the members of the Executive Committee, however, considered that the functions proposed for the agenda committee could be performed by the General Committee. Fears were expressed that the existence of two committees would create confusion and a conflict of authority, and it was thought then that a proliferation of committees should be avoided. The Executive Committee decided, therefore, to transfer to the General Committee the functions originally intended for an agenda committee.

The idea of an agenda committee for the Assembly has been revived from time to time, and in the case of another United Nations organ an agenda committee was in existence for four years. The Economic and Social Council decided in 1947 to establish an agenda committee consisting of the President, the two Vice-Presidents, and two other members of the Council. This committee met between sessions of the Council; it was authorized to hear any of the authorities that had proposed the inclusion of items, and to make recommendations on the provisional agenda. Various difficulties were encountered in the functioning of the committee; these arose in part because some of its members could not attend all of its meetings while others had ceased to be members of the Council while they were still members of the committee. Various changes were made in the method of constituting the committee and its terms of reference were widened, but these changes did not eliminate the difficulties. In any case, it was found that the recommendations of the agenda committee did not appreciably reduce discussion of the agenda in the Council itself. In 1951 the Council discontinued the committee. In its place, a short session of the Council takes place towards the end of or shortly after the main part of each regular session of the General Assembly. The Council, during this 'resumed session', considers the program of work for the following year and adopts the agenda for the forthcoming session. This procedure seems generally satisfactory.

At one time it was thought that the Interim Committee of the Assembly might function as a scrutinizing committee in relation to a particular category of questions. The Interim Committee was empowered to 'consider and report, with its conclusions,' to the Assembly on any dispute or situation which threatened world peace and had been proposed for inclusion in the agenda, provided the Committee considered the matter to be important and requiring preliminary study.[128]

When the procedure of the Assembly was being reviewed in 1949, three separate proposals for an agenda committee were made. South Africa favoured a standing agenda committee within the Secretariat, under the chairmanship of the Secretary-General.[129] Denmark, Norway, and Sweden jointly suggested, as a basis for discussion, the creation of a committee to meet a short time in advance of each session to prepare its work.[130] The United Kingdom proposed that a fifteen-member agenda committee, representative in character and including the five permanent members of the Security Council, should meet not less than three weeks before the opening of each regular session and should be dissolved on or before the opening of the session. This committee should consider matters proposed for inclusion in the agenda and make recommendations to the Assembly concerning the inclusion, non-inclusion, or postponement of each item, the priority to be given to consideration of particular items, and an estimated date for the conclusion of the session.[131]

These three proposals were not aimed directly at securing a closer scrutiny of the agenda. The main argument of those who favoured the proposals was that, the examination of the agenda should be entrusted to a committee that would be less pressed for time than is the General Committee, thus making it easier for delegations to find grounds for agreement.[132] The 1949 Committee on procedure decided to bring the question to the attention of the General Assembly and to transmit to the Assembly the various proposals which it had received. It requested the Secretary-General to prepare a study on previous proposals and to submit to the Assembly his views on the composition and functions of an agenda committee.[133]

The Secretary-General, in the report thus requested, expressed doubts that an agenda committee could deal more effectively with questions relating to the Assembly's agenda than the General Committee had done. The General Committee, in his view, enjoyed great prestige, and 'its recommendations are therefore normally endorsed by the General Assembly without prolonged debate in plenary meetings'. That was a considerable factor in accelerating the pace of the session. He was of the opinion that the consideration of the agenda by the General Committee did not delay the beginning of the work of Main Committees.[134] Most members of the Sixth Committee endorsed the Secretary-General's conclusion, though the British and Norwegian representatives still considered that the possibility of establishing an agenda committee deserved further exploration. After a short debate, the Sixth Committee approved the conclusions of the Secretary-General.[135]

During a review of procedure during the seventh session, the possibility of establishing an agenda committee was again raised. The British and New Zealand representatives urged that the possibility of establishing an agenda committee should be examined, but most representatives did not favour any change.[136] The matter came up once again in 1963, but the 1963 Committee on procedure 'did not consider it necessary to make a recommendation'.[137] It seems likely that the General Committee will find it increasingly difficult to perform an adequate scrutinizing function, though its work will doubtless continue to be useful by obviating the need for complicated and lengthy discussions in the plenary on the wording, grouping or amalgamation, and allocation of items. The time may yet come when an agenda committee will seem a useful means of facilitating the organization of the business of the session.

Voting in Connection with the Agenda

Two earlier studies prepared under the auspices of the Carnegie Endowment for International Peace referred to the possibility of voting in the plenary on agenda questions by secret ballot:

> As mentioned above, the General Assembly in a regular session has never [1949] refused to accept any item on its agenda. There are undoubtedly many reasons why this is so, but one of them is unquestionably the fact that few states care to offend the proposer of an agenda item by voting against such a proposal in public. Were the secret ballot applied to the acceptance of all items it is possible that a considerable number might be kept off the agenda.[138]
> A secret ballot in the plenary might also make it easier for a member to support the General Committee's recommendation against inclusion of an item without offending the proposing state.[139]

Although there are some sound arguments in favour of this proposal, there seems to be a widespread dislike of secret voting, based on a feeling that governments should not be afraid to 'stand up and be counted'.

It would presumably not require any change in the rules of procedure for the General Committee to recommend that certain matters be included in the agenda for debate only. There are always a number of items that are included in the agenda in order that governments may express their views rather than because any decision or recommendation by the General Assembly is thought to be necessary. Certain items of this nature might be considered and discussed during the General Debate. It is open to any Member State, either at the time the decision is taken to include an item in the agenda or when the item arises in the normal course, to move that the item be discussed but that no proposals arising from the debate be considered or put to the vote.

The decisions of the Assembly regarding the agenda are undoubtedly important, in the sense that these decisions are momentous and weighty, though not in the legal sense that they are among the matters which are decided by a two-thirds majority vote of the Members present and voting. The United Kingdom suggested to the 1949 Committee on procedure that a two-thirds majority of the

Members present and voting, rather than a simple majority, should be required in plenary meetings to include in the agenda either an Additional Item of an important and urgent character or any item which had been recommended for rejection or postponement by the General Committee.[140] That part of the British proposal relating to Additional Items was approved by the 1949 Committee and a revision of the relevant Rule was proposed.[141]

When the proposed revision came before the Assembly's Sixth Committee, however, it hardly received the consideration it deserved. The United States representative insisted that a heavy agenda, far from being a sign of weakness, was a sign of strength; and the representative of Uruguay regarded the increase in the list of items submitted to the Assembly as a matter for congratulation.

But there was a potential anomaly in the proposal, to which the representatives of Yugoslavia and Pakistan drew attention. Important and urgent Additional Items could, if the proposal were adopted, be included in the agenda only by a two-thirds vote of Members present and voting, while a special session could be summoned by a simple majority of Members (Rules 8 and 9). Too much should not be made of this, however, because it is already the case that Supplementary and Additional Items may be added to the agenda during a special session only by a two-thirds majority (Rule 19), whereas a special session itself can be summoned by a simple majority of Member States. Be that as it may, the text proposed by the Committee on procedure was rejected.[142]

It was suggested, during the consideration of the 1949 Committee's proposal, that the inclusion of items in the agenda is a procedural question and that procedural matters should be decided by a simple majority. Again, the argument should not be pressed too far; a number of the Rules relating specifically to procedural matters (Rules 15, 19, 83, and 124) provide that a two-thirds majority is required for certain decisions.

Although questions relating to the agenda are procedural, they are indubitably important. Article 18 (2) of the Charter requires that important decisions shall be made by a two-thirds majority of Members present and voting. It would thus be in accordance with the letter and spirit of Article 18 for the Assembly to determine, by a simple majority, that any decision to include items in the agenda should require a two-thirds vote in plenary meeting. This is admittedly a drastic proposal, though it would only be making a regular practice of what is already the procedure regarding Supplementary and Additional Items during special sessions. It would ensure that all items included in the agenda would receive serious attention, which is not always the case at present. Anyone familiar with the proceedings of the Assembly can think of matters which have been admitted to the agenda with the knowledge that they will receive only perfunctory attention at the end of a busy session. Moreover, virtually all of the matters included in the agenda are regarded as of sufficient importance that resolutions arising from them require a two-thirds vote for adoption. It would, by the same token, be logical to regard inclusion of the item as requiring the same majority.

TABLE 14

Allocation of agenda items, 18th regular session, 1963

Plenary Meetings

1. Opening of the session by the Chairman of the delegation of Pakistan.
2. Minute of silent prayer or meditation.
3. Credentials of representatives to the eighteenth session of the General Assembly
   (a) Appointment of the Credentials Committee;
   (b) Report of the Credentials Committee.
4. Election of the President.
5. Constitution of the Main Committees and election of officers.
6. Election of Vice-Presidents.
7. Notification by the Secretary-General under Article 12, paragraph 2, of the Charter of the United Nations [matters relative to the maintenance of international peace and security which are being dealt with by the Security Council].
8. Adoption of the agenda.
9. General debate.
10. Report of the Secretary-General on the work of the Organization.
11. Report of the Security Council.
12. Report of the Economic and Social Council [chapters XI (section I, except paragraphs 549 to 552), XII and XIII (sections I to V and X to XII) organizational questions].
13. Report of the International Atomic Energy Agency.
14. Election of five members of the International Court of Justice.
15. Election of three non-permanent members of the Security Council.
16. Election of six members of the Economic and Social Council.
17. Election of the United Nations High Commissioner for Refugees.
18. United Nations Emergency Force:
    (a) Report on the Force.*
19. Agreement between the Republic of Indonesia and the Kingdom of the Netherlands concerning West New Guinea (West Irian): report of the Secretary-General.
20. Report of the Committee on arrangements for a conference for the purpose of reviewing the Charter.

* For sub-item (b), see p. 99, 'Fifth Committee', item 4.

TABLE 14—*continued*

21. Report of the Special Committee on the Situation with regard to the Implementation of the Declaration on the granting of independence to colonial countries and peoples.
22. Report of the Preparatory Committee on the International Co-operation Year.
23. Report of the *Ad Hoc* Committee on the Improvement of the Methods of Work of the General Assembly.
24. The violation of human rights in South Viet-Nam.
25. Restoration of the lawful rights of the People's Republic of China in the United Nations.
26. Measures in connexion with the earthquake at Skoplje, Yugoslavia.
27. Measures in connexion with the hurricane which has just struck the territories of Cuba, the Dominican Republic, Haiti, Jamaica, and Trinidad and Tobago.
28. Admission of new Members to the United Nations.

First Committee

1. Question of general and complete disarmament: report of the Conference of the Eighteen-Nation Committee on Disarmament.
2. Question of convening a conference for the purpose of signing a convention on the prohibition of the use of nuclear and thermo-nuclear weapons: report of the Secretary-General.
3. International co-operation in the peaceful uses of outer space:
   (a) Report of the Committee on the Peaceful Uses of Outer Space;
   (b) Report of the Economic and Social Council [chapter VII (section IV)].
4. The Korean question: report of the United Nations Commission for the Unification and Rehabilitation of Korea.
5. Urgent need for suspension of nuclear and thermo-nuclear tests.
6. Denuclearization of Latin America.
7. Actions on the regional level with a view to improving good neighborly relations among European States having different social and political systems.

Special Political Committee

1. The policies of *apartheid* of the Government of the Republic of South Africa: reports of the Special Committee on the policies of *apartheid* of the Government of the Republic of South Africa and replies by Member States under General Assembly resolution 1761 (XVII).
2. Effects of atomic radiation:
   (a) Report of the United Nations Scientific Committee on the Effects of Atomic Radiation;
   (b) Report of the World Meteorological Organization.
3. Report of the Commissioner-General of the United Nations Relief and Works Agency for Palestine Refugees in the Near East.
4. Question of the composition of the General Committee of the General Assembly.
5. Question of equitable representation on the Security Council and the Economic and Social Council.
6. Report of the Economic and Social Council [chapter XIII (section VI) question of the representation of African States in the Council and enlargement of the Council].

TABLE 14—*continued*

Second Committee

1. Report of the Economic and Social Council [chapters I to VI, VII (sections I to III), VIII, IX (section III), XI (section I, paragraphs 549 to 552, and section II) and XIII (sections VIII and IX) economic questions].
2. Economic development of under-developed countries:
   (a) Planning for economic development: report of the Secretary-General;
   (b) Activities of the United Nations in the field of industrial development: report of the Economic and Social Council;
   (c) Decentralization of the economic and social activities of the United Nations and strengthening of the regional economic commissions;
   (d) Accelerated flow of capital and technical assistance to the developing countries: report of the Secretary-General;
   (e) Establishment of a United Nations capital development fund: report of the Committee on a United Nations Capital Development Fund and comments thereon by the Economic and Social Council.
3. Conversion to peaceful needs of the resources released by disarmament: report of the Secretary-General.
4. United Nations training and research institute: report of the Secretary-General.
5. Progress and operations of the Special Fund.
6. United Nations programmes of technical co-operation:
   (a) Review of activities;
   (b) Confirmation of the allocation of funds under the Expanded Program of Technical Assistance;
   (c) Technical assistance to Burundi and Rwanda: report of the Secretary-General.
7. Means of promoting agrarian reform.
8. Co-operation for the eradication of illiteracy throughout the world: report of the United Nations Educational, Scientific and Cultural Organization.

Third Committee

1. Report of the Economic and Social Council [chapters IX (except section III), X and XIII (section VII) social questions].
2. Report of the United Nations High Commissioner for Refugees.
3. Draft Recommendation on Consent to Marriage, Minimum Age for Marriage, and Registration of Marriages: report of the Economic and Social Council.
4. Measures to accelerate the promotion of respect for human rights and fundamental freedoms: report of the Economic and Social Council.
5. Manifestations of racial prejudice and national and religious intolerance: report of the Secretary-General.
6. Draft Declaration on the Elimination of All Forms of Racial Discrimination.
7. Draft Declaration on the Elimination of All Forms of Religious Intolerance.
8. Draft Declaration on the Right of Asylum.
9. Freedom of information
   (a) Draft Convention on Freedom of Information;
   (b) Draft Declaration on Freedom of Information.
10. Measures designed to promote among youth the ideals of peace, mutual respect and understanding between peoples.
11. Draft International Covenants on Human Rights.
12. Designation of 1968 as International Year for Human Rights.

TABLE 14—*continued*

Fourth Committee

1. Report of the Trusteeship Council.
2. Information from Non-Self-Governing Territories transmitted under Article 73 e of the Charter of the United Nations: reports of the Secretary-General and of the Committee on Information from Non-Self-Governing Territories:
   (a) Political and constitutional information;
   (b) Information on educational, economic and social advancement;
   (c) General questions relating to the transmission and examination of information.
3. Dissemination of information in the Non-Self-Governing Territories on the Declaration on the granting of independence to colonial countries and peoples: report of the Secretary-General.
4. Offers by Member States of study and training facilities for inhabitants of Non-Self-Governing Territories: report of the Secretary-General.
5. Question of the continuation of the Committee on Information from Non-Self-Governing Territories.
6. Election, if required, to fill vacancies in the membership of the Committee on Information from Non-Self-Governing Territories.
7. Special training programme for Territories under Portuguese administration: report of the Secretary-General.
8. Question of South West Africa:
   (a) Report of the Special Committee on the Situation with regard to the Implementation of the Declaration on the Granting of Independence to Colonial Countries and Peoples;
   (b) Special educational and training programmes for South West Africa: report of the Secretary-General.
9. Question of Southern Rhodesia: report of the Special Committee on the Situation with regard to the Implementation of the Declaration on the Granting of Independence to Colonial Countries and Peoples.
10. Territories under Portuguese administration: report of the Special Committee on the Situation with regard to the Implementation of the Declaration on the Granting of Independence to Colonial Countries and Peoples.
11. Question of Oman.

Fifth Committee

1. Financial reports and accounts for the financial year ended 31 December 1962, and reports of the Board of Auditors:
   (a) United Nations;
   (b) United Nations Children's Fund;
   (c) United Nations Relief and Works Agency for Palestine Refugees in the Near East;
   (d) Voluntary funds administered by the United Nations High Commissioner for Refugees.
2. Supplementary estimates for the financial year 1963.
3. Budget estimates for the financial year 1964.
4. United Nations Emergency Force
   (b) Cost estimates for the maintenance of the Force.*
5. United Nations Operation in the Congo: cost estimates.
6. Review of the pattern of conferences: report of the Secretary-General.

* For sub-item (a), see p. 96, 'Plenary meetings', item 18.

TABLE 14—*continued*

7. Appointments to fill vacancies in the membership of subsidiary bodies of the General Assembly:
   (a) Advisory Committee on Administrative and Budgetary Questions;
   (b) Committee on Contributions;
   (c) Board of Auditors;
   (d) United Nations Administrative Tribunal;
   (e) United Nations Staff Pension Committee;
   (f) Investments Committee.
8. Scale of assessments for the apportionment of the expenses of the United Nations: report of the Committee on Contributions.
9. Audit reports relating to expenditure by specialized agencies and the International Atomic Energy Agency
   (a) Earmarkings and contingency allocations from the Special Account of the Expanded Programme of Technical Assistance;
   (b) Earmarkings and allotments from the Special Fund.
10. Administrative and budgetary co-ordination of the United Nations with the specialized agencies and the International Atomic Energy Agency.
    (a) Report of the Advisory Committee on Administrative and Budgetary Questions;
    (b) Inter-organizational machinery for matters of pay and personnel administration: report of the Secretary-General.
11. Administrative and budgetary procedures of the United Nations:
    (a) Report of the Secretary-General on administrative and financial procedures to be followed by the General Assembly at the time peace-keeping operations are authorized;
    (b) Report of the Secretary-General on his consultations concerning the desirability and feasibility of establishing a peace fund.
12. Personnel questions:
    (a) Geographical distribution of the staff of the Secretariat: report of the Secretary-General;
    (b) Proportion of fixed-term staff;
    (c) Other personnel questions.
13. Report of the United Nations Joint Staff Pension Board.
14. United Nations International School: report of the Secretary-General.
15. Report of the Economic and Social Council [chapter XIV, work programme and review of priorities and financial implications of actions of the Council].
16. Third International Conference on the Peaceful Uses of Atomic Energy: report of the Secretary-General.

Sixth Committee

1. Report of the International Law Commission on the work of its fifteenth session.
2. Question of extended participation in general multilateral treaties concluded under the auspices of the League of Nations.
3. Consideration of principles of international law concerning friendly relations and co-operation among States in accordance with the Charter of the United Nations.
4. Technical assistance to promote the teaching, study, dissemination and wider appreciation of international law: report of the Secretary-General with a view to the strengthening of the practical application of international law.

5

DEBATE

The fuller the assembly of states is, the more solemn, effectual, and free the debates will be, and the resolutions must needs come with greater authority . . . and then reason, upon free debate, will be judge, and not the sword. . . . I thould think it extremely necessary . . . that neutralities in debates should by no means be endured : for any such latitude will quickly open a way to unfair proceedings. . . . The . . . advantage of a . . . Parliament . . . is it will beget and increase personal friendship between princes and states, which tends to the rooting up of wars, and planting peace in a deep and fruitful soil. . . . It were a great motive to the tranquillity of the world that they could freely converse face to face, and personally and reciprocally give and receive marks of civility and kindness. A hospitality that leaves these impressions behind it will hardly let ordinary matters prevail to mistake or quarrel one another.

WILLIAM PENN

THERE has always been a debating aspect to diplomacy. Diplomats constantly engage in verbal strife with other diplomats. Indeed, 'debate' and 'combat' have a common linguistic origin.

Nor is the practice of public diplomatic debate new, though it would no doubt have seemed shocking to diplomats of the seventeenth to nineteenth centuries. Greek diplomacy, two thousand five hundred years ago, was essentially oratorical. Ambassadors addressed large assemblies of citizens; covenants could hardly have been more openly arrived at.[144]

The public debate of contemporary 'parliamentary diplomacy' has, however, altered the nature of this verbal combat. Speeches in today's intergovernmental assemblies are rarely made with the purpose of convincing opponents by reasoned argument; they are more usually designed to convince third parties, or to appeal to people over the heads of governments, or to win the approbation of public opinion at home, or to ensure that a point of view is on record. The possibility that a direct confrontation of ideas could lead to greater understanding, or even agreement, is easily lost sight of.

Public debate is, nevertheless, an important part of the 'parliamentary diplomacy' of the General Assembly. Although it sometimes increases hostility and tension, it can also facilitate agreement. In any case, verbal combat is preferable to arbitrary violence.

Of some ninety to one hundred items now included in the agenda of a regular session of the General Assembly, about twenty-five are normally allocated directly to the plenary Assembly, and the remainder to the seven Main Committees. The items dealt with in the plenary are as follows:

   (i) Election of the President and Vice-Presidents of the Assembly and members of principal organs, and certain other elections and appointments.

  (ii) Consideration of recommendations of the General Committee on matters proposed for inclusion in the agenda.

 (iii) The General Debate.

 (iv) Reports, or parts thereof, of principal organs, and certain other reports.

  (v) Substantive items, usually about five in number.

 (vi) Miscellaneous matters of a formal nature, such as the admission of new Members.

From time to time there have been suggestions that a greater number of substantive items should be considered directly in plenary meeting. The 1949 Committee on procedure suggested that a 'means of lightening the task of any given Main Committee would be to consider directly in plenary meeting, without preliminary reference to committee, certain questions which fall within the terms of reference of the Main Committee. This procedure would . . . have the great advantage of reducing to a notable extent repetition of debate'. This recommendation now forms part of the first annex to the Rules of Procedure.[145] Discussion in the plenary is more formal than in a Main Committee; it is a useful way of permitting statements of view on matters which are uncontroversial, or on which agreement has already been achieved informally, or on which agreement is not being attempted.

Items not dealt with directly in plenary meeting are referred to one of the seven Main Committees. Proceedings in Main Committees differ in a number of ways from proceedings in plenary meetings. Members speak from their places rather than from a rostrum, and this makes for a somewhat less formal atmosphere. One-third of the members of a Committee constitute a quorum, whereas in the plenary a simple majority of Members is required (Rules 110 and 69). Decisions in Main Committees are made by a simple majority of members present and voting (except decisions to reconsider proposals which have already been adopted or rejected, which require a two-thirds majority), whereas decisions on 'important' questions in the plenary require a two-thirds majority of Members present and voting (Rules 126, 124 and 85–87). A tie vote in a Main Committee on matters other than elections is regarded as a rejection of the proposal, whereas in the plenary the vote is taken again at a subsequent meeting and, if there is a second tie, the proposal is then regarded as rejected (Rules 134 and 97). Nominations are allowed in Main Committees, but not in the plenary (Rule 94).

Each Main Committee is a committee of the whole, consisting of representatives of all Member States. A Main Committee exists only for the duration of the session; if it is desired to set up a committee of the whole Membership to transact business between sessions, the Assembly creates a subsidiary organ. Unless a specific decision is taken to the contrary, an inter-sessional committee reaches decisions by a simple majority of the members present and voting (Rules 126 and 162).

Each Main Committee deals with a particular 'category of subjects' (Rules 99 and 101). The seven Main Committees are as follows:

Political and Security Committee (including the regulation of armaments) (First Committee);

Special Political Committee;

Economic and Financial Committee (Second Committee);

Social, Humanitarian, and Cultural Committee (Third Committee);

Trusteeship Committee (including Non-Self-Governing Territories) (Fourth Committee);

Administrative and Budgetary Committee (Fifth Committee);

Legal Committee (Sixth Committee).

In the first few sessions of the Assembly, items were occasionally referred simultaneously to two Committees, which met jointly for consideration of such items. This practice, as the 1947 Committee on procedure emphasized, 'is as a general rule undesirable and often results in unnecessary duplication of debate'.[146] It is now the practice to allocate each item to one Committee.

Each Committee has developed a character and personality of its own. The two political Committees and the Fourth Committee usually engage in robust debate, though the Fourth Committee is unlike the other Committees in that much of its time is now spent in hearing and questioning petitioners. The Sixth Committee is rather like a seminar for lawyers. Debate in the Fifth Committee is often a trialogue between the Secretariat, the Chairman of the Advisory Committee on Administrative and Budgetary Questions, and other representatives.

The Third Committee has sometimes been regarded as the Assembly's problem child. This is partly because the Committee has an exceptionally disparate agenda. Certain of the social questions, such as community development and the United Nations Children's Fund (UNICEF), would easily fit into the 'category of subjects' dealt with by the Second Committee. The international control of narcotic drugs is a technical matter with legal and economic, as well as social, aspects. The work of the High Commissioner for Refugees is primarily humanitarian in character, though it has political undertones. The other items on the Third Committee's agenda relate to human rights, and the Committee has since 1954 been working its way steadily through two draft covenants. Progress has inevitably been slow, and one cannot but wonder whether a Main Committee of the Assembly is a suitable organ for giving detailed attention to the text of legal instruments. The 1949 Committee on procedure pointed out that a Main Committee, by the very fact of its size— Main Committees at that time had fifty-nine members—'was not particularly fitted to draft conventions, and that when it was entrusted with the detailed study of conventions, it often did not have time to deal satisfactorily with other questions for which it was responsible'.[147]

The Fourth Committee now spends a considerable amount of time dealing with petitioners, some of whom have already been heard by other organs of the United Nations. A Committee consisting of all Member States, meeting in public, is hardly the best body to give careful attention to some of the issues raised in oral petitions. I realize, of course, that oral petitions are intended to be a form of pressure in which political leaders from colonial territories air grievances in an international forum, but the system can be abused. The fact is that the Fourth Committee now devotes so much time to these hearings that it can hardly give sufficient attention to other matters which come before it.

TABLE 15

Hearing of petitioners during 15th, 16th and 17th regular sessions

	Fifteenth session	Sixteenth session	Seventeenth session
Number of meetings held by the Fourth Committee	153	173	104
Number of meetings of the Fourth Committee devoted wholly or partly to hearing petitioners	41	38	48
Percentage of meetings devoted wholly or partly to hearing petitioners	26·8	22·0	46·2

Some oral hearings may be inevitable, nevertheless, particularly if it is clear that:

(a) the content of the proposed statement is both important and urgent;

(b) the information to be given is not already available to the Committee;

(c) it is essential that the matter be presented in oral rather than written form.

In such cases, it would be possible for the Fourth Committee to establish sub-committees of limited membership (under Rule 104) to conduct such hearings. In any case, it facilitates the conduct of business when the Fourth Committee reaches clear decisions on its program of work at the beginning of the session, so that the Secretariat can inform petitioners of the dates on which they will be called on to speak.

It is not possible to allocate items in such a way that each Main Committee has an approximately equal load of business, nor do the Committees have the same amount of business each year.

TABLE 16

Number of meetings during sessions of the General Assembly

Session	General Com.	Plenary	First Com.	Ad Hoc or Spec Pol.Com.	Second Com.	Third Com.	Fourth Com.	Fifth Com.	Sixth Com.
1, Pt. I	17	33	11	—	6	11	12	17	12
Pt. II	10	34	35	—	23	37	15	28	21
1st Spec.	7	12	13	—	1	1	1	1	1
2	7	49	59	—	24	33	20	56	25
2nd Spec.	1	7	25	—	1	1	1	1	1
3; Pt. I	14	52	95	28	30	97	36	75	80
Pt. II	8	32	36	26	—	49	—	5	—
4	4	57	72	61	31	40	57	52	71
5	6	50	74	82	28	76	57	48	39
(resumed)	—	5	26	—	—	—	—	—	—
6	4	44	64	58	48	72	49	58	53
7, Pt. I	7	36	48	50	54	65	66	34	54
Pt. II	1	17	56	—	—	—	—	1	—
Pt. III	—	3	13	—	—	—	—	—	—
8	5	40	57	43	41	60	81	53	37
9	10	44	72	55	55	80	73	55	45
10	4	45	57	34	43	62	81	47	38
1 E.S.S. } 2 E.S.S.	—	13	—	—	—	—	—	—	—
11	5	104	52	41	66	77	100	65	29
12	6	54	77	42	59	73	91	52	41
3 E.S.S.	—	15	—	—	—	—	—	—	—
13	4	46	83	42	70	70	103	57	51
(resumed)	—	2	—	—	—	—	37	—	—
14	6	63	58	48	63	75	121	55	48
4 E.S.S.	—	6	—	—	—	—	—	—	—
15, Pt. I	7	97	54	51	71	79	95	64	40
Pt. II	1	35	26	35	—	—	58	21	—
3rd Spec.	—	11	—	—	—	—	—	—	—
16. Pt. I	9	81	69	65	79	76	103	65	45
Pt. II	2	19	13	—	—	—	47	2	—
Pt. III	2	15	—	—	—	—	23	—	—
17	5	81	63	52	85	76	104	71	46
4th Spec.	—	3	—	—	—	—	—	22	—
18	6	80	45	53	74	77	84	55	59

The First Committee has not, in the past, begun its substantive work until about the fourth or fifth week of the session, and it has usually finished in a rush. The Assembly decided in 1963 that the First Committee should meet as early as possible in the session to organize its work, determine the order of discussion, and start the consideration of its agenda. The hope was that, during the early part of the session, meetings of the First Committee might be held when there is an interruption in the General Debate; later, plenary meetings might be held during one part of the day and meetings of the First Committee during the other part of the day.[148]

The other Committees usually start work within a few days of receiving the lists of agenda items referred to them, normally by the beginning of the third week of the session. The Fifth Committee cannot complete its work until the session is about to close, as it has to deal with the financial implications of decisions of the Assembly.

Each Main Committee establishes an order of priority for the consideration of the items referred to it, taking into account the date fixed for the closing of the session (Rule 100). The Fourth Committee draws up a provisional time-table for its work. The Second, Third, and Fifth Committees decide on their programs of work, based on suggestions from their Chairmen. During the course of the session, the Chairman of the Second Committee usually submits further notes to the Committee regarding the organization of the remainder of the work.

The Assembly decided in 1963 that Main Committees should be more systematic in establishing programs of work early in the session. Each Main Committee was asked to decide the approximate dates on which it would consider the various items referred to it and the date on which it proposed to conclude its work. This program of work is to be transmitted to the General Committee to enable that Committee to make recommendations about the organization of the work of the session.[149] If a time-table is drawn up for the guidance of a Committee, night or week-end meetings can be arranged should the Committee fall behind the time-table. The very fact of scheduling a night or week-end meeting sometimes helps a Committee to catch up to its time-table without the necessity of actually holding any extra meeting.

It is natural that there should develop a feeling of professional solidarity and intimacy among representatives in different Committees who meet each other year after year. This certainly facilitates the harmonious conduct of business, though it would become unhealthy if it should lead to overt rivalry between Committees. Main Committees of the Assembly are composed of the same Member States, and there should be no question of their reaching different conclusions. One should probably regard as a lapse from normal practice the occasion during the eighteenth session when the

Second and Special Political Committees exchanged communications regarding the priority of agenda items,[150] and the assumption on the part of some representatives in the General Committee that the way the question of Oman would be dealt with would depend on whether it were referred to the Special Political Committee or the Fourth Committee.[151]

Sometimes an illusion of conflict between Committees arises from the fact that the internal co-ordination of policy within some delegations is imperfect. The increase in the number of States and of intergovernmental organizations has imposed a severe strain on the diplomatic services of many countries, and not only of those newly independent. Sometimes representatives, especially in the non-political Committees, do not have full or precise instructions from their governments; sometimes they have instructions from a particular ministry, but these may in part be inconsistent with the instructions that another member of the same delegation has received from another ministry. Possibly the greatest difficulty occurs when a representative in one Committee supports some proposal which involves the expenditure of funds, while a member of the same delegation opposes the budgetary appropriations in the Fifth Committee.

It is perhaps inevitable that each Main Committee should believe that it possesses an expertise that other Committees lack. Representatives of the Sixth Committee are more inclined to give expression to this idea than representatives in other Committees. During the sixth session, for example, when the Sixth Committee was considering the methods and procedures of the Assembly for dealing with legal and drafting questions, the main focus of debate was not (as one might have expected) on problems arising from the existence of different legal systems, but on the right of legal experts to pronounce on matters within their competence and on the tendency of the Assembly to ignore the expertise which was to be found in the Sixth Committee. One representative noted that there was a displacement in the balance of the work of the United Nations, to the disadvantage of the Sixth Committee; as a result, its agenda was diminishing.[152] Another representative pointed out during the fourteenth session that the distribution of work in the United Nations was not satisfactory. Juridical questions were sometimes discussed by non-legal Committees in which strictly technical considerations might be overshadowed by political and sometimes even purely emotional factors. While he fully recognized the fitness of the Third Committee to prepare the draft covenants on human rights, he believed that, where difficulties arose, they should at least be referred to the Sixth Committee for advice. The Sixth Committee had been created to ensure that technical legal matters should be treated by specialists.[153] A year later, the question was raised again, many representatives deploring the paucity of the Sixth Committee's agenda.[154]

The basic order of business for each item in a Main Committee is as follows. First, a general debate on an item or group of items; secondly, discussion of draft resolutions and amendments; finally, voting, including explanations of vote. Each Committee adapts this framework for its own purposes. The Fifth Committee examines the budget estimates in consecutive 'readings'. The Fourth Committee adds to the normal procedure three other stages for some items: hearing of petitioners, questioning of petitioners, and introductory statements by governments directly concerned with the matter. The Second Committee considered in 1963 a number of suggestions, submitted by the Chairman of the eighteenth session (Ismael Thajeb of Indonesia), for the better organization of its work at future session. One of the suggestions was that the general debate in the Committee might be discontinued. Mr. Thajeb commented that the general debate was 'overlong and contains much repetition', and another representative said that it was 'more a succession of monologues than an exchange of views'. The Second Committee intends to review Mr. Thajeb's suggestions and the comments on them at the beginning of the nineteenth session.[155]

Each Main Committee reports to the plenary on the items allocated to it. The Rapporteurs' reports of the Second, Fourth and the two political Committees are now limited to accounts of proposals made and of the decisions of the Committee; the Rapporteurs of the Third, Fifth, and Sixth Committees often include also summaries of the main points made in the debate. In the case of the two political Committees, the Third Committee, and the Sixth Committee, the Rapporteurs report directly to the plenary; in the other Committees, the usual practice is for the Rapporteur to submit a draft report for each item or group of items to the Committee and, if necessary, to revise it before transmitting it to the plenary.

Committees undoubtedly function best if they exercise

flexibility in procedure. The 1953 Committee on procedure considered that the tendency of Main Committees to observe independent and succeeding stages for each item often provoked duplication of speeches and increased the risk of engaging in protracted procedural discussions.

> The mechanics of a Main Committee cannot be simplified or altered beyond a certain point, it is true, but greater flexibility . . . is desirable.[156]

In order that the business of the Assembly shall be conducted in a smooth and expeditious manner, three things are necessary: first, thorough advance preparation by the Secretariat (including the distribution of relevant documents at an early stage); secondly, presiding officers with 'competence, authority, tact and impartiality . . . respect for the rights both of minorities as well as majorities, and . . . familiarity with the rules of procedure'.[157] and; finally, the exercise of good sense and restraint by representatives of Member States.

The early submission of relevant documents is most important.[158] There is no doubt that the Assembly's proceedings begin to 'drag' if essential documents have not been available sufficiently in advance of the session for governments to consider them and instruct their representatives. In some cases, Member States themselves are at fault. The Rules of Procedure require that items proposed for inclusion in the agenda should, if possible, be accompanied by basic documents (Rule 20), and for these to be of maximum value, they should be available some weeks before the opening of the session.

Sometimes documents issued by the Secretariat are not available sufficiently early. This may be caused by the fact that essential information does not reach the Secretariat on time, or by the uneven pressure of work falling on those responsible for preparing or printing the documents. Any change in the basic schedule of United Nations meetings, such as a special session of the Assembly or the late opening of a regular session and the consequent postponement of other meetings, inevitably disrupts arrangements for the production of documents.

The reasons for delay are various, but the consequence is that the Assembly wastes time because Members are insufficiently informed or instructed. In some cases of the late availability of documents, the Assembly might be well advised to postpone consideration of the item until the next session, but this is not always possible. Just before the opening of the eighteenth session (1963), for example, the Secretary-General stated that if military operations were to continue in the Congo beyond the end of the year, he would need the financial authorization very quickly, yet when the Fifth Committee came to consider the matter later in the month, it was held up because the documentation was not available.[159] In this case, the matter could not have been held over until the next session.

Presiding Officers

It is difficult to exaggerate the extent to which good chairmanship can facilitate, and bad chairmanship can obstruct, the work of the Assembly. It is true that a good chairman cannot prevent a United Nations organ from getting into a procedural tangle on occasions, since some procedural situations that arise are unpredictable and complicated.* But an incompetent presiding officer can, single-handedly, create procedural chaos if he does not understand the Rules, or does not enforce them, or acts in a dictatorial or partisan manner.

The General Assembly is composed of representatives of sovereign Members and, at any rate on important substantive issues, representatives are presumed to act in accordance with official instructions. The problem, though, is that the single category of business on which representatives are usually without instructions is procedural business. This means that once the Assembly or Committee becomes involved in a procedural discussion, delegates begin to 'free-wheel'. One can sense the atmosphere of liberation which sweeps over a meeting when debate on the substance of a question is temporarily put aside so that some knotty procedural point can be resolved. One observes representatives closing their folders of papers and lighting cigarettes so as to deal in a thoroughly relaxed and level-headed way with a matter which requires initiative, tact, and imagination rather than fidelity to official instructions.

The Assembly has been reluctant to give substantial authority of a formal kind to its presiding officers, and there has been some decrease in the formal powers of presiding officers since 1946. The

---

* I recall hearing the eminent President of the fourteenth session having to inaugurate a vote with the explanation: ' "Yes" will mean "No". . . .'

first Secretary-General told an Assembly Committee in 1947 that Paul-Henri Spaak, President of the Assembly's first session, had taken important decisions of a procedural or organizational kind without consulting the General Committee or the Assembly 'because he considered that the administration of the Assembly was in his hands'.[160] It would be unthinkable that an Assembly President would today take decisions of the kind taken by Spaak on his own authority. Indeed, the Assembly amended the Rules of Procedure in 1949 to state specifically that presiding officers exercise their functions 'under the authority of' the Assembly or Committee (Rules 36 and 109).

This decline in formal authority is not, perhaps, surprising. In the first year or so in the life of the Organization, there was evident determination on the part of the permanent members of the Security Council to stick together to the greatest possible extent, especially on matters relating to procedure and the interpretation of the Charter. The United Nations began with only a few exact precedents. With the steady accumulation of a body of precedents, presiding officers have increasingly been called upon to interpret the Rules and the customary practices rather than to establish new precedents. Finally, the Rules of Procedure have been developed and elaborated by successive revisions, thus providing established procedures for matters that were formerly decided in an *ad hoc* manner, often on the basis of proposals from the Chair.

This, however, is not the whole story. The political climate since 1945 has been characterized by great emphasis on the principle of the sovereignty and equality of nations large and small. This has been held to imply that presiding officers, even in the interests of orderly procedure and the expeditions and harmonious conduct of business, should in no way inhibit the inherent right of representatives to express freely the views of their governments on matters within the scope of the Charter. There is frequent insistence on the notion that each United Nations organ is master of its own proceedings. This is at best a half truth, but it was asserted by the 1949 Committee on procedure and the paragraph was later annexed to the Rules of Procedure.[161]

Presiding officers are given certain formal powers under the Rules of Procedure, but these formal powers are no substitute for such personal qualities as courtesy, tolerance, and fair-mindedness. The presiding officers of many deliberative bodies acquire authority and respect by long and continuous tenure of office. One of the most influential of the Speakers of the British House of Commons, Arthur Onslow, achieved his ascendancy and prestige not solely because of his undoubted talents, but also by the fact that he occupied the Chair of St. Stephen's without interruption for thirty-four years. The President of the Assembly or the Chairman of a Main Committee is elected for only one session. At the time of his election, he represents a government which is committed to certain policies. Even the most seasoned and talented diplomat, experienced in the procedures of intergovernmental assemblies, and taking full advantage of the advice and help of the Secretariat, can acquire only limited authority in matters of procedure in a session of three or four months, and he can never wholly divest himself of the policies, passions, and prejudices of his nation.

This is not to imply that good chairmanship is unattainable; but good chairmen do not grow on trees, and those who have been endowed with the requisite qualities and have enjoyed appropriate experience often prefer, or are required, to use their talents in other ways.

The formal powers granted to presiding officers are of three kinds: *obligatory*, *discretionary*, and *initiatory*. Under their *obligatory* functions, presiding officers declare the opening and closing of each meeting; direct the discussions, put questions, and announce decisions; accord the right to speak, calling upon representatives in the order in which they have signified their desire to speak; rule on points of order; when debate is limited and a representative has spoken his allotted time, call him to order without delay; ensure observance of the Rules of Procedure; and, subject to the Rules, have complete control of the proceedings and over the maintenance of order. (Rules 35, 70, 73, 74, 108, 111, 114, and 115.)

Under the *discretionary* functions, a presiding officer may call a speaker to order if his remarks are not relevant to the subject under discussion; may limit the time to be allowed to speakers regarding the adjournment or closure of the debate, the suspension or adjournment of the meeting, and explanations of vote*; may announce the list of speakers; may accord the right of reply to a representative, even if the list of speakers has been closed; may permit explanations

* The President of the Assembly may limit the time to be allowed to speakers in favour of or against a recommendation of the General Committee that an item be included in the agenda (Rule 23).

113

of vote, either before or after the voting; and may permit the discussion and consideration of amendments or of motions as to procedure even though these amendments or motions as to procedure have not been circulated in writing the previous day. (Rules 70, 75–78, 80, 90, 111, 116–119, 121, and 129.)

Apart from their obligatory and discretionary functions, presiding officers have *initiatory* powers to facilitate the smooth conduct of business. The 1949 Committee on procedure emphasized that a presiding officer is expected to exercise leadership in matters of procedure and 'should be able, at any time and without any reflection on his impartiality, to draw members' attention to measures likely to expedite their proceedings'.[162] It would be useful if representatives were to emphasize, in speeches of nomination or acceptance, the clear responsibility which presiding officers have to exercise leadership of this kind. Representatives should, as far as possible, uphold the authority and dignity of the Chair—though not all would go as far as a distinguished United States representative who stated laconically 'The Chair is always right'.[163]

Apart from the general responsibility of a presiding officer to suggest ways of proceeding expeditiously, a presiding officer has the same rights as any other representative to initiate procedural proposals. He may propose that the time to be allowed to speakers or the number of times each representative may speak on any question should be limited; he may propose the suspension or the adjournment of the meeting, the adjournment of the debate on the item under discussion, the closure of the debate, or the closure of the list of speakers. (Rules 35, 74–78, 108, 115–119.)

Since there is sometimes confusion regarding the responsibilities and rights of presiding officers, it would be useful if each presiding officer, on a convenient occasion early in the session, would state explicitly his or her conception of the responsibilities attaching to the office, particularly in matters where the Rules are imprecise or misunderstanding is likely to occur. Such a statement might include an interpretation of what constitutes a point of order (quoting, where necessary, from reports of committees of the Assembly on procedure) and a reminder that the presiding officer has a duty, under the Rules, to dispose of a point of order before allowing another one to be raised. It might include similar interpretations with regard to the right of reply and explanations of vote, and of the responsibilities of presiding officers when requests to exercise these rights are made.

Representatives might be reminded that presiding officers are under an obligation to ensure observance of the Rules of Procedure. It would be helpful if, following such a statement, a representative were to request that it be made available in verbatim form to all representatives.

Presiding officers can often save time and facilitate the handling of business by reminding the Committee, as each item is taken up, of the history of the matter, of any previous decisions of other organs of the United Nations, and of documents relevant to the item. A chairman can also suggest procedures that would enable a Committee to proceed expeditiously.[164] As each item is completed, the chairman can remind the Committee of what business still remains to be done, and in suitable cases suggest some sort of rough time-table for future work. If procedural suggestions from the Chair come 'out of the blue' and appear to be arbitrary or unfair, time will be lost. If, however, they are made after full though informal consultation, a Committee usually accepts them gratefully.

To illustrate how a proposal from the Chair can assist a Committee, I give below the statement of a presiding officer during the fourteenth session, dealing with the order of items:

THE CHAIRMAN: The next point of the agenda is the order of the items. . . .

Before proceeding with any discussion of priorities, I wish to make a few remarks which may be of assistance in this respect.

Members of the Committee are no doubt acutely aware that our agenda this session is not only heavy but contains several items of great significance for current developments in international relations. I spoke earlier about a spirit of co-operation which I hoped would contribute to the success of our deliberations . . . I am sure that all members of the Committee earnestly wish that our proceedings here would help to promote those favourable trends rather than disturb them.

One of the ways to do this would be to avoid, as far as possible, acrimonious debate, and especially perhaps debate on procedural questions. Experience has shown that sharp differences over procedure may serve to charge the air with bitterness or embarrassment and, in fact, to hinder the ultimate discussion of substantive questions, which are the main purpose of our deliberations here.

Members of the Committee will be aware that informal consultations have been taking place among delegations, reflecting various points of view, about the order of priority for the discussion of the items on our agenda. I have tried to keep in touch with those consultations. . . .

In this endeavour there has been a commendable demonstration of co-operation on the part of all concerned and I am happy to state it is my understanding that there is some consensus as to how we are to proceed in the immediate future.

In the light of the circumstances which I have mentioned and of my understanding of various positions, I have been encouraged to make a suggestion, which . . . is that we begin at once with. . . .[165]

There is one other procedural task which is the lot of presiding officers. For those who are habitually punctual, it must be a source of irritation that most United Nations meetings start late. Even as early as the second session (1947), the Secretary-General was urging that meetings begin promptly at the scheduled time,[166] and all the Committees of the Assembly on procedure have emphasized that much time is wasted because meetings begin late.[167] One representative stated in 1950 that he had spent 'some forty-six hours in committee rooms between the scheduled period for the opening of a meeting and the actual commencement, that is to say, about the equivalent of a whole week and a half of meetings'.[168]

Some representatives were under the illusion in 1950 that the late starting of meetings was due to poor transport facilities between Manhattan, Lake Success, and Flushing Meadows, and soon after the move to the new headquarters building, the delegate of Uruguay rejoiced that 'meetings can now begin within a few minutes of the specified time' and thus valuable time would be saved.[169] A few months later, however, the same representative presided over the Special Committee on Measures to Limit the Duration of Sessions which once again had to 'draw attention to the serious loss of time that results from the lack of punctuality in the opening of meetings. . . .'[170]

A short delay in starting a meeting may on occasion serve a useful purpose, particularly if delicate negotiations are in progress. The presiding officer nearly always knows when this is happening and can adjust the time of starting accordingly. It would be of convenience, in these circumstances, if there could be some means of informing representatives of the approximate time when the meeting was likely to begin.

TABLE 17

Time not utilized by the Assembly during 16th and 17th regular sessions

	Average duration of meetings	Late starting (average)	Early ending (average)	Average time lost per meeting	Total time for for session
Sixteenth session	hours min.	min.	min.	min.	hours min.
Plenary	2 9	33	23	56	107 19
First Committee	2 6	28	13	41	56 40
Special Political Com.	1 55	23	31	54	58 45
Second Committee	2 17	38	13	51	67 10
Third Committee	2 8	31	8	39	49 45
Fourth Committee	1 58	31	22	53	152 5
Fifth Committee	2 6	23	16	39	43 35
Sixth Committee	1 37	28	25	53	40 10
Seventeenth session					
Plenary	2 34	7*	12	19	25 30
First Committee	1 5	22	29	50	52 40
Special Political Com.	1 51	23	36	59	51 35
Second Committee	2 26	18	14	32	45 35
Third Committee	2 1	18	21	39	49 5
Fourth Committee	2 10	23	15	38	65 25
Fifth Committee	2 5	22	15	37	43 50
Sixth Committee	1 55	19	32	51	38 55

* Sir Zaffrula Khan, the President of the seventeenth session, made a point of starting plenary meetings as promptly as possible.

Orderly Debate

Many questions arise in connections with maintaining good order in debate, but five seem to me of special importance: the circumstances in which the Rules of Procedure may be suspended; the problem of speeches which include remarks that seem objectionable to the presiding officer or a representative; interruptions during speeches and requests to speak out of turn; procedural motions (such as that a meeting be held in private or that the debate be adjourned); and the limitation of debate.

Enforcing and suspending the Rules: The Rules of Procedure were made for the Assembly, and not the Assembly for the Rules. The Rules of Procedure provide that the Rules may be *amended* by a simple majority of Members present and voting, provided a committee has reported on the proposed amendment (Rule 164), but there is no specific provision for the *suspension* of a Rule.* Since the Assembly's presiding officers are required to ensure observance of the Rules of Procedure, and since it is occasionally in the general interest that a particular Rule should not be enforced, it would make for orderly procedure if there were an accepted means by which a Rule could be suspended.

The Canadian delegation drew the attention of the 1949 Committee on procedure to this matter.

> It would save the time of the Assembly if there were a clear provision for the suspension of the rules of procedure. The inclusion of such a rule would, by clarifying the position, render debate on this question unnecessary. Moreover, it would tend to increase respect for the rules of procedure and thus lead to a saving of time.

Canada proposed that a new Rule should provide that a Rule of Procedure should not be suspended, nor should the President put to the vote a motion for the suspension of any Rule, unless (*a*) the motion had been submitted in writing to the Secretary-General, and (*b*) copies of the motion had been distributed to all delegations at least forty-eight hours before being put to the vote. The 1949 Committee did not examine this proposal, and the Canadian representative reserved the right to raise the matter again.[171]

The precise form of the Canadian proposal might seem to place undue obstacles in the way of suspending a Rule, and it would no doubt be sufficient to provide that any Rule of Procedure could be suspended by a decision of the Assembly taken by a majority of the Members present and voting. If that were done, it would probably be desirable to limit the number of speakers in the discussion of any proposal to suspend a Rule to two or three in favour of the suspension and two or three against, allowing the presiding officer the discretion to limit the time to be allowed to speakers.

Remarks to which objection is made : There are three main grounds on which objection is made to speeches—that the remarks are irrelevant, that they are needlessly repetitious, or that they are offensive.

Presiding officers have the power, though not the obligation, to call a speaker to order if his remarks are not relevant to the subject

---

* The Rules of Procedure of the Economic and Social Council and of the Trusteeship Council include provisions for the suspension of a Rule.

under discussion (Rules 70 and 111).* The President of the Assembly, when acting as Chairman of the General Committee, should see that the substance of an item is not discussed, except in so far as this bears upon the Committee's recommendation regarding inclusion, rejection, or postponement (Rule 40).

Rules of relevancy are always difficult to apply. For one thing, honest and intelligent people differ as to whether particular matters are or are not relevant to the subject under discussion. Furthermore, the relevant merges but gradually into the irrelevant; a presiding officer can rarely be certain at exactly what moment irrelevance begins. In theory it is desirable that a presiding officer should call a speaker to order as soon as his remarks become irrelevant to the subject under discussion. Occasionally a speaker may privately warn the Chair that he proposes to make remarks which may be considered irrelevant by other representatives, but normally the presiding officer has no such warning. In view of the many claims on his attention, it is impossible for a presiding officer to detect immediately every trace of irrelevancy; often the matter comes to his attention by means of a point of order. If he has momentarily been concerned with some other matter (for example, if he has been in conversation with the secretary of the meeting), he has to improvise a ruling which will accord with the Rules of Procedure and yet offend neither the representative who was speaking nor the representative who rose on a point of order. Usually this is done by making a general appeal to all speakers to confine their remarks to the subject under discussion.

There is no specific Rule designed to prevent repetition. Indeed, many representatives would claim that they have a right to be long-winded and tediously repetitious if they so desire. There are occasions, though these are rare, when a repetitious speech may be useful as a 'screen' for informal negotiations. In the ordinary way, however, tedious repetition is to be deprecated, and presiding officers, under their general powers and in the interests of orderly procedure, may request speakers to refrain from repeating remarks with which the Committee is already familiar. As a last resort, a presiding officer or any representative may propose a limitation on the time to be allowed to each speaker; in cases of deliberate persistence in

* These Rules are similar in intent to Rule 15 (3) of the Rules of Procedure of the League Assembly. It is believed that the League rule was never invoked in the entire history of the organization.

repetition of a filibustering nature, it might be necessary to move the adjournment or closure of the debate on the item under discussion.

There is no specific Rule against making disrespectful or offensive remarks, although presiding officers have invoked the rules on relevancy (Rules 70 and 111) and the rules on the general powers of presiding officers (Rules 35 and 108) in efforts to halt abusive speeches. The South African delegation proposed to the 1949 Committee on procedure that the Rules should be amended to empower Chairmen 'To call speakers to order wherever they resort to invective or display of personal animus directed against either an individual or a State, or where they in any other way detract from the dignity of the proceedings'.[174] The Committee made no recommendation on this question. Indeed, it is hardly possible to have a rule to prevent speakers from resorting to invective against a State, but presiding officers have tried to stop offensive remarks of a personal kind directed to heads of state or heads of government. On one occasion, the President of the Assembly directed that certain offensive remarks of this character should be deleted from the official records.[173]

It is, in fact, rare for representatives to resort to gross abuse. More often the problem has arisen from the use of such phrases as 'the Russian satellites' or 'the so-called Special Representative on the Question of Hungary'. No formal Rule can compel representatives to keep within the bounds of courtesy. There is no reason why a representative should not attack the views or policies of another representative and his government, but it is discourteous and a threat to good order to make abusive personal remarks about other representatives, to accuse them of deliberate falsehood, to impute to them unworthy motives, or to charge them with intentional misrepresentation.

In recent years, a number of difficulties have arisen when strong objection has been voiced to the political content of a speech. During the course of the General Debate in 1961, a proposal was submitted that the speech of one representative should be deleted from the official records on the ground that it had been insulting. This proposal was later withdrawn in favour of one censuring the government concerned because the statement of its representative had been 'offensive, fictitious and erroneous'. This motion was approved by sixty-seven votes to one, with twenty abstentions.[174]

Interruptions during speeches and requests to speak out of turn:
Although the purpose of the Rules of Procedure is to enable business
to proceed smoothly and without interruption, it is necessary to have
an emergency procedure by which business can be interrupted if
some abnormal development occurs. If, for example, the system of
simultaneous interpretation becomes defective so that the Spanish
interpretation cannot be heard, it is essential that the situation
should be drawn to the attention of the presiding officer without
delay. Any procedure that permits a representative to interrupt
another representative or to speak out of turn is open to abuse, and in
fact the majority of so-called points of order raised in the Assembly
and its Committees are not points of order at all.

The point of order is believed to have been an English invention, and a French representative has stated that it is unknown in
French parliamentary practice.[175] According to the standard work
on British parliamentary procedure, a point of order in the British
House of Commons arises in the following way:[176]

> Although it is the duty of the presiding officer to interfere in the
> first instance for the preservation of order when, in his judg-
> ment, the occasion demands his interference, it is also the right
> of any representative who conceives that a breach of order has
> been committed, if the presiding officer refrains from inter-
> fering (either because he does not consider it necessary to do so,
> or because he does not perceive that a breach of order has been
> committed), to rise in his place, interrupting any representative
> who may be speaking, and direct the attention of the Chair to
> the matter, provided he does so the moment the alleged breach
> of order occurs.*

The General Assembly has not found it possible to define a
point of order. As one representative has put it, 'all attempts hitherto
made at international conferences and at meetings of international
organizations to define points of order have failed . . . because it has
obviously been felt that the matter should be left to the good sense
of representatives. . . .'[177] This statement is correct as far as it goes,
but there are certain attributes of a point of order which are explicit
in the Rules of Procedure. (Rules 73, 90, 114, and 129.)

    1. A point of order should not concern the substance of the
matter under discussion.

* I have adapted this quotation to the terminology of the United Nations by
changing 'Speaker' to 'presiding officer' and 'Member' to 'representative'.

2. A point of order raised while voting is in progress should concern only the actual conduct of the voting.

3. A point of order, being a matter for the decision of the presiding officer, should not deal with any matter outside the presiding officer's competence.

4. A point of order should be decided immediately; it takes precedence over all proposals or motions.

5. The presiding officer should decide a point of order in accordance with the Rules of Procedure; there is no provision in the Rules whereby the presiding officer may submit a point of order for the decision of the Assembly or Committee.

6. A representative may appeal against the ruling of the presiding officer.

7. Any such appeal should not be debated but should be immediately put to the vote.

Two Committees of the Assembly have stated their views on what constitutes a valid point of order, elaborating what is explicitly stated in the Rules.

A point of order is, basically, an intervention directed to the presiding officer requesting him to make use of some power inherent in his office or specifically given him under the rules of procedure. It may, for example, relate to the material conditions under which the meeting is taking place. It may be a request that the presiding officer should accord the speaker some privilege which it is in the officer's power to grant. Under a point of order, a representative may request the presiding officer to apply a certain rule of procedure or he may refer to the manner in which the presiding officer should apply a given rule, or the rules of procedure as a whole. . . .

Presiding officers must give an immediate ruling on every point of order, and if the ruling is challenged, they must put it to the vote; no discussion may take place. Hence, there can be no question of seconding or debating a point of order. Moreover, as the presiding officer must immediately dispose of each point of order as it is raised, two or more points of order can never be before the Chair at the same time.[178]

It is discourteous, to say the least, to rise to a point of order in the middle of a speech if it could equally effectively be done at the end, but there could be no possible objection were a representative to rise to a point of order in the middle of a speech to say that the system of simultaneous interpretation was not working. A representative should not, however, interrupt a speech merely to ask that he be accorded the right of reply at a later stage or to request the presiding officer to clarify some point in connexion with an impending vote.

Two special difficulties have been encountered in connection with points of order. The first arises when a presiding officer either fails to rule immediately on a point of order, or fails to put to the vote immediately an appeal against his ruling; these actions are required under Rules 73 and 114. If a representative raises a new point of order before an outstanding point of order has been disposed of, and if the presiding officer does not insist on disposing of an outstanding point of order before admitting a new one, procedural chaos results. I have been assured that a Main Committee once had eighty-four different undecided points of order awaiting rulings from the Chair.

A second difficulty may arise when a representative (either deliberately or in ignorance) raises a matter under the guise of a point of order which is not a point of order at all. It is in this regard that the art of good chairmanship is so important. If an inexperienced representative raises what purports to be a point of order but which is in reality nothing of the kind, the presiding officer may explain why the alleged point of order is inadmissible. If, on the other hand, such a point is raised by an experienced representative who is deliberately abusing the Rules, the presiding officer faces a more difficult task. If the point appears to be a gross abuse of procedure and a threat to good order, the presiding officer is likely to reply rather succinctly that the matter raised is inadmissible as a point of order; on the other hand, a presiding officer, on a rare occasion, may decide not to reject such a point if he considers that by accepting it he would facilitate the conduct of business and if he feels confident that he would be supported in so doing by a substantial majority of representatives.

The practice has developed of presiding officers permitting representatives to speak out of turn 'on a point of information' or 'on a request for clarification' or 'on a point of personal privilege'. There is no provision for these practices in the Rules, since any legitimate such point or request can be raised as a point of order.

Difficulties may also arise regarding the right of reply. The normal practice, in accordance with Rules 70 and 111, is for the presiding officer to call upon representatives in the order in which they signify their desire to speak. The Assembly, in urging representatives to take the floor in the order in which they are inscribed on the list of speakers, has taken it for granted that representatives prevented from doing so would normally be placed at the end of the list, unless they had arranged to change places with other representatives.[179] If, during the course of debate, a speech is made to which another representative wishes to make a reply, and if the list of speakers has been declared closed, the presiding officer has the discretionary power of according the right of reply if he considers this desirable (Rules 75 and 116). The right of reply before the list of speakers has been closed is not provided for in the Rules of Procedure. In practice, a representative usually wishes to reply at once to any speech he considers misrepresents the policy of his government or is based on inaccurate information, whether or not the list of speakers has been closed. In such circumstances, presiding officers have been inclined to accord the right of reply, though the practice is now carried to excess. It is, after all, a privilege and not a right to speak out of turn. I would make four suggestions designed to prevent undue abuse of the practice.

1. Presiding officers should not allow representatives to interrupt the speeches of other representatives in order to make statements of reply.

2. Although a presiding officer might, on a convenient occasion, wish to inform the meeting that a representative had asked to be allowed to exercise the right of reply, an oral statement of reply should, if possible, be made at the end of the meeting.

3. Representatives should be encouraged to make statements of reply in written rather than oral form, and such replies should be incorporated into the official records.[179]

4. Presiding officers might be given the power to limit the time allowed to representatives making oral statements of reply.

Representatives spend a great deal of time hearing other representatives explain why they are going to vote, or have already voted, in a particular way. This is permitted under Rule 90 (Rule 129 in Committees), which reads in part:

The President may permit Members to explain their votes, either before or after the voting, except when the vote is taken by secret ballot. The President may limit the time to be allowed for such explanations. The President shall not permit the proposer of a proposal or of an amendment to explain his vote on his own proposal or amendment.

Proposals to limit the time allowed for explanations of vote have been made from time to time. Greece suggested a time limit of five minutes in 1949.[180] The New Zealand representative commented in 1952 that he was 'astounded' at the length of speeches delivered in explanations of vote, and added that these explanations often contained 'elaborate disputations, rhetorical questions and appeals to the conscience of mankind'.[181]

It should be emphasized that:

1. The presiding officer is not obliged to permit explanations of vote.

2. It is within the discretion of the presiding officer whether explanations of vote are heard before or after voting.

3. Explanations of vote are not admissible in connexion with elections by secret ballot.

4. The proposer of a proposal or of an amendment may not explain his vote on his own proposal or amendment.

5. The presiding officer may limit the time to be allowed for explanations of vote.

6. Explanations of vote may be made in writing and circulated as official documents.

Australia proposed in 1952 that only those Members who had not participated in the debate on a subject should be permitted to explain their votes.[182] This proposal may seem unduly drastic, but it might be possible to impose a time limit on explanations of vote by representatives who have already spoken in the debate. In any event, presiding officers should not allow representatives to reopen a discussion which has already concluded under the guise of explaining their votes. It would be logical and orderly if, in the normal way, explanations of vote were heard after the voting.

Procedural motions : There has been in the past, and no doubt there will continue to be in the future, some confusion between a point of order and a procedural motion; one reason for this is that in some parliamentary bodies no distinction is made between the two.[183] As far as the General Assembly is concerned, however, the two are distinct. A point of order is a request to the presiding officer to give a ruling; a procedural motion is a proposal which is either automatically accepted by the Chair or, if opposed, is put to the vote.

Motions as to procedure which are automatically accepted by the Chair and not put to the vote are as follows:

(a) the withdrawal by its proposer of an unamended motion before voting on it has commenced (Rules 82 and 123);

(b) the re-introduction of a motion thus withdrawn (Rules 82 and 123); and

(c) a request for a roll-call vote (Rules 89 and 128).

One kind of procedural proposal is, like a point of order, decided at the discretion of the presiding officer. A presiding officer may 'permit the discussion and consideration of amendments, or of motions as to procedure, even though these amendments and motions have not been circulated or have only been circulated the same day' (Rules 80 and 121). Any proposal for the immediate discussion and consideration of an amendment or motion as to procedure which has not been circulated in writing in the normal way is decided by the presiding officer at his discretion and is not put to the vote.

There is one recurring cause of confusion regarding procedural motions. Speakers are called upon in the order in which they have signified their desire to speak, the only exception being that the discussion of any matter may be interrupted should a representative rise to a point of order. How, then, can a representative move a procedural motion, such as the closure of debate? If he places his name on the list of speakers, the motion may be irrelevant when his turn comes; if he rises at once on a point of order, he may only raise a matter on which the presiding officer is competent to rule, and therefore may not make a proposal which has to be decided by vote.

It seems that the correct way of moving a motion as to procedure is to do so in the following stages. First, a representative rises to a point of order and then states his wish to move a procedural motion, specifying the nature of the motion and the Rule or Rules under which it will be moved. The presiding officer then states whether the proposed motion is admissible. If the ruling of the presiding officer is affirmative, the representative then proposes the motion.

Limitation of debate : No question of procedure arouses more intense feelings than the question of limiting debate.

On the one hand, it has been maintained that it was in the interests of the dignity and prestige of the Assembly to limit the duration of its sessions and so make possible the attendance at its sessions of eminent statesmen of all countries. On the other hand, it was asserted that the sovereign rights of Members to free expression of views and the rights and duties of the Assembly in regard to full discussion of the questions brought before it had to be maintained.[184]

The possibility of imposing some general limitation on the length of speeches has been considered by each Committee of the Assembly on procedure, and the conclusion has been reached on each occasion that no general limitation of debate is feasible.[185] The reason is obvious. If the Rules limit debate at one particular stage, representatives will use another occasion to express their views:

Whatever restrictions were imposed, a representative would always find some way of giving full expression to his views. If restrictions were imposed on the length or number of speeches made by each representative, speakers would resort to points of order, explanations of vote, the right of reply and the like. Even if a point of order was defined as relating only to questions within the President's or the Chairman's competence, a clever speaker would still be able to adjust his speech in order to bring it within that fairly wide definition, and it would only waste more time in the end if the President or the Chairman were to attempt to call him to order.

Again, although an explanation of vote should be brief, the speaker himself was the only judge of what it should cover, and there was no possibility of imposing restrictions in that respect without rendering the right of explanation useless. The right of reply was also difficult to define, and speakers could easily make use of it to evade any limitations on the general debate.[186]

There have been occasions when Committees have successfully applied a time limit, but discussion of a proposal to limit speeches can be exceedingly time-consuming. During the sixth session, for example, the Chairman of the *Ad Hoc* Political Committee proposed that there be a time limit of five minutes on speeches in explanation of vote or under the right of reply during discussion of a question relating to Germany, and this proposal was upheld by the Committee by a large majority. One representative began a speech of protest and, after he had spoken for five minutes, he was called

TABLE 18

Practice regarding limitation of debate

	Rule No.		Number of speakers or number of times each representative may speak	Time to be allowed to each speaker
	Plenary	Committees		
(a) General practice	35 74	108 115	The presiding officer or any other representative may propose the limitation of the number of times each representative may speak on any question. The Assembly (Committee) may impose such a limitation	The presiding officer or any other representative may propose the limitation of the time to be allowed to each speaker. The Assembly (Committee) may impose such a limitation. When debate is limited and a representative has spoken his allotted time, the presiding officer shall call him to order without delay.
(b) Recommendation of the General Committee that an item be included in the agenda	23	—	Three in favour, three against	The President may limit the time to be allowed to speakers.
(c) Appeal against ruling of presiding officer on a point of order	73	114	The appeal shall be immediately put to the vote	No debate permitted.
(d) Adjournment of debate on the item under discussion	76	117	Proposer of motion, two in favour, two against	The presiding officer may limit the time to be allowed to speakers.

(e) Closure of debate on the item under discussion	118	77	Two speakers opposing the closure	The presiding officer may limit the time to be allowed to speakers.
(f) Suspension or adjournment of the meeting	119	78	Proposer of the motion, no debate, motion shall be immediately put to the vote	The presiding officer may limit the time to be allowed to the proposer of the motion.
(g) Division of proposals and amendments	130	91	Two in favour, two against	—
(h) Reconsideration of proposals	124	83	Two speakers opposing the motion for reconsideration	—
(i) Explanations of vote	129	90	Proposer of a proposal or of an amendment may not explain his vote on his own proposal or amendment	The presiding officer may limit the time to be allowed to speakers.
(j) Report of a Main Committee in plenary meeting	—	68	Discussion takes place only if at least one-third of the Members present and voting consider such a discussion to be necessary. Any proposal to this effect shall not be debated, but shall be immediately put to the vote	No debate permitted.

to order by the Chairman and told that his time was up. The representative protested vigorously and proposed the adjournment of the debate so that his delegation could consult the President of the Assembly about the procedural situation. After a confused debate, the Committee voted to give the aggrieved representative an opportunity to explain his views. He then proceeded to speak—at great length.[187]

The present practice regarding limitation of debate is set out in Table 18. A number of minor changes of practice regarding limitation of debate may be worth considering. In the first place, the Economic and Social Council has a time limit of five minutes on interventions on procedural questions. This Rule is seldom applied, but the knowledge of its existence has been one means of discouraging lengthy speeches on procedure. Canada proposed in 1949 that the Assembly should adopt a similar Rule.[188]

In the absence of a general time limit on procedural interventions, it would be possible to give presiding officers authority to limit the time to be allowed for such statements. They already have this right in connexion with explanations of vote, and it would seem reasonable to give them the same right regarding:

(a) points of order;
(b) the right of reply;
(c) motions for the division of proposals and amendments, or to reconsider a proposal that has been adopted or rejected.

With regard to (c), presiding officers already have the right to *propose* the limitation of the time to be allowed to speakers in these matters, and a slight increase in the reserve powers of presiding officers could hardly be open to objection.

'Extended Remarks'

It was suggested in a study sponsored by the Carnegie Endowment for International Peace in 1949 that some system should be adopted by which representatives could incorporate into the official record statements which had not been delivered orally.[189] This possibility was considered by the 1953 and 1963 Committees on procedure. The 1953 Committee concluded that 'serious problems would arise regarding such questions as, for example, the relevance of remarks which had been submitted in writing and the exercise of the right of reply with respect to them'.[190] The majority of the members of the 1963 Committee considered that to incorporate into the official records written statements supplementing or replacing oral statements would have the effect of altering considerably the nature of the Assembly's debates and would also raise 'a certain number of practical problems which would be difficult to solve'.[191]

The 1963 Committee did not specify what the 'practical problems' would be, but it may be questioned whether the objections are insuperable. It should surely be possible to devise means to ensure that irrelevant remarks could be excluded and to permit the right of reply or counter-reply. In any case, delegations already have the right to request the Secretary-General to circulate relevant documents. The practice of incorporating undelivered speeches into the official records of the Assembly is not new. I know of two cases of such statements being incorporated in the records of the Assembly, and the system is also used by other organs.[192]

6

DECISIONS

The composition . . . does, at first, look seem to carry with it no small difficulty what votes to allow for the inequality of princes and states. . . . [A] vote . . . in my opinion, should be by the ballot . . . which, in a great degree, prevents the ill effects of corruption, because if any of the delegates . . . could be so vile false, and dishonourable as to be influenced by money, they have the advantage of taking their money that will give it them and of voting undiscovered to the interest of their principles and their own inclinations; as they that do understand the balloting box do very well know. . . . It seems to me that nothing in this Imperial Parliament should pass but by three quarters of the whole. . . . In all great points, especially before a final resolve, they may be obliged to transmit to their principals the merits of such important cases depending, and receive their last instructions : which may be done in four and twenty days at the most. . . . If any of the sovereignties that constitute these imperial states shall refuse to submit their claim or pretensions to them or abide and perform the judgment thereof, and seek their remedy by arms, or delay their compliance beyond the time prefixed in their resolutions, all other sovereignties, united as one strength, shall compel the submission and performance of the sentence, with damages to the suffering party. . . .

WILLIAM PENN

WHEN DEBATE HAS CONCLUDED, some procedural mechanism is needed in order to dispose of the matter and pass to other business. Such a mechanism may be nothing more than a proposal of the presiding officer or another representative that the Assembly or Committee take no further action on the matter. More usually, however, it is a proposal in express terms, deciding on or recommending some course of action, or expressing an opinion; and any such proposal is either accepted without opposition or put to the vote. In this chapter I am concerned, first, with the rationale of voting; secondly, with the relationship between 'decisions' and 'agreement', and the methods by which the Assembly, in appropriate cases, makes no decision, or makes only a formal or procedural decision, or seeks to postpone or avoid a decision; and, finally, I touch briefly on the difficult question of how the General Assembly may ensure compliance with its conclusions.

I suppose that the idea of decision by majority vote arose by empirical observation of the fact that the majority, being more numerous and therefore usually more powerful than the minority, was able to have its way. In the most primitive societies, it was the practice to punish, kill, or eat the dissenting minority; at a later stage of development, it was realized that the preservation of the community depended on co-operation rather than coercion and that minorities should be granted the right of silent existence, though not the right to challenge overtly the will of the majority; finally, a stage was reached in which the homogeneity of the community was given a high value, and minorities sought, by persuasion, to become majorities. It is, after all, more civilized to count heads rather than break them, to appeal to the ballot rather than the bullet.

Voting is ostensibly a means of resolving a difference of opinion by the will of the majority and with the acquiescence of the minority. It is thus an attractive system for majorities, or those who expect to become majorities. There are, nevertheless, some differences which no reasonable person would consider should or could be resolved by vote. The weight of numbers has no bearing on questions of fact, such as who wrote the plays ascribed to Shakespeare, or what is the specific gravity of beer, or whether a particular scientific theory is true.

Moreover, the majority is not always right. Alexis de Tocqueville wrote of the possible tyranny of the majority and of the safeguards which might mitigate such tyranny.[193] It is certainly important to distinguish between the rule of law and the rule of the majority, in international as in other forms of politics.

On some matters, unanimity is generally regarded as desirable. This requirement is often encountered in the jury system, for example. Certain organizations never vote. There is no voting at Commonwealth conferences. Informal groups of States at United Nations headquarters do not normally vote on substantive issues. The Society of Friends (Quakers) does not resolve differences of opinion by voting; discussion continues until a decision is reached which is acceptable to all.

The use of voting in diplomatic matters is a novel procedure. Before the twentieth century, the principle of unanimity applied in inter-State relations. The same principle was, in theory, the general rule in the League of Nations, and in the case of the permanent members still holds in the United Nations Security Council on most non-procedural matters.

The Charter of the United Nations specifies that decisions of the Assembly shall be made by voting. The term 'decisions', as used in the Charter, has a broad meaning and 'refers to all types of action which the General Assembly takes . . . under the Charter. . . .'[194] Very few resolutions of the Assembly include the verb *decides*, though every resolution is the record of a 'decision' within the meaning of Article 18.

An election or appointment, whether by secret ballot or acclamation, is also a decision; but its nature is different from a decision, expressed in a resolution, relating to some action or recommendation by the Assembly. A ballot is, to a considerable extent, a mathematical process in the sense that it is not possible to 'amend' a candidate for office; each ballot cast is, in this formal sense, unconditional. It is true that there may be informal or under-the-counter understandings and conditions. A may vote for B on condition that B will support A (or perhaps C) on another issue; or on the understanding that B intends, on some future occasion, to act in a particular way; or on the assumption that a second ballot will probably be required, in which event support will be switched to D.

When two or more elective places are to be filled, the 'amending' concept enters in to a degree. When the General Assembly elects its Vice-Presidents or the members of the Economic and Social Council, for example, each vote for a group of States may be unconditional in the formal sense, but the distribution of choices within the vote may represent an element of adjustment to meet the views of others.

All the same, voting to elect States or persons to offices is to a considerable extent a mathematical process. The mathematical element in voting takes on a different significance once the possibility of amendment exists. In matters where amendment is permitted, there is always the possibility of adjusting the text of a proposal in the interests of wider agreement. No representative in a United

Nations organ can know for certain the form a resolution will take until the final vote is taken. The drafting of proposals and amendments, and the anticipation of procedural situations, is today an important diplomatic art. Yet even the most skilled representative cannot foresee every contingency, since there are elements of irrationality and fortuity in any human situation. The mere order of voting is often important. Moreover, there is a voting paradox (which I need not elaborate here) by which, if there are more than two choices, the final result may in part be determined by the order in which the alternatives are put to the vote.

A resolution of the Assembly usually consists of one or more preambular paragraphs and one or more operative paragraphs. The preambular paragraphs may refer to Articles of the Charter, or to principles of international law, or to previous decisions of United Nations organs, or to some other sentiment having a bearing on the operative paragraphs. The operative paragraphs of a resolution are, broadly speaking, of two kinds. They may, in the first place, relate to some action which the Assembly, under the Charter, is competent to take; the approval of the budget or the establishment of a subsidiary organ are actions of this kind. The operative paragraphs may, alternatively, be such recommendations as the Assembly, under the Charter, is competent to make; they may be straightforward recommendations (the General Assembly . . . appeals to, or calls upon, or invites, or suggests, or urges) or they may be in the nature of expressions of opinion (the General Assembly . . . affirms, or commends, or declares, or deplores, or regrets).*

The following resolution of the seventeenth session consists of six preambular paragraphs; four paragraphs (1 to 4) which express opinions; two paragraphs (5 and 6) which address recommendations to some Member States, one paragraph (9) with a recommendation to all Member States, and one paragraph (8) with recommendations to a subsidiary organ; and one paragraph (7) which decides on action which the Assembly is competent to take under Article 22 of the Charter, and one paragraph (10) which, though in the form of a request, is in substance a decision under Article 98 of the Charter.

---

* The League Assembly made 'decisions' by a unanimous vote, but a recommendation (or *voeu*) could be adopted by a simple majority.

The situation with regard to the implementation of the Declaration on the Granting of Independence to Colonial Countries and Peoples : Report of the Special Committee established under General Assembly resolution 1654 (XVI)

The General Assembly

Recalling its resolution 1514 (XV) of 14 December 1960, containing the Declaration on the granting of independence to colonial countries and peoples, and its resolution 1654 (XVI) of 27 November 1961 by which it established the Special Committee of Seventeen on the implementation of this Declaration,

Conscious of the fact that the Declaration on the granting of independence to colonial countries and peoples and the subsequent establishment of the Special Committee have raised great hopes everywhere, and in particular among peoples who have not yet attained their independence, for the elimination of all forms of colonialism and foreign domination without delay,

Having considered the report of the Special Committee,

Noting with profound regret that, in spite of the efforts of the United Nations, the provisions of the Declaration have not been fully implemented in a large number of territories and that in certain cases even preliminary measures have not yet been taken to realize its objectives,

Deeply concerned by the negative attitude and the deliberate refusal of certain Administering Powers to co-operate with the Special Committee,

Reaffirming its conviction that any delay in the implementation of the Declaration constitutes a continuing source of international conflict, seriously impeding international co-operation and creating in many regions of the world increasingly dangerous situations likely to threaten international peace and security,

1. *Expresses its appreciation* to the Special Committee on the situation with regard to the implementation of the Declaration on the granting of independence to colonial countries and peoples for the work it has accomplished;

2. *Takes note with approval* of the methods and procedures which the Special Committee has adopted for the discharge of its functions;

3. *Solemnly reiterates and reaffirms* the objectives and principles enshrined both in the Declaration contained in resolution 1514 (XV) of 14 December 1960 and in resolution 1654 (XVI) of 27 November 1961;

4. *Deplores* the refusal of certain Administering Powers to co-operate in the implementation of the Declaration in territories under their administration;

5. *Calls upon* the Administering Powers concerned to cease forthwith all armed action and repressive measures directed against peoples who have not yet attained their independence, and particularly against the political activities of their rightful leaders;

6. *Urges* all Administering Powers to take immediate steps in order that all colonial territories and peoples may accede to independence without delay in accordance with the provisions of paragraph 5 of the Declaration;

7. *Decides* to enlarge the membership of the Special Committee established by resolution 1654 (XVI) by the addition of seven new members to be nominated by the President of the General Assembly;

8. *Invites* the enlarged Special Committee:

(a) To continue to seek the most suitable ways and means for the speedy and total application of the Declaration to all territories which have not yet attained independence;

(b) To propose specific measures for the complete application of the Declaration on the granting of independence to colonial countries and peoples;

(c) To submit to the General Assembly in due course, and not later than its eighteenth session, a full report containing its suggestions and recommendations on all the territories mentioned in paragraph 5 of the Declaration;

(d) To apprise the Security Council of any developments in these territories, which may threaten international peace and security;

9. *Requests* all Member States, and especially the Administering Powers, to afford the Special Committee their fullest co-operation;

10. *Requests* the Secretary-General to continue to provide the Special Committee with all the facilities and the personnel necessary for the implementation of the present resolution.

The question of competence

I stated in Chapter 4 that the inclusion of an item in the agenda of the Assembly does not necessarily mean that the Assembly is competent to adopt a resolution. Article 12 (1) of the Charter, for example, provides that 'While the Security Council is exercizing in respect of any dispute or situation the functions assigned to it in the present Charter, the General Assembly shall not make any recommendations with regard to that dispute or situation unless the Security Council so requests'. The Assembly has not applied this provision of the Charter in a completely consistent manner, although one precedent gives some indication of how Member States interpret the phrase 'shall not make any recommendations'. A Main Committee of the Assembly decided during the fourth session, in connection with a matter with which the Security Council was concerned, that a proposal containing the words 'Deems it essential to take the following measures' would have constituted a recommendation within the meaning of Article 12 (1); but that a resolution welcoming an announcement and a forthcoming event, and commending the parties concerned and a United Nations organ, did not constitute a recommendation within the meaning of Article 12 (1).[196]

Article 2 (7) states that the United Nations is not authorized to intervene in matters that are essentially within the domestic jurisdiction of a State except in regard to the application of enforcement measures if peace is threatened. Most Member States have held either that discussion does not constitute intervention, or at any rate that the Assembly can reach a decision on competence only after discussion has taken place. It is entirely consistent with either one of these positions to insist, after the discussion has been concluded, that the Assembly is not competent to adopt a resolution which includes a recommendation.

Some governments have held that, while Article 2 (7) does not prevent the Assembly from making a recommendation of a general nature regarding the domestic matters of all States, the Assembly is not competent to make a specific recommendation regarding the domestic matters of a particular State, since that would constitute intervention. For example, the delegate of Sweden declared in 1953 that:

> The United Nations could not . . . refrain from concerning itself with respect for human rights. . . . His delegation also considered that the Assembly had every right to make general recommendations in the matter. . . . However, his delegation was not prepared to accept resolutions recommending a Member State to adopt specific measures.[197]

A Member State might thus regard discussion of some question as not constituting intervention, or might consider that discussion was necessary as a preliminary to taking a decision on competence; yet when it came to voting, it might regard as *ultra vires* all resolutions of any kind, or all resolutions containing general recommendations, or all resolutions containing specific recommendations regarding the domestic affairs of a particular State.

Whatever views may be taken about the interpretation of Articles 2 (7) and 12 (1) in regard to the adoption of resolutions, Rules 81 and 122 provide that, at any time before a vote is taken on a proposal, it is in order to move that the Assembly or Committee is not competent to adopt such a proposal. Such a motion calling for a decision on competence must be put to the vote before a vote is taken on the proposal in question.

The Search for Agreement

'The art of diplomacy', an American diplomat has written, 'consists of making the policy of one government understood and if possible accepted by other governments'.[181] Applying this definition to the General Assembly, one may say that one purpose of debate is to help governments to understand the policies of other governments, and that one purpose of adopting resolutions is to express the greatest possible degree of consensus. In traditional diplomacy, it was often in the interests of all parties that any differences should be kept private while the search for agreement continued. In contemporary diplomacy, by contrast, it is often difficult to avoid a premature disclosure of differences, and this may hamper the search for agreement.

If conference diplomacy is to serve the interests of governments, constant efforts are needed to devise procedures and practices which can resolve as well as expose differences. Thus when a situation of conflict is being debated in the Assembly, attention should initially be directed towards the reconciling of differences. If the situation is deteriorating while the matter is under consideration, it may be desirable to mobilize the support of governments in favour of an appeal to the parties to exercise restraint, or to discontinue threatening actions, or in other ways to refrain from aggravating the situation. This may be followed at a later stage by the creation of machinery of a fact-finding character, either because some of the facts are in dispute or because of a wish to establish the culpability of one or more of the parties. In some circumstances it may be useful to establish new negotiating machinery, in other circumstances to recommend to the parties the general principles of a settlement. But whichever approach or combination of approaches may be used, someone has to take the initiative. Sometimes this may be done by one or more of the States directly involved; at other times the initiative may come from relatively disinterested third parties; at still other times the Secretary-General or a senior official of the Secretariat may informally initiate procedures designed to facilitate a solution. Occasionally the problem is not to find candidates to exercise this function of leadership but to co-ordinate a number of simultaneous but unrelated efforts.

Moreover, sponsorship of a proposal often becomes a matter of prestige, so that Member States compete for the privilege. In the first years of the United Nations, a draft resolution or amendment usually had a small number of sponsors, but the practice gradually developed of trying to secure a representative group of sponsors, and more recently of having not simply a representative group but the largest possible number of sponsors.* Moreover, there have been cases of Members announcing that they were sponsoring a proposal when their formal sponsorship was not desired by some or all of the original sponsors.

---

* The summit was reached in 1959 when a proposal on disarmament was sponsored by all Member States. This was a *reductio ad absurdum*, since the Member States were presumably addressing the proposal to themselves.

The larger the number of sponsors, the less procedural flexibility there is. For one thing, a proposed amendment cannot be accepted without the approval of all of the original sponsors. Pressure on Members to co-sponsor a proposal has another consequence because a State might cheerfully acquiesce in a slightly objectionable phrase in a resolution sponsored by another State, but would find it much more difficult to be on record as sponsoring an objectionable phrase.

Difficulties have occasionally arisen when a Member has failed to vote for a proposal which it has sponsored. During the fifteenth session, for example, the chairman of a Main Committee ruled that an amendment was out of order because one of the sponsoring delegations had abstained in the vote on the amendment. This ruling was upheld by the Committee by fourteen votes to thirteen, with thirty-four abstentions, after which the chairman stated that he was withdrawing his ruling. After the vote had taken place, the delegation concerned stated that it withdrew its sponsorship of the amendment in question.[199] It is to be hoped that this incident is not taken as a useful precedent!

There are differences of opinion regarding the extent to which a presiding officer should initiate substantive proposals designed to foster agreement. His primary responsibility is to give leadership in matters of procedure, and this may be endangered if he takes an excessive interest in matters of substance. The Rapporteur does not have the same responsibility for procedural leadership, though nowhere are the functions or duties of the Rapporteur defined in the Rules of Procedure.

The Rapporteur filled a vital role in the practice of the League of Nations. In the case of the League Council, a Rapporteur was normally appointed for each matter with which the Council was dealing. In committees of the Assembly, normal procedure was to appoint a Rapporteur for each major subject or group of subjects rather than to have one Rapporteur for all the matters committed to it, as is the practice in committees of the United Nations Assembly.

The League Assembly sometimes appointed the Rapporteur at the beginning of the discussion, sometimes at the end; the Council usually appointed a Rapporteur at the end of the general discussion. In any event, it was the normal practice for the Rapporteur to begin his duties before formal proposals were submitted, and as a result proposals were submitted to him rather than to the body which had appointed him. A Rapporteur was a delegate, or was appointed a delegate by his government, but Östen Undén of Sweden suggested that a different practice might sometimes have been appropriate:

> The system of appointing Rapporteurs from among the members of the Council itself . . . would not appear to be entirely rational. . . . In many cases it would, no doubt, be more satisfactory to entrust such duties to private individuals or to a special conciliation commission consisting of members in no way dependent on their Governments, who after exhaustive negotiations with the parties would endeavour to bring about an amicable settlement of the dispute and would ultimately put forward proposals for such a settlement. . . .
>
> The Inter-American Treaty on Good Offices and Mediation of 1936 includes an interesting provision in this respect: 'When a controversy arises between them that cannot be settled by the usual diplomatic means, the High Contracting Parties may have recourse to the good offices or mediation of an eminent citizen of any of the other American countries, preferably chosen from a general list made up in accordance with the following article.'[200]

The League Rapporteur, like his counterpart in the United Nations, was expected to submit an objective report of the debate, and in this task he was assisted by the Secretariat. But, in cases of disagreement, his duties did not end there.

> The task of the Rapporteur was to elucidate the issues involved in the dispute and to make proposals for its solution. To this end it was his duty to study the documents relating to the dispute, to engage in private conversations with the disputants and to guide discussion in the Council. In several instances, he was authorized to call upon outside experts for advice and assistance. Between sessions . . . the Rapporteur in several instances entered into negotiations with the disputants in the capital of his own country. . . . In his report the Rapporteur would submit . . . proposals for the solution of the dispute in the form of a draft resolution. When the report came before the Council the Rapporteur might intervene at any time in the discussion. It was a common practice . . . to adopt the draft resolution submitted by the Rapporteur without discussion, after the President had invited the parties to make their observations and state any objections they might have to raise.[201]

The Rapporteur in the League system thus exercised a variety of functions. He accumulated and reported information which was formally communicated to him, and he requested whatever additional information he deemed necessary. This was an important weapon in the hands of the Rapporteur. 'Even when facts were asked for, the object was not fact-finding, but pressure on the disputants to mend the facts.'[202] An advisory opinion could be sought on legal aspects from a committee of jurists or from the Permanent Court of International Justice. Diplomatic pressures of various kinds might be brought to bear on the parties.

The object of the system was to produce a report, with proposals, that would be generally accepted. In the Assembly this was not normally difficult. The Council Rapporteur had a harder task. Disputes tended to be protracted while the search for agreement continued, but disputes of the kind which were dealt with by the League Council were likely to be protracted whatever the procedure.

In 1948 the British delegation suggested that the rapporteur system which had been used by the League should be revived.

The United Kingdom representative explained, first, that any conflict with existing procedures should be avoided, and, second, that conciliation proceedings should not be rigid or formal in character. What was proposed was that a practice be established under which the parties would at the outset automatically meet with the conciliator and ascertain whether their differences could be eliminated.[203]

After extensive discussion of the British proposal, the Interim Committee proposed changes in the Assembly's Rules of Procedure which would have empowered the President of the Assembly to appoint a Rapporteur or conciliator accepted by the parties in any questions relating to the maintenance of international peace and security brought before the Assembly. The Interim Committee, in a separate proposal, referred approvingly to the experience of the League Council 'whereby cases were presented . . . by a rapporteur who had the function of conciliator, and that this practice allowed private conversations among the parties and the rapporteur and avoided the crystallization of views that tend to result from taking a stated public position'; the Interim Committee went on to recommend that 'such a practice be developed in the Security Council as an integral part of the system of pacific settlement'.[204]

When the proposed change in the Rules of Procedure of the

Assembly came before the *Ad Hoc* Political Committee during the third session, the British representative proposed that a decision on the matter be postponed, and this was approved.[205] The official records give no indication why the British delegation did not persist with the proposal, but the Assembly can, of course, adopt the method whenever it wishes to do so, no revision of the Rules being needed to permit this.

One potential danger of likening the General Assembly to a parliamentary or legislative body is that it may encourage the idea that every debate must terminate with a decision of substance which is arrived at by means of a vote. I take the view that some of the contentious questions with which the Assembly has been concerned have been prematurely pressed to a vote on a proposal of substance. When a matter is proposed for inclusion in the agenda; and when such a proposal is considered informally within the groups and in the lobbies, and formally by the General Committee and by the plenary Assembly; and when the item has been the subject of debate —a substantial impact is made whether or not a resolution of substance is adopted. Indeed, it seems to me desirable to facilitate practices whereby the Assembly can debate a question without necessarily reaching a conclusion of substance.

A number of democratic legislatures have found it useful to devise procedures by which a general discussion on some topic can take place without the necessity of putting a question to the vote at the conclusion of the debate. In the British House of Commons, for example, every debate takes place on a motion moved by a Member. Circumstances may arise, however, when a debate is desired but no decision is necessary. The Opposition Party may wish to ventilate a subject without challenging the authority of the government, or the government may wish to test the feeling of the House though without causing a division on a motion in express terms. In such circumstances a debate may be arranged, by informal agreement between the parties, on the motion 'That this House do now adjourn' without any intention of pressing to a conclusion a motion which, if approved, would result in the termination of the sitting. This 'substantive' motion for the adjournment is a technical form devised for the purpose of enabling the House to discuss matters without recording a decision in express terms. When its purpose has been served, the motion is withdrawn and the House turns its attention to other business.

This kind of adjournment debate is in some respects akin to the General Debate held in plenary meetings of the General Assembly. In the case of the Assembly, however, a debate can take place without a motion of any kind being moved, and can be terminated simply by acquiescence in a declaration of the presiding officer that the matter has been disposed of.

Although the normal practice of the Assembly is that items included in the agenda (other than elections and appointments) are debated and then decided by the adoption of substantive resolutions, there are significant exceptions to this general rule. An item may be included in the agenda, but there may be no debate and either no resolution or only a formal resolution; or an item may be debated in the ordinary way but, for some reason or another, disposed of either without the adoption of a resolution or by the adoption of a resolution of which the operative parts are formal or procedural in character. It should be noted that the Rules of Procedure of the Economic and Social Council specifically provide for the submission of 'motions requiring that no decision be taken on the substance of . . . proposals'.[207]

No debate, no resolution: Article 98 requires the Secretary-General to make an annual report to the General Assembly on the work of the Organization. This report now constitutes item 10 of the agenda. Under Article 12 (2) of the Charter, the Secretary-General is required, with the consent of the Security Council, to notify the Assembly at each session of any matters relative to the maintenance of international peace and security which are being dealt with by the Security Council. This notification constitutes item 7 of the agenda. Neither the report nor the notification is debated by the Assembly, and no resolution is adopted in connection with either.

Important substantive items may be disposed of without debate and without a resolution. During the thirteenth session (1958), for example, Secretary-General Hammarskjold submitted a report summarizing the experience derived from the establishment and operation of the United Nations Emergency Force, and the item was referred to the Special Political Committee. The Secretary-General made a few remarks about the study and stated that he and his colleagues were at the disposal of the Committee, should there be any need for clarifications. The Secretary-General concluded: 'I feel no need for the General Assembly to take any action at the present time.' The Chairman then stated that in view of the Secretary-General's statement, the Committee now need hardly enter into a discussion of the question; since no one had asked for the floor, he took it that the Committee was in agreement that the item was disposed of.[208]

No debate, only a formal resolution: The Security Council reports annually to the Assembly; the report is not discussed but a formal resolution is adopted in the following terms:

> *The General Assembly,*
>
> *Takes note* of the report of the Security Council to the General Assembly covering the period . . .

Debate, no resolution: There are three ways by which a matter included in the agenda may be debated and then disposed of without the adoption of a resolution: if no draft resolutions are submitted, if all draft resolutions are withdrawn, or if none of the draft resolutions obtains the required majority.

An item included in the agenda may be the subject of debate but no resolutions may be submitted either because that is the normal practice for the item, or, in special circumstances, because there is informal agreement that this is appropriate in a particular case. An example of the first kind is the General Debate. When all delegations wishing to participate have done so, the President simply declares: 'The General Debate is concluded' or words to that effect. The Assembly then proceeds to other business.

The Assembly may occasionally find that, having debated a matter, all draft resolutions are withdrawn. During the twelfth session, for example, Syria proposed that the Assembly should take up the question of 'threats to the security of Syria and to international peace' caused by 'the heavy, unprecedented and unwarranted concentration of Turkish troops . . . in close proximity to the Syrian-Turkish border'. The Syrian delegate stated that it was urgently necessary for the Assembly to set up a commission to investigate the Turkish threat to Syria. His government had turned to the Assembly only after exhausting all other diplomatic resources. The Turkish representative affirmed the friendly feelings of his country towards Syria, and welcomed the proposal that the Assembly should take up the Syrian request. After other representatives had spoken, the General Committee agreed to recommend that the item be included in the agenda and discussed in plenary meeting.

The matter was considered in a rather strident atmosphere at six plenary meetings of the Assembly during the succeeding two weeks. Syria proposed that a commission be set up to investigate the situation on the spot. Canada and six other States submitted a draft resolution which would have expressed confidence that the Secretary-General, in the exercise of his responsibilities under the Charter, would be available to undertake discussions with the parties. Throughout the period of the public debate, there took place intensive private consultations in an effort to ease the tension and assist the two countries to compose their differences. At the conclusion of the debate, the Indonesian representative appealed to the parties to the dispute and to the sponsors of draft resolutions not to press any of the proposals to a vote. Syria, Turkey, and the seven sponsors of the second draft resolution agreed to the Indonesian proposal; the President of the Assembly stated, 'I feel sure that the Assembly will regard this . . . as a satisfactory outcome'; and the Assembly happily proceeded to other business.[209]

A similar situation may arise in the case of a dispute in which disinterested governments attempt to produce a compromise proposal acceptable to the parties. If it should transpire that one of the parties finds the proposed compromise unacceptable, the sponsors may prefer to withdraw a draft even if it seems likely that it would secure the necessary majority. Thus a report of the Fourth Committee concerning the frontier between Italian Somaliland and Ethiopia in 1958 included the following paragraphs:

13. At the same meeting, the sponsors of the three-Power draft resolution withdrew their proposal in view of the fact that, despite their efforts to revise it to meet objections, they had not been able to produce a text acceptable to both parties concerned. 14. In the absence of any other proposal, the Committee is therefore unable to present a draft resolution for adoption by the General Assembly.[210]

When the same question came before the Assembly's Fourth Committee a year later, no proposals were submitted formally, although several informal suggestions were made. The representatives of Japan and New Zealand, in particular, had consulted with the parties concerned and with other delegations in the hope that a proposal acceptable to both parties could be worked out. These efforts were, in the event, abortive and the Rapporteur reported to the plenary that 'the Fourth Committee regrets to inform the General Assembly that it has no draft resolution to recommend'.[211] It is clear from the wording of the Rules and the practice of the Assembly that a Main Committee is under no necessity to recommend a draft resolution to the plenary Assembly.

Another way in which a matter may be debated but no resolution adopted arises when a draft resolution passes in a Main Committee, where a simple majority is sufficient, but later fails in the plenary, where a two-thirds majority is required for 'important' questions.

It should be emphasized that once a draft resolution has been adopted by a Committee, it becomes the proposal of the Committee and not of the original sponsor or sponsors; the question whether or not to vote in the plenary on a draft resolution recommended by a Main Committee is for the plenary to decide.

Debate, followed by a formal or procedural decision: Finally, a substantive conclusion may be avoided or postponed by a decision which, if in the form of a resolution, is merely formal or procedural. Opinions may differ as to precisely what constitutes such a decision, but I suggest that it is one which does not go beyond: (*a*) an expression of satisfaction that certain steps are taking place or contemplated; (*b*) an expression of confidence that the matter will be resolved in accordance with certain principles; (*c*) a decision not to consider the matter further or to postpone further consideration. Examples of decisions of this kind are:

(a) *The General Assembly,*
    Having examined the Moroccan question,
    Noting that some delegations declared that negotiations between France and Morocco would be initiated regarding this question,
    Expressing confidence that a satisfactory solution will be achieved,
    Decides to postpone for the time being further consideration of this item.[212]

(b) *The General Assembly.*
    Considering that, for the time being, it does not appear appropriate to adopt a resolution on the question of Cyprus,
    Decides not to consider further the item. . . .[213]

(c) *The General Assembly*,

Decides not to consider further the item entitled 'The question of Algeria', and is therefore no longer seized of this item on the agenda of its tenth session.[214]

(d) *The General Assembly*,

1. *Decides* to give further consideration at its thirteenth session to items 19, 20 and 21 of the agenda of the twelfth session;

2. *Requests* the Secretary-General to include these items in the provisional agenda of the thirteenth session of the General Assembly.[215]

(e) *The General Assembly*,

Takes note of the statements made by the Heads of the delegations of the Soviet Union and the United States on the question of disarmament, and

Decides to take up for consideration the problem of disarmament, and all pending proposals relating to it, at its sixteenth session.[216]

(f) *The General Assembly*,

Recalling its resolution 1217 (XII) of 14 December 1957 and Economic and Social Council resolution 820 (XXXI) of 28 April, 1961,

Recommends that the item entitled 'Population growth and economic development' should be included in the agenda of its seventeenth session in view of the fact that a draft resolution on this item was distributed to the Second Committee on 1 December 1961 but could not be considered because of lack of time.[217]

(g) *The General Assembly*,

Having made progress in the preparation of the draft Convention on Freedom of Information at its fourteenth, fifteenth and sixteenth sessions,

Bearing in mind that a draft resolution on the future organization of work on this subject has been submitted to the General Assembly at its seventeenth session,

Having been unable to consider the draft Convention and the draft Declaration as well as the draft resolution at its seventeenth session,

Decides to give priority to the agenda item entitled 'Draft Convention on Freedom of Information' and 'Draft Declaration on Freedom of Information' and to devote as many meetings as necessary to these items at its eighteenth session.[218]

(h) *Extract from* letter dated 10 December 1963 from the Chairman of the First Committee to the President of the General Assembly, '. . . At its 1346th meeting held on 5 December 1963, the First Committee decided to recommend to the General Assembly that consideration of this item [Actions on the regional level with a view to improving good neighbourly relations among European States having different social and political systems] be deferred until the nineteenth session of the General Assembly.'[219]

Developing a Tradition of Compliance

The problem of compliance in the Assembly arises from the fact that the world of States is in a period of transition. Nations treasure the concept of sovereignty as much as ever they did; yet nations never were, and are not now, wholly sovereign. One limitation on the sovereignty of Members of the United Nations is given legal expression in the Charter, by which they agree to accept certain over-riding obligations and carry out certain decisions of United Nations organs.[220] The limitation on sovereignty is, perhaps, even more drastic in its non-legal forms. Nations are not entirely free to act as they will in external affairs: they are inhibited by the concrete power of others, and by such intangible qualities as reason and justice.

A government should constantly review the national interest in the light of the national interests of others. A chief purpose of diplomacy is to make what is apparently incompatible compatible. National interest is transcended by international interest.

This is the theory. In practice, international issues rarely present themselves in such simple terms. The United Nations is a centre for harmonizing the actions of nations in the attainment of certain common ends, but true harmony in international affairs is elusive. The General Assembly is not a world parliament. It cannot legislate, but it can 'recommend'. Its recommendations may relate to general principles of international co-operation, or they may be specific measures for the peaceful adjustment of a situation which seems likely to impair friendly relations among nations or lead to a breach of peace. Increasingly the Assembly has interpreted its right of recommendation as including the right to deplore or condemn.

A substantive resolution adopted by the General Assembly

usually attempts to express the greatest possible degree of consensus of Member States. Numbers are often significant, since decisions on 'important' questions require a two-thirds majority, but there are other considerations besides numbers. The minority is sometimes wiser than the majority. Moreover, although the votes of States are equal in a numerical or juridical sense, they have different values in a political or moral sense.

The Assembly wavers between conflicting conceptions of its main role. 'It seems obvious', H. Field Haviland has written, 'that the principal task of the Assembly is to harmonize conflicting views rather than to impose a decision contrary to these views. Yet at times pressure may be necessary to break a deadlock.'[221] The predicaments the Assembly often faces can be simply stated. Should the Assembly frame its decision in such a way as to make compliance as easy as possible, or in such a way as to endorse the highest standards of conduct? Should it seek by quiet diplomacy to persuade an erring government to mend its ways, or should it publicly deplore all departures from the noble principles on which the Organization is based? Does reconciliation or censure best serve the interests of Member States and of the United Nations itself?

There is no general answer to these questions. Each issue is unique each time it arises. Certainly there are policies and incidents which come to the attention of the Assembly which cause a general sense of moral affront. Military or other forms of aggression, the subjugation of a helpless people, doctrines of race superiority, the contemptuous disregard of agreements—these cannot be condoned by those who care for the principles on which the United Nations was founded. But the essential task, it seems to me, is not to strike an attitude; it is to rectify the situation which is objectionable. The former is relatively easy, the latter requires such rare qualities as imagination, wisdom, and patience. As a former United States Secretary of State has noted,

> To express collective indignation may bring the glow of moral principles vindicated without effort; but it is usually futile, and, more often than not, harmful.[222]

This is not to say that intractable problems should be swept under the carpet nor that the Assembly should turn a blind eye when the principles of the Charter are flouted. But it is difficult to believe that resolutions which regret, deplore, or condemn, repeated year after year in some cases, have a consistently beneficial effect. Repetition can be vain.

The General Assembly cannot, by fiat, abolish prejudice, or set free the slaves, or liberate the oppressed; but it can declare that these are desirable goals and it can often take technical steps to bring their attainment nearer. The heart of the problem is to frame the Assembly's decisions in such a way that they exert pressure without increasing intransigence.

The adoption of a resolution expressing an opinion may represent pressure, or a resolution may authorize action which amounts to pressure. The General Assembly may use the prestige of the Organization and its Secretary-General in an attempt to secure compliance with principles stated in the Charter. The Assembly may establish a subsidiary organ to elucidate the facts or to exercise good offices. It may call for a report on the implementation of a resolution. But whatever form the decision takes, restraint of language is important. In examining those resolutions of the Assembly which have not been complied with, I cannot help wondering whether it was always wise to formulate the decision in such blunt language. If defiance of a United Nations recommendation is to be regarded as a grave matter, it will be because compliance is the normal policy of a civilized government. What is needed is a tradition of compliance.

Methods of Making Decisions

The Rules of Procedure provide for five methods of making decisions; in practice, a method of making decisions which is not provided for in the Rules of Procedure is also used. In addition, the Assembly has recently decided to experiment with mechanical voting.

1. Voting is 'normally . . . by show of hands'* : In a vote by a show of hands, the presiding officer requests those in favour of a proposal to raise their hands, then those who are against the proposal, and

---

* The Rules of Procedure provide that representatives may vote 'yes', 'no', or 'abstention'. There is no proxy voting, so that Members who are absent cannot participate in the voting; Members who are absent are permitted to indicate at a later stage how they would have voted had they been present when the vote was taken, although such indication does not alter the result of the vote.

finally those wishing to abstain; those who do not raise their hands are considered absent. The secretary of the meeting counts the votes and communicates the result to the presiding officer.

2. *Voting may be 'by standing'* : In a vote by standing, the presiding officer first requests those in favour of a proposal to rise from their seats, then those who are against the proposal, and finally those wishing to abstain; those not rising are considered absent. The counting of votes is done in the same way as in a vote by show of hands. I know of no case in which the Assembly or one of its committees has actually used this method.

3. *In connection with a vote other than a secret ballot, 'any representative may request a roll-call'* : A vote by roll-call is taken in the English alphabetical order of the names of Members, beginning with the Member whose name is drawn by lot by the presiding officer from a special box. The name of each Member is called by the secretary of the meeting, and representatives reply 'yes', 'no', or 'abstain'. If no reply is heard, the name is repeated; if again no reply is heard, that Member is considered absent. The vote of each Member is marked by the secretary on a special form; upon conclusion of the roll-call, the votes are counted by the secretary and the result communicated to the presiding officer.

4. *'All elections shall be held by secret ballot'; 'There shall be no nominations' for elections held in plenary meetings* : In the case of voting conducted by secret ballot, the presiding officer designates two tellers from among the representatives. Ballot papers are distributed to the delegations by conference officers, and a member of each delegation writes on the paper the name of the State(s) or person(s) his delegation wishes to vote for. A ballot box is placed at the head of the meeting, and the secretary calls the names of Members in the English alphabetical order, beginning with the Member whose name is drawn by lot by the presiding officer from a special box. Representatives deposit their ballots in the ballot box in the presence of the tellers. When the voting is completed, the box is opened in the presence of the tellers, who count the votes with the assistance of the Secretariat, and communicate the result to the presiding officer.

The system of election by secret ballot used in committees of the Assembly, and in plenary meetings where only one elective place is to be filled and a simple majority is sufficient, is known as Second or Exhaustive Ballot. In the first ballot, votes may be cast for any eligible candidate.* If no candidate obtains a simple majority of Members present and voting, the ballot is inconclusive and a second ballot is taken restricted to the two candidates obtaining the largest number of votes. If in the second ballot the votes are equally divided, and a simple majority is required, the presiding officer decides between the candidates by drawing lots.

If in plenary meeting of the Assembly two or more elective places are to be filled, those obtaining in the first ballot the majority required are elected. If more candidates obtain the required majority than there are places to be filled, it has been the practice to regard as elected those candidates obtaining the greatest number of votes, to a number equal to the places to be filled.[223] If all the places are not filled, additional ballots are held to fill the remaining places, the voting being restricted to the candidates obtaining the greatest number of votes in the previous ballot, to a number not more than twice the places remaining to be filled. Similarly, if only one place is to be filled and a two-thirds majority is required, and if in the first ballot no candidate obtains the majority required, additional ballots are held, restricted to the two candidates obtaining the largest number of votes, until one candidate secures two-thirds of the votes cast. These additional ballots are known as restricted ballots. If three restricted ballots are inconclusive, not more than three unrestricted ballots are held in which votes may be cast for any eligible candidate, followed by not more than three additional restricted ballots, followed by not more than three unrestricted ballots, and so on until all the places have been filled.

A system of election which combines a secret ballot, a ban on nominations, the requirement of a two-thirds majority for election in certain cases, and an alternation between restricted and unrestricted ballots in groups of three, is inevitably cumbersome.

5. *When the Assembly is not in session, decisions relating to the place of meeting of the Assembly or the summoning of a special session may be made by consultation of Members:* Sessions of the Assembly may be held elsewhere than at headquarters, and special sessions may be summoned, at the request of a majority of Members or at the request of any Member with the concurrence of a majority of Members.

---

* The word 'candidate' is a little misleading in connection with ballots in plenary meeting, since candidates are not publicly named. Aspirants for elective places are, however, usually candid in private. In any case, the word 'candidate' is used in the Rules of Procedure.

6. *A method of making a decision which is not explicitly provided for in the Rules is by acquiescence (or, in the case of elections, by acclamation):* When a presiding officer believes that a proposal does not meet with objection, he may decide not to put the question to a vote; he declares that, if there is no objection, the proposal will be adopted. If objection is made, a vote is held in accordance with the Rules of Procedure. Occasionally, after a resolution has been adopted by acquiescence, abstentions or negative votes have been recorded at the request of one or more Members.

7. *Mechanical voting:* The possibility of introducing mechanical voting was considered by the 1949 Committee on procedure, and again in 1955 in connection with the correction of votes, but on neither occasion was there sufficient support to justify a change of practice.[224] The 1963 Committee on procedure took a more favourable view, and the Assembly decided to install electrical voting equipment in the General Assembly Hall on an experimental basis for one year and to carry out additional preparatory work so as to permit an expansion of the system later if the experiment proved successful.[225]

Mechanical voting is accurate and saves time. As the General Assembly has grown in size, the Secretariat has found it more and more difficult to count the votes when decisions are taken by show of hands. A roll-call vote requires an average of eight and a half minutes and a vote by show of hands at least five minutes, whereas not more than one minute would be needed for either type of vote if a mechanical system were used. Table 19 shows the number of votes taken during the fifteenth, sixteenth, and seventeenth sessions; during the seventeenth session, the Fifth Committee could have saved some nine hours or more if a mechanical system had been available.[226]

Mechanical voting can be used for an ordinary vote, whether by roll-call or not, and also for such subsidiary purposes as to determine the presence of a quorum. Each representative has before him a switch with positions marked 'yes', 'no', and 'abstention'. The presiding officer has a device for initiating the vote and being informed of the result. In the case of voting by roll-call, the vote of each member is indicated by lights of differing colours on a wall panel; last minute changes of vote are possible. The totals are counted automatically and recorded.

When the question of mechanical voting was first considered in

1949, it was estimated that equipment for the General Assembly Hall would cost $55,200. In 1963 the installation cost for the General Assembly Hall was estimated at $40,700; the equipment would cost $228,000 to purchase outright, or could be rented and maintained at $38,000 for the first year and $16,000 in succeeding years.[227]

TABLE 19

Number of votes taken during the 15th, 16th and 17th regular sessions

	Fifteenth session	Sixteenth session	Seventeenth session
Plenary meetings			
Roll-call votes	146	74	38
Votes by show of hands	99	84	83
First Committee			
Roll-call votes	36	32	15
Votes by show of hands	18	27	22
Special Political Committee			
Roll-call votes	24	19	18
Votes by show of hands	34	23	17
Second Committee			
Roll-call votes	12	22	25
Votes by show of hands	34	19	40
Third Committee			
Roll-call votes	18	13	5
Votes by show of hands	34	62	90
Fourth Committee			
Roll-call votes	54	11	8
Votes by show of hands	77	13	21
Fifth Committee			
Roll-call votes	8	8	13
Votes by show of hands	54	54	128
Sixth Committee			
Roll-call votes	0	1	0
Votes by show of hands	4	4	4

The 1963 decision to experiment with mechanical voting was opposed by the Soviet bloc and the Congo (Leopoldville), but the general view was that a mechanical system would prove to be convenient and accurate, and would save time.[228] Some of the opposition to mechanical voting doubtless arises from the fact that delegates are not familiar with it; there was similar opposition to simultaneous interpretation in the early days.[229]

8. *Non-participation in the vote.* During the eighteenth session, the President, after consultation with the Chairmen of Main Committees, laid down the following procedure in cases of non-participation in the vote.[230]

(a) A delegation which wishes its non-participation in a vote to be recorded in the summary record or verbatim record should make a statement to that effect, either before or after the vote.

(b) When such a statement is recorded in the summary record or verbatim record, it will also appear in the Committee's report to the General Assembly if the delegation so desires, subject to the Committee's approval.

(c) During the roll-call the names of all delegations including those absent will be called, even if any delegation has already stated its intention not to participate in the vote.

(d) As far as the counting of the votes is concerned, those delegations which answer the roll-call by stating 'Not participating' will be considered as absent. In other words, the result of the vote will contain only the names of the delegations under the three following headings provided for in Rules 89 and 128: 'Yes', 'No', 'Abstention'. There will not be another heading called 'Present and not voting'; but, if a delegation expressly requests that its non-participation in a vote be recorded, its statement in this connexion will appear in the verbatim record of the relevant meeting.

7

ELECTIONS
AND APPOINTMENTS

If men of sense and honour and substance are chosen . . . one may be a check upon the other, and all prudently limited by the sovereignty they represent.

WILLIAM PENN

THERE ARE, in addition to the General Assembly, five 'principal organs' of the United Nations: the three Councils, the International Court of Justice, and the Secretariat. The General Assembly is composed of all the Members of the Organization. The Assembly elects some members of the Security and Trusteeship Councils, all the members of the Economic and Social Council, and participates in the election of the Judges of the International Court. The Secretary-General of the Organization is appointed by the General Assembly upon the recommendation of the Security Council, and the staff is appointed by the Secretary-General under regulations established by the Assembly.[231]

In every case, the composition of a body is intimately related to its functions. I am, however, concerned in this book with the procedure and practice of the General Assembly and not with the activities of organs some or all of whose members are elected or appointed by the Assembly. I intend, therefore, to discuss the functions of United Nations organs only to the extent that these have a direct bearing on the Assembly's electoral responsibilities.

The Security Council

The Assembly fills six seats on the Security Council by election. Members are elected for terms of two years, three elected members retiring each year; and retiring members are not eligible for immediate re-election. The non-elective seats are held by the five permanent members: the Republic of China, France, the Soviet Union, the United Kingdom, and the United States (Article 23). The election of non-permanent members of the Security Council is one of the 'important' questions for which a two-thirds majority of the Members of the Assembly present and voting is required (Article 18).

The importance of the Security Council hardly needs stressing. Member States have, in the Charter, specifically conferred on the Council primary responsibility for the maintenance of international peace and security, and have agreed to accept and carry out its decisions (Articles 24 and 25).

The Charter lays down principles that should govern the election of non-permanent members of the Council:

> due regard being specially paid, in the first instance to the contribution of Members of the United Nations to the maintenance of international peace and security and to the other purposes of the Organization, and also to equitable geographical distribution.[232]

The history of this part of the Charter is of some interest. The British delegation at Dumbarton Oaks had suggested that the Charter should specify that in the election of non-permanent members of the Security Council, due regard should be paid to the *military* contributions of States to the maintenance of international peace and security. Both the United States and the Soviet Union had reservations about the proposal in this form, and the British delegate therefore suggested the omission of 'military'. It seemed for a time that this revised formula might be acceptable, but it was withdrawn when the Soviet delegate stated that he would accept it on the understanding that it would apply to all sixteen Soviet republics, which at that time were being sponsored by the USSR as potential Members of the Organization.[233]

The idea of linking the election of non-permanent members of the Council to contributions to peace and security was revived at

San Francisco, though 'military' was left out. Britain suggested adding 'equitable geographical distribution' as another criterion, and the reference to 'the other purposes of the Organization' was inserted because of the difficulties the League of Nations had experienced in collecting financial contributions.[234]

Even without an agreement or understanding about the distribution of elective places, there are obvious difficulties in defining or applying such a subjective criterion as 'the contribution of Members ... to the maintenance of international peace and security and to the other purposes of the Organization'. During the first session of the Assembly, the following five States received more than the required two-thirds majority on the first ballot: Brazil, Egypt, Mexico, the Netherlands, and Poland; Australia and Canada were runners-up. Australia withdrew after the third ballot, and Canada was accordingly elected.[235] The pattern of election at the first session was thus as follows:

Latin America	2
Middle East	1
Eastern Europe	1
Western Europe	1
Commonwealth	1

This pattern was, in fact, based on an informal understanding between the Council's permanent members.

Table 20 shows the distribution of non-permanent seats on the Security Council since the Organization was founded. It will be seen that there have always been two elected members from Latin America, and at least one from Western Europe. The Commonwealth was represented until 1964, sometimes by an older Commonwealth State, sometimes by one of the newer Commonwealth States of Asia or Africa. The Middle East has been continuously represented only if the area is stretched beyond its normal limits. Eastern Europe has been represented for half the period, but for three years by a State which parted company from the Soviet bloc in 1948. If the Byelorussian and Ukrainian Republics are regarded as States in no way different from other Members of the United Nations, then a strict application of the principle of equitable geographical distribution, without reference to other considerations, would now entitle Eastern Europe to a seat on the Council frequently, but not

TABLE 20

Non-permanent members of the Security Council, 1946–64

	Latin America	*Asia and Africa*	*Eastern Europe*	*Western Europe*	*'Older Common-wealth' States*
1946	Brazil Mexico	Egypt	Poland	Netherlands	Australia
1947	Brazil Colombia	Syria	Poland	Belgium	Australia
1948	Argentina Colombia	Syria	Ukraine	Belgium	Canada
1949	Argentina Cuba	Egypt	Ukraine	Norway	Canada
1950	Cuba Ecuador	Egypt India	Yugoslavia	Norway	
1951	Brazil Ecuador	India	Yugoslavia	Netherlands Turkey	
1952	Brazil Chile	Pakistan		Greece Netherlands Turkey	
1953	Chile Colombia	Lebanon Pakistan		Denmark Greece	
1954	Brazil Colombia	Lebanon		Denmark Turkey	New Zealand
1955	Brazil Peru	Iran		Belgium Turkey	New Zealand
1956	Cuba Peru	Iran	Yugoslavia (resigned)	Belgium	Australia
1957	Colombia Cuba	Iraq Philippines		Sweden	Australia
1958	Colombia Panama	Iraq Japan		Sweden	Canada
1959	Argentina Panama	Japan Tunisia		Italy	Canada
1960	Argentina Ecuador	Tunisia Ceylon	Poland (resigned)	Italy	
1961	Chile Ecuador	Ceylon Liberia (resigned) United Arab Republic		Turkey	
1962	Chile Venezuela	Ghana United Arab Republic	Romania (resigned)	Ireland	
1963	Brazil Venezuela	Ghana Morocco Philippines		Norway	
1964	Bolivia Brazil	Ivory Coast Morocco	Czecho-slovakia (will resign at end of 1964 in favour of Malaysia)	Norway	

continuously. The Soviet complaint, however, has been based not so much on the Charter as on the informal understanding reached in 1946 by the Council's permanent members. The Soviet Union maintains that the five permanent members of the Security Council

> undertook to support the election to the Council of candidates nominated by the countries of the five main regions of the world. In accordance with that plan it was agreed that in the election of non-permanent members support would be given to two countries from the Latin-American region . . . while one seat would be allotted to the British Commonwealth, one to the Middle East, one to Western Europe, and one to Eastern Europe.[236]

The Soviet Union has, moreover, always maintained that the Assembly should, as a matter of course, endorse the choices already made informally and privately by groups.

The United States, for its part, has maintained that the 1946 agreement was intended to apply to the first election: that the only factors now to be taken into account in connexion with the elections are those specified in Article 23 (1) of the Charter; that the States of the Soviet bloc have not contributed to the maintenance of international peace and security; and that the Charter refers to equitable geographical *distribution* and not *representation*, and that this principle has been maintained by the election of such States as Greece, Turkey, and Yugoslavia. Underneath these legal arguments has been the wish to have the Security Council so constituted that there are six members which can be relied upon to stand with the United States in the case of threats to the peace.

It should be emphasized at this point that some States which were not parties to the 1946 understanding have not felt bound by it. The Indian representative stated this explicitly during the second session (1947) after withdrawing from the contest to permit the election of the Ukraine to the Council:

> We have been told that the allocation of seats on the Security Council is based on some arrangement privately arrived at among some of the Powers. But the distribution of Council seats by secret diplomacy to which the members of the General Assembly are not a party cannot, I am sure, find any support in this august body.
>
> Without in any way desiring to offend any of the Powers concerned, the delegation of India must challenge this arrangement.

Our withdrawal should not be taken to mean, nor does it imply, that we accept the so-called agreement between certain Powers for the distribution of seats.[237]

The Charter requirement that a two-thirds majority of the Members present and voting is required for the election of non-permanent members of the Security Council means that, if a seat is contested, balloting can be a tedious and lengthy process. Indeed, a determined minority of one-third of the Members plus one has the power to compel the Assembly to engage in inconclusive ballots for an indefinite period and, in the case of extreme intransigence, might render the Security Council ineffective.

During the second session (1947) there were eleven inconclusive ballots for one of the seats before India withdrew in favour of the Ukrainian SSR. There were thirteen inconclusive ballots during the fifth session (1950) before Lebanon withdrew in favour of Turkey. It was not until the nineteenth ballot during the sixth session (1951) that Greece received a two-thirds majority.

During the tenth session (1955) 36 ballots were necessary. Balloting began on 14 October. On the first ballot, thirty-nine votes were needed for election, and Cuba and Australia obtained the required majority; Poland and the Philippines had thirty-four and thirty-three votes respectively. After four ballots, Poland withdrew in the hope that Yugoslavia might be acceptable as a compromise candidate. Twenty-five further inconclusive ballots were held, with Yugoslavia varying between twenty-three and twenty-eight votes and the Philippines varying between twenty-five and thirty-three votes; on all these ballots, except the nineteenth, the Philippines was in the lead, but was always at least seven votes short of the required two-thirds majority.

After the twenty-ninth inconclusive ballot had taken place on 6 December, the President of the Assembly drew the attention of hungry delegates to the serious situation.

> If no agreement is reached, I for my part am ready to assist the Assembly [the verb was nicely chosen] in reaching a decision by called a meeting which would not rise until the vacant seat has been filled. . . .[238]

The session was due to close on 10 December, but two days before this the closing date was changed to 16 December. The admission of sixteen new Member States on 14 December introduced a new element into balloting for the Council. For the next five ballots, which were held on the morning of 16 December, the required two-thirds majority fluctuated between forty-four and forty-six. On the thirty-second ballot, the Philippines obtained forty votes, its highest vote, but still six short of two-thirds.

At 9 o'clock on the evening of 16 December (the revised date for the closing of the session), after all other business of the session had been disposed of, the Assembly returned to the election. Thirty-four ballots had been taken without the remaining seat on the Council being filled. The President announced that there had been consultations with a number of delegations, including the two rivals for the seat, with the object of finding an acceptable solution.

> It was felt that this purpose would be achieved if lots were drawn in the President's office between the two candidates I have already mentioned to decide which should withdraw from the present elections. After completing the first year of the term, the other candidate would offer its resignation from the Security Council. The agreement is that the vacant seat would then be filled for the remainder of the term by the election of the other candidate at the eleventh session.
>
> The spirit of this compromise solution, for which I do not hesitate to assume a moral responsibility that will certainly be shared by the other representatives, must ensure that the agreement will be faithfully observed.
>
> In accordance with the procedure I have outlined, lots were drawn in the President's office; as a result, the Philippines has withdrawn its candidature at this time in favour of Yugoslavia.
>
> I am sure that the Assembly, in approving this procedure, will recognize that it does not set a precedent and will further agree that, in view of the unusual circumstances, the arrangement should be accepted and carried out.[239]

Following the President's statement, several representatives mounted the rostrum to express reservations about the procedure which had been outlined. A few stated flatly that it was illegal; others announced that they had no instructions in connexion with such a new and unexpected development; others expressly stated that they could not at that time commit their governments regarding the future, and in particular regarding how they would vote in 1956 if Yugoslavia should resign the seat after one year. After an inconclusive debate, the Philippines suggested that a further ballot be held. This time Yugoslavia received thirty-four votes and the Philippines nineteen (forty votes required for election). The President thereupon declared that he released the two parties from the agreement. The Assembly, having at 10.30 p.m. rejected a motion to suspend the meeting and resume it one hour later, decided to extend the session until 20 December.[240]

On the morning of 20 December the Assembly returned to the question, and on the thirty-sixth ballot Yugoslavia received forty-three votes, five more than the required majority. The three-month session closed, as is the custom, with one minute of silent prayer or meditation.

Having served on the Council during 1956, Yugoslavia informed the Secretary-General that she would not be in a position to serve on the Council in 1957.[241] A by-election to fill the vacancy was therefore held in accordance with Rule 141, and the Philippines was elected on the first ballot, obtaining one vote more than the required majority. Following the election, the Soviet representative stated that there had been a flagrant violation of the rights of the Eastern European Members. He referred to the informal agreement of 1946 and said that the decision just reached illustrated the fact that the United Nations was dwindling in importance.[242]

A similar situation developed during the fourteenth session (1959). The terms of office of Canada, Japan, and Panama were due to expire at the end of 1959. After a certain amount of preliminary manœuvring, it was agreed informally that Ceylon and Ecuador should succeed Canada and Panama respectively, and they were duly elected on the first ballot. Poland and Turkey were candidates for the other seat.

Poland's candidature was announced in July, though for some months before that Polish diplomats in New York and elsewhere had been preparing the ground. At one time it seemed likely that Greece would be Poland's rival for the seat, but at the last moment Greece withdrew and Turkey was substituted. It was the view of Turkey's supporters that the seat for which she was a candidate should, if possible, be filled by an Eastern European country. One difficulty was that Turkey had, for a time in 1959, been a candidate for one of the vice-presidencies of the Assembly reserved for 'Western European and other States' but at the last moment had switched her candidature to one of the Afro-Asian vacancies. By contesting an East

European vacancy on the Security Council, Turkey was in effect claiming to belong to three different regions at once. The announcement of Turkey's candidature was not made until after the session had begun, and this meant that some States which might have supported her had already made commitments to Poland.

Fifty-two ballots were needed to resolve the question. The two-thirds majority required for election varied between fifty and fifty-four votes, with the result that a State which could get at least twenty-nine votes on every ballot could prevent any other State from being elected. In the event, Poland's vote never fell below thirty-six, and—until the last ballot—Turkey's vote never fell below thirty-three. To put it another way, Poland's highest vote was six short of the necessary majority, and Turkey's highest vote was ten short of the necessary majority. About a dozen States were 'floating' voters, but even if all these had 'floated' in the same direction on any single ballot, this would still not have given either candidate the required majority.

Balloting began on 12 October. Thirty-one ballots were held during that month, twelve more during November, and six more on 1 December. The Assembly was due to close on 5 December, though the closing date was eventually changed to 12 December. As the session progressed, the word 'compromise' was heard more frequently. Turkey had let it be known in mid-November that she would consider 'splitting the term' with Poland, and discussions about this were entered into during the last few days of the session. Even if agreement could be reached on this, it still remained to be settled which of the two would be elected in 1959 and serve the first year, what guarantees there would be that this country would resign at the end of 1960, what guarantees there would be that the other country would be elected during the fifteenth session to serve during 1961, whether any of the arrangements should be linked with any other question, and what implications the arrangements would have for the elections after 1961.

At the night meeting at the end of the session, 12–13 December, the Assembly was able to endorse an agreement which had been negotiated in private. The President stated that, because of the impasse, consultations had taken place between the two candidates and their supporters. As a result it had been agreed that Poland was the only candidate during the fourteenth session, but that Poland would resign at the end of 1960. Turkey would be the only candidate during the fifteenth session for the vacancy thus created. 'In the vote, it is understood that the Members of the Assembly will confirm that agreement.'[244]

Before the vote was taken, several not entirely consistent statements were made. The Soviet representative said that the election of Poland would end the discrimination against Eastern Europe; the Soviet Union supported the plan for a split term as a temporary way out of the situation. The United States representative denied that there had been any discrimination against any area or nation; the United States intended to examine each candidacy in the future in the light of the circumstances prevailing at the time. The Polish representative said he was convinced that there was agreement that there would not, in the future, be any discrimination against Eastern Europe in elections to the Security Council. Poland would give an assurance that, should she be elected, she would resign after one year. The Turkish representative said that his country's agreement with Poland did not extend to the question of principle involved; Turkey maintained its position in that matter. The representatives of Canada, Brazil, and the United Kingdom expressed gratification that the deadlock had been ended.[245]

At 2.30 a.m., the Assembly proceeded to the election by secret ballot, Poland obtaining seventy-one votes, thus being elected on the fifty-second ballot. Three diehards maintained their support for Turkey: Greece and the Yemen obtained one vote each; four Members abstained, and two were absent.

The decision in 1955 to split the 1956–57 term between Yugoslavia and the Philippines had been reluctantly accepted by the Assembly as an exceptional measure and on the understanding, as the President put it, 'that it does not set a precedent'. The adoption of the same expedient in 1959 soon came to be regarded as a normal arrangement. In 1960, after thirteen inconclusive ballots, it was announced that Liberia and Ireland would split the 1961–62 term. The following year, after nine inconclusive ballots, it was announced that Romania and the Philippines would split the 1962–63 term. The 1964–65 term was split between Czechoslovakia and Malaysia; in 1964, for the first time, the United Kingdom was the only Commonwealth State on the Council.

The position now is that it is impossible to distribute the six seats to be filled by election in such a way that all the main groups are continuously represented. There has been growing pressure since 1956 to enlarge the Security Council, and in 1963 the Assembly decided to submit for the ratification of Member States amendments to the Charter to provide for increasing the Security Council to fifteen members, the non-permanent members to be elected according to a fixed pattern. Such a change is impossible without the support of all the permanent members of the Security Council, and the Soviet Union has opposed any modification of the Charter without the participation of the People's Republic of China.[246] Pending a review of the Charter, the Soviet Union has suggested that the non-permanent seats should be redistributed.

Region	1946 understanding	Soviet proposal for redistribution, 1963	General Assembly proposal for enlargement, 1963
Asia	—	1	⎫
Middle East	1	1	⎬ 5
Africa	—	1	⎭
Latin America	2	1	2
Eastern Europe	1	1	1
Western Europe	1	1	⎫ 2
Other States	—	—	⎬
Commonwealth	1	—	—

Latin America has always had one-third of the elective places on the Council, and this was reasonable in the early years. With the large increase in the Membership of the United Nations since 1955, and assuming that the Security Council is not enlarged by Charter amendment, it is inevitable that pressure will mount to give Latin America one seat rather than two.

Any increase in the number of permanent or non-permanent members of the Council would necessarily mean a consequential revision of Article 27 relating to voting and the veto. However desirable such changes may be, they would not eliminate controversy regarding the distribution of elective places. There will always be more candidates than vacancies.

The Economic and Social Council

Serious difficulties have not often arisen in connexion with the election of members of the Economic and Social Council. The Council consists of eighteen members elected for three-year terms. A retiring member is eligible for immediate re-election (Article 61).

Elections to the Council are among the important questions for which a two-thirds majority vote of Members of the Assembly present and voting is required (Article 18). No criteria are laid down for the selection of members or the distribution of seats.

Until 1961, the permanent members of the Security Council, were continuously re-elected to the Economic and Social Council, and were also members of most of the Council's subsidiary organs. Except for the period 1950–52, there had been five members from Western Europe, including France and the United Kingdom. Except for 1946, there had been three East European members, including the Soviet Union. From 1950 there had been, in addition to China, at least three other members from the Afro-Asian area. Latin America had had four members. There had been at least one 'older Commonwealth' member, and the United States had been continuously re-elected.

In addition to the United Kingdom and at least one 'older Commonwealth' State, there had usually been at least one Asian or African member of the Commonwealth on the Council. In the election during the fourteenth session (1955), however, India and Japan were both candidates for the seat being vacated by Pakistan. After six inconclusive ballots in which Japan led, the Indian representative stated that as Japan had consistently obtained a simple majority of votes, and in order to establish a good practice and a good convention, India would withdraw.[247] Japan was accordingly elected on the seventh ballot, thus reducing the Commonwealth representation to two for the period 1960–61. India returned to the Council in 1962.

Two changes in the distribution of seats took place during the 1960 elections. China was dropped from the Council and has not been elected since then. There was also a deadlock over filling the last place; by the end of the year, after thirteen ballots, only seventeen places had been filled, India and Belgium being the contenders. Seven more inconclusive ballots were held in March 1961. On 4 April 1961, the seventeen members of the Council held an informal meeting but were unable to proceed with business because of doubts as to the legality of meeting without the full membership prescribed by the Charter.

TABLE 21

Members of the Economic and Social Council, 1946–1964

	Latin America	Asia and Africa	Eastern Europe	Western Europe	'Older Common-wealth' States	United States
1946	Chile Colombia Cuba Peru	China India Lebanon	Czechoslovakia Ukraine USSR Yugoslavia	Belgium (resigned) France Greece Norway United Kingdom	Canada	United States
1947	Chile Cuba Peru Venezuela	China India Lebanon	Byelorussia Czechoslovakia USSR	France Netherlands Norway Turkey United Kingdom	Canada New Zealand	United States
1948	Brazil Chile Peru Venezuela	China Lebanon	Byelorussia Poland USSR	Denmark France Netherlands Turkey United Kingdom	Australia Canada New Zealand	United States
1949	Brazil Chile Peru Venezuela	China India Lebanon	Byelorussia Poland USSR	Belgium Denmark France Turkey United Kingdom	Australia New Zealand	United States
1950	Brazil Chile Mexico Peru	China India Iran Pakistan	Czechoslovakia Poland USSR	Belgium Denmark France United Kingdom	Australia Canada	United States

TABLE 21—continued

Members of the Economic and Social Council, 1946–1964

	Latin America	Asia and Africa	Eastern Europe	Western Europe	'Older Commonwealth' States	United States
1951	Chile Mexico Peru Uruguay	China India Iran Pakistan Philippines	Czechoslovakia Poland USSR	Belgium France Sweden United Kingdom	Canada	United States
1952	Argentina Cuba Mexico Uruguay	China Egypt Iran Pakistan Philippines	Czechoslovakia Poland USSR	Belgium France Sweden United Kingdom	Canada	United States
1953	Argentina Cuba Uruguay Venezuela	China Egypt India Philippines	Poland USSR Yugoslavia	Belgium France Sweden Turkey United Kingdom	Australia	United States
1954	Argentina Cuba Ecuador Venezuela	China Egypt India Pakistan	Czechoslovakia USSR Yugoslavia	Belgium France Norway Turkey United Kingdom	Australia	United States
1955	Argentina Dominican Rep. Ecuador Venezuela	China Egypt India Pakistan	Czechoslovakia USSR Yugoslavia	France Turkey Netherlands Norway	Australia	United States

Table 21—continued
Members of the Economic and Social Council, 1946–1964

	Latin America	Asia and Africa	Eastern Europe	Western Europe	'Older Commonwealth' States	United States
1956	Argentina Brazil Dominican Rep. Ecuador	China Egypt Indonesia Pakistan	Czechoslovakia USSR Yugoslavia	United Kingdom France Greece Netherlands Norway United Kingdom	Canada	United States
1957	Argentina Brazil Dominican Rep. Mexico	China Egypt Indonesia Pakistan	Poland USSR Yugoslavia	Finland France Greece Netherlands United Kingdom	Canada	United States
1958	Brazil Chile Costa Rica Mexico	China Indonesia Pakistan Sudan	Poland USSR Yugoslavia	Finland France Greece Netherlands United Kingdom	Canada	United States
1959	Chile Costa Rica Mexico Venezuela	Afghanistan China Pakistan Sudan	Bulgaria Poland USSR	Finland France Netherlands Spain United Kingdom	New Zealand	United States
1960	Brazil Chile Costa Rica Venezuela	Afghanistan China Japan Sudan	Bulgaria Poland USSR	Denmark France Netherlands Spain United Kingdom	New Zealand	United States

TABLE 21—continued

Members of the Economic and Social Council, 1946–1964

	Latin America	Asia and Africa	Eastern Europe	Western Europe	'Older Common-wealth' States	United States
1961	Brazil El Salvador Uruguay Venezuela	Afghanistan Ethiopia Japan Jordan	Bulgaria Poland USSR	Denmark France Italy Spain United Kingdom	New Zealand	United States
1962	Brazil Colombia El Salvador Uruguay	Ethiopia India Japan Jordan Senegal	Poland USSR Yugoslavia	Denmark France Italy United Kingdom	Australia	United States
1963	Argentina Colombia El Salvador Uruguay	Ethiopia India Japan Jordan Senegal	Czechoslovakia USSR Yugoslavia	Austria France Italy United Kingdom	Australia	United States
1964	Argentina Colombia Chile Ecuador	Algeria India Iraq Japan Senegal	Czechoslovakia USSR Yugoslavia	Austria France Luxembourg United Kingdom	Australia	United States

The Assembly met again on 18 April to complete the election, and the President announced that agreement had been reached along the following lines:

The Western European group is prepared to agree that if Belgium and India decide not to press their candidatures at this session of the Assembly, and another European candidate is elected now, then the Western European group will be prepared to support two candidates from among the members of the Asian-African group at next autumn's election for the seats now occupied by Afghanistan and Spain. . . . In keeping with this understanding, the candidature of Italy has been presented for the existing vacancy . . .[248]

The President's statement related only to the completion of the election for 1961–62 and to the election for 1962–63, but it may be assumed that, for the time being, the allocation of seats compares with the earlier period as follows:

	Distribution of seats 1953–1960	Distribution of seats since 1962
Western Europe	3	2
Eastern Europe	2	2
Asia and Africa	3	5
Latin America	4	4
'Older Commonwealth' States	1	1
Permanent members of the Security Council	5	4

From the very first session of the Assembly, there has been pressure to increase the size of the Economic and Social Council. This would, of course, be possible only by amending Article 61 of the Charter. It has been argued that an increase in the number of the members would make it possible for the Council to be more representative of the whole Membership of the United Nations, which in turn would increase the authority of the Council and improve the quality of its work. The Soviet bloc has opposed any increase, but the opposition has not been related to the merits of the proposals but has arisen from the general opposition to any amendment to the Charter so long as the present representation of China continues.

It may be doubted whether the Council has in reality been as unrepresentative as is sometimes implied. If account is taken of such factors as fair regional representation and the contribution of States to the regular activities and extra-budgetary programs for which the Economic and Social Council has general responsibility, the present composition may be regarded as reasonable. Although many Member States believe that the Afro-Asian countries have not been sufficiently represented, and that this has accounted for some of the Council's problems, the record of the Council does not suggest that it has been indifferent to the needs and problems of the less-developed countries.

The real problem is that the Council has to reconcile divergent conceptions of its own rôle and functions. It has aspired to become a periodic 'summit' conference on major economic and social questions; it has initiated international consultation on technical questions; it has been concerned with reviewing and co-ordinating the activities of the specialized agencies and its own functional and regional commissions; it has been a debating club, passing resolutions of a general character. Because the growth of economic regionalism has led to the creation of organs of regional economic co-operation (both within the framework of the United Nations and outside it), and because the General Assembly provides an attractive forum for major policy initiatives in the economic and social field, the Economic and Social Council has increasingly tended to become a procedural body concerned with the review and co-ordination of programs of work.

It would be possible to accept the likelihood that the Council will continue to devote its main attention to programs of work rather than major problems of policy, and to initiate some new means of consultation and co-operation on important economic and social questions, supplementing the machinery already in existence. A number of ideas directed towards this end were, indeed, considered during 1959. The British and Dutch representatives on the Council, as well as Secretary-General Hammarskjold, expressed doubt as to whether the Council had been living up to its responsibilities.[249] Hammarskjold suggested that the time had come for the United Nations to deal more directly with the formulation of international economic policies, or at least to serve in a more systematic way as a forum for the co-ordination of such policies.

I believe that short special meetings at the ministerial level, within or under the aegis of the Economic and Social Council, might make an invaluable contribution to the formulation of international economic policies adequate to vital requirements for concerted action. . . .'[250]

The Council, at its session in December 1959, approved a resolution asking the Secretary-General to organize a meeting of the Council at the ministerial level. But it must be admitted that, in spite of careful advance preparation, the idea never really got off the ground. Instead of engaging in real debate, the Council was subjected to a series of elevating monologues. Senior ministers will attend meetings of the Council only if there is important work to be done.

If the main problem is that wider participation in the work of the Council is desirable, two alternative possibilities that do not involve amendments to the Charter may be envisaged.

In the first place, the Charter provides that members of the Economic and Social Council serve for three-year terms (as do the elected members of the Trusteeship Council), compared with two-year terms for the non-permanent members of the Security Council. It might be possible to develop a convention that some of the members elected to the Economic and Social Council from the under-represented regions would resign after two years in favour of other States from the same regions. This would not change the distribution of places on the Council but would increase the speed of rotation of seats.

A second possibility would be based on Article 69 of the Charter and Rules 75 and 76 of the Council's Rules of Procedure. These provisions empower the Council to invite a Member of the United Nations which is not a member of the Council to participate in the Council's deliberations. Such a Member may take part in debate and submit proposals, but does not have the right to vote. In accordance with these provisions, the Assembly might designate a number of Asian and African States not elected to the Council as 'Consulting Members', which would participate regularly in the business of the Council.

Such an arrangement, like the one examined earlier, would not alter the voting situation in the Council. The less-developed countries of Asia and Africa might still continue to regard the Assembly as a more advantageous forum for debate and decision than the Council, but they would know that their problems and needs would have fuller expression in the Council before decisions were taken.

Another step would be to enlarge some of the functional bodies appointed by the Council, so as to provide for a more equitable distribution of seats. Decisions to this end were taken by the Assembly in 1963.[251] It is in the subsidiary organs that much of the substantive work is done, and the Council itself is reluctant to over-ride the advice of bodies with larger membership than itself.

The Trusteeship Council

So fast has been the development of trust territories toward self-government or independence that a problem has been encountered regarding the composition of the Trusteeship Council which seems not to have been foreseen by the founding fathers of the United Nations.

At the San Francisco Conference, the United States proposed that the Trusteeship Council should consist of specially qualified representatives designated by the States administering trust territories and by an equal number of other States named for three-year periods by the General Assembly.[252] The Soviet Union, for its part, proposed that the Big Five should be permanent members of the Council. Representatives of States administering trust territories and permanent members of the Security Council not administering such territories would be balanced by an equal number of representatives of other States named by the General Assembly.[253]

In view of the Soviet proposal that permanent members of the Security Council should also be permanent members of the Trusteeship Council, the original United States proposal was modified to provide for a Trusteeship Council in essentially the same form as was subsequently provided in Article 86 (1) of the Charter.

> The Trusteeship Council shall consist of the following Members of the United Nations:
> (a) those Members administering trust territories;
> (b) such of those Members mentioned by name in Article 23 [the five permanent members of the Security Council] as are not administering trust territories; and
> (c) as many other Members elected for three-year terms by the General Assembly as may be necessary to ensure that the total number of members of the Trusteeship Council is equally divided between those Members of the United Nations which administer trust territories and those which do not.

The theoretical possibility that the objectives of the trusteeship system might eventually be achieved in respect of some territories does not seem to have been discussed at San Francisco. It was, however, raised by the British delegation to the Executive Committee of the Preparatory Commission of the United Nations the following September. In a memorandum on the composition of the Trusteeship Council, the United Kingdom pointed out that reductions in the number of members administering trust territories might occur, and would be of two kinds. If a permanent member of the Council should cease to be an administering State, it would displace two elected members. If a non-permanent member of the Council should cease to be an administering State, it would, unless subsequently elected by the Assembly as a non-administering member, lose its seat on the Council and would displace one elected member. The decision which elected member should be displaced 'would presumably lie with the General Assembly'.[254]

The possibility raised by the British delegation seemed remote in 1945 and it evidently evoked no discussion. Interest at that time was concentrated on getting the trusteeship system into effective operation, and there was no overt interest in such long-term problems as how the system might be dismantled as its objectives were progressively achieved.[255]

By the end of 1946, it became possible to constitute the Trusteeship Council. Australia, Belgium, France, New Zealand, and the United Kingdom had submitted trusteeship agreements which had been approved by the Assembly, and they thus became Administering Authorities; China, the Soviet Union, and the United States were members of the Council by virtue of their permanent membership of the Security Council; Mexico and Iraq were elected to the Council for a three-year term each to establish parity. After approval and ratification of the trusteeship agreement for the Pacific Islands under United States administration in 1947, the United States became an Administering Authority and, in order to maintain parity, Costa Rica and the Philippines were elected to the Council. Italy, as Administering Authority for the Trust Territory of Somaliland but not a Member of the United Nations, began to participate without vote in relevant proceedings of the Trusteeship Council in 1950. After the admission of Italy to the United Nations in 1955, Italy became an *ex-officio* member of the Council and Burma was elected as an additional non-administering member in order to keep the balance.

TABLE 22

Elected Members of the Trusteeship Council, 1947–1965

Year*	Latin America	Asia and Africa
1947	Mexico	Iraq
1948	Costa Rica	Iraq
	Mexico	Philippines
1949	Costa Rica (resigned)	Iraq
	Mexico	Philippines
1950	Argentina	Iraq
	Dominican Republic	Philippines
1951	Argentina (resigned)	Iraq
	Dominican Republic	Thailand
1952	El Salvador	Iraq
	Dominican Republic	Thailand
1953	El Salvador	Syria
	Dominican Republic	Thailand
1954	El Salvador	India
	Haiti	Syria
1955	El Salvador	India
	Haiti	Syria
1956	Guatemala	Burma
	Haiti	India
		Syria
1957	Guatemala	Burma
	Haiti	India
		Syria
1958	Guatemala	Burma
	Haiti	India
		Syria
1959	Haiti	Burma
	Paraguay	India
		United Arab Republic
1960	Bolivia	Burma
	Paraguay	India
		United Arab Republic
1961	Bolivia	Burma
	Paraguay	India
		United Arab Republic
1962	Bolivia	India
1963–5		Liberia

* According to the Rules of Procedure of the General Assembly, the term of office of Members of the Council shall begin on 1 January following their election, except as provided in Rule 148: 'When a Trusteeship Agreement has been approved and a Member of the United Nations has become an Administering Authority of a Trust Territory . . . the General Assembly shall proceed to such election or elections to the Trusteeship Council as may be necessary. . . . Members elected at any such election . . . shall take office immediately upon their election and shall complete their terms . . . as if they had begun their terms of office on 1 January following their election'.

The principle of parity of membership between administering and non-administering members has been observed in almost all of the Visiting Missions and other subsidiary organs of the Council.

In two cases, non-administering members have resigned from the Council before expiration of their terms of office. On each occasion, the Assembly has elected a member to fill the remainder of the term, though it may be questioned whether this practice conforms strictly to the letter of Article 86 of the Charter ('as many other Members elected for three-year terms') or the Rule of Procedure of the Assembly based on that Article (now Rule 149).

When elections to the Council for the years 1959–61 took place in 1958, it was known that Somaliland under Italian trusteeship would achieve independence on July 1, 1960; Italy would then cease to be a member of the Trusteeship Council. The lapse of Italy's membership in 1960 would require either that one of the members elected by the Assembly in 1958 or 1959 should serve only so long as Italy continued to exercise administering responsibilities, or that means would have to be devised to displace an elected member as from the date of Italy's disappearance. The President of the Assembly referred to this impending difficulty when the election took place.

> In the foreseeable future . . . one of the Members ceases to be an Administering Authority and therefore ceases to be a member of the Council. This will occur in 1960. In the light of the elections which will take place today, it will be necessary for the General Assembly, at its next regular session, to consider the procedure to be followed in order that the . . . balance may be maintained after the number of Administering Authorities has been reduced.

There was no discussion of the President's statement, and the election of Paraguay, Burma, and the United Arab Republic took place in the normal manner.[256]

In the event, the question of the composition of the Council during 1960 was to become more complicated than had been envisaged in 1958. The Cameroons and Togoland under French administration were destined to become independent on 1 January and 27 April, 1960 respectively. France, as a permanent member of the Security Council, would continue as a member of the Trusteeship Council, but as a non-administering member, thus displacing two elected members of the Council.

Thus the situation before the Assembly in 1959 was as follows. Two elected members of the Council (Haiti and India) were due to retire at the end of the year. The Assembly could elect two members to succeed them, to serve during the period of about four months during which France would continue to exercise administering responsibilities. Such a procedure would not accord exactly with the letter of the Charter ('elected for three-year terms . . .'), but there were precedents for elections for less than three years. This procedure would ensure parity until 1 July 1960, when Italy's membership would lapse. If it were necessary for the Council to meet during the second half of 1960, however, parity could be maintained only by the displacement of one of the members elected the previous year for the period 1959–61.

Two means of displacing elected members were envisaged. In the first place, lots could be drawn. This method is prescribed in the Assembly's Rules of Procedure in certain cases of equally divided votes in elections (Rules 95 and 133). It was resorted to in 1955 in an attempt to break the deadlock over the Security Council election, and it has also been used to determine the order in which members of an Assembly committee should retire.[257] It is, however, one thing to use this method if it is prescribed in the Rules or accepted by the candidates before an election takes place, and quite another thing to resort to it after valid elections have been held and without the express consent of the parties.

Alternatively, the Assembly might have decided that all elected members should retire simultaneously, and a new election held to fill the proper number of vacancies.

Either of these methods of reducing the number of elected members was open to some objection. During discussion of this matter in 1959, the Indian representative, after informing the Assembly that India was a candidate for election, stated that 'once a country is elected for a three-year period there is no provision . . . for premature termination of membership without consent. . . . The compulsive premature cessation or termination of membership would indeed infringe on the fundamental right of an elected member under the Charter.'[258]

The provisional agenda of the 1959 session included, in the normal way, an item entitled 'Election of two members of the Trusteeship Council', to which was appended a footnote reading as follows:

Procedure to be devised in order to comply with the provisions of Article 86 of the Charter as France and Italy will cease to be Administering Authorities in 1960. . . .[259]

This footnote was not included in the agenda recommended by the General Committee and approved by the plenary Assembly.[260]

The question raised in the footnote in the provisional agenda did not come formally before the Assembly until 9 p.m. on the final evening of the session. Consideration of the question was interrupted for about an hour in order to complete the election of members of the Security Council; except for this break, the matter occupied the attention of weary delegates until 4.15 a.m.

It was probably difficult, during a night meeting at the end of a busy three-month session, to give the matter the attention it deserved. Some representatives were familiar with the problem in all its ramifications, but others were apparently taken by surprise. The representative of Israel, for example, said that his delegation had had no opportunity to study the implications of what was being proposed.[261]

There were, in effect, three proposals before the Assembly. The first was submitted by the Soviet Union in two different but similar versions. One would have decided to elect two members of the Trusteeship Council upon the expiry of the terms of office of Haiti and India, and to have resumed the fourteenth session of the Assembly on 28 April 1960 to decide on the composition of the Trusteeship Council thereafter; the other would have convened a special session of the Assembly on 28 April 1960.[262] The first Soviet proposal was not adopted as it failed to obtain the required two-thirds majority; the second Soviet proposal was rejected.

A different proposal was submitted by Tunisia, and the Assembly approved by majorities of at least two-thirds of the Members present and voting each of the following paragraphs.[263]

The General Assembly,
Guided by the provisions of Article 86 of the Charter of the United Nations,
Considering the desirability of studying the situation which would result both from the fact that it will soon be impossible to observe simultaneously the principles of parity and of the inclusion of the permanent members of the Security Council in the membership of the Trusteeship Council, and from the fact that the category of elected members whose role in the work of

181

the Trusteeship Council has proved important will be eliminated in the very near future,

Decides [to] elect two members of the Trusteeship Council at the present session, in accordance with Article 86 of the Charter;

Decides to resume consideration of the whole question of membership of the Trusteeship Council at its next session.

The Assembly then voted on the draft resolution as a whole, but it failed to obtain the required two-thirds majority and so was not adopted.

Having rejected the two versions of the Soviet proposal and the amended Tunisian proposal, the Assembly proceeded to elect Bolivia and India to the Trusteeship Council, succeeding Haiti and India. The future was left to take care of itself.

This was, in fact, the result which several Member States had favoured, though the result was achieved by unsatisfactory means. The representatives of Ceylon, India, and the United Kingdom had specifically urged the Assembly to hold elections in the ordinary way.[264] In the event, the Assembly took that course in the absence of agreement on any other proposal.

When the Assembly met a year later, the Secretary-General drew attention to the problem which had been swept under the carpet in 1959. In a request for the inclusion in the Assembly's agenda of an item entitled 'The Question of the composition of the Trusteeship Council', the Secretary-General stated that the Council was no longer composed in accordance with the Charter.[265] Since the attainment of independence by Somaliland, the Council had been constituted as follows:

Administering members	*Non-administering members*				
Australia	China	⎤			
Belgium	France	⎬ Permanent members of Security			
New Zealand	USSR	⎦ Council			
United Kingdom	3 elected members retiring at the end of 1961				
United States	2	,,	,,	,,	,, 1962
—	—				
Total 5	8				
—	—				

The provision for parity laid down in the Charter was no longer being observed.

It was not until 7 April 1962 that the Assembly reached this matter. The President then announced that informal discussions had been taking place and suggested that 'Members may feel that no action need be taken . . . at the present session'. If that were agreed, the Trusteeship Council would 'continue to function during 1961 on the basis of its present membership of thirteen'.[266] In spite of reservations on the part of some Members, this procedure was accepted.

During the course of 1962, Western Samoa administered by New Zealand achieved independence, and Ruanda-Urundi administered by Belgium achieved independence as the two States of Rwanda and Burundi. Territories remaining under trusteeship thereafter were as follows:

Territory	*Administering Authority*
Nauru	Australia, on behalf also of New Zealand and the United Kingdom
New Guinea	Australia
Pacific Islands	United States

The Trusteeship Council is therefore constituted as follows:

Administering members	*Non-administering members*
Australia	China
New Zealand	France
United Kingdom	USSR
United States	One member elected by the Assembly (Liberia for 1963–65)

It may be questioned whether this composition accords with the strict letter of the Charter. The trusteeship agreement for Nauru designates Australia, New Zealand, and the United Kingdom jointly as 'the Administering Authority', but New Zealand and the United Kingdom are not now 'Members administering trust territories'. But to drop New Zealand and the United Kingdom from the Council would mean the end of parity, since the Council would then consist of Australia and the United States as States administering trust territories, four permanent members of the Security Council as non-administering members, and not a single member elected by the Assembly.

The fact is that the question of the composition of the Trusteeship Council, which aroused such interest in 1959–61, subsided once the Assembly had decided to create a special committee on the liquidation of colonialism and to abandon the principle of parity, which the Charter provides for the Trusteeship Council and which had also been observed for the Committee on Information from Non-Self-Governing Territories.

Judges of the International Court

The Assembly, in conjunction with the Security Council, elects the judges of the International Court of Justice. The procedure of nomination and election is very cumbersome.

The Statute of the International Court declares that the Court should be composed of independent judges, elected regardless of their nationality from among persons of high moral character, who possess the qualifications required in their respective countries for appointment to the highest judicial offices, or are jurisconsults of recognized competence in international law. The electors should bear in mind not only that the persons to be elected should individually possess the qualifications required, but also that in the body as a whole the representation of the main forms of civilization and of the principal legal systems of the world should be assured.[267]

Candidates are nominated by the national groups in the Permanent Court of Arbitration established by the Hague Conferences of 1899 and 1907; or, in the case of Members of the United Nations not represented in the Permanent Court of Arbitration, by national groups appointed by their governments under the same conditions prescribed for members of the Permanent Court of Arbitration.[268] Each nominating group consists of not more than four persons, selected by governments, 'of known competency in questions of international law, of the highest moral reputation. . . .'

These national groups are somewhat amorphous.

[They] have actually no organic consistency; each is rather four separate individuals having no provision for acting together as a unit. They have no address. . . . [They] are supposed to act independently of their governments; presumably they would transmit their nominations to the Secretary-General directly. No procedure for this has been provided. . . .[269]

This system of nominations inevitably leads to the valid nomination of many more candidates than there are vacancies. Thus there were seventy-eight nominations in 1946 for the original fifteen vacancies. In the 1963 elections to fill five vacancies, there were twenty-five nominations.

Rule 94 of the Rules of Procedure of the Assembly, which prohibits nominations in plenary meetings, has not been applied in connexion with the election of judges of the Court, although the only nominations permitted are those made in accordance with the Statute of the Court; a candidate whose name does not appear on the ballot paper may not be nominated in a meeting of the Assembly.

Regular elections take place every three years and are for five vacancies; an election to fill a single vacancy is held if a judge ceases to serve before the completion of his term.[270] The Secretary-General of the United Nations submits to the General Assembly and the Security Council the nominations which he has received, and the *curricula vitae* of the candidates. On the day of the elections, the General Assembly and the Security Council proceed, independently of one another, to elect five members of the Court, and the candidates who obtain an 'absolute majority of votes' in both bodies are elected. The expression 'absolute majority of votes' is not used in the United Nations Charter, the Rules of Procedure of the General Assembly, or the Provisional Rules of Procedure of the Security Council, except in connexion with the election of members of the Court. In practice, 'absolute majority' has been interpreted as meaning a majority of all the qualified electors, whether or not they vote. The qualified electors in the General Assembly are the Members of the United Nations, together with Liechtenstein, San Marino, and Switzerland, which are parties to the Statute of the Court but not Members of the United Nations.[271] In the Security Council, six votes constitute an absolute majority, no distinction being made between permanent and non-permanent members. This is the only matter on which six votes in the Security Council are sufficient to make a decision; indeed, there is an inconsistency between Article 10 of the Statute of the Court ('an absolute majority of votes . . . in the Security Council') and Article 27 of the Charter ('an affirmative vote of seven members').

The electors in the General Assembly and the Security Council indicate the candidates for whom they wish to vote by placing crosses against their names on the ballot papers. Each elector may vote for not more than five candidates on the first ballot. A ballot paper on which more names are marked than there are vacancies is considered invalid. With an exception noted below in the event of a deadlock, only those candidates who have been nominated and whose names appear in the list prepared by the Secretary-General are eligible for election. The withdrawal of a candidate, either before balloting begins or between ballots, has been allowed.

If the number of candidates obtaining an absolute majority is less than the number of persons to be elected, unrestricted ballots are held. During the election in 1960, two candidates received an absolute majority of votes in the General Assembly in the first ballot, leaving three vacancies to be filled. The President stated that, in accordance with Rule 96, voting would be restricted to the six candidates who had received the largest number of votes after the two who had received an absolute majority. This had the effect of eliminating an Indian candidate, and the Indian representative in the Assembly said that the wrong procedure was being followed. In his view, Rule 96 did not apply; the Statute of the Court said nothing about restricted ballots. The President replied that Rule 96, providing for restricted ballots after an inconclusive vote, had been consistently followed in the past and in his opinion was still valid. The Indian representative asked that the question should be put to the vote, and the Assembly decided that Rule 96 did not apply. The three parties to the Statute of the Court but not Members of the United Nations abstained on the vote.[272]

If in the first ballot in either the General Assembly or the Security Council, less than five candidates receive an absolute majority of votes, a second ballot is held, and balloting continues until five candidates have obtained an absolute majority. When this occurs in either organ, and not until that time, the President of that organ notifies the President of the other organ of the names of the five candidates. Such notification is not communicated by the President to the members of the other organ until that organ has itself given five candidates the required majority of votes.

It is, of course, possible for more than the required number of candidates to receive an absolute majority of votes in the same ballot. The practice, in such an event, has been to continue voting until the required number of candidates, and no more, receive an absolute majority.[273] This practice can produce anomalies, and Lebanon protested during the eighteenth session that it was 'illogical, unjust and undemocratic' and had in 1963 'led to a surprising result'.[274]

The President of each organ makes no communication to the President of the other organ until the required number of candidates, and no more, has received an absolute majority. If, upon comparison of the names of the candidates receiving the required majority in each organ, it is found that less than five candidates have received absolute majorities, the organs proceed, again independently of one another, in a second meeting, and if necessary a third meeting, to elect candidates by further ballots for the remaining vacancies, the results being again compared after the required number of candidates has received an absolute majority in each organ.

TABLE 23

Members of the International Court of Justice, 1964

	Nationality	Year of expiration of term (*on 5 Feb.*)
B. Winiarski*	Poland	1967
A. H. Badawi*	United Arab Republic	1967
V. K. Wellington Koo	China	1967
J. Spiropoulos	Greece	1967
Sir Percy Spender	Australia	1967
Sir Gerald Fitzmaurice	United Kingdom	1973
V. M. Koretsky	USSR	1970
K. Tanaka	Japan	1970
J. L. Bustamente y Rivero	Peru	1970
Ph. C. Jessup	United States	1970
G. Morelli	Italy	1970
Sir Muhammad Zafrulla Khan†	Pakistan	1973
Luis Padilla Nervo	Mexico	1973
Isaac Forster	Senegal	1973
André Gros	France	1973

* Judges who have served continuously since the establishment of the Court.
† Also served 7 October 1954 to 5 February 1961.

This procedure continues until the two organs have given an absolute majority of votes to the same five candidates. If, after the third of these meetings, one or more seats remain unfilled, however, the Assembly and the Council may, at any time, at the request of either body, form a joint conference consisting of six members, three appointed by each body. This joint conference may, by an absolute majority, agree upon one candidate for each seat still vacant and submit his name for the approval of the Assembly and the Council. If unanimously agreed, the joint conference may submit the name of a candidate not included in the list of nominations, provided that the candidate fulfils the required conditions. If a joint conference is satisfied that it will not be successful in procuring an election, those members of the International Court who have already been elected proceed, within a period fixed by the Security Council, to fill the vacant seat by selection from among those candidates who obtained votes in the General Assembly or the Security Council. In the event of a tie vote, the eldest judge has a casting vote.

These procedures are unquestionably complicated and time-consuming. The nominating procedure is designed to achieve, to the greatest extent possible, the independence of judges. The election procedure is intended to ensure the election of judges representing the main forms of civilization and the principal legal systems of the world. It may be noted that the Statute of the Court forms an integral part of the Charter of the United Nations (Article 92) and can be amended only by the same procedure as is laid down for amendments to the Charter (Article 69 of the Statute).

The composition of the Court has been as follows:

Latin America	initially 4, now 2
Asia and Africa	initially 2, now 5
Eastern Europe	initially 3, now 2
Western Europe	usually 4
Older Commonwealth countries	1
United States	1

The Secretary-General

The Charter states that the Secretary-General 'shall be appointed by the General Assembly upon the recommendation of the Security Council' (Article 97). The Assembly decided during the first session that 'both nomination and appointment should be discussed at private meetings, and a vote . . . , if taken, shall be by secret ballot'.[275] The Assembly's Rules of Procedure accordingly provide that 'the General Assembly shall consider the [Security Council's] recommendation and vote upon it by secret ballot in private meeting'. (Rule 142.)

The Security Council's recommendation is embodied in a communiqué, and the President of the Council informs the President of the Assembly of the Council's decision. No verbatim record of the Council's discussion is issued. The practice of the Council has been to recommend only one candidate.

When the first Secretary-General was appointed, the Assembly accepted a suggestion of the President that it should ballot in public meeting rather than in private. Subsequent appointments have been made in public meetings. Members of the Assembly ballot by voting either in favour of or against the recommendation of the Council. Decisions are by simple majority of the Members present and voting, unless the Assembly determines otherwise;[276] in act, the decision has been unanimous on each occasion.

After the Assembly has appointed the Secretary-General, a formal ceremony of installation takes place. The Secretary-General takes the oath of office, and immediately assumes his title and functions.

TABLE 24

Appointment of the Secretary-General

	Security Council meeting number and date	General Assembly plenary meeting number and date
Appointment of Trygve Lie	4th 30 January 1946	20th 1 February 1946
Continuation in office of Trygvie Lie		298th 1 November 1950
Appointment of Dag Hammarskjold	617th 31 March 1953	423rd 7 April 1953
Reappointment of Dag Hammarskjold	792nd 26 September 1957	690th 26 September 1957
Appointment of U Thant as acting Secretary-General	972nd 3 November 1961	1046th 3 November 1961
Appointment of U Thant as Secretary-General	1026th 30 November 1962	1182nd 30 November 1962

Select Committees

A committee may consist of all members of the appointing body, or it may be a single individual. A committee is merely an agency to which something is committed.

The Rules of Procedure provide for:

(a) Main Committees, upon which all Members of the United Nations may be represented;

189

(b) Procedural Committees (the General Committee and the Credentials Committee);

(c) Committees concerned with finacial matters (the Advisory Committee on Administrative and Budgetary Questions, and the Committee on Contributions.

In addition, the Assembly may establish such committees or other subsidiary organs as it deems necessary for the performance of its functions (Article 22 of the Charter and Rules 98, 104, and 162).

During the first five sessions, the Assembly and the Main Committees established a considerable number of sub-committees for drafting or negotiating purposes (see Table 25). It is interesting to note that as the Assembly has increased in size, there has been much less recourse to sub-committees during sessions of the Assembly. The Assembly recommended in 1963 that Main Committees should consider the establishment of sub-committees or working groups of limited size but representative of their membership, for the purpose of facilitating the work.[277]

TABLE 25

Sub-committees and working groups, 1st to 5th regular sessions

Session	Ple-nary	Gen- Com.	First Com.	Ad hoc Pol. Com.	2nd Com.	3rd Com.	4th Com.	5th Com.	6th Com.	Total
1	—	5	7	—	2	4	3	4	5	31
								1 joint sub-com.		
2	—	—	2	—	—	2	2	—	4	10
3	1	1	6	1	2	5	—	2	1	20
					1 joint sub-com.					
4	1	—	3	1	—	—	3	1	3	12
5	—	—	—	2	2	3	1	1	1	10

A subsidiary organ meeting between sessions of the Assembly may consist of one or more persons elected or appointed in their individual capacities; the International Law Commissions is so composed. Or a subsidiary organ may be composed of States. It may be a committee of the whole Membership, such as the Committee on Arrangements for a Conference for the Purpose of Reviewing the Charter; more usually, however, subsidiary organs are composed of a limited number of Member States. In some cases their composition may be wholly or partly determined automatically. There have been a number of committees composed of the Member States whose representatives served on the General Committee at the most recent regular session of the Assembly, and half of the members of the now defunct Committee on Information from Non-Self-Governing Territories were the States transmitting information under Article 73 (e). In the case of the Eighteen-Nation Disarmament Committee, the United States and the Soviet Union jointly proposed that the Assembly endorse the agreement already reached on the composition of a new negotiating body, and this was done.

Generally speaking, however, Select Committees are elected or appointed by the General Assembly, sometimes on the nomination of the President. Subsidiary organs composed of States are usually called committees, but several are called commissions, and there is one council and one working group; these semantic variations seem to have no particular significance.*

The appropriate size of a Select Committee depends on its functions and purposes. Most Committees are too large to begin with, and they tend to increase in size as efforts are made to extend their representative character. The British House of Commons has a standing order that 'No select committee shall, without leave of the House, consist of more than fifteen members. . . .'[279] and Alexander Loveday has commented that 'international committees of more than fifteen members are certain to waste time. . . . When a committee exceeds fifteen in number, it tends to change its nature altogether. It ceases to be a working group and becomes a debating society.'†

The composition of a committee, like its size, depends on its purposes and functions. Occasionally the only factor to be taken into account in constituting a subsidiary organ is that it should be as representative as possible of the whole membership. In the case of organs of small size, this is difficult to achieve in practice. Even a fifteen-nation committee cannot include a representative of a group or region numbering seven or less unless some other group or region

---

* Sir Eyre Crowe once explained to Mr (later) Sir Harold Nicolson the difference between a commission and a committee in the following terms: 'My dear Nicolson, a Commission is a body which is despatched to a definite place, a body that sits at the centre is a Committee.' (278)

† There is no magic in the number fifteen, but it is a fact that fifteen people can just manage to sit round one table and engage in discussion; when there are sixteen people, it seems that two tables are required.

TABLE 26

Membership of some organs established by the General Assembly, 1 January 1964

	1. Ad hoc Committee to examine the question of Oman	2. Advisory Commission on the Relief and Works Agency for Palestine Refugees in Near East	3. Advisory Committee on the U.N. Emergency Force	4. Commission for the Unification and Rehabilitation of Korea	5. Committee for International Co-operation Year	6. Committee on a UN Capital Development Fund	7. Committee on the Peaceful Uses of Outer Space	8. Conciliation Committee for Palestine	9. Eighteen-Nation Committee on Disarmament	10. Executive Committee of the Programme of the High Commissioner for Refugees	11. Governing Council of the Special Fund	12. Peace Observation Commission	13. Scientific Advisory Committee	14. Scientific Committee on the Effects of Atomic Radiation	15. Special Committee on principles of international law concerning friendly relations and co-operation among States	16. Special Committee on the policies of apartheid of the Govt. of Republic of South Africa	17. Special Committee on technical assistance in the field of international law	18. Special Committee on the situation with regard to the implementation of the declaration on the granting of independence to colonial countries and peoples	19. Working Group on the examination of administrative and budgetary procedures
Afghanistan	1x														15x		17x		
Albania							7x												
Algeria										10x						16x			
Argentina					5x	6x	7x				11x			14x	15x				19x
Australia				4x			7x			10x				14x	15x			18x	
Austria							7x			10x									
Belgium		2x					7x			10x				14x			17x		
Bolivia																			
Brazil			3x			6x	7x		9x	10x	11x		13x	14x					
Bulgaria							7x		9x										19x
Burma						6x			9x									18x	
Burundi																			
Byelorussian SSR																			
Cambodia									9x									18x	

	1x	2x	3x	4x	5x	6x	7x	8x	9x	10x	11x	12x	13x	14x	15x	16x	17x	18x	19x
Cameroon																			19x
Canada			3x		5x	6x	7x			10x	11x		13x	14x	15x				19x
Central African Republic					5x														
Ceylon			3x		5x														
Chad				4x			7x												
Chile						6x				10x		12x						18x	19x
China										10x									
Colombia			3x																
Congo (Brazzaville)																			
Congo (Leopoldville)																16x			
Costa Rica	1x																		
Cuba																			
Cyprus					5x	6x	7x		9x			12x		14x	15x				
Czechoslovakia					5x										15x				
Dahomey																		18x	
Denmark						6x				10x	11x								
Dominican Republic																	17x		
Ecuador																			
El Salvador									9x									18x	
Ethiopia					5x														
Finland								8x	9x	10x	11x	12x	13x	14x	15x				19x
France		2x																	
Gabon											11x					15x	16x	17x	
Ghana						6x				10x									
Greece															15x				
Guatemala																16x			
Guinea																16x			
Haiti												12x							
Honduras																16x	17x		
Hungary							7x												

TABLE 26—continued

Committees (column numbers):

1. Ad hoc Committee to examine the question of Oman
2. Advisory Commission on Relief and Works Agency for Palestine Refugees in Near East
3. Advisory Committee on the U.N. Emergency Force
4. Commission for the Unification and Rehabilitation of Korea
5. Committee for International Co-operation Year
6. Committee on a UN Capital Development Fund
7. Committee on the Peaceful Uses of Outer Space
8. Conciliation Committee for Palestine
9. Eighteen-Nation Committee on Disarmament
10. Executive Committee of the Programme of the High Commissioner for Refugees
11. Governing Council of the Special Fund
12. Peace Observation Commission
13. Scientific Advisory Committee
14. Scientific Committee on the Effects of Atomic Radiation
15. Special Committee on principles of international law concerning friendly relations and co-operation among States
16. Special Committee on the policies of apartheid of the Govt. of Republic of South Africa
17. Special Committee on technical assistance in the field of international law
18. Special Committee on the situation with regard to the implementation of the declaration on the granting of independence to colonial countries and peoples
19. Working Group on the examination of administrative and budgetary procedures

	1	2	3	4	5	6	7	8	9	10	11	12	13	14	15	16	17	18	19
Iceland																			
India			×		×	×	×		×		×	×	×	×	×			×	×
Indonesia						×	×				×								
Iran										×								×	
Iraq						×												×	
Ireland					×												×		
Israel												×							
Italy									×	×	×	×			×			×	×
Ivory Coast						×	×			×								×	
Jamaica						×													
Japan						×	×				×			×	×				×
Jordan		×																	
Kenya																			
Kuwait																			
Laos																			

Country	1x	2x	3x	4x	5x	6x	7x	9x	10x	11x	12x	14x	15x	16x	18x	19x
Lebanon		2x							10x				15x			
Liberia					5x		7x									
Libya																
Luxembourg															18x	
Madagascar									10x				15x		18x	
Malaysia														16x	18x	
Mali																
Mauritania																
Mexico					5x		7x	9x		11x		14x	15x			19x
Mongolia							7x									19x
Morocco							7x									
Nepal	1x															
Netherlands				4x		6x			10x	11x			15x	16x		
New Zealand										11x	12x					
Nicaragua																
Niger																
Nigeria	1x					6x		9x	10x				15x	16x		
Norway			3x						10x	11x						
Pakistan			3x	4x		6x					12x					19x
Panama																
Paraguay						6x										
Peru																
Philippines				4x						11x				16x		
Poland							7x	9x					15x		18x	
Portugal																
Romania							7x	9x					15x			
Rwanda																
Saudi Arabia																
Senegal	1x									11x						
Sierra Leone							7x								18x	

TABLE 26—continued

	1. Ad hoc Committee to examine the question of Oman.	2. Advisory Commission on the Relief and Works Agency for Palestine Refugees in Near East	3. Advisory Committee on the U.N. Emergency Force	4. Commission for the Unification and Rehabilitation of Korea	5. Committee for International Co-operation Year	6. Committee on a UN Capital Development Fund	7. Committee on the Peaceful Uses of Outer Space	8. Conciliation Committee for Palestine	9. Eighteen-Nation Committee on Disarmament	10. Executive Committee of the Programme of the High Commissioner for Refugees	11. Governing Council of the Special Fund	12. Peace Observation Commission	13. Scientific Advisory Committee	14. Scientific Committee on the Effects of Atomic Radiation	15. Special Committee on principles of international law concerning friendly relations and co-operation among States	16. Special Committee on the policies of apartheid of the Govt. of Republic of South Africa	17. Special Committee on technical assistance in the field of international law	18. Special Committee on the situation with regard to the implementation of the declaration on the granting of independence to colonial countries and peoples	19. Working Group on the examination of administrative and budgetary procedures
Somalia																			
South Africa																16x			
Spain																			
Sudan		2x				6x													
Sweden							7x		9x	10x	11x	12x		14x	15x				19x
Syria																		18x	
Tanganyika										10x								18x	
Thailand				4x															
Togo								8x											
Trinidad and Tobago											11x								
Tunisia										10x								18x	
Turkey		2x		4x						10x									
Uganda																			
Ukrainian SSR																			

	2x	5x	6x	7x	8x	9x	10x	11x	12x	13x	14x	15x		18x	19x
Union of Soviet Socialist Republics														18x	19x
United Arab Republic	2x	5x	6x	7x		9x		11x	12x	13x	14x	15x		18x	19x
United Kingdom	2x		6x	7x		9x	10x	11x	12x	13x	14x	15x		18x	19x
United States of America	2x		6x	7x	8x	9x	10x	11x	12x	13x	14x	15x		18x	19x
Upper Volta															
Uruguay								11x	12x					18x	
Venezuela							10x					15x		18x	
Yemen															
Yugoslavia			6x				10x					15x		18x	
Zanzibar															

Notes. 1. The Executive Committee of the Programme of the High Commissioner for Refugees and the Governing Council of the Special Fund were established by the General Assembly, but their members are elected by the Economic and Social Council. In addition to the members noted above, the Federal Republic of Germany, the Holy See, and Switzerland are members of the Executive Committee of the Programme of the High Commissioner for Refugees; the Federal Republic of Germany is a member of the Governing Council of the Special Fund. The Executive Board of the United Nations Children's Fund (UNICEF) is elected by the Economic and Social Council.

2. Agreement on the composition of the Eighteen-Nation Committee on Disarmament was endorsed by General Assembly resolution 1722 (XVI) of 20 December 1961. France has declined to participate.

3. Two subsidiary organs of the General Assembly are composed of the Member States whose representatives served on the General Committee at the most recent regular session of the General Assembly; (i) the Committee on applications for review of administrative tribunal judgments; and (ii) the Committee on the question of defining aggression.

4. The Committee on Arrangements for a Conference for the purpose of Reviewing the Charter consists of all Members of the United Nations.

is prepared to accept less than the share to which it is entitled. Moreover, the choices within regions may give rise to dissension.

Usually, however, the problem is not simply to make the committee reasonably representative; account has also to be taken of other factors. In constituting the Scientific Advisory Committee, the Committee on the Peaceful Uses of Outer Space, and the Scientific Committee on Effects of Atomic Radiation, for example, account had to be taken of the degree of scientific and technological development in the countries to be appointed. Furthermore, some subsidiary organs are deliberately unrepresentative in order that they may have the best chance to discharge their functions with hope of success. The Palestine Conciliation Commission is an example of this kind. Some subsidiary organs of the Assembly, such as the Advisory Committee on UNEF and the Commission for the Unification and Rehabilitation of Korea, deliberately excluded the permanent members of the Security Council. Several organs, such as the Advisory Commission on the United Nations Relief and Works Agency for Palestine Refugees in the Near East, consist only of States directly concerned with the tasks entrusted to the committee.

There can be no uniform method of constituting organs with widely differing functions. The membership of each organ should be determined in the light of three main considerations: does the organ possess, or can it develop, the necessary expertise to discharge the functions entrusted to it; is it small enough so that there can emerge a reasonable degree of intimacy, cohesion, and consensus; and is its composition such that its reports and recommendations will command wide support by the full membership of the Assembly?

8

FINANCIAL PROCEDURE

The third benefit is that it saves money, both to the prince and people. . . .

WILLIAM PENN

CONTROL of the purse-strings has traditionally been an important political weapon. The Council of the League of Nations at first intended to exercise general financial control, but the Assembly soon asserted its primacy in financial matters. The United Nations Charter gives to the General Assembly a key role in financial matters. It expressly entrusts the Assembly with responsibility for considering and approving the budget, apportioning the expenses among the Members, considering and approving financial and budgetary arrangements with specialized agencies, and examining 'the administrative budgets' of such agencies 'with a view to making recommendations to the agencies concerned'.[281] An Advisory Committee on Administrative and Budgetary Questions (usually known simply as 'the Advisory Committee') is responsible for expert examination of the budget, and in other ways assists the General Assembly and the Fifth Committee.[282]

The Budget Estimates

The regular budget of the United Nations, covering one calendar year, provides for the day-to-day running expenses of the Organization, including the International Court of Justice, and for implementing the decisions of the various organs. The departmental estimates are reviewed by the Controller and approved by the Secretary-General. The budget estimates are to be submitted to the

Advisory Committee at least twelve weeks before the opening of each regular annual session of the Assembly; the practice during recent years has been for the estimates to be made available to the Committee in the latter part of May. The estimates, together with the Advisory Committee's report on them, are submitted to Member States at least five weeks before the opening of each regular session of the Assembly, that is to say, usually by the middle of August.[283]

If decisions affecting the estimates should be taken after they have been prepared but before they have been considered by the Assembly, revised estimates are prepared in the same way as the original estimates and are submitted to the Advisory Committee and, with the Advisory Committee's report on them, to Member States. If, after the budget has been adopted, there should arise unforeseen or extraordinary expenses for which funds are not available in the regular budget, supplementary estimates are issued. Supplementary estimates are reviewed by the Advisory Committee and then submitted to the General Assembly.[284]

The consistent practice has been that budget estimates are not considered by the Fifth Committee or the plenary Assembly until the Advisory Committee has first had the opportunity of examining them and making a report. The Advisory Committee thus plays a vitally important part in the budget process. It consists of twelve persons, each appointed by name by the General Assembly to serve in an individual capacity, and the Rules of Procedure provide that it shall include at least three financial experts of recognized standing. Members are selected on the basis of broad geographical representation, personal qualifications, and experience; no two members may be nationals of the same State.[285] The Secretary-General informs Member States when vacancies occur by death, resignation, or expiration of term, and invites the Fifth Committee to suggest the names of persons to fill the vacancies. The Fifth Committee conducts a secret ballot and submits for the approval of the Assembly a draft resolution containing the names of the persons recommended for appointment.

There has been some continuity in the membership of the Advisory Committee. Mr. Thanasiss Aghnides was Chairman from the Committee's inception until the end of 1963, and the Committee has always included nationals of France, the United Kingdom, the United States, and the Soviet Union.

The Committee is composed of individuals, but they are almost always also officials of their own governments. The meetings of the Advisory Committee are closed, but one assumes that some members of the Committee, being familiar with the policies of their governments, take care to act in accordance with those policies. Secretary-General Lie came to the conclusion that it was inappropriate that members of the Advisory Committee should serve also as national representatives in the Fifth Committee, and he suggested in 1952 that membership of the Advisory Committee should disqualify a person from service in the Fifth Committee. The Fifth Committee took no immediate action on this matter, and Secretary-General Hammarskjold later stated that he did not wish to maintain the suggestion of his predecessor; the matter accordingly lapsed.[286]

The Advisory Committee usually holds two main sessions during the year. The session in the summer is devoted mainly to an examination of the budget estimates for the ensuing year. During the second session, normally beginning during the week preceding the opening of the regular session of the Assembly and continuing through the session, the Committee considers revised and supplementary estimates, and also reviews the budgets of the specialized agencies. Occasionally the Advisory Committee has met during the spring in Geneva to deal with special matters mainly pertaining to the European Office of the United Nations.

The gross amount of the annual appropriation for the regular budget increased fairly steeply in the early years of the United Nations, and then levelled off at between $40 million and $50 million for the period 1949–56. Since 1957, the regular budget has again been rising.

Part of the increase has been due simply to rising costs, but there has also been a considerable expansion of economic and social programs, especially for regional activities. Forty per cent of the regular budget is now required for economic and social programs and about forty per cent for administrative and conference services. The expenditure by main fields of activity in 1962 is shown in Table 28.

The Assembly has laid it down that no council or other competent body shall take a decision involving expenditure unless it has before it a report from the Secretary-General on the administrative and financial implications of the proposal;[288] all the main organs

TABLE 27

Gross Budget Appropriation, 1946–1964

	$ (million)
1946	19·4
1947	27·7
1948	34·8
1949	43·5
1950	41·6
1951	47·8
1952	48·1
1953	48·3
1954	47·8
1955	47·0
1956	48·6
1957	50·8
1958	55·1
1959	60·8
1960	63·1
1961	73·0
1962	82·1
1963	93·9
1964	101·3

TABLE 28

Expenditure by main fields of activity, 1962 [287]

	$ (million)
General Assembly	7·3
Security Council	1·8
Trusteeship and non-self-governing territories	1·3
Field missions	3·9
Economic and social activities, including refugees	33·5
Legal, including International Court of Justice	2·4
Public information	6·2
Administration and services	19·7
Miscellaneous (buildings, special conferences, etc.)	6·1

except the Security Council have incorporated this requirement in their rules of procedure. As far as the Assembly itself is concerned, the relevant Rule reads as follows:

No resolution involving expenditure shall be recommended by a committee for approval by the General Assembly unless it is accompanied by an estimate of expenditures prepared by the Secretary-General. No resolution in respect of which expenditures are anticipated by the Secretary-General shall be voted by the General Assembly until the Administrative and Budgetary [Fifth] Committee has had an opportunity of stating the effect of the proposal upon the budget estimates of the United Nations.[289]

It is necessary that, in addition to the ordinary budget appropriations, there should be some procedure for dealing with emergency expenses. This could in theory be done either by calling the Assembly into special session whenever required or by delegating the Assembly's financial authority. A special problem concerns actions relating to peace and security authorized by the Security Council when the General Assembly is not in session.

Each year the Assembly authorizes the Secretary-General, under certain conditions, to incur unforeseen or extraordinary expenses over and above the credits voted in the regular budget.[290] *Unforeseen* expenses are expenses arising from programs provided for in the budget but in excess of the amount appropriated; *extraordinary* expenses are those arising from decisions of a competent organ for new activities not contemplated when the budget was approved.

Until 1960, the Assembly's resolution contained no upper limit for unforeseen and extraordinary expenses. When the Security Council initiated the operation in the Congo, the Secretary-General obtained the concurrence of the Advisory Committee to incur expenses up to a limit of $40 million, pending financial action by the General Assembly. This incident highlighted the extent of the discretionary powers granted to the Secretary-General and the Advisory Committee. In the light of a review of the problem by the Advisory Committee,[291] the Assembly decided in 1961 that the Secretary-General would continue to have authority to incur peace-keeping expenses up to $2 million annually. Beyond that figure, and up to $10 million, the concurrence of the Advisory Committee should be obtained. Expenditure exceeding $10 million should not be incurred without the convening of a special session of the Assembly.

The annual resolution on unforeseen and extraordinary expenses now authorizes the Secretary-General to enter into commitments in the following financial year for:

(a) certain commitments specified in the resolution, such as expenses of the International Court of Justice or special conferences;

(b) such commitments, not exceeding a total of $2 million, as the Secretary-General certifies relate to the maintenance of peace and security;

(c) other expenses for which the concurrence of the Advisory Committee is obtained;

provided that if, as a result of a decision of the Security Council, commitments relating to the maintenance of peace and security should exceed $10 million, a special session of the General Assembly shall be convened.

TABLE 29

Unforeseen and extraordinary expenses, 1947–1963[292]

	Certified by Secretary-General	Prior concurrence of Advisory Committee*	Total
	$	$	$
1947	—	—	2,817,346
1948	—	—	4,634,944†
1949	105,000	250,870	355,870
1950	300,000	457,300	757,300
1951	182,500	14,000	196,500
1952	410,000	196,540	606,540
1953	46,000	70,790	116,790
1954	153,000	58,250	211,250
1955	175,500	194,580	370,800
1956	555,000	383,250	938,250
1957	599,600	152,700	712,300
1958	599,800	3,967,900‡	4,567,700
1959	423,800	191,700	615,500
1960	622,000	515,350§	1,137,350
1961	276,800	219,040	495,840
1962	1,018,200	1,132,000	2,150,200
1963	—	343,900	343,900

* Includes amounts authorized in respect of the International Court of Justice or other specific provisions of the resolution.

† Advisory Committee concurrence to $4 million on Palestine missions.

‡ Includes $3.6 million for Observation Group in Lebanon.

§ In addition, the concurrence of the Advisory Committee was obtained in commitments of up to $40 million for operations in the Congo; subsequently the Assembly decided to finance these operations through an *ad hoc* account.

A problem of any system of financial control is that a committee whose duty it is to review estimates of expenditure usually feels that it has to justify its existence by proposing some reductions.

The officials who prepare the estimates, knowing that some cuts are likely, may be tempted to inflate the figures. This has not, hitherto, been a particularly serious problem for the United Nations.

A second problem is to keep financial control separate from policy decision. A budget review committee should examine the estimates and may recommend economies that might be effected, but only in a way that is consistent with the decisions of policy on which the estimates are based. This problem can never disappear entirely, since honest people may disagree on the exact location of the line which separates policy from administration.

A further difficulty, which is peculiar to international organizations, arises when different members of the same delegation advocate inconsistent policies in various organs. This may arise because of a lack of co-ordination within delegations, or because representatives have not received sufficiently precise instructions. It is interesting, for example, to note the impassioned appeals for economy by certain representatives in the Fifth Committee during October 1959,[293] and to compare it with the indignation of the representatives of the same Member States in the Fourth Committee during the same month when the Under-Secretary for Conference Services appealed to delegations to bear in mind budgetary restrictions before incurring abnormal expenditures.[294]

The Advisory Committee usually recommends to the Assembly that some of the estimates be reduced. The Secretary-General may, in the light of such recommendations, agree that some of the reductions are reasonable, though he may point out that the reductions recommended by the Advisory Committee are based on certain assumptions, and if the assumptions turn out to be incorrect, supplementary estimates may be required. Occasionally, the Secretary-General may insist on maintaining some of the original estimates, in spite of a recommendation of the Advisory Committee that they be reduced. In that event the Assembly, acting on a recommendation of its Fifth Committee, would be the arbiter.

The Assembly considers the budget estimates in the following stages:

1. The Secretary-General introduces the budget estimates with an oral statement in the Fifth Committee.

2. The Chairman of the Advisory Committee introduces the Committee's report on the budget estimates with an oral statement in the Fifth Committee.

3. The Fifth Committee considers the budget estimates in the light of the report and recommendations of the Advisory Committee. It begins with a general discussion.

4. The Fifth Committee next makes a detailed examination (the 'first reading') of the budget estimates.*

5. The Fifth Committee reviews the budget estimates in a 'second reading', in the light of the provisional decisions taken during the 'first reading'.

6. The recommendations of the Fifth Committee are embodied in a draft report of the Rapporteur which, after approval by the Fifth Committee, is submitted to the plenary Assembly.

7. Finally, the Rapporteur's report is considered by the Assembly in plenary meeting and a resolution is adopted, a two-thirds majority being required for decisions on budgetary questions.[295]

Debate on the budget estimates enables delegations to express their views on a wide range of financial and administrative questions. At the same time, it is of little value, except for purposes of propaganda, to make speeches in the Fifth Committee to the effect that some activity of the United Nations is undesirable and that therefore there should be no financial provision for it in the budget. There is little point in making generalized complaints of extravagance or suggestions for an across-the-board reduction of a fixed percentage. There is little to be gained by proposing a budget ceiling. Opposition to the policy on which the estimates are based should be voiced in the organs which decide the policy; the task of the Fifth Committee is to review the financial and administrative implementation of policy.

Contributions

The General Assembly is concerned not only with voting the necessary budget appropriations; it is also responsible for raising the money or, to be more precise, for apportioning the expenses among Member States.[296] The Assembly decided during the first session

---

* The expressions 'first reading', 'second reading', etc., originated in the British Parliament. Before the invention of mechanical printing, every proposal to change the statute law was read in full by the Clerk each time it was debated.

that the apportionment of expenses should be 'broadly according to capacity to pay', and a standing expert Committee on Contributions was set up to advise on the matter.[297] The Committee on Contributions consists of ten members, selected on the basis of broad geographical representation, personal qualifications, and experience. No two members may be nationals of the same State. Members of the Committee are appointed by the same procedure as is used to appoint members of the Advisory Committee.[298]

Members of the Committee on Contributions are appointed in their personal capacities by the General Assembly. The question was raised in the Fifth Committee during the sixth session (1951) whether it would be permissible under the Rules of Procedure and resolutions of the Assembly for a member of the Committee to appoint a substitute to take his place in case of absence, without authorization from the General Assembly. The Chairman of the Committee on Contributions explained that the Committee had accepted substitute members since its inception; this was always reported to the Assembly, she said, and no criticism of the procedure had been voiced in the Assembly.[299] The practice has continued, but the Committee has accepted the designation of substitutes 'on the basis that the substitute would remain in consultation with the member he was representing'.[300] Nationals of France, the United Kingdom, the United States, and the Soviet Union have served on the Committee since its inception.

The Preparatory Commission of the United Nations had taken the view that in apportioning the expenses two opposite tendencies should be guarded against. 'Some members may desire unduly to minimise their contributions, whereas others may desire to increase them unduly for reasons of prestige.'[301] It need hardly be said that, in the event, it has been more necessary to guard against the former tendency than the latter.

In apportioning the expenses, the Committee on Contributions uses national incomes estimates as a guide and takes account of the following main factors:[302]

(a) Comparative income per head of population;

(b) The assessment for countries with low *per capita* income may be reduced by amounts which, for countries with the very lowest incomes per inhabitant, approach a maximum of 50 per cent;

(c) The minimum assessment should be 00·4 per cent;

(d) In principle, the maximum contribution of any one Member State should not exceed 30 per cent of the total;*

(e) In normal times the *per capita* contribution of any Member State should not exceed the *per capita* contribution of the Member with the highest assessment (that is to say, the United States);†

(f) The ability of Member States to secure foreign currency.

The Preparatory Commission suggested that in determining the scale of assessments, account should be taken of temporary dislocation of national economies arising out of the second world war, but the Committee on Contributions has concluded that the consequences of war dislocations are now largely reflected in the national income figures.[304]

The Committee on Contributions works to the greatest extent possible on the basis of objective data, but has been given discretion to consider all facts relevant to 'capacity to pay' in arriving at its recommendations, and in 1963 it was asked to give due attention to the developing countries in view of their special economic and financial problems.[305] Some difficulties necessarily arise because the statistical information available to the Committee is of varying degrees of reliability, and it is by no means a straightforward matter converting estimates of national income into a common currency. In addition, the Committee has to deal with some questions which are partially subjective, such as 'ability . . . to secure foreign currency'. A certain amount of judgment must clearly be exercised.

Contributions are payable in United States dollars, but the Secretary-General may, at his discretion, and after consultation with the Chairman of the Committee on Contributions, accept a portion

---

* The United States assessment has been progressively reduced from 39·89 per cent in 1946–8 to 32·02 in 1962–4, and it is intended that it shall eventually drop to 30 per cent. But for this ceiling, the US assessment would now be about 38·5 per cent.

The US Congress has always wished to limit the US share of the budgets of international organizations to one-third. See Public Law 495, 82d Cong., 2d Session, pp. 2–3: 'No representative of the United States Government in any international organization after fiscal year 1953 shall make any commitment requiring the appropriation of funds by the United States in excess of 33⅓ per centum of the budget. . . .' This provision was dropped in 1954 because of assurances that future United States assessments for the United Nations would not exceed 33⅓ per cent.

† The Committee on Contributions reported in 1961 that only Canada was at that time affected by the *per capita* ceiling principle.[303]

in other currencies. Efforts have been made to broaden the range and amounts of acceptable currencies, on the understanding that the United Nations will be safeguarded against exchange losses and will not be forced to accept inconvertible currencies for which the Organization can find no use.[306]

Certain Member States, by virtue of their former membership of the League of Nations, receive credits as a share of those assets of the League which were transferred to the United Nations. These credits are to be liquidated over a period which will end in 1965.[307]

The Committee on Contributions submits a report to each regular session of the Assembly, and this forms the basis for the Assembly's apportionment of expenses. After the adoption of the budget, the Secretary-General informs Member States of their commitments in respect of annual contributions and advances to the Working Capital Fund, and requests them to remit the sums due.[308] At the beginning of each financial year and at intervals throughout the year, Member States are informed of the amounts of any arrears. The Secretary-General issues a monthly statement showing the amounts assessed, payments received, and balances due.[309]

The Committee on Contributions is responsible for advising the Assembly on the action to be taken with regard to the application of the Charter provisions relating to arrears.[310] The Charter states that a Member which is in arrears shall have no vote in the General Assembly 'if the amount of its arrears equals or exceeds the amount of the contributions due from it for the preceding two full years'. The General Assembly may, nevertheless, permit such a Member State to vote if it is satisfied that failure to pay is due to 'conditions beyond the control of the Member'. The Financial Regulations, as interpreted by the Secretary-General, provide that amounts due during any particular year are not regarded as arrears; as of 1 January each year, unpaid balances from the previous year are considered to be one year in arrears.[311]

The Committee on Contributions has reported annually that no action was required regarding arrears, except in 1958 when the Committee stated that Bolivia had not paid part of the contribution for 1955 as well as the total contribution for 1956, 1957, and 1958; before the opening of the session of the General Assembly in 1958, arrangements had been made for payment of the arrears.[312] In September 1960, the Secretary-General reported that one Member State was in arrears to the extent that Article 19 of the Charter

TABLE 30

Scale of Assessments, 1946–1964
(Percentage of Regular Budget)

	1946	1947	1948	1949	1950	1951	1952
Afghanistan	—	0·05	0·05	0·05	0·05	0·06	0·08
Albania	—	—	—	—	—	—	—
Algeria	—	—	—	—	—	—	—
Argentina	1·94	1·85	1·85	1·85	1·85	1·85	1·62
Australia	2·00	1·97	1·97	1·97	1·97	1·92	1·77
Austria	—	—	—	—	—	—	—
Belgium	1·42	1·35	1·35	1·35	1·35	1·35	1·35
Bolivia	0·08	0·08	0·08	0·08	0·08	0·08	0·06
Brazil	1·94	1·85	1·85	1·85	1·85	1·85	1·62
Bulgaria	—	—	—	—	—	—	—
Burma	—	—	—	0·15	0·15	0·15	0·15
Burundi	—	—	—	—	—	—	—
Byelorussian SSR	0·23	0·22	0·22	0·22	0·22	0·24	0·34
Cambodia	—	—	—	—	—	—	—
Cameroun	—	—	—	—	—	—	—
Canada	3·35	3·20	3·20	3·20	3·20	3·30	3·35
Central African Republic	—	—	—	—	—	—	—
Ceylon	—	—	—	—	—	—	—
Chad	—	—	—	—	—	—	—
Chile	0·47	0·45	0·45	0·45	0·45	0·41	0·35
China	6·30	6·00	6·00	6·00	6·00	6·00	5·75
Colombia	0·39	0·37	0·37	0·37	0·37	0·37	0·37
Congo (Brazzaville)	—	—	—	—	—	—	—
Congo (Leopoldville)	—	—	—	—	—	—	—
Costa Rica	0·04	0·04	0·04	0·04	0·04	0·04	0·04
Cuba	0·30	0·29	0·29	0·29	0·29	0·31	0·33
Cyprus	—	—	—	—	—	—	—
Czechoslovakia	0·95	0·90	0·90	0·90	0·90	0·99	1·05
Dahomey	—	—	—	—	—	—	—
Denmark	0·81	0·79	0·79	0·79	0·79	0·79	0·79
Dominican Republic	0·05	0·05	0·05	0·05	0·05	0·05	0·05
Ecuador	0·05	0·05	0·05	0·05	0·05	0·05	0·05
El Salvador	0·05	0·05	0·05	0·05	0·05	0·05	0·05
Ethiopia	0·08	0·08	0·08	0·08	0·08	0·08	0·10
Finland	—	—	—	—	—	—	—
France	6·30	6·00	6·00	6·00	6·00	6·00	5·75
Gabon	—	—	—	—	—	—	—
Ghana	—	—	—	—	—	—	—
Greece	0·17	0·17	0·17	0·17	0·17	0·18	0·18
Guatemala	0·05	0·05	0·05	0·05	0·05	0·06	0·06
Guinea	—	—	—	—	—	—	—
Haiti	0·04	0·04	0·04	0·04	0·04	0·04	0·04
Honduras	0·04	0·04	0·04	0·04	0·04	0·04	0·04
Hungary	—	—	—	—	—	—	—
Iceland	0·04	0·04	0·04	0·04	0·04	0·04	0·04
India	4·09	3·95	3·95*a*	3·25	3·25	3·41	3·53

a Including Pakistan

TABLE 30—*continued*

1953	1954	1955	1956	1957	1958	1959	1960	1961	1962	1963	1964
0·08	0·08	0·08	0·06	0·06	0·06	0·06	0·06	0·06	0·05	0·05	0·05
—	—	—	0·04	0·04	0·04	0·04	0·04	0·04	0·04	0·04	0·04
—	—	—	—	—	—	—	—	—	—	—	0·10
1·45	1·40	1·32	1·17	1·17	1·14	1·11	1·11	1·11	1·01	1·01	1·01
1·75	1·75	1·80	1·65	1·65	1·61	1·79	1·79	1·79	1·66	1·66	1·66
—	—	—	0·36	0·36	0·35	0·43	0·43	0·43	0·45	0·45	0·45
1·37	1·38	1·38	1·27	1·27	1·24	1·30	1·30	1·30	1·20	1·20	1·20
0·06	0·06	0·05	0·05	0·05	0·05	0·04	0·04	0·04	0·04	0·04	0·04
1·45	1·40	1·32	1·09	1·09	1·06	1·02	1·02	1·02	1·03	1·03	1·03
—	—	—	0·14	0·14	0·14	0·16	0·16	0·16	0·20	0·20	0·20
0·13	0·13	0·13	0·10	0·10	0·10	0·08	0·08	0·08	0·07	0·07	0·07
—	—	—	—	—	—	—	—	—	—	—	0·04
0·43	0·50	0·53	0·48	0·48	0·47	0·47	0·47	0·47	0·52	0·52	0·52
—	—	—	0·04	0·04	0·04	0·04	0·04	0·04	0·04	0·04	0·04
—	—	—	—	—	—	—	—	0·04	0·04	0·04	0·04
3·30	3·30	3·63	3·15	3·15	3·09	3·11	3·11	3·11	3·12	3·12	3·12
—	—	—	—	—	—	—	—	0·04	0·04	0·04	0·04
—	—	—	0·11	0·11	0·11	0·10	0·10	0·10	0·09	0·09	0·09
—	—	—	—	—	—	—	—	0·04	0·04	0·04	0·04
0·33	0·33	0·30	0·30	0·30	0·29	0·27	0·27	0·27	0·26	0·26	0·26
5·62	5·62	5·62	5·14	5·14	5·01	5·01	5·01	5·01	4·57	4·57	4·57
0·35	0·41	0·41	0·37	0·37	0·36	0·31	0·31	0·31	0·26	0·26	0·26
—	—	—	—	—	—	—	—	0·04	0·04	0·04	0·04
—	—	—	—	—	—	—	—	0·04	0·07	0·07	0·07
0·04	0·04	0·04	0·04	0·04	0·04	0·04	0·04	0·04	0·04	0·04	0·04
0·34	0·34	0·30	0·27	0·27	0·26	0·25	0·25	0·25	0·22	0·22	0·22
—	—	—	—	—	—	—	—	0·04	0·04	0·04	0·04
1·05	1·05	0·94	0·84	0·84	0·82	0·87	0·87	0·87	1·04	1·04	1·04
—	—	—	—	—	—	—	—	0·04	0·04	0·04	0·04
0·78	0·78	0·74	0·66	0·66	0·64	0·60	0·60	0·60	0·58	0·58	0·58
0·05	0·05	0·05	0·05	0·05	0·05	0·05	0·05	0·05	0·05	0·05	0·05
0·04	0·04	0·04	0·05	0·05	0·05	0·06	0·06	0·06	0·06	0·06	0·06
0·05	0·06	0·06	0·06	0·06	0·06	0·05	0·05	0·05	0·04	0·04	0·04
0·10	0·10	0·12	0·11	0·11	0·11	0·06	0·06	0·06	0·05	0·05	0·05
—	—	—	0·37	0·37	0·36	0·36	0·36	0·36	0·37	0·37	0·37
5·75	5·75	5·90	5·70	5·70	5·56	6·40	6·40	6·40	5·94	5·94	5·94
—	—	—	—	—	—	—	—	0·04	0·04	0·04	0·04
—	—	—	—	0·07	0·07	0·07	0·07	0·07	0·09	0·09	0·09
0·19	0·21	0·21	0·20	0·20	0·19	0·23	0·23	0·23	0·23	0·23	0·23
0·06	0·07	0·07	0·07	0·07	0·07	0·05	0·05	0·05	0·05	0·05	0·05
—	—	—	—	—	—	0·04	0·04	0·04	0·04	0·04	0·04
0·04	0·04	0·04	0·04	0·04	0·04	0·04	0·04	0·04	0·04	0·04	0·04
0·04	0·04	0·40	0·04	0·04	0·04	0·04	0·04	0·04	0·04	0·04	0·04
—	—	—	0·46	0·46	0·39	0·42	0·42	0·42	0·51	0·51	0·51
0·04	0·04	0·04	0·04	0·04	0·04	0·04	0·04	0·04	0·04	0·04	0·04
3·45	3·40	3·30	2·97	2·97	2·90	2·46	2·46	2·46	2·03	2·03	2·03

TABLE 30—*continued*

	1946	1947	1948	1949	1950	1951	1952
Indonesia	—	—	—	—	—	0·60	0·60
Iran	0·47	0·45	0·45	0·45	0·45	0·45	0·40
Iraq	0·17	0·17	0·17	0·17	0·17	0·17	0·14
Ireland	—	—	—	—	—	—	—
Israel	—	—	—	—	0·12	0·12	0·17
Italy	—	—	—	—	—	—	—
Ivory Coast	—	—	—	—	—	—	—
Jamaica	—	—	—	—	—	—	—
Japan	—	—	—	—	—	—	—
Jordan	—	—	—	—	—	—	—
Kenya	—	—	—	—	—	—	—
Kuwait	—	—	—	—	—	—	—
Laos	—	—	—	—	—	—	—
Lebanon	0·06	0·06	0·06	0·06	0·06	0·06	0·06
Liberia	0·04	0·04	0·04	0·04	0·04	0·04	0·04
Libya	—	—	—	—	—	—	—
Luxembourg	0·05	0·05	0·05	0·05	0·05	0·05	0·05
Madagascar	—	—	—	—	—	—	—
Malaysia	—	—	—	—	—	—	—
Mali	—	—	—	—	—	—	—
Mauritania	—	—	—	—	—	—	—
Mexico	0·66	0·63	0·63	0·63	0·63	0·63	0·65
Mongolia	—	—	—	—	—	—	—
Morocco	—	—	—	—	—	—	—
Nepal	—	—	—	—	—	—	—
Netherlands	1·47	1·40	1·40	1·40	1·40	1·35	1·27
New Zealand	0·52	0·50	0·50	0·50	0·50	0·50	0·50
Nicaragua	0·04	0·04	0·04	0·04	0·04	0·04	0·04
Niger	—	—	—	—	—	—	—
Nigeria	—	—	—	—	—	—	—
Norway	0·52	0·50	0·50	0·50	0·50	0·50	0·50
Pakistan	—	—	—	0·70	0·70	0·74	0·79
Panama	0·05	0·05	0·05	0·05	0·05	0·05	0·05
Paraguay	0·04	0·04	0·04	0·04	0·04	0·04	0·04
Peru	0·21	0·20	0·20	0·20	0·20	0·20	0·20
Philippines	0·30	0·29	0·29	0·29	0·29	0·29	0·29
Poland	1·00	0·95	0·95	0·95	0·95	1·05	1·36
Portugal	—	—	—	—	—	—	—
Romania	—	—	—	—	—	—	—
Rwanda	—	—	—	—	—	—	—
Saudi Arabia	0·08	0·08	0·08	0·08	0·08	0·08	0·08
Senegal	—	—	—	—	—	—	—
Sierra Leone	—	—	—	—	—	—	—
Somalia	—	—	—	—	—	—	—
South Africa	1·15	1·12	1·12	1·12	1·12	1·04	0·90
Spain	—	—	—	—	—	—	—
Sudan	—	—	—	—	—	—	—
Sweden	—	2·35	2·04	2·00	1·98	1·85	1·73
Syria	0·12	0·12	0·12	0·12	0·12	0·11	0·09
Tanganyika	—	—	—	—	—	—	—

TABLE 30—*continued*

1953	1954	1955	1956	1957	1958	1959	1960	1961	1962	1963	1964
0·60	0·60	0·56	0·51	0·51	0·50	0·47	0·47	0·47	·045	0·45	0·45
0·33	0·28	0·25	0·27	0·27	0·26	0·21	0·21	0·21	0·20	0·20	0·20
0·12	0·12	0·11	0·12	0·12	0·12	0·09	0·09	0·09	0·09	0·09	0·09
—	—	—	0·19	0·19	0·18	0·16	0·16	0·16	0·14	0·14	0·14
0·17	0·17	0·17	0·16	0·16	0·16	0·14	0·14	0·14	0·15	0·15	0·15
—	—	—	2·08	2·08	2·03	2·25	2·25	2·25	2·24	2·24	2·24
—	—	—	—	—	—	—	—	0·06	0·04	0·04	0·04
—	—	—	—	—	—	—	—	—	—	—	0·05
—	—	—	—	1·97	1·92	2·19	2·19	2·19	2·27	2·27	2·27
—	—	—	0·04	0·04	0·04	0·04	0·04	0·04	0·04	0·04	0·04
—	—	—	—	—	—	—	—	—	—	—	n.a.
—	—	—	—	—	—	—	—	—	—	—	—
—	—	—	0·04	0·04	0·04	0·04	0·04	0·04	0·04	0·04	0·04
0·05	0·05	0·05	0·05	0·05	0·05	0·05	0·05	0·05	0·05	0·05	0·05
0·04	0·04	0·04	0·04	0·04	0·04	0·04	0·04	0·04	0·04	0·04	0·04
—	—	—	0·04	0·04	0·04	0·04	0·04	0·04	0·04	0·04	0·04
0·05	0·06	0·06	0·06	0·06	0·06	0·06	0·06	0·06	0·05	0·05	0·05
—	—	—	—	—	—	—	—	0·06	0·04	0·04	0·04
—	—	—	—	0·22	0·17	0·17	0·17	0·17	0·13	0·13	0·13
—	—	—	—	—	—	—	—	0·04	0·04	0·04	0·04
—	—	—	—	—	—	—	—	—	—	0·04	0·04
0·70	0·75	0·80	0·70	0·70	0·68	0·71	0·71	0·71	0·74	0·74	0·74
—	—	—	—	—	—	—	—	—	—	0·04	0·04
—	—	—	—	0·12	0·12	0·14	0·14	0·14	0·14	0·14	0·14
—	—	—	0·04	0·04	0·04	0·04	0·04	0·04	0·04	0·04	0·04
1·25	1·25	1·25	1·15	1·15	1·12	1·01	1·01	1·01	1·01	1·01	1·01
0·48	0·48	0·48	0·43	0·43	0·42	0·42	0·42	0·42	0·41	0·41	0·41
0·04	0·04	0·04	0·04	0·04	0·04	0·04	0·04	0·04	0·04	0·04	0·04
—	—	—	—	—	—	—	—	0·04	0·04	0·04	0·04
—	—	—	—	—	—	—	—	0·21	0·21	0·21	0·21
0·50	0·50	0·50	0·49	0·49	0·48	0·49	0·49	0·49	0·45	0·45	0·45
0·79	0·75	0·67	0·55	0·55	0·54	0·40	0·40	0·40	0·42	0·42	0·42
0·05	0·05	0·05	0·05	0·05	0·05	0·04	0·04	0·04	0·04	0·04	0·04
0·04	0·04	0·04	0·04	0·04	0·04	0·04	0·04	0·04	0·04	0·04	0·04
0·18	0·18	0·18	0·15	0·15	0·15	0·11	0·11	0·11	0·10	0·10	0·10
0·39	0·45	0·45	0·41	0·41	0·40	0·43	0·43	0·43	0·40	0·40	0·40
1·58	1·73	1·73	1·56	1·56	1·52	1·37	1·37	1·37	1·28	1·28	1·28
—	—	—	0·25	0·25	0·24	0·20	0·20	0·20	0·16	0·16	0·16
—	—	—	0·50	0·50	0·49	0·34	0·34	0·34	0·32	0·32	0·32
—	—	—	—	—	—	—	—	—	—	—	0·04
0·07	0·07	0·07	0·07	0·07	0·07	0·06	0·06	0·06	0·07	0·07	0·07
—	—	—	—	—	—	—	—	0·06	0·05	0·05	0·05
—	—	—	—	—	—	—	—	—	—	0·04	0·04
—	—	—	—	—	—	—	—	0·04	0·04	0·04	0·04
0·83	0·78	0·78	0·71	0·71	0·67	0·56	0·56	0·56	0·53	0·53	0·53
—	—	—	1·14	1·14	1·11	0·93	0·93	0·93	0·86	0·86	0·86
—	—	—	—	0·11	0·11	0·06	0·06	0·06	0·07	0·07	0·07
1·65	1·65	1·59	1·46	1·46	1·43	1·39	1·39	1·39	1·30	1·30	1·30
0·08	0·08	0·08	0·08	0·08	0·08	—	—	—	0·05	0·05	0·05
—	—	—	—	—	—	—	—	—	—	0·04	0·04

TABLE 30—*continued*

	1946	1947	1948	1949	1950	1951	1952
Thailand (Siam)	—	—	0·27	0·27	0·27	0·24	0·21
Togo	—	—	—	—	—	—	—
Trinidad and Tobago	—	—	—	—	—	—	—
Tunisia	—	—	—	—	—	—	—
Turkey	0·93	0·91	0·91	0·91	0·91	0·91	0·75
Uganda	—	—	—	—	—	—	—
Ukrainian SSR	0·88	0·84	0·84	0·84	0·84	0·92	1·30
Union of Soviet Socialist Republics	6·62	6·34	6·34	6·34	6·34	6·98	9·85
United Arab Republic (Egypt)	0·81	0·79	0·79	0·79	0·79	0·71	0·60
United Kingdom	11·98	11·48	11·48	11·37	11·37	11·37	10·56
United States of America	39·89	39·89	39·89	39·89	39·79	38·92	36·90
Upper Volta	—	—	—	—	—	—	—
Uruguay	0·18	0·18	0·18	0·18	0·18	0·18	0·18
Venezuela	0·28	0·27	0·27	0·27	0·27	0·30	0·32
Yemen	—	—	0·04	0·04	0·04	0·04	0·04
Yugoslavia	0·34	0·33	0·33	0·33	0·33	0·36	0·43
Zanzibar	—	—	—	—	—	—	—

'might be deemed to apply' but that assurances had been given that a payment was in transit which would reduce its arrears below the stipulated limit.[313]

In May 1963, the Secretary-General informed the President of the Assembly that Haiti was more than two years in arrears. The President replied that he would have drawn the attention of the Assembly to the loss of voting rights had a formal count of vote taken place in the presence o af representative of Haiti. He had, however, been informed that Haiti would very shortly make a payment. Commenting on this exchange of communications, the Soviet Government maintained that 'automatic deprivation of a Member State's right to vote in the General Assembly' would be 'arbitrary and unlawful, contrary to the Charter, . . .'[314]

Working Capital Fund and the Bond Issue

In order that United Nations activities should not be halted because of the late receipt of contributions and also to provide a reserve for unforeseen and extraordinary expenses, a Working Capital Fund has been established. The Fund is composed of advances from Member States, in accordance with the ordinary Scale of Assessments.[315]

For reasons outside the control of the United Nations, only about one-quarter of the payments to the regular budget are received

TABLE 30—*continued*

1953	1954	1955	1956	1957	1958	1959	1960	1961	1962	1963	1964
0·18	0·18	0·18	0·16	0·16	0·16	0·16	0·16	0·16	0·16	0·16	0·16
—	—	—	—	—	—	—	—	0·04	0·04	0·04	0·04
—	—	—	—	—	—	—	—	—	—	—	0·04
—	—	—	—	0·05	0·05	0·05	0·05	0·05	0·05	0·05	0·05
0·65	0·65	0·65	0·63	0·63	0·61	0·59	0·59	0·59	0·40	0·40	0·40
—	—	—	—	—	—	—	—	—	—	—	0·04
1·63	1·88	2·00	1·85	1·85	1·80	1·80	1·80	1·80	1·98	1·98	1·98
12·28	14·15	15·08	13·96	13·96	13·62	13·62	13·62	13·62	14·97	14·97	14·97
0·50	0·47	0·40	0·36	0·36	0·35	0·32b	0·32b	0·32b	0·25	0·25	0·25
10·30	9·80	8·85	7·81	7·81	7·62	7·78	7·78	7·78	7·58	7·58	7·58
35·12	33·33	33·33	33·33	33·33	32·51	32·51	32·51	32·51	32·02	32·02	32·02
—	—	—	—	—	—	—	—	0·04	0·04	0·04	0·04
0·18	0·18	0·18	0·16	0·16	0·16	0·12	0·12	0·12	0·11	0·11	0·11
0·35	0·39	0·44	0·43	0·43	0·42	0·50	0·50	0·50	0·52	0·52	0·52
0·04	0·04	0·04	0·04	0·04	0·04	0·04	0·04	0·04	0·04	0·04	0·04
0·44	0·44	0·44	0·36	0·36	0·35	0·35	0·35	0·35	0·38	0·38	0·38
—	—	—	—	—	—	—	—	—	—	—	n.a.

b Including Syria

during the first six months of the year; the cash position thus reaches a dangerously low point in June.[316] There is the further problem of arrears on the regular budget, which amounted to $19·3 million at the end of 1963.

Until 1963, the Working Capital Fund had varied in amount between $20 million and $25 million, but in 1962 the Secretary-General asked that the amount should be substantially increased.[317] The Advisory Committee favoured an increase to $40 million, pending a further review of the question; this was approved by the Assembly.[318]

TABLE 31

Level of Working Capital Fund, 1946–1964

	$ (million)
1946	25·0
1947–1951	20·0
1952	21·2
1953–1955	21·5
1956	20·0
1957–1958	22·0
1959	23·5
1960–1962	25·0
1963–1964	40·0

In view of the serious financial situation of the United Nations in 1961, the General Assembly authorized the issue of United Nations bonds not exceeding $200 million, 'for purposes normally related to the Working Capital Fund'. The Assembly decided to include in the regular budget for 1963 and future years an amount sufficient to pay interest charges and the instalments of principal due. The bonds bear interest at 2 per cent per annum, and the principal is repayable in twenty-five instalments. Bonds were offered to Members of the United Nations and related agencies, and provision was also made for the sale of bonds to non-profit institutions or associations under certain conditions.[319]

As of 20 January 1964, 58 Member States and 4 non-Member States had purchased bonds to the amount of $151.5 million. Purchases and outstanding pledges are shown in Table 32.

TABLE 32

United Nations Bond Issue, purchase and pledges, 20 January 1964

A. Member States	purchase	pledge outstanding
Afghanistan	25,000	—
Albania	—	—
Algeria	—	—
Argentina	—	—
Australia	4,000,000	—
Austria	900,000	—
Belgium	—	—
Bolivia	—	—
Brazil	—	100,000
Bulgaria	—	—
Burma	100,000	—
Burundi	—	—
Byelorussian SSR	—	—
Cambodia	5,000	—
Cameroun	9,569	—
Canada	6,240,000	—
Central African Republic	—	—
Ceylon	25,000	—
Chad	—	—
Chile	—	—
China	500,000	—
Colombia	—	—
Congo (Brazzaville)	—	—
Congo (Leopoldville)	—	—
Costa Rica	—	—
Cuba	—	—
Cyprus	26,175	—
Czechoslovakia	—	—
Dahomey	—	—
Denmark	2,500,000	—
Dominican Republic	—	—
Ecuador	—	12,000

TABLE 32—*continued*

A. *Member States*	*purchase*	*pledge outstanding*
El Salvador	—	—
Ethiopia	200,000	—
Finland	1,480,000	—
France	—	—
Gabon	—	—
Ghana	100,000	—
Greece	10,000	—
Guatemala	—	—
Guinea	—	—
Haiti	—	—
Honduras	10,000	—
Hungary	—	—
Iceland	80,000	—
India	2,000,000	—
Indonesia	200,000	—
Iran	250,000	250,000
Iraq	100,000	—
Ireland	300,000	—
Israel	200,000	—
Italy	8,960,000	—
Ivory Coast	60,000	—
Jamaica	20,000	—
Japan	5,000,000	—
Jordan	75,000	—
Kenya	—	—
Kuwait	1,000,000	—
Laos	—	—
Lebanon	8,271	—
Liberia	—	200,000
Libya	25,000	—
Luxembourg	100,000	—
Madagascar	—	—
Malaysia	340,000	—
Mali	20,000	—
Mauritania	4,082	—
Mexico	—	—
Mongolia	—	—
Morocco	280,000	—
Nepal	—	—
Netherlands	2,020,000	—
New Zealand	1,000,000	—
Nicaragua	—	—
Niger	—	—
Nigeria	1,000,000	—
Norway	1,800,000	—
Pakistan	500,000	—
Panama	—	25,000
Paraguay	—	—
Peru	—	—

TABLE 32—*continued*

A. *Member States*	*purchase*	*pledge outstanding*
Philippines	750,000	—
Poland	—	—
Portugal	—	—
Romania	—	—
Rwanda	—	—
Saudi Arabia	20,000	—
Senegal	—	—
Sierra Leone	28,000	—
Somalia	—	—
South Africa	—	—
Spain	—	—
Sudan	50,000	—
Sweden	5,800,000	—
Syria	—	—
Tanganyika	2,800	—
Thailand	160,000	—
Togo	10,000	—
Trinidad and Tobago	8,750	—
Tunisia	485,000	—
Turkey	100,000	—
Uganda	10,000	—
Ukrainian SSR	—	—
USSR	—	—
United Arab Republic	250,000	—
United Kingdom	12,000,000	—
United States	75,493,897	*
Upper Volta	—	—
Uruguay	—	—
Venezuela	300,000	—
Yemen	—	—
Yugoslavia	200,000	—
Zanzibar	—	—
	137,141,544	

B. *Non-member States*		
Germany, Federal Republic of	12,000,000	—
Korea, Republic of	400,000	—
Switzerland	1,900,000	—
Viet Nam, Republic of	10,000	—
	$151,451,544	

* If outstanding pledges are honoured, the United States will purchase further bonds in the amount of $1,050,750, making total sales $153,089,294.

Audit Procedures

The Assembly has established audit procedures to ensure that the sums appropriated are spent in accordance with its decisions. The Assembly appoints a Board of Auditors consisting of the Auditor-General or corresponding officer of three Member States.[320] The annual accounts are certified by the Controller, approved by the Secretary-General, and submitted to the Board of Auditors not later than 31 March following the end of the financial year. The Secretary-General must provide the Board of Auditors with a statement of any amounts written off because of losses or deficiencies. The Board of Auditors reports to the Advisory Committee and the General Assembly on its scrutiny of the accounts, including trust and special accounts. The Board is specifically required to report on the accuracy of the accounts and records, cases of fraud, wasteful or improper expenditure of United Nations' money or assets, and any defect in the accounting system.[321]

Relations with UN agencies

The General Assembly is required by the Charter to 'examine the administrative budgets of . . . specialized agencies with a view to making recommendations to the agencies concerned'.[322] By the terms of their agreements with the United Nations, the International Bank for Reconstruction and Development and the International Monetary Fund are not required to transmit their budgets for examination by the United Nations. The agreement between the United Nations and the International Atomic Energy Agency provides that the administrative aspects of the Agency's budget shall be examined by the United Nations. These functions are entrusted to the Advisory Committee.[323] which also examines the budget estimates of the Technical Assistance Board and the administrative budget of the United Nations Special Fund. The Advisory Committee reports on these matters to the General Assembly.

The Advisory Committee thus conducts a broad review of the problems of administrative and budgetary co-ordination of the United Nations family of agencies. The exchange of information between the agencies on financial procedures, personnel matters, and such question as common premises is facilitated, though without any interference with the autonomy of the separate agencies. The Advisory Committee cannot compel an agency to change its administrative and budgetary procedures, but it can make available the experience of different agencies and emphasize the importance of the highest practicable degree of co-ordination and uniformity of practice.

Extra-budgetary programmes

Trust funds, reserve accounts, and special accounts may be set up outside the regular budget; in the absence of a decision to the contrary, such funds and accounts are administered in accordance with the ordinary Financial Regulations.[324] This section deals with the following extra-budgetary programs:

High Commissioner for Refugees

U.N. Relief and Works Agency for Palestine Refugees
in the Near East

U.N. Children's Fund
(UNICEF)

Expanded Program of Technical Assistance

Special Fund

UN Fund for the Congo

The extra-budgetary programs with which this section deals are financed by voluntary contributions of governments, and also of non-governmental agencies and private individuals. From 1952 to 1961 a negotiating committee for extra-budgetary funds sought to secure contributions from governments for UN welfare programs. This method has now been discontinued in favour of annual pledging sessions or other fund-raising techniques.[325]

The total of extra-budgetary programs represents a considerably higher level of annual expenditure than does the regular UN budget. The three programs concerned with economic development and welfare now receive contributions from a wide range of Member States, and their annual budgets are increasing. Secretary-General Thant has suggested that the combined budgets of the Expanded Program of Technical Assistance and the Special Fund should be increased by at least £25 million a year during the World Development Decade.

The two refugee programs draw funds from fewer States. In the case of the agency for Arab refugees from Palestine, the United States contributes 70 per cent of the annual budget, and the United Kingdom and Canada a further 20 per cent. Several non-Members contribute generously to the extra-budgetary programs.

There have in the past been some difficulties arising from the receipt of contributions for economic development programs in non-convertible currencies, especially but not exclusively from Soviet bloc countries. It is understandable that contributing countries with balance-of-payments problems should wish to limit the drain on their foreign reserves. At the same time, the agencies cannot operate at peak efficiency so long as there are restrictions on their use of contributions.

Suggestions have been made from time to time for consolidating the budgets of some or all of the voluntary programs, and even for financing by compulsory assessments. There is, indeed, little logic in the present practice of including certain administrative and operational expenses in the regular budgets of the UN and the related agencies, and meeting other expenses from voluntary contributions. There would, however, be formidable political obstacles to any scheme for financing the present extra-budgetary programs by means of compulsory assessments. The most practicable step in the immediate future would probably be to merge the Technical Assistance Programs and the Special Fund.

Peace-keeping Expenses

There are several ways of meeting the expenses of UN peace-keeping operations. The regular budget includes a section 'Special missions and related activities' for such operations as the Truce Supervision Organization in Palestine, the Military Observer Group in India and Pakistan, the Commission for the Unification and Rehabilitation of Korea, and the Special Representative of the Secretary-General in Amman. Other short-term operations, such as the Observer Group in Lebanon, have been met under the procedure for 'unforeseen and extraordinary expenses'. In several recent cases, the parties to the dispute have shared the costs of United Nations action.

But in the case of the Emergency Force in the Middle East and the operation in the Congo, the scale and expected duration of United Nations action has been such as to require special financial procedures. When the Assembly decided in 1956 to establish 'an emergency international force to secure and supervise the cessation of hostilities' in the Middle East, there were no exact precedents. The Suez question had been considered by the Security Council and, following vetoes by Britain and France, had been placed before the Assembly under the Uniting for Peace procedure. Secretary-General Hammarskjold suggested to the Assembly that a nation providing a contingent for the UN Emergency Force should be responsible for 'all costs of equipment and salaries'; other expenses should be financed 'outside the normal budget of the United Nations' and allocated to Member States on the basis of the ordinary scale of assessments.[326] The Assembly accepted this procedure for the first $10 million and invited Member States to make voluntary contributions to meet any costs beyond that amount.[327] For 1958 and 1959 the Assembly decided to allocate all the expenses in accordance with the regular scales of assessments.[328] For subsequent years the Assembly agreed on special reductions for the less-developed countries, to be met by voluntary contributions.[329] The United States provided special assistance or voluntary contributions to UNEF of $22.7 million up to 30 June 1962; the United Kingdom provided $2.3 million during the same period.

The decisions of the Assembly on the financing of UNEF did not command unanimous assent. The countries of the Soviet bloc held in 1956, and still hold, that only the Security Council has the authority to establish United Nations forces. They have regarded as illegal the procedures used both to establish the UN Emergency Force and to allocate the expenses; and they have accordingly refused to pay their assessments.

A large number of Latin American and Afro-Asian countries, while not challenging the legality of the procedures adopted, considered that to allocate all of the expenses according to the regular scale of assessments would impose an unreasonable burden on the poorer countries. They held that a major portion of the expenses should be borne either by the permanent members of the Security Council[330] or by the countries deemed responsible for creating the situation which had required UN peace-keeping action. These differences of view had not been resolved in 1960 when the Congo crisis occurred.

The UN operation in the Congo was authorized by the Security Council, and Secretary-General Hammarskjold obtained the concurrence of the Advisory Committee to incur expenses up to $40 million in 1960 under the procedure for meeting unforeseen and extraordinary expenses. He later submitted budget estimates totalling $66.6 million for the period 14 July to 31 December 1960. The Advisory Committee recommended that the amount be reduced to $60 million and the total was further reduced by waivers of reimbursement as follows:

	$
Canada	650,000
USSR	1,301,750
United Kingdom	520,000
United States	10,317,622

In addition to the waivers, the United States made a voluntary contribution of $3.9 million for 1960 in order to reduce the burden on the less-developed countries; the United States made similar voluntary contributions of $26.7 million for the period 1 January 1961 to 30 June 1962.

By the time the Assembly came to consider the financing of the Congo operation at the end of 1960, it had become clear that it was costing more than the whole of the regular United Nations budget. Moreover, the Soviet Union had by this time withdrawn its support of the operation, and Mr. Khrushchev had attacked Secretary-General Hammarskjold and put forward the *troika* proposal. The Assembly decided in 1960 to apportion the Congo expenses according to the regular scale of assessments, but with reductions for the less-developed countries to be met by voluntary contributions.[331] Similar decisions were later taken by the Assembly for the period 1 January 1961, to 30 June 1962.[332] The Assembly also decided in 1960 that a working group should consider the whole question of the administrative and budgetary procedures of the United Nations.[333]

The fact was that the question of paying for peace-keeping operations was not simply a financial one. It was also a political crisis arising from divergent views regarding the proper role and procedures of the United Nations in maintaining international peace and security. The working group which the Assembly established in 1960 was not able to resolve these fundamental differences, and it presented no agreed conclusions. What it managed to do was to 'identify the principles and issues at stake', and a majority of members were of the opinion that the International Court of Justice should be asked for an advisory opinion on the legal nature of financial obligations arising out of peace-keeping operations.[334] The Assembly, accordingly, decided in 1961 to ask the International Court to advise whether the peace-keeping expenses for UNEF and the Congo constituted 'expenses of the Organization' within the meaning of Article 17 of the Charter.[335] This action, it was hoped, would lead to a clarification of the legal issues, but as the Assembly was unable to agree on how the Congo expenses should be apportioned after 30 June 1962, some further action was needed if the Congo operations were to continue after that date. It was in this situation that U Thant proposed a United Nations bond issue, and this was approved by the General Assembly.[336]

The World Court's advisory opinion on peace-keeping expenses, though not unanimous, was of great importance.[337] The Court recognized that any interpretation of the Charter was likely to have political significance. At the same time, it considered that it had been invited to undertake an essentially judicial task; it had been asked to give an advisory opinion upon a concrete legal question.

The Court rejected the contention that the Charter implied the qualifying adjective 'regular' or 'administrative' before the references to budget and expenses, and it considered that the practice of the Organization had been entirely consistent with the plain meaning of the text.

It had been argued that expenses resulting from operations for maintaining international peace and security are not 'expenses of the Organization'. This argument rested in part upon the view that when the maintenance of peace and security is involved, only the Security Council can authorize action. The Court pointed out that the Security Council has primary authority for maintaining peace and security, and only the Security Council can require enforcement by coercive action against an aggressor. But the Security Council's responsibility is not exclusive, and the Charter makes it abundantly clear that the General Assembly is also to be concerned with international peace and security. The provisions of the Charter which distribute functions and powers to the Security Council and the General Assembly do not exclude from the General Assembly the power to provide for the financing of measures designed to maintain peace and security, and the Court could find no basis for limiting the budgetary authority of the General Assembly in this respect. Whenever the United Nations takes action to fulfil one of its stated purposes, the expenses incurred are 'expenses of the Organization', even if the action should have been taken by the wrong organ.

The operations in the Middle East and the Congo were undertaken to fulfil a prime purpose of the United Nations, that is to say, to promote and maintain peace, though they were not enforcement actions. The Court was of the opinion, by nine votes to five, that the expenditures incurred are 'expenses of the Organization'.

The Assembly, by seventy-six votes to seventeen with eight abstentions, accepted this advisory opinion in 1962.[338] But although the Assembly had authorized the Secretary-General to incur expenses for the Congo operation and UNEF during 1962, it had taken no decision regarding the apportioning of these expenses beyond 30 June 1962. The Assembly therefore took three actions in 1962.[339]

1. It authorized a continuing expenditure for the Congo and UNEF up to 30 June 1963;

2. It established an enlarged working group to study special methods for financing peace-keeping operations, as well as the situation arising from the accumulation of arrears,

3. It decided to convene a special session of the Assembly during the first half of 1963 to consider the financial situation in the light of the working group's report.

The working group met in 1963 in the knowledge that at the end of the previous year there had been accumulated arrears exceeding $100 million due from Member States for peace-keeping operations, and $17.7 million of arrears for the regular budget. The working group, like its predecessor in 1962, was unable to present unanimous conclusions.[340] It did, however, prepare the ground for the series of important decisions taken during a special session of the Assembly in 1963. These decisions, to be sure, were taken in the face of strong opposition on the part of the countries of the Soviet bloc. Indeed, the Soviet representative stated early in the session that, from 1963 on, the Soviet Union:

1. Would not pay that part of its contribution to the regular budget to finance the redemption of UN bonds;

2. Would not pay that part of its contribution to the regular budget used for certain specified purposes (The UN Field Service, the Truce Supervision Organization, the Commission for the Unification and Rehabilitation of Korea, and the Memorial Cemetery in Korea);

3. Would pay its contribution for the regular UN technical assistance program 'in its national currency' so that the money could be used only for 'the dispatch of Soviet equipment and experts'.[341]

In spite of this firm Soviet position, the Assembly, by substantial majorities, took the following decisions.[342]

1. For the second half of 1963, $9.5 million and $33 million were appropriated for UNEF and the Congo respectively. Of these amounts, $2.5 million and $3 million respectively were apportioned among Member States in accordance with the regular scale of assessments, and the balances were similarly apportioned, with the important exception that the 'economically less developed' countries were to have reductions of 55 per cent, to be met by voluntary contributions. Of 104 Member States whose assessments had been fixed at that time, 78 were classified as 'economically less developed', the exceptions being Australia, Canada, Japan, New Zealand, South Africa, the United States, and all European countries except Albania, Bulgaria, Cyprus, Greece, Portugal, Spain, Turkey, and Yugoslavia.

2. The period during which UN bonds might be sold was extended until 31 December 1963.*

3. The Assembly appealed to Member States in arrears to arrange to pay their assessments before 31 October 1963, without prejudice to their political or juridical objections.

4. The Assembly approved the following principles, *inter alia*, as guidelines for the sharing of the costs of future peacekeeping operations involving heavy expenditures:

(a) The financing of such operations is the collective responsibility of all Member States of the United Nations;

---

* On 17 December 1963 the Assembly further extended the period to the end of 1964.[343]

(b) Whereas the economically more developed countries are in a position to make relatively larger contributions, the economically less developed countries have a relatively limited capacity to contribute toward peace-keeping operations involving heavy expenditures;

(c) Without prejudice to the principle of collective responsibility, every effort should be made to encourage voluntary contributions from Member States;

(d) The special responsibilities of the permanent members of the Security Council for the maintenance of peace and security should be borne in mind in connexion with their contributions to the financing of peace and security operations;

(e) Where circumstances warrant, the General Assembly should give special consideration to the situation of any Member States which are victims of, and those which are otherwise involved in, the events or actions leading to a peace-keeping operation.

5. The working group was asked to recommend a special method for financing expensive peace-keeping operations.

6. The Secretary-General was asked to explore the possibility of establishing a peace fund, financed through voluntary contributions, to enable him to discharge promptly his responsibilities under the Charter in case of breaches of the peace.*

Later in 1963, during the eighteenth regular session, the Assembly authorized the financing of the Congo operation until 30 June 1964, and of UNEF until 31 December 1964. $3 million was apportioned among Member States in accordance with the regular scale for the Congo, and $2 million according to the regular scale for UNEF. $12 million and $15.75 million respectively were apportioned on the same basis, except for reductions of 55 per cent for the Congo and 57.5 per cent for UNEF for the less developed countries, to be met by voluntary contributions.[345]

---

* In pursuance of this request, the Secretary-General asked Member States to send him their observations on the desirability and feasibility of establishing such a peace fund. The Fifth Committee decided on 2 December 1963 to refer to the working group the replies received and the record of the discussion in the Fifth Committee.[344]

TABLE 33

Contributions due to the United Nations Emergency Force Special Account, December 31, 1963

Member States	1 July to 31 Dec. 1963 US $	1 January to 30 June 1962 US $	1961 US $
Afghanistan	2,821·00	907·00	5,583 ·50
Albania	2,256·00	735·00	7,484·00
Argentina	56,974·00	18,442·00	103,291·00
Australia	—	—	—
Austria	—	—	—
Belgium	—	—	—
Bolivia	2,256·00	735·00	7,484·00
Brazil	58,102·00	—	—
Bulgaria	11,282·00	3,720·00	29,938·00
Burma	—	—	—
Byelorussian Soviet Socialist Republic	49,322·00	50,170·00	87,943·00
Cambodia	—	—	—
Cameroun	—	—	—
Canada	140,421·95	—	—
Central African Republic	2,256·00	—	—
Ceylon	—	—	—
Chad	2,256·00	777·00	—
Chile	14,667·00	4,765·00	25,125·00
China	257,793·00	217,133·00	466,207·50
Colombia	9,947·00	—	—
Congo (Brazzaville)	2,256·00	—	—
Congo (Leopoldville)	3,949·00	—	—
Costa Rica	2,256·00	735·00	3,722·00
Cuba	12,410·00	4,008·00	46,778·00
Cyprus	2,256·00	—	—
Czechoslovakia	110,972·00	113,093·00	162,787·00
Dahomey	—	—	—
Denmark	—	—	—
Dominican Republic	2,821·00	919·00	9,356·00
Ecuador	2,175·88	—	—
El Salvador	2,256·00	724·00	—
Ethiopia	2,821·00	—	—
Finland	—	—	—
France	—	—	—
Gabon	—	—	—
Ghana	5,077·00	—	—
Greece	12,974·00	—	—
Guatemala	2,821·00	919·00	4,653·00
Guinea	2,256·00	735·00	7,484·00
Haiti	2,256·00	735·00	3,722·00
Honduras	2,256·00	735·00	3,722·00
Hungary	53,115·00	54,126·00	78,587·00
Iceland	—	—	—
India	—	—	—

TABLE 33—*continued*

1960 US $	1959 US $	1958 US $	1957 US $	*Total due* US$
5,926·00	9,092·00	15,000·00	2,814·00	42,143·50
3,951·00	6,062·00	10,000·00	5,876·00	36,364·00
109,594·00	168,180·00	285,000·00	171,869·00	913,350·00
—	—	—	—	—
—	—	—	—	—
3,939·00	6,056·00	12,500·00	—	32,970·00
—	—	—	—	58,102·00
15,826·00	24,257·00	35,000·00	20,565·00	140,588·00
—	—	—	—	—
46,419·00	71,219·00	117,500·00	70,510·00	493,083·00
—	—	—	—	—
—	—	—	—	140,421·95
—	—	—	—	2,256·00
—	—	—	—	—
—	—	—	—	3,033·00
26,643·00	35,269·00	—	—	106,469·00
989,797·00	759,151·00	1,252,500·00	405,048·00	4,347,629·50
—	—	—	—	9,947·00
—	—	—	—	2,256·00
—	—	—	—	3,949·00
3,171·09	—	—	—	9,884·09
24,679·00	37,874·00	65,000·00	12,662·00	203,411·00
—	—	—	—	2,256·00
85,983·00	131,856·00	205,000·00	123,393·00	933,084·00
—	—	—	—	—
—	—	—	—	13,096·00
—	—	—	—	2,175·88
—	—	—	—	2,980·00
—	—	—	—	2,821·00
—	—	—	—	—
—	—	—	—	—
—	—	—	—	—
—	—	—	—	5,077·00
—	—	—	—	12,974·00
4,915·00	7,566·00	—	—	20,874·00
—	—	—	—	10,475·00
3,951·00	6,062·00	—	—	16,726·00
3,951·00	—	—	—	10,664·00
41,516·00	63,627·00	97,500·00	67,572·00	456,043·00
—	—	—	—	—

TABLE 33—*continued*

Member States	1 July to 31 Dec. 1963 US $	1 January to 30 June 1962 US $	1961 US $
Indonesia	25,384·00	—	—
Iran	11,282·00	—	—
Iraq	5,077·00	1,654·00	16,840·00
Ireland	13,279·00	—	—
Israel	—	—	—
Italy	212,461·00	—	—
Ivory Coast	2,256·00	—	—
Japan	—	—	—
Jordan	2,256·00	735·00	7,484·00
Laos	2,256·00	—	—
Lebanon	2,821·00	919·00	4,653·00
Liberia	2,256·00	—	—
Libya	—	—	—
Luxembourg	4,742·00	—	—
Madagascar	—	—	—
Malaysia	—	—	—
Mali	2,256·00	15·50	—
Mauritania	2,256·00	780·00	416·00
Mexico	41,744·00	13,629·00	132,849·00
Mongolia	2,256·00	780·00	416·00
Morocco	7,898·00	—	—
Nepal	2,256·00	735·00	200·20
Netherlands	—	—	—
New Zealand	—	—	—
Nicaragua	2,256·00	735·00	1,860·75
Niger	2,256·00	777·00	3,762·00
Nigeria	—	—	—
Norway	—	—	—
Pakistan	23,692·00	—	—
Panama	2,256·00	735·00	3,722·00
Paraguay	2,256·00	735·00	3,722·00
Peru	5,641·00	1,826·00	20,582·00
Philippines	—	—	—
Poland	121,406·00	60,854·00	256,343·00
Portugal	9,026·00	—	—
Romania	30,351·00	30,816·00	63,618·00
Saudi Arabia	3,949·00	1,297·00	11,227·00
Senegal	2,821·00	971·00	—
Sierra Leone	2,256·00	—	—
Somalia	2,256·00	—	—
South Africa	—	—	—
Spain	48,512·00	15,720·00	174,013·00
Sudan	3,949·00	1,297·00	11,227·00
Sweden	—	—	—
Syria*	2,821·00	915·00	—

* For the years 1959, 1960 and 1961 assessments have been shown against the United Arab Republic.

TABLE 33—*continued*

1960 US $	1959 US $	1958 US $	1957 US $	Total due US $
—	—	—	—	25,384·00
—	—	—	—	11,282·00
8,854·00	13,623·00	30,000·00	5,627·00	81,675·00
—	—	—	—	13,279·00
—	—	—	—	—
—	—	—	—	212,461·00
—	—	—	—	2,256·00
—	—	—	—	—
3,951·00	6,062·00	10,000·00	5,876·00	36,364·00
—	—	—	—	2,256·00
4,938·00	6,514·00	—	—	19,845·00
—	—	—	—	2,256·00
—	—	—	—	—
—	—	—	—	4,742·00
—	—	—	—	—
—	—	—	—	—
—	—	—	—	2,271·50
—	—	—	—	3,452·00
70,158·00	107,564·00	170,000·00	32,828·00	568,772·00
—	—	—	—	3,452·00
—	—	—	—	7,898·00
—	—	—	—	3,191·20
—	—	—	—	—
—	—	—	—	—
—	—	—	—	4,851·75
444·00	—	—	—	7,239·00
—	—	—	—	—
—	—	—	—	23,692·00
3,939·00	6,056·00	12,500·00	1,289·00	30,497·00
3,951·00	6,062·00	10,000·00	—	26,726·00
10,817·00	16,649·00	37,500·00	7,034,00	100,049·00
135,134·00	207,514·00	380,000·00	229,159·00	1,390,410·00
—	—	—	—	9,026·00
33,406·00	51,442·00	122,500·00	73,448·00	405,581·00
5,915·00	9,087·00	17,500·00	10,283·00	59,258·00
—	—	—	—	3,792·00
—	—	—	—	2,256·00
—	—	—	—	2,256·00
—	—	—	—	—
91,643·00	140,826·00	277,500·00	167,462·00	915,676·00
5,868·00	9,067·00	27,500·00	16,159·00	75,067·00
—	—	—	—	—
—	—	20,000·00	11,752·00	35,488·00

TABLE 33—*continued*

Member States	1 July to 31 Dec. 1963 US $	1 January to 30 June 1962 US $	1961 US $
Tanganyika	—	—	—
Thailand	9,026·00	—	—
Togo	2,256·00	777·00	3,762·00
Tunisia	2,821·00	—	—
Turkey	—	—	—
Ukrainian Soviet Socialist Republic	187,800·00	191.019·00	336,801·00
Union of Soviet Socialist Republics	1,419,878·00	1,444,204·00	2,548,457·00
United Arab Republic	14,102·00	4,574·00	59,876·00
United Kingdom of Great Britain and Northern Ireland	—	—	—
United States of America	3,037,040·00	—	—
Upper Volta	2,256·00	777·00	7,524·00
Uruguay	6,205·00	2,010·00	11,167·00
Venezuela	—	—	—
Yemen	2,256·00	735·00	7,484·00
Yugoslavia	—	—	—
	6,127,361·83	2,254,134·50	4,741,872·95

TABLE 33—*continued*

1960 US $	1959 US $	1958 US $	1957 US $	Total due US $
444·00	—	—	—	7,239·00
—	—	—	—	2,821·00
—	—	—	—	—
177,778·00	272,747·00	450,000·00	271,759·00	1,887,904·00
2,706,146·00	2,063,805·00	3,405,000·00	2,050,676·00	15,638,166·00
31,477·00	48,432·00	87,500·00	52,883·00	298,844·00
—	—	—	—	—
—	—	—	—	3,037,040·00
444·00	—	—	—	11,001·00
11,806·00	—	—	—	31,188·00
—	—	—	—	—
3,951·00	6,062·00	10,000·00	5,876·00	36,364·00
—	—	—	—	—
4,681,325·09	4,297,783·00	7,162,500·00	3,822,420·00	33,087,397·37

TABLE 34

Contributions due to the Congo ad hoc Account, December 31, 1963

Member States	1 July to 31 Dec. 1963 US $	1 Nov. 1961 to 30 June 1962 US $	1 Jan. to 31 Oct. 1961 US $	12 July to 31 Dec. 1960 US $	Total due US $
Afghanistan	8,238·00	7,949·00	11,887·00	14,529·00	42,603·50
Albania	6,589·00	6,366·00	7,925·00	19,373·00	40,253·00
Argentina	166,384·00	160,664·00	219,911·00	18,797·00	565,756·00
Australia	—	—	—	—	—
Austria	148,262·00	359,637·00	65,335·00		573,234·00
Belgium	395,367·00	958,903·00	1,287,766·00	629,615·00	3,271,651·00
Bolivia	6,589·00	6,366·00	7,925·00	10,664·40	31,484·40
Brazil	169,679·00	163,940·00	202,080·00	44,922·50	580,621·50
Bulgaria	32,947·00	31,865·00	31,699·00	77,491·00	174,002·00
Burma	—	—	—	—	—
Byelorussian Soviet Socialist Republic	171,326·00	415,604·00	465,577·00	227,630·00	1,280,137·00
Cambodia	—	—	—	—	—
Cameroun	—	—	—	—	—
Canada	250,429·76	—	—	—	250,429·76
Central African Republic	6,589·00	—	—	—	6,589·00
Ceylon	—	—	—	—	—
Chad	6,483·23	—	—	—	6,483·23
Chile	42,831·00	41,372·00	53,492·00	65,383·00	203,078·00
China	752,846·00	1,823,774·00	2,481,426·00	1,396,543·50	6,454,589·50
Colombia	42,831·00	—	—	—	42,831·00
Congo (Brazzaville)	6,589·00	—	—	—	6,589·00
Congo (Leopoldville)	11,532·00	—	—	—	11,532·00
Costa Rica	6,589·00	6,366·00	7,611·50	—	20,566·50
Cuba	36,242·00	34,989·00	49,529·00	121,080·00	241,840·00
Cyprus	6,589·00	—	—	—	6,589·00

Czechoslovakia	385,483·00	935,266·00	861,813·00	421,358·00	2,603,920·00
Dahomey	4,488·34	—	—	—	4,488·34
Denmark	—	—	—	—	—
Dominican Republic	8,238·00	7,958·00	9,905·00	24,216·00	50,317·00
Ecuador	4,679·96	—	—	—	4,679·96
El Salvador	6,589·00	6,358·00	—	—	12,947·00
Ethiopia	8,238·00	—	—	—	8,238·00
Finland	—	—	—	—	—
France	1,957,068·00	4,746,601·00	6,339,772·00	3,099,642·00	16,143,083·00
Gabon	14,827·00	—	—	—	14,827·00
Ghana	37,889·00	—	—	—	37,889·00
Greece	8,238·00	7,958·00	9,905·00	12,108·00	38,209·00
Guatemala	6,589·00	—	—	—	6,589·00
Guinea	6,589·00	—	—	—	6,589·00
Haiti	6,589·00	6,366·00	7,925·00	9,686·50	30,566·50
Honduras	6,589·00	6,366·00	7,925·00	9,686·50	30,566·50
Hungary	184,595·00	447,646·00	83,210·00	203,414·00	918,775·00
Iceland	—	—	—	—	—
India	74,131·00	—	—	—	74,131·00
Indonesia	32,947·00	31,823·00	41,605·00	25,853·50	132,228·50
Iran	14,827·00	14,324·00	17,831·00	43,589·00	90,571·00
Iraq	46,126·00	—	—	—	46,126·00
Ireland	—	—	—	—	—
Israel	738,019·00	—	—	—	738,019·00
Italy	6,589·00	—	—	—	6,589·00
Ivory Coast	—	—	—	—	—
Japan	6,589·00	—	—	—	6,589·00
Jordan	6,589·00	6,366·00	7,925·00	19,373·00	40,253·00
Laos	6,589·00	—	—	—	6,589·00
Lebanon	8,238·00	3,870·02	—	—	12,108·02
Liberia	6,589·00	—	—	—	6,589·00
Libya	—	—	—	—	—

TABLE 34—continued

Member States	1 July to 31 Dec. 1963 US $	1 Nov. 1961 to 30 June 1962 US $	1 January to 31 Oct. 1961 US $	14 July to 31 Dec. 1960 US $	Total due US $
Luxembourg	16,474·00	—	—	—	16,474·00
Madagascar	6,589·00	6,394·00	10,936·00	—	23,919·00
Malaysia	—	—	—	—	—
Mali	6,589·00	6,396·00	7,925·00	—	20,910·00
Mauritania	6,589·00	6,400·00	877·00	—	13,866·00
Mexico	121,906·00	117,801·00	149,664·00	343,866·00	724,237·00
Mongolia	6,589·00	6,400·00	877·00	—	13,866·00
Morocco	23,063·00	22,282·00	27,736·00	67,805·00	140,886·00
Nepal	6,589·00	6,366·00	137·16	—	13,092·16
Netherlands	—	—	—	—	—
New Zealand	—	—	—	—	—
Nicaragua	6,589·00	6,366·00	7,925·00	9,686·50	30,566·50
Niger	6,589·00	6,396·00	7,925·00	1,065·00	21,975·50
Nigeria	—	—	—	—	—
Norway	—	—	—	—	—
Pakistan	69,190·00	—	—	—	69,190·00
Panama	6,589·00	6,366·00	7,925·00	9,686·50	30,566·50
Paraguay	6,589·00	6,366·00	7,925·00	—	20,880·00
Peru	16,474·00	15,907·00	21,793·00	26,637·50	80,811·50
Philippines	—	—	—	—	—
Poland	421,726·00	510,845·00	678,553·00	663,517·00	2,274,641·00
Portugal	26,358·00	25,431·00	39,624·00	96,864·00	188,277·00
Romania	105,432·00	255,713·00	336,800·00	164,668·00	862,613·00
Saudi Arabia	11,532·00	11,149·00	11,887·00	29,059·00	63,627·00
Senegal	8,238·00	7,994·00	—	—	16,232·00
Sierra Leone	6,589·00	—	—	—	6,589·00
Somalia	6,589·00	6,396·00	1,111·07	—	14,096·07

South Africa	174,621·00	423,528·00	554,730·00	271,219·00	1,424,098·00
Spain	141,674·00	136,816·00	184,250·00	450,417·00	913,157·00
Sudan	—	—	—	—	—
Sweden	—	—	—	—	—
Syria*	8,238·00	7,955·00	—	—	16,193·00
Tanganyika	—	—	—	—	—
Thailand	26,358·00	—	—	—	26,358·00
Togo	6,589·00	6,396·00	7,925·00	1,065·00	21,975·50
Tunisia	8,238·00	—	—	—	8,238·00
Turkey	—	—	—	—	—
Ukrainian Soviet Socialist Republic	652,356·00	1,582,482·00	1,783,061·00	871,774·00	4,889,673·00
Union of Soviet Socialist Republics	4,932,209·00	11,904,509·00	13,491,828·00	6,596,425·00	36,984,971·00
United Arab Republic*	41,184·00	39,775·00	63,398·00	154,982·00	299,339·00
United Kingdom	142,755·31	—	—	—	142,755·31
United States of America	10,549,720·00	—	—	—	10,549,720·00
Upper Volta	6,589·00	4,207·00	—	—	10,796·00
Uruguay	18,121·00	17,499·00	23,774·00	29,059·00	88,453·00
Venezuela	85,663·00	—	—	—	85,663·00
Yemen	6,589·00	6,366·00	7,925·00	19,373·00	40,253·00
Yugoslavia	62,600·00	60,505·00	69,341·00	169,512·00	361,958·00
	23,611,962·60	25,519,703·02	29,776,831·73	16,471,576·90	95,380,074·25

* For the years 1960 and 1961 assessments have been shown against the United Arab Republic.

The main question which would arise during 1964 was likely to be whether Article 19 would take its course, resulting in the withdrawal of voting rights in the Assembly in respect of countries two years in arrears. This was a question regarding which legal and political issues were closely intertwined. The Soviet Government had taken the legal position that Articles 18 and 19 of the Charter, relating to voting in the General Assembly, should be considered together. Article 18 states that among the important questions for which a two-thirds vote is needed in the Assembly is 'suspension of the rights and privileges of membership. . . .' Loss of voting rights in the Assembly for States more than two years in arrears should not, according to the Soviet view, be automatic but should require a two-thirds majority vote in the Assembly.

9

THE FUTURE
OF THE ASSEMBLY

*It now rests to conclude the discourse in which, if I have not
pleased my reader or answered his expectation, it is some
comfort to me I meant well, and have cost him but little money
and time.*

WILLIAM PENN

THE GENERAL ASSEMBLY occupies a key position in the
network of organs of the United Nations. Some of its main
procedural problems have arisen from the fact that it has had to do
things for which it is not fully equipped, legally or politically. This,
in itself, should occasion no regret. Political institutions progress
towards maturity by a process of trial and error, but perfect maturity
is a mirage that is never achieved. Success consists in striving.

Of all organs of the United Nations, the Assembly has received
the greatest impact from the increase in the number of sovereign
States since the war. The new and emerging States pin great hopes
on the United Nations. Some, like Indonesia, have owed their very
existence to the United Nations; many others regard the United
Nations as a midwife. The United Nations helped them to achieve
sovereignty: it should also ensure that they achieve security and
prosperity.

Moreover, the United Nations can help these new and emerging
States to find their place in the world. Secretary-General Hammarskjold often referred to the important role of the United Nations
during this period of transition.

The United Nations is now, or will be, their Organization. The United Nations can give them a framework for their young national life which gives a deeper sense and a greater weight to independence.[346]

To belong to the United Nations is a mark of sovereignty. Each State, as it attains independence, applies for Membership, and failure to gain admission might be thought to cast doubts on the reality of the applicant's independence. Moreover, the Charter provides no procedure for withdrawal from the Organization, whereas nearly a score of States withdrew from the League, in many cases for reasons which now seem trifling.

One of the bases of the United Nations is the principle of the sovereign equality of its Members. This is a juridical concept which, if applied consistently, would mean that no State should be coerced by external means to act contrary to its own wishes. In practice, no principle can be fully and consistently applied since equally valid principles may be in conflict. But, leaving this aside, it should be stressed that juridical equality is not the same as political equality. The newer States do not differ from other States in this respect. Each Member of the General Assembly has one vote, and no distinction is made between large and small, strong and weak, old and new, wise and foolish. The relationship between power and influence has never been a direct one, but in traditional diplomacy a State could be influential in spite of its folly; in conference diplomacy a State may be influential in spite of its weakness.

New concepts of neutrality are emerging. Neutrality has traditionally referred to the legal situation of non-belligerent States in time of war; permanent neutrality involved an obligation, contracted in peace-time, not to take part in future wars. In either case, a balance of legal rights and duties was involved, though a neutral State did not have to adopt an attitude of ideological indifference.[347]

The new neutrality of the non-aligned and uncommitted States does not arise from legal obligations but from a belief that the Cold War has little relevance for them, or at least that it is neither necessary nor in their interests to take sides. They are not, of course, neutral about everything; they are agreed, for example, that colonialism must go as soon as possible. But by and large they seek to remain aloof from the ideological and power struggle between the Communist camp and the West.

If the Cold War should, in time, abate, if the Soviet Union and the United States should find more and more matters in which their interests coincided, a host of new problems would arise for the medium and smaller countries. There might then be a suspicion that the super-powers were arranging things between themselves at the expense of other States, which had not even been consulted. There have been one or two recent hints of this in United Nations affairs, but it is not at present an acute problem for the new countries.

It is clear that the impetus and focus of the United Nations will increasingly be determined by the aspirations and ambitions of States which played little or no role in traditional diplomacy. These newer and emerging States face internal and external problems different from those of the older States. The latter have inherited a legacy of obligations, enmities, and grievances. The newer States, by and large, start from scratch, without allies, without obligations, and with few specific grievances. To be sure, they soon find that other States proffer alliance, they soon incur obligations, they soon discover or invent grievances. But from the moment of birth, these States are thrust upon the world stage. Their representatives in the General Assembly are asked to pronounce on a variety of questions which may be of only marginal interest. I recall Neville Chamberlain's reference, at the time of the Munich crisis, to 'a quarrel in a far-away country between people of whom we know nothing'.[348] Today it does not seem surprising that governments and peoples should be concerned about distant tragedies or quarrels; there are no longer any far-away countries.

The point I wish to stress, however, is not that we are all involved in mankind, for to understand this is a mark of civilization. What I am concerned about is the temptation to cover the incapacity to deal with one's own problems by moralizing about other people's. A diplomat for whom I have great admiration said to me some years ago that the internal problems facing his government and people at home seemed insoluble, but that the one thing his country could do to make the world a better place for all was to vote in the General Assembly for Algerian independence. These remarks were not made cynically, and I have not repeated them cynically. All the same, they seem to me to exemplify one of the dangers to which any political body is subject. It is only too easy for governments to dramatize and thus exaggerate the inadequacies and mistakes of others, and this is a special temptation in an Assembly which conducts much of its business in public.

The Assembly is now so large that means must be devised to use to the best advantage organs with limited membership, including the Security Council and the Economic and Social Council. It may well be that the Security Council can never fill the role which the founding fathers intended for it. It is often said that the Council was predicated on the assumption that the Great Powers would co-operate in peace as they had in war, but that the icy blasts of the Cold War have unexpectedly swept away the foundations of co-operation. I doubt whether the expectations of foreign offices were ever as rosy as such statements imply, but the task now is not to regret the past or deplore the present, but to see what can be done to ensure that there is a future.

The Security Council could be used to better effect. Secretary-General Hammarskjold pointed out several years ago that an important feature of the Council was that it had been able to exert its influence during the intervals when it did not meet in public. 'It may be asked if the time is not now ripe to give formal expression to this fact by the organization of regular meetings of the Council in executive session.'[349]

One difficulty is that the Council is not constituted in such a way as to represent adequately the real world. The People's Republic of China is absent, and it now seems impossible to distribute the six elective places so as to give fair representation to all the main regions and groups. The countries of the Soviet bloc have opposed any amendment to the Charter so long as the representation of China has not been rectified. Until recently it had been thought that the People's Republic of China, even if it were seated in the Security Council, would favour a redistribution of seats rather than an enlargement of the Council. As this book went to press, however, there was some evidence that this assumption might have to be revised. An editorial in *Jenmin Jihpao* on 18 December 1963, the day after the Assembly had voted in favour of enlarging the Security Council and the Economic and Social Council, stated that although a re-allocation of seats would be preferable, the People's Republic of China would support the demand of the Afro-Asian countries for enlarging the Councils.[350]

It is merely a truism to say that the burdens on the Assembly would be eased if there were greater reliance on the Rule of Law and greater use of the legal institutions of the United Nations. The Rule of Law, as it evolved in national societies, was based on two ideals.

First, that executive power should be derived from and exercised in accordance with law. Secondly, that law itself should respect the supreme dignity and worth of the human person.

The Rule of Law in international relations is usually taken to mean simply 'the observance by States of international law as it exists today'.[351] This, to be sure, is not an onerous obligation; but the ultimate goal must be that relations among States should be governed by accepted rules of conduct, that controversies should be submitted to judicial tribunals for settlement, and that means of enforcing judicial decisions should be devised. This would require that what constitutes 'the law' should be known with reasonable certainty and applied without discrimination. Judicial tribunals should act impartially and with complete independence. They should ascertain the facts by means of evidence presented by the parties, and should hear legal arguments on questions of law. Their decisions should dispose of the matter by a finding upon facts in dispute and an application of law to the facts so found, including when necessary a ruling upon any disputed question of law; and the parties should agree to accept and comply with the decision of such a tribunal.[352]

The International Court has, perhaps, been maligned beyond its deserts. It is true that our age is highly political; nations have been reluctant to submit crucial issues for judicial settlement. All the same, the Court has performed some vital tasks. In any case, the value of a judicial system cannot be judged simply by counting the number of times it is overtly resorted to. The usefulness of the Court should be determined, in the first place, by the wrongs that were not done and the disputes that were not allowed to fester simply because the Court existed.

The General Assembly itself must keep its procedures and practices under constant review. Secretary-General Thant commented in 1962: 'The present procedures might have suited an Assembly with fewer members and confronted by less momentous issues. They do not suit the present. . . . A streamlining of procedures has thus become progressively more urgent and necessary.'[353]

Main Committees should seek the greatest possible degree of flexibility. The Second Committee recently decided to review its organization and methods of work, particularly regarding the Committee's general debate and the order and manner of discussion of agenda items.[354] More use might be made by Main Committees of working groups or sub-committees of limited membership, particularly for drafting or revising conventions and other texts.[355] It might also be possible to make use of committees of limited size for hearing oral statements and petitions. It can hardly be denied that some petitioners do not add anything new and in fact abuse their privilege.[356]

Matters proposed for inclusion in the agenda should be scrutinized more carefully than has been the practice in the past. The Assembly has been reluctant to reject requests for the inclusion of items in the agenda, but there are intermediate steps between unconditional inclusion and outright rejection. The Assembly may include an item in the agenda for consideration during the course of the General Debate or on some other occasion, with the proviso that it is for discussion only. The Assembly may refer an item, without debate of its substance, for consideration and report by an organ meeting between sessions, or may postpone consideration by deciding to include it in the provisional agenda of a future session. The Secretary-General reported in 1956 that, in informal consultations with the Permanent Representatives of Member States, it had been suggested that certain items be considered on a biennial rather than an annual basis.[357]

A little time might be saved if the General Debate in the plenary were combined with whatever consideration was needed of the reports of the Secretary-General, the three Councils, and possibly other organs. The Chairman of the Second Committee during the eighteenth session suggested that the general debate should be discontinued in the Second Committee, and that statements of economic policy should be made in the General Debate in the plenary.[358]

There are very few possibilities of improving the conduct of debate by changing the Rules of Procedure. Arbitrary limitation of the length or number of speeches is a drastic measure which would not lead to any significant saving of time. Much would be gained, however, if the Rules relating to points of order, the right of reply, and explanations of vote were better understood and more strictly applied.

The one area in which the Assembly might effect a significant improvement in procedure is that of the means by which it reaches conclusions. Most of the matters with which the Assembly deals must, in the last resort, be decided by vote. If there is a difference of opinion among Member States about an item in the budget, for example, this cannot be settled except by a vote. But in contentious questions of a political or quasi-political nature, the primary task is to cause an improvement in the situation rather than to place on the public record the views of Member States. It is interesting, in this connexion, to note that such bodies as the Committee on the Peaceful Uses of Outer Space and the Committee on the Elimination of Colonialism have agreed that they will aim at conducting their work in such a way as to reach agreement without need for voting.[359] The United Nations is a centre for harmonizing the actions of nations, not just a place where differences are recorded. The impact of quiet diplomacy and public debate may be much reduced or altogether lost if a substantive proposal is pressed to a vote prematurely.

The competition for Assembly offices, for places on the Councils, and for membership of subsidiary organs has caused some distortion of what is important; the contest has tended to become an end in itself, leading to preoccupation with such mutually exclusive concepts as equitable geographical representation and 'parity'. The important thing is that organs should be so constituted that they can function effectively and enjoy general confidence, and this is rarely achieved by the automatic application of mathematical formulas. The one procedural device which might facilitate elections and appointments would be to create a committee to advise on nominations.

The Assembly should review its subsidiary organs from time to time to ensure that there is no unnecessary duplication. Secretary-General Thant pointed out in August 1962 that there were four committees concerned with colonial territories, and that to combine them would both relieve the delegations concerned of unnecessary burdens and reduce costs and staff requirements.[360] The Assembly did not take the hint in 1962, and it was necessary for a representative of the Secretary-General to return to the charge the following year.[361] As a result, the Committee on Information from Non-Self-Governing Territories was discontinued.

These matters of procedure have no intrinsic importance; they are merely means to achieve the ends for which the United Nations was created. The chief purpose of good procedure is not to save time, but to ensure that international business is well handled.

A NOTE ON
FURTHER READING

THE main bibliographic sources on the procedure and practice of the General Assembly are the official records of Assembly debates. It is impossible, in the space available, to list all the debates which have had a direct or indirect bearing on procedure. Appendix 3 gives the numbers of the Main Committees and plenary meetings of the Assembly at which some of the more important procedural questions have been discussed.

Four committees of the General Assembly have reported on the procedures, methods, and organization of the Assembly, as follows:

Session	Name of Committee	Date of report	References
2	Committee on Procedures and Organization	23 Sept. 1947	Plenary meetings, Annex 4, A/388
4	Special Committee on Methods and Procedures	12 Aug. 1949	Supplement No. 12, A/937
8	Special Committee on Measures to Limit the Duration of Regular Sessions	26 June 1953	Annexes, Agenda item 54, A/2402
18	*Ad Hoc* Committee on the Improvement of the Methods of Work	28 May 1963	Annexes, Agenda item 25, A/5423

Extracts from these reports will be found in Appendices 7–10, pp. 305–348.

The standard work on the League Assembly is *The Assembly of the League of Nations*, by Margaret E. Burton, University of Chicago Press, 1941. A useful study of the procedure and organization of inter-governmental assemblies is *A Guide to the Practice of International Conferences*, by Vladimir D. Pastuhov, Carnegie Endowment for International Peace, 1945.

The Carnegie Endowment for International Peace has sponsored two studies relating wholly or partly to the procedure and practice of the General Assembly of the United Nations. Both were issued for limited circulation. The first, *Memorandum Concerning the Conduct of the Business of the General Assembly of the United Nations*, was prepared by Waldo Chamberlin in 1949; it is now out of print. The second, *Some Implications of Expanding United Nations Membership*, was prepared by Eric Stein in 1956; a few copies are still available. An important book on the politics, rather than the procedure, of the Assembly is *The Political Role of the General Assembly*, by H. Field Haviland, Jr., Carnegie Endowment for International Peace, 1951.

APPENDICES

Articles of the Charter
quoted or referred to in the text

WE, THE PEOPLES OF THE UNITED NATIONS, DETER-
MINED to save succeeding generations from the scourge of war,
which twice in our life-time has brought untold sorrow to mankind, and

to reaffirm faith in fundamental human rights, in the dignity and
worth of the human person, in the equal rights of men and women
and of nations large and small, and

to establish conditions under which justice and respect for the
obligations arising from treaties and other sources of international
law can be maintained, and

to promote social progress and better standards of life in larger
freedom,

AND FOR THESE ENDS to practice tolerance and live together
in peace with one another as good neighbors, and

to unite our strength to maintain international peace and security,
and

to ensure, by the acceptance of principles and the institution of
methods, that armed force shall not be used, save in the common
interest, and

to employ international machinery for the promotion of the
economic and social advancement of all peoples,

HAVE RESOLVED TO COMBINE OUR EFFORTS TO
ACCOMPLISH THESE AIMS. Accordingly, our respective
Governments, through representatives assembled in the city of

San Francisco, who have exhibited their full powers found to be in good and due form, have agreed to the present Charter of the United Nations and do hereby establish an international organization to be known as the United Nations.

Chapter I. Purposes and Principles

Article 1

The Purposes of the United Nations are:

1. To maintain international peace and security, and to that end: to take effective collective measures for the prevention and removal of threats to the peace, and for the suppression of acts of aggression or other breaches of the peace, and to bring about by peaceful means, and in conformity with the principles of justice and international law, adjustment or settlement of international disputes or situations which might lead to a breach of the peace;

2. To develop friendly relations among nations based on respect for the principle of equal rights and self-determination of peoples, and to take other appropriate measures to strengthen universal peace;

3. To achieve international co-operation in solving international problems of an economic, social, cultural, or humanitarian character, and in promoting and encouraging respect for human rights and for fundamental freedoms for all without distinction as to race, sex, language, or religion; and

4. To be a center for harmonizing the actions of nations in the attainment of these common ends.

Article 2

The Organization and its Members, in pursuit of the Purposes stated in Article 1, shall act in accordance with the following Principles.

1. The Organization is based on the principle of the sovereign equality of all its Members.

2. All Members, in order to ensure to all of them the rights and benefits resulting from membership, shall fulfil in good faith the obligations assumed by them in accordance with the present Charter.

3. All Members shall settle their international disputes by peaceful means in such a manner that international peace and security, and justice, are not endangered.

4. All Members shall refrain in their international relations from the threat or use of force against the territorial integrity or political

independence of any state, or in any other manner inconsistent with the Purposes of the United Nations.

5. All Members shall give the United Nations every assistance in any action it takes in accordance with the present Charter, and shall refrain from giving assistance to any state against which the United Nations is taking preventive or enforcement action.

6. The Organization shall ensure that states which are not Members of the United Nations act in accordance with these Principles so far as may be necessary for the maintenance of international peace and security.

7. Nothing contained in the present Charter shall authorize the United Nations to intervene in matters which are essentially within the domestic jurisdiction of any state or shall require the Members to submit such matters to settlement under the present Charter; but this principle shall not prejudice the application of enforcement measures under Chapter VII.

Chapter II. Membership

*   *   *

Article 4

1. Membership in the United Nations is open to all other peace-loving states which accept the obligations contained in the present Charter and, in the judgment of the Organization, are able and willing to carry out these obligations.

2. The admission of any such state to membership in the United Nations will be effected by a decision of the General Assembly upon the recommendation of the Security Council.

Article 5

A Member of the United Nations against which preventive or enforcement action has been taken by the Security Council may be suspended from the exercise of the rights and privileges of membership by the General Assembly upon the recommendation of the Security Council. The exercise of these rights and privileges may be restored by the Security Council.

Article 6

A Member of the United Nations which has persistently violated the Principles contained in the present Charter may be expelled from the Organization by the General Assembly upon the recommendation of the Security Council.

Chapter III. Organs

Article 7

1. There are established as the principal organs of the United Nations: a General Assembly, a Security Council, an Economic and Social Council, a Trusteeship Council, an International Court of Justice, and a Secretariat.

2. Such subsidiary organs as may be found necessary may be established in accordance with the present Charter.

*   *   *

Chapter IV. The General Assembly

Article 9

1. The General Assembly shall consist of all the Members of the United Nations.

2. Each Member shall have not more than five representatives in the General Assembly.

Article 10

The General Assembly may discuss any questions or any matters within the scope of the present Charter or relating to the powers and functions of any organs provided for in the present Charter, and, except as provided in Article 12, may make recommendations to the Members of the United Nations or to the Security Council or to both on any such questions or matters.

Article 11

1. The General Assembly may consider the general principles of cooperation in the maintenance of international peace and security, including the principles governing disarmament and the regulation of armaments, and may make recommendations with regard to such principles to the Members or to the Security Council or to both.

2. The General Assembly may discuss any questions relating to the maintenance of international peace and security brought before it by any Member of the United Nations, or by the Security Council, or by a state which is not a Member of the United Nations in accordance with Article 35, paragraph 2, and, except as provided in Article 12, may make recommendations with regard to any such questions to the state or states concerned or to the Security Council or to both. Any such question on which action is necessary shall be referred to the Security Council by the General Assembly either before or after discussion.

3. The General Assembly may call the attention of the Security Council to situations which are likely to endanger international peace and security.

4. The powers of the General Assembly set forth in this Article shall not limit the general scope of Article 10.

Article 12

1. While the Security Council is exercising in respect of any dispute or situation the functions assigned to it in the present Charter, the General Assembly shall not make any recommendation with regard to that dispute or situation unless the Security Council so requests.

2. The Secretary-General, with the consent of the Security Council, shall notify the General Assembly at each session of any matters relative to the maintenance of international peace and security which are being dealt with by the Security Council and shall similarly notify the General Assembly, or the Members of the United Nations if the General Assembly is not in session, immediately the Security Council ceases to deal with such matters.

Article 13

1. The General Assembly shall initiate studies and make recommendations for the purpose of:

  (a) promoting international co-operation in the political field and encouraging the progressive development of international law and its codification;
  (b) promoting international co-operation in the economic, social, cultural, educational, and health fields, and assisting in the realization of human rights and fundamental freedoms for all without distinction as to race, sex, language, or religion.

2. The further responsibilities, functions, and powers of the General Assembly with respect to matters mentioned in paragraph 1 (b) above are set forth in Chapters IX and X.

Article 14

Subject to the provisions of Article 12, the General Assembly may recommend measures for the peaceful adjustment of any situation, regardless of origin, which it deems likely to impair the general welfare or friendly relations among nations, including situations resulting from a violation of the provisions of the present Charter setting forth the Purposes and Principles of the United Nations.

Article 15

1. The General Assembly shall receive and consider annual and special reports from the Security Council; these reports shall include an account of the measures that the Security Council has decided upon or taken to maintain international peace and security.

2. The general Assembly shall receive and consider reports from the other organs of the United Nations.

Article 16

The General Assembly shall perform such functions with respect to the international trusteeship system as are assigned to it under Chapters XII and XIII, including the approval of the trusteeship agreements for areas not designated as strategic.

Article 17

1. The General Assembly shall consider and approve the budget of the Organization.

2. The expenses of the Organization shall be borne by the Members as apportioned by the General Assembly.

3. The General Assembly shall consider and approve any financial and budgetary arrangements with specialized agencies referred to in Article 57 and shall examine the administrative budgets of such specialized agencies with a view to making recommendations to the agencies concerned.

Article 18

1. Each member of the General Assembly shall have one vote.

2. Decisions of the General Assembly on important questions shall be made by a two-thirds majority of the members present and voting. These questions shall include: recommendations with respect to the maintenance of international peace and security, the election of the non-permanent members of the Security Council, the election of the members of the Economic and Social Council, the election of members of the Trusteeship Council in accordance with paragraph 1 (c) of Article 86, the admission of new Members to the United Nations, the suspension of the rights and privileges of membership, the expulsion of Members, questions relating to the operation of the trusteeship system, and budgetary questions.

3. Decisions on other questions, including the determination of additional categories of questions to be decided by a two-thirds majority, shall be made by a majority of the members present and voting.

Article 19

A Member of the United Nations which is in arrears in the payment of its financial contributions to the Organization shall have no vote in the General Assembly if the amount of its arrears equals or exceeds the amount of the contributions due from it for the preceding two full years. The General Assembly may, nevertheless, permit such a Member to vote if it is satisfied that the failure to pay is due to conditions beyond the control of the Member.

Article 20

The General Assembly shall meet in regular annual sessions and in such special sessions as occasion may require. Special sessions shall be convoked by the Secretary-General at the request of the Security Council or of a majority of the Members of the United Nations.

Article 21

The General Assembly shall adopt its own rules of procedure. It shall elect its President for each session.

Article 22

The General Assembly may establish such subsidiary organs as it deems necessary for the performance of its functions.

Chapter V. The Security Council

Article 23

1. The Security Council shall consist of eleven Members of the United Nations. The Republic of China, France, the Union of Soviet Socialist Republics, the United Kingdom of Great Britain and Northern Ireland, and the United States of America shall be permanent members of the Security Council. The General Assembly shall elect six other Members of the United Nations to be non-permanent members of the Security Council, due regard being specially paid, in the first instance to the contribution of Members of the United Nations to the maintenance of international peace and security and to the other purposes of the Organization, and also to equitable geographical distribution.

2. The non-permanent members of the Security Council shall be elected for a term of two years. In the first election of the non-permanent members, however, three shall be chosen for a term of one year. A retiring member shall not be eligible for immediate re-election.

3. Each member of the Security Council shall have one representative.

Article 24

1. In order to ensure prompt and effective action by the United Nations, its Members confer on the Security Council primary responsibility for the maintenance of international peace and security, and agree that in carrying out its duties under this responsibility the Security Council acts on their behalf.

2. In discharging these duties the Security Council shall act in accordance with the Purposes and Principles of the United Nations. The specific powers granted to the Security Council for the discharge of these duties are laid down in Chapters VI, VII, VIII, and XII.

3. The Security Council shall submit annual and, when necessary special reports to the General Assembly for its consideration.

Article 25

The Members of the United Nations agree to accept and carry out the decisions of the Security Council in accordance with the present Charter.

*   *   *

Article 27

1. Each member of the Security Council shall have one vote.

2. Decisions of the Security Council on procedural matters shall be made by an affirmative vote of seven members.

3. Decisions of the Security Council on all other matters shall be made by an affirmative vote of seven members including the concurring votes of the permanent members; provided that, in decisions under Chapter VI, and under paragraph 3 of Article 52, a party to a dispute shall abstain from voting.

Article 28

1. The Security Council shall be so organized as to be able to function continuously. Each member of the Security Council shall for this purpose be represented at all times at the seat of the Organization.

2. The Security Council shall hold periodic meetings at which each of its members may, if it so desires, be represented by a member of the government or by some other specially designated representative.

3. The Security Council may hold meetings at such places other than the seat of the Organization as in its judgment will best facilitate its work.

*   *   *

Chapter VI. Pacific Settlement of Disputes

Article 33

1. The parties to any dispute, the continuance of which is likely to endanger the maintenance of international peace and security, shall, first of all, seek a solution by negotiation, enquiry, mediation, conciliation, arbitration, judicial settlement, resort to regional agencies or arrangements, or other peaceful means of their own choice.

2. The Security Council shall, when it deems necessary, call upon the parties to settle their dispute by such means.

Article 34

The Security Council may investigate any dispute, or any situation which might lead to international friction or give rise to a dispute, in order to determine whether the continuance of the dispute or situation is likely to endanger the maintenance of international peace and security.

Article 35

1. Any Member of the United Nations may bring any dispute, or any situation of the nature referred to in Article 34, to the attention of the Security Council or of the General Assembly.

2. A state which is not a Member of the United Nations may bring to the attention of the Security Council or of the General Assembly any dispute to which it is a party if it accepts in advance, for the purposes of the dispute, the obligations of pacific settlement provided in the present Charter.

3. The proceedings of the General Assembly in respect of matters brought to its attention under this Article will be subject to the provisions of Articles 11 and 12.

* * *

Article 49

The Members of the United Nations shall join in affording mutual assistance in carrying out the measures decided upon by the Security Council.

* * *

Chapter IX. International Economic and Social Co-operation

Article 60

Responsibility for the discharge of the functions of the Organization set forth in this Chapter shall be vested in the General

Assembly and, under the authority of the General Assembly, in the Economic and Social Council, which shall have for this purpose the power set forth in Chapter X.

Chapter X. The Economic and Social Council
Article 61

1. The Economic and Social Council shall consist of eighteen Members of the United Nations elected by the General Assembly.

2. Subject to the provisions of paragraph 3, six members of the Economic and Social Council shall be elected each year for a term of three years. A retiring member shall be eligible for immediate re-election.

3. At the first election, eighteen members of the Economic and Social Council shall be chosen. The term of office of six members so chosen shall expire at the end of one year, and of six other members at the end of two years, in accordance with arrangements made by the General Assembly.

4. Each member of the Economic and Social Council shall have one representative.

*   *   *

Article 69

The Economic and Social Council shall invite any Member of the United Nations to participate, without vote, in its deliberations on any matter of particular concern to that Member.

*   *   *

Chapter XI. Declaration Regarding Non-Self-Governing Territories

Article 73

Members of the United Nations which have or assume responsibilities for the administration of territories whose peoples have not yet attained a full measure of self-government recognize the principle that the interests of the inhabitants of these territories are paramount, and accept as a sacred trust the obligation to promote to the utmost, within the system of international peace and security established by the present Charter, the well-being of the inhabitants of these territories, and, to this end:

(a) to ensure, with due respect for the culture of the peoples concerned, their political, economic, social, and educational advancement, their just treatment, and their protection against abuses;

257

(b) to develop self-government, to take due account of the political aspirations of the peoples, and to assist them in the progressive development of their free political institutions, according to the particular circumstances of each territory and its peoples and their varying stages of advancement;

(c) to further international peace and security;

(d) to promote constructive measures of development, to encourage research, and to co-operate with one another and, when and where appropriate, with specialized international bodies with a view to the practical achievement of the social, economic, and scientific purposes set forth in this Article; and

(e) to transmit regularly to the Secretary-General for information purposes, subject to such limitation as security and constitutional considerations may require, statistical and other information of a technical nature relating to economic, social, and educational conditions in the territories for which they are respectively responsible other than those territories to which Chapters XII and XIII apply.

Article 74

Members of the United Nations also agree that their policy in respect of the territories to which this Chapter applies, no less than in respect of their metropolitan areas, must be based on the general principle of good-neighborliness, due account being taken of the interests and well-being of the rest of the world, in social, economic, and commercial matters.

*   *   *

Chapter XII. International Trusteeship System

Article 85

1. The functions of the United Nations with regard to trusteeship agreements for all areas not designated as strategic, including the approval of the terms of the trusteeship agreements and of their alteration or amendment, shall be exercised by the General Assembly.

2. The Trusteeship Council, operating under the authority of the General Assembly, shall assist the General Assembly in carrying out these functions.

Chapter XIII. The Trusteeship Council

Article 86

1. The Trusteeship Council shall consist of the following Members of the United Nations:

(a) those Members administering trust territories;
(b) such of those Members mentioned by name in Article 23 as are not administering trust territories; and
(c) as many other Members elected for three-year terms by the General Assembly as may be necessary to ensure that the total number of members of the Trusteeship Council is equally divided between those Members of the United Nations which administer trust territories and those which do not.

2. Each member of the Trusteeship Council shall designate one specially qualified person to represent it therein.

*　　　*　　　*

Chapter XIV. The International Court of Justice

Article 92

The International Court of Justice shall be the principal judicial organ of the United Nations. It shall function in accordance with the annexed Statute, which is based upon the Statute of the Permanent Court of International Justice and forms an integral part of the present Charter.

Article 93

1. All Members of the United Nations are *ipso facto* parties to the Statute of the International Court of Justice.

2. A state which is not a Member of the United Nations may become a party to the Statute of the International Court of Justice on conditions to be determined in each case by the General Assembly upon the recommendation of the Security Council.

Article 94

1. Each Member of the United Nations undertakes to comply with the decision of the International Court of Justice in any case to which it is a party.

2. If any party to a case fails to perform the obligations incumbent upon it under a judgment rendered by the Court, the other party may have recourse to the Security Council, which may, if it deems necessary, make recommendations or decide upon measures to be taken to give effect to the judgment.

Article 95

Nothing in the present Charter shall prevent Members of the United Nations from entrusting the solution of their differences to other tribunals by virtue of agreements already in existence or which may be concluded in the future.

Article 96

1. The General Assembly or the Security Council may request the International Court of Justice to give an advisory opinion on any legal question.

2. Other organs of the United Nations and specialized agencies, which may at any time be so authorized by the General Assembly, may also request advisory opinions of the Court on legal questions arising within the scope of their activities.

Chapter XV. The Secretariat

Article 97

The Secretariat shall comprise a Secretary-General and such staff as the Organization may require. The Secretary-General shall be appointed by the General Assembly upon the recommendation of the Security Council. He shall be the chief administrative officer of the Organization.

Article 98

The Secretary-General shall act in that capacity in all meetings of the General Assembly, of the Security Council, of the Economic and Social Council, and of the Trusteeship Council, and shall perform such other functions as are entrusted to him by these organs. The Secretary-General shall make an annual report to the General Assembly on the work of the Organization.

Article 99

The Secretary-General may bring to the attention of the Security Council any matter which in his opinion may threaten the maintenance of international peace and security.

Article 100

1. In the performance of their duties the Secretary-General and the staff shall not seek or receive instructions from any government or from any other authority external to the Organization. They shall refrain from any action which might reflect on their position as international officials responsible only to the Organization.

2. Each Member of the United Nations undertakes to respect the exclusively international character of the responsibilities of the Secretary-General and the staff and not to seek to influence them in the discharge of their responsibilities.

Article 101

1. The staff shall be appointed by the Secretary-General under regulations established by the General Assembly.

2. Appropriate staffs shall be permanently assigned to the Economic and Social Council, the Trusteeship Council, and, as required, to other organs of the United Nations. These staffs shall form a part of the Secretariat.

3. The paramount consideration in the employment of the staff and in the determination of the conditions of service shall be the necessity of securing the highest standards of efficiency, competence, and integrity. Due regard shall be paid to the importance of recruiting the staff on as wide a geographical basis as possible.

* * *

Article 103

In the event of a conflict between the obligations of the Members of the United Nations under the present Charter and their obligations under any other international agreement, their obligations under the present Charter shall prevail.

* * *

Chapter XVIII. Amendments

Article 108

Amendments to the present Charter shall come into force for all Members of the United Nations when they have been adopted by a vote of two-thirds of the members of the General Assembly and ratified in accordance with their respective constitutional processes by two-thirds of the Members of the United Nations, including all the permanent members of the Security Council.

Article 109

1. A general conference of the Members of the United Nations for the purpose of reviewing the present Charter may be held at a date and place to be fixed by a two-thirds vote of the members of the General Assembly and by a vote of any seven members of the Security Council. Each Member of the United Nations shall have one vote in the conference.

2. Any alteration of the present Charter recommended by a two-thirds vote of the conference shall take effect when ratified in accordance with their respective constitutional processes by two-thirds of the Members of the United Nations, including all the permanent members of the Security Council.

3. If such a conference has not been held before the tenth annual session of the General Assembly following the coming into

force of the present Charter, the proposal to call such a conference shall be placed on the agenda of that session of the General Assembly, and the conference shall be held if so decided by a majority vote of the members of the General Assembly and by a vote of any seven members of the Security Council.

* * *

Articles of the Statute of the International Court of Justice quoted or referred to

Chapter I. Organization of the Court

Article 2

The Court shall be composed of a body of independent judges, elected regardless of their nationality from among persons of high moral character, who possess the qualifications required in their respective countries for appointment to the highest judicial offices, or are juris consults of recognized competence in international law.

Article 3

1. The Court shall consist of fifteen members, no two of whom may be nationals of the same state.

2. A person who for the purposes of membership in the Court could be regarded as a national of more than one state shall be deemed to be a national of the one in which he ordinarily exercises civil and political rights.

Article 4

1. The members of the Court shall be elected by the General Assembly and by the Security Council from a list of persons nominated by the national groups in the Permanent Court of Arbitration, in accordance with the following provisions.

2. In the case of Members of the United Nations not represented in the Permanent Court of Arbitration, candidates shall be nominated by national groups appointed for this purpose by their governments under the same conditions as those prescribed for members of the Permanent Court of Arbitration by Article 44 of the Convention of The Hague of 1907 for the pacific settlement of international disputes.

3. The conditions under which a state which is a party to the present Statute but is not a Member of the United Nations may participate in electing the members of the Court shall, in the absence of a special agreement, be laid down by the General Assembly upon recommendation of the Security Council.

Article 5

1. At least three months before the date of the election, the Secretary-General of the United Nations shall address a written request to the members of the Permanent Court of Arbitration belonging to the states which are parties to the present Statute, and to the members of the national groups appointed under Article 4, paragraph 2, inviting them to undertake, within a given time, by national groups, the nomination of persons in a position to accept the duties of a member of the Court,

2. No group may nominate more than four persons, not more than two of whom shall be of their own nationality. In no case may the number of candidates nominated by a group be more than double the number of seats to be filled.

Article 6

Before making these nominations, each national group is recommended to consult its highest court of justice, its legal faculties and schools of law, and its national academies and national sections of international academies devoted to the study of law.

Article 7

1. The Secretary-General shall prepare a list in alphabetical order of all the persons thus nominated. Save as provided in Article 12, paragraph 2, these shall be the only persons eligible.

2. The Secretary-General shall submit this list to the General Assembly and to the Security Council.

Article 8

The General Assembly and the Security Council shall proceed independently of one another to elect the members of the Court.

Article 9

At every election, the electors shall bear in mind not only that the persons to be elected should individually possess the qualifications required, but also that in the body as a whole the representation of the main forms of civilization and of the principal legal systems of the world should be assured.

Article 10

1. Those candidates who obtain an absolute majority of votes in the General Assembly and in the Security Council shall be considered as elected.

2. Any vote of the Security Council, whether for the election of judges or for the appointment of members of the conference envis-

aged in Article 12, shall be taken without any distinction between permanent and non-permanent members of the Security Council.

3. In the event of more than one national of the same state obtaining an absolute majority of the votes both of the General Assembly and of the Security Council, the eldest of these only shall be considered as elected.

Article 11

If, after the first meeting held for the purpose of the election, one or more seats remain to be filled, a second and, if necessary, a third meeting shall take place.

Article 12

1. If, after the third meeting, one or more seats still remain unfilled, a joint conference consisting of six members, three appointed by the General Assembly and three by the Security Council, may be formed at any time at the request of either the General Assembly or the Security Council, for the purpose of choosing by the vote of an absolute majority one name for each seat still vacant, to submit to the General Assembly and the Security Council for their respective acceptance.

2. If the joint conference is unanimously agreed upon any person who fulfils the required conditions, he may be included in its list, even though he was not included in the list of nominations referred to in Article 7.

3. If the joint conference is satisfied that it will not be successful in procuring an election, those members of the Court who have already been elected shall, within a period to be fixed by the Security Council, proceed to fill the vacant seats by selection from among those candidates who have obtained votes either in the General Assembly or in the Security Council.

4. In the event of an equality of votes among the judges, the eldest judge shall have a casting vote.

Article 13

1. The members of the Court shall be elected for nine years and may be re-elected; provided, however, that of the judges elected at the first election, the terms of five judges shall expire at the end of three years and the terms of five more judges shall expire at the end of six years.

2. The judges whose terms are to expire at the end of the above-mentioned initial periods of three and six years shall be chosen by lot to be drawn by the Secretary-General immediately after the first election has been completed.

3. The members of the Court shall continue to discharge their duties until their places have been filled. Though replaced, they shall finish any cases which they may have begun.

4. In the case of the resignation of a member of the Court, the resignation shall be addressed to the President of the Court for transmission to the Secretary-General. This last notification makes the place vacant.

Article 14

Vacancies shall be filled by the same method as that laid down for the first election, subject to the following provision: the Secretary-General shall, within one month of the occurrence of the vacancy, proceed to issue the invitations provided for in Article 5, and the date of the election shall be fixed by the Security Council.

Article 15

A member of the Court elected to replace a member whose term of office has not expired shall hold office for the remainder of his predecessor's term.

* * *

Chapter V. Amendment

Article 69

Amendments to the present Statute shall be effected by the same procedure as is provided by the Charter of the United Nations for amendments to that Charter, subject however to any provisions which the General Assembly upon recommendation of the Security Council may adopt concerning the participation of states which are parties to the present Statute but are not Members of the United Nations.

Appendix 3

General Assembly meetings at which some important procedural questions were discussed.

Subject	Session	Meeting Numbers	Resolution
Provisional Rules of Procedure	1, Part 1	6th Com., mtgs. 2–5, 9, 10; plenary mtgs. 2, 18, 19	17 (I)
Measures to economize time	1, Part 11	Plenary mtg. 67.	102 (I)
	2	6th Com., mtgs. 56, 57; plenary mtg. 118	173 (II)
Methods and Procedures	3, Part 1	*Ad Hoc* Political Com., mtg. 23; plenary mtg. 201	271 (III)
	4	6th Com., mtgs. 142–158, 166; plenary mtgs. 235, 236	362 (IV)
'Uniting for Peace'	5	1st Com., mtgs. 354–371; plenary mtgs. 299–302	377 (V)
Amendments to and parts of proposals relating to 'important questions': majority required	5	6th Com., mtgs. 213, 214; plenary mtg. 290	475 (V)
Methods and procedures for dealing with legal and drafting questions	6	6th Com., mtgs. 256–263, 266, plenary mtg. 356	597 (VI)
	7	6th Com., mtgs. 306–312; plenary mtg. 391	684 (VII)
Measures to limit the duration of regular sessions	6	5th Com., mtg. 340; plenary mtg. 373	
	7	6th Com., mtgs. 346–354; plenary mtgs. 387, 388, 410	689 (VII)

Subject	Session	Meeting Numbers	Resolution
	8	6th Com., mtgs. 360–366; plenary mtg. 453	791 (VIII)
Reports and petitions from S.W. Africa	9	4th Com., mtgs. 399–403; plenary mtg. 494	844 (IX)
Correction of votes	9	6th Com., mtg. 439; plenary mtg. 512	901 (IX)
	10	6th Com., mtgs. 455–458; plenary mtg. 549	983 (X)
Number of Vice-Presidents; composition of the General Committee		Special Political Com., mtgs. 79–83; 6th Com. mtg. 480; plenary mtg. 623	1104 (XI)
	12	Plenary mtg. 728	1192 (XII)
Presidency: equitable geographical distribution	14	Special Political Com., mtgs. 163–169; plenary mtg. 852	
Composition of the Trusteeship Council	15	Plenary mtg. 979	
Enlargement of the Advisory Committee on Administrative and Budgetary Questions	16	5th Com., mtgs. 866–868; plenary mtg. 1067	1659 (XVI)
Methods of work	18	Plenary mtg. 1256	1898 (XVIII)
Mechanical means of voting	18	5th Com., mtgs. 1043, 1044; plenary mtg. 1278	1957 (XVIII)
Composition of the General Committee	18	Special Political Com. mtgs. 419–429; plenary mtg. 1285	1990 (XVIII)

Successive Texts of the
Rules of Procedure
of the General Assembly

13. As amended during the twelfth session by resolution 1192 (12 Dec. 1957) — A/520/Rev. 6; A/4700

14. As amended during the sixteenth session by resolution 1659 (28 Nov. 1961) — A/520/Rev. 6 and Corr. 1; A/4700/ Corr. 1

15. As amended during the eighteenth session by resolution 1990 (17 Dec. 1963) — A/520/Rev. 7

Rules of Procedure
of the General Assembly[362]
(embodying amendments and additions adopted by the
General Assembly up to and including its eighteenth
session)

EXPLANATORY NOTES

1. The Table of Contents, Introduction, Annexes I and II, and the Index to the Rules of Procedure, are not reproduced here.
2. Rules 49, 84, 85, 87, 145, 147, and 162, which reproduce textually provisions of the Charter, are printed in heavy type and are, in addition, provided with a footnote. A footnote has also been added in the case of other Rules which, based directly on provisions of the Charter, do not reproduce those provisions textually.
3. Rules for committee meetings which are identical or similar to Rules for plenary meetings are not reproduced. Rules 98–105, 110, 126, 133 and 134 for committee meetings differ from the corresponding Rules for plenary meetings and are therefore reproduced. Figures between square brackets in sections dealing with Rules for plenary meetings refer to identical or corresponding Rules for committee meetings, and vice versa.
4. Rule 163 states that 'The . . . notes in italics to these rules shall be disregarded in the interpretation of the rules.'

I. SESSIONS

REGULAR SESSIONS

Date of meeting

RULE 1*

The General Assembly shall meet every year in regular session commencing on the third Tuesday in September.

Duration of session

RULE 2

On the recommendation of the General Committee, the General Assembly shall, at the beginning of each session, fix a closing date for the session.

* Rule based directly on a provision of the Charter (Art. 20).

Place of meeting

RULE 3

Sessions shall be held at the Headquarters of the United Nations unless convened elsewhere in pursuance of a decision of the General Assembly at a previous session or at the request of a majority of the Members of the United Nations.

RULE 4

Any Member of the United Nations may, at least one hundred and twenty days before the date fixed for the opening of a regular session, request that the session be held elsewhere than at the Headquarters of the United Nations. The Secretary-General shall immediately communicate the request, together with his recommendations, to the other Members of the United Nations. If within thirty days of the date of his communication a majority of the Members concur in the request, the session shall be held accordingly.

Notification of session

RULE 5

The Secretary-General shall notify the Members of the United Nations, at least sixty days in advance, of the opening of a regular session.

Adjournment of session

RULE 6

The General Assembly may decide at any session to adjourn temporarily and resume its meetings at a later date.

Special sessions

Summoning by the General Assembly

RULE 7*

The General Assembly may fix a date for a special session.

Summoning on request from the Security Council or Members

RULE 8

(*a*) Special sessions of the General Assembly shall be held within fifteen days of the receipt by the Secretary-General of a request for such a session from the Security Council, or of a request from a majority of the Members of the United Nations, or of the concurrence of a majority of Members as provided in rule 9.

(*b*) Emergency special sessions pursuant to General Assembly resolution 377 A (V) shall be convened within twenty-four hours of

---

* Rule based directly on a provision of the Charter (Art. 20).

the receipt by the Secretary-General of a request for such a session from the Security Council, on the vote of any seven members thereof, or of a request from a majority of the Members of the United Nations expressed by vote in the Interim Committee or otherwise, or of the concurrence of a majority of Members as provided in rule 9.

Request by Members
RULE 9

(*a*) Any Member of the United Nations may request the Secretary-General to summon a special session. The Secretary-General shall immediately inform the other Members of the United Nations of the request and inquire whether they concur in it. If within thirty days of the date of the communication of the Secretary-General a majority of the Members concur in the request, a special session of the General Assembly shall be summoned in accordance with rule 8.

(*b*) This rule shall apply also to a request by any Member for an emergency special session pursuant to resolution 377 A (V). In such a case the Secretary-General shall communicate with the other Members by the most expeditious means of communication available.

Notification of session
RULE 10

The Secretary-General shall notify the Members of the United Nations, at least fourteen days in advance, of the opening of a special session summoned at the request of the Security Council, and, at least ten days in advance, in the case of a request by a majority of the Members or the concurrence of a majority in the request of any Member. In the case of an emergency special session convened pursuant to rule 8 (*b*), the Secretary-General shall notify the Members of the United Nations at least twelve hours in advance of the opening of the session.

Notification to other bodies
RULE 11

Copies of the notice summoning each session shall be addressed to all other principal organs of the United Nations and to the specialized agencies referred to in Article 57, paragraph 2, of the Charter.

II. AGENDA

REGULAR SESSIONS

Provisional agenda

RULE 12

The provisional agenda for a regular session shall be drawn up by the Secretary-General and communicated to the Members of the United Nations at least sixty days before the opening of the session.

RULE 13

The provisional agenda of a regular session shall include:

(*a*) Report of the Secretary-General on the work of the Organization;

(*b*) Reports from the Security Council,
> the Economic and Social Council,
> the Trusteeship Council,
> the International Court of Justice,
> the subsidiary organs of the General Assembly,
> specialized agencies (where such reports are called for under agreements entered into);

(*c*) All items the inclusion of which has been ordered by the General Assembly at a previous session;

(*d*) All items proposed by the other principal organs of the United Nations;

(*e*) All items proposed by any Member of the United Nations;

(*f*) All items pertaining to the budget for the next financial year and the report on the accounts for the last financial year;

(*g*) All items which the Secretary-General deems it necessary to put before the General Assembly; and

(*h*) All items proposed under Article 35, paragraph 2, of the Charter by States not Members of the United Nations.

Supplementary items

RULE 14

Any Member or principal organ of the United Nations or the Secretary-General may, at least thirty days before the date fixed for the opening of a regular session, request the inclusion of supplementary items in the agenda. These items shall be placed on a supplementary list, which shall be communicated to the Members of the United Nations at least twenty days before the date fixed for the opening of the session.

Additional items

RULE 15

Additional items of an important and urgent character, proposed for inclusion in the agenda less than thirty days before the opening of a regular session or during a regular session, may be placed on the agenda, if the General Assembly so decides by a majority of the Members present and voting. No additional item may be considered until seven days have elapsed since it was placed on the agenda, unless the General Assembly, by a two-thirds majority of the Members present and voting, decides otherwise, and until a committee has reported upon the question concerned.

SPECIAL SESSIONS

Provisional agenda

RULE 16

The provisional agenda of a special session, summoned at the request of the Security Council, shall be communicated to the Members of the United Nations at least fourteen days before the opening of the session. The provisional agenda of a special session summoned at the request of a majority of the Members, or the concurrence of a majority in the request of any Member, shall be communicated at least ten days before the opening of the session. The provisional agenda of an emergency special session shall be communicated to the Members of the United Nations simultaneously with the communication summoning the session.

RULE 17

The provisional agenda for a special session shall consist only of those items proposed for consideration in the request for the holding of the session.

Supplementary items

RULE 18

Any Member or principal organ of the United Nations or the Secretary-General may, at least four days before the date fixed for the opening of a special session, request the inclusion of supplementary items in the agenda. Such items shall be placed on a supplementary list which shall be communicated to the Members of the United Nations as soon as possible.

Additional items

RULE 19

During a special session items on the supplementary list and additional items may be added to the agenda by a two-thirds majority of the Members present and voting. During an emergency special session additional items concerning the matters dealt with in resolution 377 A (V) may be added to the agenda by a two-thirds majority of the Members present and voting.

Explanatory memoranda

RULE 20

All items proposed for inclusion in the agenda shall be accompanied by an explanatory memorandum and, if possible, by basic documents or by a draft resolution.

Approval of the agenda

RULE 21

At each session the provisional agenda and the supplementary list, together with the report of the General Committee thereon, shall be submitted to the General Assembly for approval as soon as possible after the opening of the session.

Amendment and deletion of items

RULE 22

Items on the agenda may be amended or deleted by the General Assembly by a majority of the Members present and voting.

Debate on inclusion of items

RULE 23

Debate on the inclusion of an item in the agenda, when that item has been recommended for inclusion by the General Committee, shall be limited to three speakers in favour of and three against the inclusion. The President may limit the time to be allowed to speakers under this rule.

Modification of the allocation of expenses

RULE 24

No proposal for a modification of the allocation of expenses for the time being in force shall be placed on the agenda unless it has been communicated to the Members of the United Nations at least ninety days before the date fixed for the opening of the session.

III. DELEGATIONS

Composition

RULE 25*

The delegation of a Member shall consist of not more than five representatives and five alternate representatives, and as many

* Rule based directly on a provision of the Charter (Art. 9, para. 2).

advisers, technical advisers, experts and persons of similar status as may be required by the delegation.

Alternates

RULE 26

An alternate representative may act as a representative upon designation by the Chairman of the delegation.

IV. CREDENTIALS

Submission of credentials

RULE 27

The credentials of representatives, and the names of members of a delegation shall be submitted to the Secretary-General if possible not less than one week before the date fixed for the opening of the session. The credentials shall be issued either by the Head of the State or Government or by the Minister for Foreign Affairs.

Credentials Committee

RULE 28

A Credentials Committee shall be appointed at the beginning of each session. It shall consist of nine members, who shall be appointed by the General Assembly on the proposal of the President. The Committee shall elect its own officers. It shall examine the credentials of representatives and report without delay.

Provisional admission to a session

RULE 29

Any representative to whose admission a Member has made objection shall be seated provisionally with the same rights as other representatives, until the Credentials Committee has reported and the General Assembly has given its decision.

V. PRESIDENT AND VICE-PRESIDENTS

Temporary President

RULE 30

At the opening of each session of the General Assembly the Chairman of that delegation from which the President of the previous session was elected shall preside until the General Assembly has elected a President for the session.

Elections

RULE 31

The General Assembly shall elect a President and seventeen Vice-Presidents, who shall hold office until the close of the session at which they are elected.* The Vice-Presidents shall be elected, after the election of the Chairmen of the seven Main Committees referred to in rule 101, on the basis of ensuring the representative character of the General Committee.

Acting President

RULE 32 [107]

If the President finds it necessary to be absent during a meeting or any part thereof, he shall appoint one of the Vice-Presidents to take his place.

RULE 33 [107]

A Vice-President acting as President shall have the same powers and duties as the President.

Replacement of the President

RULE 34 [107]

If the President is unable to perform his functions, a new President shall be elected for the unexpired term.

General powers of the President

RULE 35 [108]

In addition to exercising the powers which are conferred upon him elsewhere by these rules, the President shall declare the opening and closing of each plenary meeting of the session, shall direct the discussions in plenary meeting, ensure observance of these rules, accord the right to speak, put questions and announce decisions. He shall rule on points of order, and, subject to these rules, shall have complete control of the proceedings at any meeting and over the maintenance of order thereat. The President may, in the course of

* Rule based directly on a provision of the Charter (Art. 21, second sentence).
In the Annex to resolution 1990 (XVIII), the General Assembly decided as follows:

1. In the election of the President of the General Assembly, regard shall be had for equitable geographical rotation of this office among the following four regions: African and Asian States, Eastern European States, Latin American States, Western European and other States.

2. The seventeen Vice-Presidents shall be elected according to the following pattern, subject to paragraph 3 below:
(a) Seven from African and Asian States;
(b) One from Eastern European States;
(c) Three from Latin American States;
(d) Two from Western European and other States;
(e) Five from the permanent members of the Security Council.

3. The region from which the President is elected will, however, reduce by one the number of Vice-Presidents allocated in paragraph 2 of the present annex.

the discussion of an item, propose to the General Assembly the limitation of the time to be allowed to speakers, the limitation of the number of times each representative may speak on any question, the closure of the list of speakers or the closure of the debate. He may also propose the suspension or the adjournment of the meeting or the adjournment of the debate on the item under discussion.

RULE 36 [109]

The President, in the exercise of his functions, remains under the authority of the General Assembly.

The President shall not vote

RULE 37 [106]

The President, or Vice-President acting as President, shall not vote but shall appoint another member of his delegation to vote in his place.

VI. GENERAL COMMITTEE

Composition

RULE 38

The General Committee shall comprise the President of the General Assembly, who shall preside, the seventeen Vice-Presidents and the Chairmen of the seven Main Committees. No two members of the General Committee shall be members of the same delegation, and it shall be so constituted as to ensure its representative character.* Chairmen of other committees, upon which all Members have the right to be represented and which are established by the General Assembly to meet during the session, shall be entitled to attend meetings of the General Committee and may participate without vote in the discussion.

Substitute members

RULE 39

If a Vice-President of the General Assembly finds it necessary to be absent during a meeting of the General Committee he may designate a member of his delegation as his substitute. The Chairman of a Main Committee shall, in case of absence, designate the Vice-Chairman of the Committee as his substitute. A Vice-Chairman shall not have the right to vote if he is of the same delegation as another member of the Committee.

Functions

RULE 40

The General Committee shall, at the beginning of each session,

* See Rules 31 and 105.

consider the provisional agenda, together with the supplementary list, and shall make recommendations to the General Assembly with regard to each item proposed, concerning its inclusion in the agenda, the rejection of the request for inclusion, or the inclusion of the item in the provisional agenda of a future session. It shall, in the same manner, examine requests for the inclusion of additional items in the agenda, and shall make recommendations thereon to the General Assembly. In considering matters relating to the agenda of the General Assembly, the General Committee shall not discuss the substance of any item, except in so far as this bears upon the question whether the General Committee should recommend the inclusion of the item in the agenda, the rejection of the request for inclusion, or the inclusion of the item in the provisional agenda of a future session, and what priority should be accorded to an item the inclusion of which has been recommended.

RULE 41

The General Committee shall make recommendations to the General Assembly concerning the closing date of the session. It shall assist the President and the General Assembly in drawing up the agenda for each plenary meeting, in determining the priority of its items, and in the co-ordination of the proceedings of all committees of the General Assembly. It shall assist the President in the general conduct of the work of the General Assembly which falls within the competence of the President. It shall not, however, decide any political question.

RULE 42

The General Committee shall meet periodically throughout each session to review the progress of the General Assembly and its committees and to make recommendations for furthering such progress. It shall also meet at such other times as the President deems necessary or upon the request of any other of its members.

Participation by representatives of Members requesting the inclusion of items in the agenda

RULE 43

A Member of the General Assembly which has no representative on the General Committee, and which has requested the inclusion of an item in the agenda, shall be entitled to attend any meeting of the General Committee at which its request is discussed, and may participate, without vote, in the discussion of that item.

Formal revision of resolutions of the General Assembly

RULE 44

The General Committee may revise the resolutions adopted by

the General Assembly, changing their form but not their substance. Any such changes shall be reported to the General Assembly for its consideration.

VII. SECRETARIAT

Duties of the Secretary-General

RULE 45

The Secretary-General shall act in that capacity in all meetings of the General Assembly,* its committees and sub-committees. He may designate a member of the staff to act in his place at these meetings.

RULE 46

The Secretary-General shall provide and direct the staff required by the General Assembly and any committees or subsidiary organs which it may establish.

Duties of the Secretariat

RULE 47

The Secretariat shall receive, translate, print and distribute documents, reports and resolutions of the General Assembly, its committees and organs; interpret speeches made at the meetings; prepare, print and circulate the summary records of the session; have the custody and proper preservation of the documents in the archives of the General Assembly; publish the reports of the meetings; distribute all documents of the General Assembly to the Members of the United Nations, and, generally, perform all other work which the General Assembly may require.

Annual report of the Secretary-General

RULE 48

The Secretary-General shall make an annual report, and such supplementary reports as are required, to the General Assembly on the work of the Organization.* He shall communicate the annual report to the Members of the United Nations at least forty-five days before the opening of the session.

Notification under Article 12 of the Charter

RULE 49†

THE SECRETARY-GENERAL, WITH THE CONSENT OF THE SECURITY COUNCIL, SHALL NOTIFY THE GENERAL ASSEMBLY AT EACH SESSION OF

---

* Rules based directly on a provision of the Charter (Art. 98).
† Rule reproducing textually a provision of the Charter (Art. 12, para. 2).

ANY MATTERS RELATIVE TO THE MAINTENANCE OF INTERNATIONAL PEACE AND SECURITY WHICH ARE BEING DEALT WITH BY THE SECURITY COUNCIL, AND SHALL SIMILARLY NOTIFY THE GENERAL ASSEMBLY, OR THE MEMBERS OF THE UNITED NATIONS IF THE GENERAL ASSEMBLY IS NOT IN SESSION, IMMEDIATELY THE SECURITY COUNCIL CEASES TO DEAL WITH SUCH MATTERS.

Regulations concerning the Secretariat

RULE 50*

The General Assembly shall establish regulations concerning the staff of the Secretariat.

Official and working languages

RULE 51

Chinese, English, French, Russian and Spanish shall be the official languages of the General Assembly, its committees and sub-committees. English, French and Spanish shall be the working languages.

Interpretation from a working language

RULE 52

Speeches made in any of the working languages shall be interpreted into the other two working languages.

Interpretation from official languages

RULE 53

Speeches made in either of the other two official languages shall be interpreted into the three working languages.

Interpretation from other languages

RULE 54

Any representative may make a speech in a language other than the official languages. In this case, he shall himself provide for interpretation into one of the working languages. Interpretation into the other working languages by the interpreters of the Secretariat may be based on the interpretation given in the first working language.

Language of verbatim records

RULE 55

Verbatim records shall be drawn up in the working languages. A translation of the whole or part of any verbatim record into either of the other two official languages shall be furnished if requested by any delegation.

* Rule based directly on a provision of the Charter (Art. 101, para. 1).

Language of summary records

RULE 56

Summary records shall be drawn up as soon as possible in the official languages.

Language of Journal

RULE 57

The Journal of the General Assembly shall be issued in the working languages.

Language of resolutions and important documents

RULE 58

All resolutions and other important documents shall be made available in the official languages. Upon the request of any representative, any other document shall be made available in any or all of the official languages.

Publications in languages other than the official languages

RULE 59

Documents of the General Assembly, its committees and sub-committees, shall, if the General Assembly so decides, be published in any languages other than the official languages.

IX. RECORDS

Verbatim records

RULE 60

Verbatim records of all plenary meetings shall be drawn up by the Secretariat and submitted to the General Assembly after approval by the President. Verbatim records shall also be made of the proceedings of the Main Committees established by the General Assembly. Other committees or sub-committees may decide upon the form of their records.

Resolutions

RULE 61

Resolutions adopted by the General Assembly shall be communicated by the Secretary-General to the Members of the United Nations within fifteen days after the termination of the session.

X. PUBLIC AND PRIVATE MEETINGS: PLENARY MEETINGS; MEETINGS OF COMMITTEES AND SUB-COMMITTEES

General principles

RULE 62

The meetings of the General Assembly and its Main Committees shall be held in public unless the body concerned decides that exceptional circumstances require that the meeting be held in private. Meetings of other committees and sub-committees shall also be held in public unless the body concerned decides otherwise.

Private meetings

RULE 63

All decisions of the General Assembly taken at a private meeting shall be announced at an early public meeting of the General Assembly. At the close of each private meeting of the Main Committees, other committees and sub-committees, the Chairman may issue a communiqué through the Secretary-General.

XI. MINUTE OF SILENT PRAYER OR MEDITATION

Invitation to silent prayer or meditation

RULE 64

Immediately after the opening of the first plenary meeting and immediately preceding the closing of the final plenary meeting of each session of the General Assembly, the President shall invite the representatives to observe one minute of silence dedicated to prayer or meditation.

XII. PLENARY MEETINGS
CONDUCT OF BUSINESS

Emergency special sessions

RULE 65

Notwithstanding the provisions of any other rule and unless the General Assembly decides otherwise, the Assembly, in case of an emergency special session, shall convene in plenary session only and proceed directly to consider the item proposed for consideration in the request for the holding of the session, without previous reference to the General Committee or to any other committee; the President and Vice-Presidents for such emergency special sessions shall be, respectively, the Chairmen of those delegations from which were elected the President and Vice-Presidents of the previous session.

Report of the Secretary-General

RULE 66

Proposals to refer any portion of the report of the Secretary-General to one of the Main Committees without debate shall be decided upon by the General Assembly without previous reference to the General Committee.

Reference to committees

RULE 67

The General Assembly shall not, unless it decides otherwise, make a final decision upon any item on the agenda until it has received the report of a committee on that item.

Discussion of committee reports

RULE 68

Discussion of a report of a Main Committee in a plenary meeting of the General Assembly shall take place if at least one-third of the Members present and voting at the plenary meeting consider such a discussion to be necessary. Any proposal to this effect shall not be debated, but shall be immediately put to the vote.

Quorum

RULE 69 [110]

A majority of the Members of the General Assembly shall con-constitute a quorum.

RULE 70 [111]

No representative may address the General Assembly without having previously obtained the permission of the President. The President shall call upon speakers in the order in which they signify their desire to speak. The President may call a speaker to order if his remarks are not relevant to the subject under discussion.

Precedence

RULE 71 [112]

The Chairman and the Rapporteur of a committee may be accorded precedence for the purpose of explaining the conclusion arrived at by their committee.

Statements by the Secretariat

RULE 72 [113]

The Secretary-General, or a member of the Secretariat designated by him as his representative, may, at any time, make either oral or written statements to the General Assembly concerning any question under consideration by it.

Points of order

RULE 73 [114]

During the discussion of any matter, a representative may rise to a point of order, and the point of order shall be immediately decided by the President in accordance with the rules of procedure. A representative may appeal against the ruling of the President. The appeal shall be immediately put to the vote and the President's ruling shall stand unless overruled by a majority of the Members present and voting. A representative rising to a point of order may not speak on the substance of the matter under discussion.

Time limit on speeches

RULE 74 [115]

The General Assembly may limit the time to be allowed to each speaker and the number of times each representative may speak on any question. When debate is limited and a representative has spoken his allotted time, the President shall call him to order without delay.

Closing of list of speakers

RULE 75 [116]

During the course of a debate the President may announce the list of speakers and, with the consent of the General Assembly, declare the list closed. He may, however, accord the right of reply to any Member if a speech delivered after he has declared the list closed makes this desirable.

Adjournment of debate

RULE 76 [117]

During the discussion of any matter, a representative may move the adjournment of the debate on the item under discussion. In addition to the proposer of the motion, two representatives may speak in favour of, and two against, the motion, after which the motion shall be immediately put to the vote. The President may limit the time to be allowed to speakers under this rule.

Closure of debate

RULE 77 [118]

A representative may at any time move the closure of the debate on the item under discussion, whether or not any other representative has signified his wish to speak. Permission to speak on the closure of the debate shall be accorded only to two speakers opposing the closure, after which the motion shall be immediately put to the vote. If the General Assembly is in favour of the closure, the President shall declare the closure of the debate. The President may limit the time to be allowed to speakers under this rule.

Suspension or adjournment of the meeting

RULE 78 [119]

During the discussion of any matter, a representative may move the suspension or the adjournment of the meeting. Such motions shall not be debated, but shall be immediately put to the vote. The President may limit the time to be allowed to the speaker moving the suspension or adjournment of the meeting.

Order of procedural motions

RULE 79 [120]

Subject to rule 73, the following motions shall have precedence in the following order over all other proposals or motions before the meeting:

    (*a*) To suspend the meeting;
    (*b*) To adjourn the meeting;
    (*c*) To adjourn the debate on the item under discussion;
    (*d*) For the closure of the debate on the item under discussion.

Proposals and amendments

RULE 80 [121]

Proposals and amendments shall normally be introduced in writing and handed to the Secretary-General, who shall circulate copies to the delegations. As a general rule, no proposal shall be dis cussed or put to the vote at any meeting of the General Assembly unless copies of it have been circulated to all delegations not later than the day preceding the meeting. The President may, however, permit the discussion and consideration of amendments, or of motions as to procedure, even though these amendments and motions have not been circulated or have only been circulated the same day.

Decisions on competence

RULE 81 [122]

Subject to rule 79, any motion calling for a decision on the com petence of the General Assembly to adopt a proposal submitted to it shall be put to the vote before a vote is taken on the proposal in question.

Withdrawal of motions

RULE 82 [123]

A motion may be withdrawn by its proposer at any time before voting on it has commenced, provided that the motion has not been amended. A motion which has thus been withdrawn may be reintro duced by any Member.

Reconsideration of proposals

RULE 83 [124]

When a proposal has been adopted or rejected it may not be reconsidered at the same session unless the General Assembly, by a two-thirds majority of the Members present and voting, so decides.

Permission to speak on a motion to reconsider shall be accorded only to two speakers opposing the motion, after which it shall be immediately put to the vote.

VOTING

Voting rights

RULE 84* [125]

EACH MEMBER OF THE GENERAL ASSEMBLY SHALL HAVE ONE VOTE.

Two-thirds majority

RULE 85*

DECISIONS OF THE GENERAL ASSEMBLY ON IMPORTANT QUESTIONS SHALL BE MADE BY A TWO-THIRDS MAJORITY OF THE MEMBERS PRESENT AND VOTING. THESE QUESTIONS SHALL INCLUDE: RECOMMENDATIONS WITH RESPECT TO THE MAINTENANCE OF INTERNATIONAL PEACE AND SECURITY, THE ELECTION OF THE NON-PERMANENT MEMBERS OF THE SECURITY COUNCIL, THE ELECTION OF THE MEMBERS OF THE ECO-NOMIC AND SOCIAL COUNCIL, THE ELECTION OF MEMBERS OF THE TRUSTEESHIP COUNCIL IN ACCORDANCE WITH PARAGRAPH IC OF ARTICLE 86 OF THE CHARTER, THE ADMISSION OF NEW MEMBERS TO THE UNITED NATIONS, THE SUSPENSION OF THE RIGHTS AND PRIVILEGES OF MEMBERSHIP, THE EXPULSION OF MEMBERS, QUESTIONS RELATING TO THE OPERATION OF THE TRUSTEESHIP SYSTEM, AND BUDGETARY QUESTIONS.

RULE 86

Decisions of the General Assembly on amendments to proposals relating to important questions, and on parts of such proposals put to the vote separately, shall be made by a two-thirds majority of the Members present and voting.

Simple majority

RULE 87* [126]

DECISIONS OF THE GENERAL ASSEMBLY ON QUESTIONS OTHER THAN THOSE PROVIDED FOR IN RULE 85, INCLUDING THE DETERMINA-TION OF ADDITIONAL CATEGORIES OF QUESTIONS TO BE DECIDED BY A TWO-THIRDS MAJORITY, SHALL BE MADE BY A MAJORITY OF THE MEMBERS PRESENT AND VOTING.

Meaning of the expression 'Members present and voting'

RULE 88 [127]

For the purpose of these rules, the phrase 'Members present and

* Rules 84, 85, and 87 reproduce the three paragraphs of Art. 18 of the Charter.

voting' means Members casting an affirmative or negative vote. Members which abstain from voting are considered as not voting.

Method of voting

RULE 89 [128]

The General Assembly shall normally vote by show of hands or by standing, but any representative may request a roll-call. The roll-call shall be taken in the English alphabetical order of the names of the Members, beginning with the Member whose name is drawn by lot by the President. The name of each Member shall be called in any roll-call and one of its representatives shall reply 'Yes', 'No' or 'Abstention'. The result of the voting shall be inserted in the record in the English alphabetical order of the names of the Members.

Conduct during voting

RULE 90 [129]

After the President has announced the beginning of voting, no representative shall interrupt the voting except on a point of order in connexion with the actual conduct of the voting. The President may permit Members to explain their votes, either before or after the voting, except when the vote is taken by secret ballot. The President may limit the time to be allowed for such explanations. The President shall not permit the proposer of a proposal or of an amendment to explain his vote on his own proposal or amendment.

Division of proposals and amendments

RULE 91 [130]

A representative may move that parts of a proposal or of an amendment shall be voted on separately. If objection is made to the request for division, the motion for division shall be voted upon. Permission to speak on the motion for division shall be given only to two speakers in favour and two speakers against. If the motion for division is carried, those parts of the proposal or of the amendment which are subsequently approved shall be put to the vote as a whole. If all operative parts of the proposal or of the amendment have been rejected, the proposal or the amendment shall be considered to have been rejected as a whole.

Voting on amendments

RULE 92 [131]

When an amendment is moved to a proposal, the amendment shall be voted on first. When two or more amendments are moved to a proposal, the General Assembly shall first vote on the amendment furthest removed in substance from the original proposal and then on the amendment next furthest removed therefrom, and so on, until all the amendments have been put to the vote. Where, however, the adoption of one amendment necessarily implies the rejection of another amendment, the latter amendment shall not be put to the vote. If one or more amendments are adopted, the amended proposal shall then be voted upon. A motion is considered an amendment to a proposal if it merely adds to, deletes from or revises part of that proposal.

Voting on proposals

RULE 93 [132]

If two or more proposals relate to the same question, the General Assembly shall, unless it decides otherwise, vote on the proposals in the order in which they have been submitted. The General Assembly may, after each vote on a proposal, decide whether to vote on the next proposal.

Elections

RULE 94 [105]

All elections shall be held by secret ballot. There shall be no nominations.

RULE 95 [133]

When only one person or Member is to be elected and no candidate obtains in the first ballot the majority required, a second ballot shall be taken which shall be restricted to the two candidates obtaining the largest number of votes. If in the second ballot the votes are equally divided, and a majority is required, the President shall decide between the candidates by drawing lots. If a two-thirds majority is required, the balloting shall be continued until one candidate secures two-thirds of the votes cast; provided that, after the third inconclusive ballot, votes may be cast for any eligible person or Member. If three such unrestricted ballots are inconclusive, the next three ballots shall be restricted to the two candidates who obtained the greatest number of votes in the third of the unrestricted ballots, and the following three ballots thereafter shall be unrestricted, and so on until a person or Member is elected. These provisions shall not prejudice the application of rules 144, 145, 147 and 149.

RULE 96

When two or more elective places are to be filled at one time under the same conditions, those candidates obtaining in the first ballot the majority required shall be elected. If the number of candidates obtaining such majority is less than the number of persons or Members to be elected, there shall be additional ballots to fill the remaining places, the voting being restricted to the candidates obtaining the greatest number of votes in the previous ballot, to a number not more than twice the places remaining to be filled; provided that, after the third inconclusive ballot, votes may be cast for any eligible person or Member. If three such unrestricted ballots are inconclusive, the next three ballots shall be restricted to the candidates who obtained the greatest number of votes in the third of the unrestricted ballots, to a number not more than twice the places remaining to be filled, and the following three ballots thereafter shall be unrestricted, and so on until all the places have been filled. These provision shall not prejudice the application of rules, 144, 145, 147 and 149.

Equally divided votes

RULE 97 [134]

If a vote is equally divided on matters other than elections, a second vote shall be taken at a subsequent meeting which shall be held within forty-eight hours of the first vote, and it shall be expressly mentioned in the agenda that a second vote will be taken on the matter in question. If this vote also results in equality, the proposal shall be regarded as rejected.

XIII. COMMITTEES

Creation

RULE 98

The General Assembly may set up such committees as it deems necessary for the performance of its functions.

Categories of subjects

RULE 99

Items relating to the same category of subjects shall be referred to the committee or committees dealing with that category of subjects. Committees shall not introduce new items on their own initiative.

Priorities

RULE 100

Each Main Committee, taking into account the closing date for the session fixed by the General Assembly on the recommendation of the General Committee, shall adopt its own priorities and meet as may be necessary to complete the consideration of the items referred to it.

Main Committees

RULE 101

The Main Committees of the General Assembly are:

(*a*) Political and Security Committee (including the regulation of armaments) (First Committee);
(*b*) Special Political Committee;
(*c*) Economic and Financial Committee (Second Committee);
(*d*) Social, Humanitarian and Cultural Committee (Third Committee);
(*e*) Trusteeship Committee (including Non-Self-Governing Territories) (Fourth Committee);
(*f*) Administrative and Budgetary Committee (Fifth Committee);
(*g*) Legal Committee (Sixth Committee).

Representation of Members

RULE 102

Each Member may be represented by one person on each Main Committee and on any other committee that may be constituted upon which all Members have the right to be represented. It may also assign to these committees advisers, technical advisers, experts or persons of similar status.

RULE 103

Upon designation by the Chairman of the delegation, advisers, technical advisers, experts or persons of similar status may act as members of committees. Persons of this status shall not, however, unless designated as alternate representatives, be eligible for appointment as Chairmen, Vice-Chairmen or Rapporteurs of committees or for seats in the General Assembly.

Sub-committees

RULE 104

Each committee may set up sub-committees, which shall elect their own officers.

Officers

RULE 105 [94]

Each committee shall elect its own Chairman, Vice-Chairman and Rapporteur. These officers shall be elected on the basis of equitable geographical distribution, experience and personal competence.*These elections shall be held by secret ballot.

* In the Annex to resolution 1990 (XVIII), the General Assembly decided that the seven Chairmen of the Main Committees should be elected according to the following pattern:
(*a*) Three representatives from African and Asian States;
(*b*) One representative from Eastern European States;
(*c*) One representative from Latin American States;
(*d*) One representative from Western European and other States;
(*e*) The seventh chairmanship shall rotate every alternate year among representatives of States mentioned in (*c*) and (*d*) above.

The Chairman of a Main Committee shall not vote
RULE 106 [37]

Absence of officers
RULE 107 [32–34]

Functions of the Chairman
RULES 108 and 109 [35 and 36]

Quorum
RULE 110 [69]

One third of the members of a committee shall constitute a quorum. The presence of a majority of the members of the committee is, however, required for a question to be put to the vote.

Speeches
RULE 111 [70]

Precedence
RULE 112 [71]

Statements by the Secretariat
RULE 113 [72]

Points of order
RULE 114 [73]

Time limit on speeches
RULE 115 [74]

Closing of list of speakers
RULE 116 [75]

Adjournment of debate
RULE 117 [76]

Closure of debate
RULE 118 [77]

Suspension or adjournment of the meeting
RULE 119 [78]

Order of procedural motions
RULE 120 [79]

Proposals and amendments
RULE 121 [80]

Decisions on competence
RULE 122 [81]

Withdrawal of motions
RULE 123 [82]

Reconsideration of proposals
RULE 124 [83]

Voting rights
RULE 125 [84]

Majority required

RULE 126 [87]

Decisions in the committees of the General Assembly shall be made by a majority of the members present and voting.

Meaning of the expression 'members present and voting'

RULE 127 [88]

Method of voting

RULE 128 [89]

Conduct during voting

RULE 129 [90]

Division of proposals and amendments

RULE 130 [91]

Voting on amendments

RULE 131 [92]

Voting on proposals

RULE 132 [93]

Elections

RULE 133 [95]

When only one person or member is to be elected and no candidate obtains in the first ballot the majority required, a second ballot shall be taken, which shall be restricted to the two candidates obtaining the largest number of votes. If in the second ballot the votes are equally divided, and a majority is required, the Chairman shall decide between the candidates by drawing lots.

Equally divided votes

RULE 134 [97]

If a vote is equally divided on matters other than elections, the proposal shall be regarded as rejected.

XIV. ADMISSION OF NEW MEMBERS TO THE UNITED NATIONS

Applications

RULE 135

Any State which desires to become a Member of the United Nations shall submit an application to the Secretary-General. This application shall contain a declaration, made in a formal instrument, that it accepts the obligations contained in the Charter.

Notifications of applications

RULE 136

The Secretary-General shall send for information a copy of the application to the General Assembly, or to the Members of the United Nations if the General Assembly is not in session.

Considerations and decision by the General Assembly
RULE 137
If the Security Council recommends the applicant State for membership the General Assembly shall consider whether the applicant is a peace-loving State and is able and willing to carry out the obligations contained in the Charter, and shall decide, by a two-thirds majority of the Members present and voting, upon its application for membership.

RULE 138
If the Security Council does not recommend the applicant State for membership or postpones the consideration of the application, the General Assembly may, after full consideration of the special report of the Security Council, send back the application to the Security Council, together with a full record of the discussion in the General Assembly, for further consideration and recommendation or report.

Notification of decision and effective date of membership
RULE 139
The Secretary-General shall inform the applicant State of the decision of the General Assembly. If the application is approved, membership will become effective on the date on which the General Assembly takes its decision on the application.

XV. ELECTIONS TO PRINCIPAL ORGANS
GENERAL PROVISIONS
Terms of office
RULE 140
Except as provided in rule 148, the term of office of members of Councils shall begin on 1 January following their election by the General Assembly, and shall end on 31 December following the election of their successors.

By-elections
RULE 141
Should a member cease to belong to a Council before its term of office expires, a by-election shall be held separately at the next session of the General Assembly to elect a member for the unexpired term.

APPOINTMENT OF THE SECRETARY-GENERAL
Appointment of the Secretary-General
RULE 142
When the Security Council has submitted its recommendation

on the appointment of the Secretary-General, the General Assembly shall consider the recommendation and vote upon it by secret ballot in private meeting.

THE SECURITY COUNCIL

Annual elections

RULE 143*

The General Assembly shall each year, in the course of its regular session, elect three non-permanent members of the Security Council for a term of two years.

Qualifications for membership

RULE 144†

In the election of non-permanent members of the Security Council, in accordance with Article 23, paragraph 1, of the Charter, due regard shall be specially paid, in the first instance, to the contribution of Members of the United Nations to the maintenance of international peace and security and to the other purposes of the Organization, and also to equitable geographical distribution.

Re-eligibility

RULE 145‡

A RETIRING MEMBER OF THE SECURITY COUNCIL SHALL NOT BE ELIGIBLE FOR IMMEDIATE RE-ELECTION.

THE ECONOMIC AND SOCIAL COUNCIL

Annual elections

RULE 146§

The General Assembly shall each year, in the course of its regular session, elect six members of the Economic and Social Council for a term of three years.

Re-eligibility

RULE 147‖

A RETIRING MEMBER OF THE ECONOMIC AND SOCIAL COUNCIL SHALL BE ELIGIBLE FOR IMMEDIATE RE-ELECTION.

---

* Rule based directly on a provision of the Charter (Art. 23, para. 2).
† Rule based directly on a provision of the Charter (Art. 23, para. 1).
‡ Rule reproducing textually a provision of the Charter (Art. 23, para. 2, last sentence).
§ Rule based directly on a provision of the Charter (Art. 61, para. 2).
‖ Rule reproducing textually a provision of the Charter (Art. 61, para. 2, last sentence).

THE TRUSTEESHIP COUNCIL

Occasions for elections

RULE 148

When a Trusteeship Agreement has been approved and a Member of the United Nations has become an Administering Authority of a Trust Territory in accordance with Article 83 or 85 of the Charter, the General Assembly shall proceed to such election or elections to the Trusteeship Council as may be necessary, in accordance with Article 86. A Member or Members elected at any such election at a regular session shall take office immediately upon their election and shall complete their terms in accordance with the provisions of rule 140, as if they had begun their terms of office on January 1 following their election.

Term of office and re- eligibility

RULE 149*

A non-administering member of the Trusteeship Council shall be elected for a term of three years and shall be eligible for immediate re-election.

Vacancies

RULE 150

At each session the General Assembly shall, in accordance with Article 86 of the Charter, elect members to fill any vacancies.

THE INTERNATIONAL COURT OF JUSTICE

Method of election

RULE 151

The election of the members of the International Court of Justice shall take place in accordance with the Statute of the Court.

RULE 152

Any meeting of the General Assembly held in pursuance of the Statute of the International Court of Justice for the purpose of the election of members of the Court shall continue until as many candidates as are required for all the seats to be filled have obtained in one or more ballots an absolute majority of votes.

XVI. ADMINISTRATIVE AND BUDGETARY QUESTIONS

Regulations for financial administration

RULE 153

The General Assembly shall establish regulations for the financial administration of the United Nations.

* Rule based directly on a provision of the Charter (Art. 86, para. 1 c).

Estimates of expenditure

RULE 154

No resolution involving expenditure shall be recommended by a committee for approval by the General Assembly unless it is accompanied by an estimate of expenditures prepared by the Secretary-General. No resolution in respect of which expenditures are anticipated by the Secretary-General shall be voted by the General Assembly until the Administrative and Budgetary Committee has had an opportunity of stating the effect of the proposal upon the budget estimates of the United Nations.

Information on the cost of resolutions

RULE 155

The Secretary-General shall keep all committees informed of the detailed estimated cost of all resolutions which have been recommended by the committees for approval by the General Assembly.

Advisory Committee on Administrative and Budgetary Questions

RULE 156

The General Assembly shall appoint an Advisory Committee on Administrative and Budgetary Questions (hereinafter called the 'Advisory Committee'), with a membership of twelve, including at least three financial experts of recognized standing.

Composition of the Advisory Committee

RULE 157

The members of the Advisory Committee, no two of whom shall be nationals of the same State, shall be selected on the basis of broad geographical representation, personal qualifications and experience, and shall serve for three years corresponding to three financial years, as defined in the regulations for the financial administration of the United Nations. Members shall retire by rotation and shall be eligible for reappointment. The three financial experts shall not retire simultaneously. The General Assembly shall appoint the members of the Advisory Committee at the regular session immediately preceding the expiration of the term of office of the members, or, in case of vacancies, at the next session.

Functions of the Advisory Committee

RULE 158

The Advisory Committee shall be responsible for expert examination of the budget of the United Nations, and shall assist the

Administrative and Budgetary Committee of the General Assembly. At the commencement of each regular session it shall submit to the General Assembly a detailed report on the budget for the next financial year and on the accounts of the last financial year. It shall also examine on behalf of the General Assembly the administrative budgets of specialized agencies and proposals for financial and budgetary arrangements with such agencies. It shall perform such other duties as may be assigned to it under the regulations for the financial administration of the United Nations.

Committee on Contributions

RULE 159

The General Assembly shall appoint an expert Committee on Contributions, consisting of ten members.

Composition of the Committee on Contributions

RULE 160

The members of the Committee on Contributions, no two of whom shall be nationals of the same State, shall be selected on the basis of broad geographical representation, personal qualifications and experience, and shall serve for a period of three years corresponding to three financial years, as defined in the regulations for the financial administration of the United Nations. Members shall retire by rotation and shall be eligible for reappointment. The General Assembly shall appoint the members of the Committee on Contributions at the regular session immediately preceding the expiration of the term of office of the members, or, in case of vacancies, at the next session.

Functions of the Committee on Contributions

RULE 161

The Committee on Contributions shall advise the General Assembly concerning the apportionment, under Article 17, paragraph 2, of the Charter, of the expenses of the Organization among Members, broadly according to capacity to pay. The scale of assessments, when once fixed by the General Assembly, shall not be subject to a general revision for at least three years, unless it is clear that there have been substantial changes in relative capacities to pay. The Committee shall also advise the General Assembly on the assessments to be fixed for new Members, on appeals by Members for a change of assessments, and on the action to be taken with regard to the application of Article 19 of the Charter.

XVII. SUBSIDIARY ORGANS OF THE GENERAL ASSEMBLY

Creation and rules of procedure

RULE 162

THE GENERAL ASSEMBLY MAY ESTABLISH SUCH SUBSIDIARY ORGANS AS IT DEEMS NECESSARY FOR THE PERFORMANCE OF ITS FUNCTIONS.* The rules relating to the procedure of committees of the General Assembly, as well as rules 45 and 62, shall apply to the procedure of any subsidiary organ, unless the General Assembly or the subsidiary organ decides otherwise.

XVIII. INTERPRETATIONS AND AMENDMENTS

Notes in italics

RULE 163

The description of the rules in the tables of contents and the notes in italics to these rules shall be disregarded in the interpretation of the rules.

Method of amendment

RULE 164

These rules of procedure may be amended by a decision of the General Assembly taken by a majority of the Members present and voting, after a committee has reported on the proposed amendment.

*   *   *

ANNEX III[363]

PROCEDURE FOR THE EXAMINATION OF REPORTS AND PETITIONS RELATING TO THE TERRITORY OF SOUTH WEST AFRICA

Special rules adopted by the General Assembly at its ninth session

PROCEDURE WITH REGARD TO REPORTS

Special rule A : The General Assembly shall receive annually from the Committee on South West Africa the report on South West Africa submitted to the Committee by the Union of South Africa (or a report on conditions in the Territory of South West Africa prepared by the Committee in accordance with paragraph 12 (*c*) of General Assembly resolution 749 A (VIII)), together with the observations of the Committee on the report as well as the comments

---

* Rule reproducing textually a provision of the Charter (Art. 22).

of the duly authorized representative of the Union of South Africa, should that Government decide to follow the General Assembly's recommendation and appoint such a representative.

Special rule B : The General Assembly shall, as a rule, be guided by the observations of the Committee on South West Africa and shall base its conclusions, as far as possible, on the Committee's observations.

PROCEDURE WITH REGARD TO PETITIONS

Special rule C : The General Assembly shall receive annually from the Committee on South West Africa a report with regard to petitions submitted to it. The summary records of the meetings at which the petitions were discussed shall be attached.

Special rule D : The General Assembly shall, as a rule, be guided by the conclusions of the Committee on South West Africa and shall base its own conclusions, as far as possible, on the conclusions of the Committee.

PRIVATE MEETINGS

Special rule E : Having regard to rule 62 of the rules of procedure of the General Assembly, meetings at which decisions concerning persons are considered shall be held in private.

VOTING PROCEDURE

Special rule F : Decisions of the General Assembly on questions relating to reports and petitions concerning the Territory of South West Africa shall be regarded as important questions within the meaning of Article 18, paragraph 2, of the Charter of the United Nations.

Extracts from the
Report of the Secretary-General
on Measures to Economize the time
of the General Assembly[364]

8 July 1947

1. HISTORY OF THE RESOLUTION

At the request of the Canadian Government an item was included in the agenda of the second part of the first session of the General Assembly on 'Measures to economize the time of the General Assembly'. This item was referred to the General Committee for its consideration and was studied both by the Committee itself and by a special sub-committee formed for the purpose, a member of the Canadian delegation being present on each occasion to explain the views which had inspired the Canadian Government to raise the question.

The General Committee submitted its report to the General Assembly on 14 December 1946. On the recommendation of the Committee the General Assembly resolved to direct the Secretary-General to make a study of the measures to economize time and of the provisional rules of procedure, on the basis of the Canadian memoranda, the suggestions received from Members, the views expressed in the General Committee and the experience acquired and precedents established during the first session.

* * *

4. SUMMARY OF PRINCIPAL SUGGESTIONS FOR ECONOMIZING TIME OF THE GENERAL ASSEMBLY

A. AGENDA

An effort should be made to limit the Agenda of a session to those important items which can be dealt with by the General Assembly within five to seven weeks. The following suggestions would tend to restrict the agenda in this way and allow Members more time for the preliminary study of agenda items:

1. It is desirable that all possible items should be submitted in time for inclusion in the provisional agenda which is circu-

lated sixty days in advance of the opening of the session, or as soon as possible thereafter for inclusion in the supplementary list. . . .

2. During the course of a session additional items should be added to the agenda only if their urgency requires it. When request is made for the inclusion of such an item, the General Committee should be informed of the circumstances which made it impossible to include the item in the provisional agenda or the supplementary list. The General Committee should recommend to the plenary meeting the inclusion of the item in the agenda only if it is convinced that the urgency of the matter is such as to require the Assembly to give it consideration regardless of the fact that previous notice of the item had not been given.

* * *

B. DEBATE

Full debate of matters before the General Assembly is necessary and desirable, and no steps should be taken that call into question this fundamental democratic right. Measures can, however, be adopted which, while protecting the rights of each Member, would accelerate the debate and avoid unnecessary repetitions. The General Assembly can, through the use of efficient procedures, allow a full expression of opinion while at the same time reducing the length of debate on many subjects. In this connexion the Secretary-General suggests the following:

1. The circulation of documentation well in advance of the opening of a session will allow delegations to make the preparation necessary for the conduct of clear, concise debate. . . .

2. Adoption by the General Assembly of clear, practical rules of procedure, appropriate to the needs which are peculiar to the Assembly, will avoid procedural difficulties and much debate on the interpretation and application of the rules.

* * *

4. Close collaboration should be maintained between the Chairmen and secretaries of committees. The latter, through continuous service with specific committees from session to session are able to assist the Chairmen in the interpretation of the rules of procedure and in making available to committees in the most useful way the services of the Secretariat.

5. Duplication of debate can be avoided and more satisfactory schedule of meetings established by avoiding the reference of the same agenda item to two committees at the same time.

C. MATERIAL ARRANGEMENTS AND SCHEDULE

The speed with which the General Assembly progresses in its work is determined in no small degree by the material arrangements made for its meetings and by the manner in which the schedule of the Assembly is drawn up. Many of the difficulties which have been encountered will decrease or disappear when the permanent head-quarters are established in Manhattan. However, the following measures would in any case tend to expedite the work of the Assembly:

1. The use of simultaneous interpretation would result in a greater economy of time than any other single measure that could be adopted. . . .

2. Changes in the announced schedule of meetings should be avoided except in unusual circumstances. Close co-operation between the Chairman and secretaries of committees is essential whenever meetings are required in order that proper clearance is obtained from the office in the Secretariat responsible for the co-ordination of the overall schedule of the General Assembly.

3. The total time lost between the scheduled hour for beginning of meetings and the actual opening of the meetings is not inconsiderable. . . .

4. The bureaus of main committees should consider as early as possible in the committees' work the question of how the pro-gramme of the committee might be expedited through the establishment of sub-committees. It is, of course, impossible to adopt fixed rules on this matter; but the Chairman of a Main committee, together with the Vice-Chairman, Rapporteur and Secretary should not fail to give special attention to it as they plan the programme of the committee in the early stage of its work.

*   *   *

7. The Secretary-General recommends that Members en-deavour to submit the texts of documents intended for circulation as far as possible in advance of the meeting at which they are to be discussed. Every effort will be made by the Secretariat to carry out the prompt translation, reproduction and circulation of documents.

8. The reading in plenary and committee meetings of rap-porteurs' reports and other documents which had previously been circulated to Members does not appear necessary in the considera-tion of any matter. . . .

Extracts from the
Report of the Committee
on Procedures and Organization
of the Great Assembly[365]

23 September 1947

INTRODUCTION

1. On 15 December 1946, the General Assembly approved resolution 102 (I) on measures to economize the time of the General Assembly.

*　　　*　　　*

PART I

5. The Committee devoted its first meeting to a discussion of its terms of reference and the organization of its work. The majority of its members considered that the terms of reference prescribed by the General Assembly made the Committee responsible for a review and study of the provisional rules of procedure for the General Assembly on the basis of the Secretary-General's report, as well as of technical and practical measures to economize the time of the General Assembly which had been proposed by Members of the United Nations, the Secretary-General and the members of the Committee themselves. Other members of the Committee, however, were of the opinion that the Committee's responsibilities were limited to a study of methods of work and internal organization of the Assembly, with a view to proposing measures which would result in an economy of time. These members felt that the Committee should examine only such rules of procedure as might be instrumental in expediting the work of the Assembly.

6. Part II of this report consists of a series of suggestions, the adoption of which would, in the opinion of the Committee, assist considerably in expediting the work of the Assembly and permit the full consideration of important problems on the agenda without requiring the representatives to stay away from their home countries for inconveniently long periods. Part III contains a proposed redraft of the provisional rules of procedure. The Committee felt that every improvement in the rules which would make debates on procedures unnecessary would result in a definite economy of time . . .

7. The Secretary-General communicated to the Committee a

letter from the Chairman of the Advisory Committee on Administrative and Budgetary Questions, suggesting changes in chapter VII of the provisional rules of procedure which would alter the title of the Advisory Committee and amend certain rules regarding its standing functions. The Committee took note of the proposed revisions but reviewed provisional rules 37 to 40 merely from the point of view of drafting. The opinion was expressed that the Fifth Committee should study the rules contained in chapter VII from the point of view of substance before their final adoption.

8. The Committee refrained from considering the rules contained in chapter IX (Languages) and X (Records). The Committee felt that these rules had serious political and financial aspects which should be considered by the appropriate Committees of the Assembly. . . .

9. Chapter XVII (Admission of new Members to the United Nations) was not examined by the Committee. A Committee entrusted with the task of preparing rules governing the admission of New Members had been established by the General Assembly on 15 December 1946 and had, after consultation with the corresponding Committee of the Security Council, presented its report directly to the General Assembly.

*   *   *

PART II

Agenda

11. The Committee is of the opinion that wherever possible items proposed for inclusion in the agenda should be submitted in time for inclusion in the provisional agenda which is communicated to Members sixty days in advance of the opening of the session. If this is impossible, every effort shoud be made to ensure that they are included in the supplementary list.

12. It is recognized that no rigid rules can be established on this question, but the observance of these principles would lead to the saving of time, inasmuch as Member Governments would thus have sufficient notice of proposed agenda items to enable them to prepare more thoroughly for the debate on these items.

13. The Committee discussed the desirability of a suitable time limit for the submission of requests for the inclusion of additional items—for instance, the end of the general debate—but decided to make no specific recommendation on this subject.

Documentation

14. The circulation of essential documents well in advance of their discussion in the General Assembly or its Committees would

greatly facilitate and expedite the work of the Assembly. When items are submitted for inclusion in the agenda, supporting documentation should be forwarded at the same time or shortly thereafter, whenever possible. While the Committee fully realizes that this is difficult and in some cases impossible, it wishes to call the attention of the General Assembly to the desirability of this principle as an objective.

* * *

Organization of Committees

16. The Committee considered the desirability of suggesting that at future sessions of the General Assembly a start should be made with the work of some at least of the Main Committees before the close of the general debate, but decided at this stage to make no recommendation on the subject.

17. While it is desirable that as many Main Committees as possible should meet simultaneously, the fact should not be overlooked that too many meetings held at one time may place too heavy a burden on the members of the General Assembly, and particularly those Member States having small delegations. If the debates are to be maintained on the high level necessary for the Assembly to conduct its business wisely and efficiently, the schedule of meetings must be so arranged as to allow the members of delegations attending them the necessary time for study and consultation. Failure to do this would be to under-estimate the importance of the deliberations of the General Assembly and of its Committees. Nevertheless, the Committee calls attention to the fact that the number of Main Committees meeting simultaneously affects materially the duration of the General Assembly. A relatively light schedule of meetings in the early weeks of the Assembly leads inevitably to an unduly heavy schedule in its later stages. The scheduling of meetings should therefore take into account: (1) the capacity of delegations to cope with the work involved; (2) the desirability of establishing a relatively uniform work-load during the entire session; and (3) the relationship of the daily schedule to the duration of the Assembly.

18. Every effort should be made by the officers of the General Assembly and by the Secretariat to announce the schedule of meetings well in advance, and to avoid as far as possible any modification therein. During the early stages of committee work, the schedule of meetings might be announced for one week in advance. However, the establishment of sub-committees, the termination of the work of some of the Main Committees, and the variable load of those still in session may require adjustments in the schedule in the later stages

of the work of the General Assembly. It would seem impracticable, during this period, to establish a rigid schedule for more than two or three days in advance.

19. The time lost between the hour scheduled for the beginning of a meeting and the actual opening of the meeting is not inconsiderable. Members of the General Assembly are urged to arrive promptly, and it is suggested that the President of the Assembly and the Chairmen of Committees open the meetings as soon as a quorum is present.

Limitation of debate

20. The provisional rules of procedure provide that the General Assembly may at any time limit the time allowed to speakers. The Committee recognizes that there are occasions on which this rule can be applied in the interest of economizing time without detriment to the rights of any member of the Assembly. The Committee, however, desires to call the attention of the Assembly to the serious difficulties attendant upon any general rule limiting the length of speeches, and it did not consider it advisable to recommend such a time limit.

Establishment of sub-committees

21. The Main Committees should consider carefully at an early stage in their work how their programmes might be expedited by the establishment of sub-committees. It is, of course, impossible to adopt fixed rules on this matter. If the debate in full committee showed that there was general agreement on the question under discussion but disagreement on points of detail, it would clearly be desirable to set up a small drafting committee to prepare a resolution for submission to the Main Committee. Technical questions on which there is no substantial disagreement should be referred to sub-committees as quickly as possible. In some cases the work of sub-committees would be facilitated by working informally, and on occasion, in private.

Conduct of business

22. The Committee noted with satisfaction that the Secretary-General is preparing for the information of members a handbook containing a record of the application of the rules of procedure in this and previous sessions of the General Assembly. If this handbook is completed and placed in use, the Assembly might wish to consider whether it has served to facilitate the conduct of the business of the General Assembly.

23. Continued close collaboration between the Chairmen and the Secretariat is desirable and the assistance of the Committee secretaries and legal advisers should be available at all times.

Allocation of agenda items among Committees

24. The reference of the same agenda item to two Committees at the same time is as a general rule undesirable and often results in unnecessary duplication of debate. In addition, experience has shown that if an item is also referred to another Committee in general terms, that Committee does not always limit itself to the consideration of the aspects of the question in regard to which it is especially competent.

25. The Committee suggests that, as a general rule, one Main Committee, or one joint committee (e.g. the Joint Second and Third Committee) be given responsibility for reporting on a given agenda item and that, if the opinion of another Committee is needed, the latter be seized only of a precise and limited question. A suggestion, which received some support, was made to the effect that a small advisory committee of jurists should be established to which the first five Main Committees could submit the legal aspects of questions under consideration. Other members of the Committee felt, however, that such a committee was not necessary.

Committee reports

26. The Committee recommends that rapporteurs' reports and other documents which have been circulated to members in advance should not be read in plenary and committee meetings. This would not, of course, limit the right of members to read such documents or such passages from them as they may consider necessary.

Simultaneous interpretation

27. The Committee examined the important question of the use by the General Assembly of simultaneous interpretation, which would contribute greatly to economizing the time of the General Assembly, and was informed of certain experimental planning which had been carried out by the Secretary-General in this field. As this question is on the provisional agenda of the second regular session of the General Assembly, the Committee refrains from conclusions and limits itself to making the observations which follow.

28. It was pointed out to the Committee by several of its members that experience, not only in the United Nations but in other international bodies over a period of years, seems to have

demonstrated that although the system of simultaneous interpretation has real merit, its use in all circumstances is not without serious disadvantages. Among the disadvantages mentioned are the following:

(a) The interpreter is obliged to follow the speaker in much the same word order as that in which the original speech is made. While in some languages this creates no insurmountable difficulties, in others it renders translation extremely difficult, especially since the rules of phrasing in certain languages differ so greatly from those in others. In following word for word in a simultaneous interpretation, the interpreter is unable, as can the interpreter in a consecutive interpretation, to follow the general line of argument and set it forth clearly for those who are listening.

(b) The interpreter, not knowing in advance what documents will be quoted, is unable to have at hand the official texts cited by the speaker. This creates serious difficulties when the discussion relates to draft resolutions or amendments. In consecutive interpretation, the interpreter's colleagues are able to collect the necessary documents for him during the course of the original speech.

(c) The representative does not hear the interpretation and is unable to control its accuracy or correct the errors of the interpreter.

(d) A physical and psychological barrier is created between the speaker and his colleagues, and representatives miss the opportunity of familiarizing themselves with the habits of thought and the languages spoken by the other representatives.

29. The Committee was in full agreement that the system of simultaneous interpretation can be used to advantage during a general debate in plenary or committee meetings, and that it would result in a considerable shortening of the length of the sessions of the General Assembly, but that it is not suitable when detailed negotiations or the reconciliation of various drafts are necessary.

30. It is clear that the introduction of simultaneous interpretation will make it necessary for the Secretariat to make provisions which would facilitate the passage from simultaneous to consecutive interpretation, and vice versa, during the same meeting, as well as to complement simultaneous interpretation by the occasional use of consecutive interpretation if this should be necessary.

*　　　*　　　*

Drafting of resolutions

33. Experience has shown that the time of the General Assembly is sometimes unnecessarily occupied by the re-drafting, during meetings of committees, of draft resolutions because of unintentional ambiguities in the text. The assistance of the Legal Department of the Secretariat which is available at any time to national delegations may usefully be asked for to avoid this as far as possible.

34. The Committee considered that the time of the General Assembly would be economized if the final texts of resolutions were drawn up simultaneously in the two working languages and the two versions kept in continuous comparison in order to avoid ambiguities in both texts.

35. The General Committee has already been given power under existing rule 36 of the provisional rules of procedure to 'revise the resolutions adopted by the General Assembly, changing their form but not their substance'. The rule goes on to say: 'Any such changes shall be reported to the General Assembly for its consideration.' Clearly, the General Committee could not itself undertake this task. It was suggested to the Committee that the General Committee might usefully appoint a drafting committee which, with the assistance of the Secretariat, could, in the interval between the adoption of a resolution by a Main Committee and the submission of that resolution to the Assembly, examine the French and English texts of the resolution and submit it to the General Committee for transmission to the Assembly with whatever drafting changes in both texts the drafting committee might consider necessary. The recommendations for drafting changes could be submitted to the Assembly together with the report as drawn up by the Main Committee

APPENDIX 8

Extracts from the
Report of the Special Committee
on Methods and Procedures
of the General Assembly[366]*

12 *August* 1949

I. INTRODUCTION

1. In its resolution 271 (III) of 29 April 1949, the General Assembly expressed its concern at the increasing length of General Assembly sessions and at the growing tendency towards protracted debates in its plenary meetings and committees, and established a Special Committee consisting of the representatives of fifteen Members. The Special Committee was instructed to:

(*a*) Consider methods and procedures which would enable the General Assembly and its committees to discharge their functions more effectively and expeditiously;

(*b*) Submit, if possible, a preliminary report to the General Assembly during the second part of its third session;

(*c*) Transmit a report to the Secretary-General, not later than 15 August 1949, for circulation to Members for consideration at the fourth regular session of the General Assembly.

The Secretary-General was invited to collaborate closely with the Special Committee in its work.

*   *   *

5. During twenty-three meetings held in June, July and August 1949, the Special Committee studied carefully the various factors affecting the duration of the General Assembly. It dealt successively with questions concerning the establishment of the agenda of sessions, the internal organization of the Assembly, the means of shortening debates in plenary meetings and committees and the clarification of rules of procedure, the application of which has given rise to difficulties in the past, thereby causing prolonged procedural debates. The conclusions which the Special Committee has the honour to bring to the General Assembly's attention in the following

* The footnotes in the document have not been reproduced, with the exception of one which appears on p. 323.

paragraphs consist of proposed amendments to the rules of procedure, interpretations of certain rules at present in force, and recommendations and advice to representatives to the General Assembly, especially those who are called upon as Chairmen to conduct debates in plenary meetings and committees.

6. In submitting its proposals, the Special Committee wishes to state that throughout its work its members have constantly had in mind the essential role entrusted to the General Assembly under the Charter, and the prestige and high authority that should belong to the only principal organ of the United Nations on which are represented on an equal footing all the Members of the Organization.

The Special Committee has been careful that none of its proposals should have the effect of diminishing the competence or functions of the General Assembly, or in any way hindering the natural development of that vital organ of the United Nations. The Special Committee examined only those proposals designed to save time, which, in the opinion of its members, took these fundamental principles into consideration.

The Special Committee believes that the adoption of its recommendations will fully safeguard the rights possessed by Members of the United Nations—whether on a given question they belong to the majority or the minority—to draw the General Assembly's attention to problems within its competence, to express their views and to participate fully in the adoption of resolutions on matters of which the General Assembly has been seized. The sole purpose of the Special Committee's recommendations is to adapt the organization and procedures of the General Assembly to its increasing responsibilities, as the Special Committee believes that such adaptation is indispensable in order to enable the Assembly to discharge its functions more effectively and expeditiously.

In this regard, it seemed particularly important to the Special Committee that General Assembly sessions should be planned in such a way as to facilitate the participation, as representatives of Member States, of persons holding the highest Government posts or representing the most diverse fields of national activity, whose normal functions prevent them from remaining at United Nations Headquarters for extensive periods.

7. The Special Committee does not consider that the present length of General Assembly sessions can be ascribed primarily to the rules of procedure. It is due, above all, to the number and complexity of the questions submitted to the Assembly and to the political problems raised by these questions. Nevertheless, the Special Committee thinks that the present methods and procedures of the Assembly

might be usefully improved if the Assembly accepted the amendments to the rules of procedure proposed by the Special Committee and if it endorsed the interpretations and opinions suggested by the Special Committee.

8. The Special Committee is not recommending substantial modifications to the rules of procedure. It considers that, on the whole, the present rules of procedure, based as they are on the experience of other international organizations and on the relatively recent work of the Preparatory Commission of the United Nations and of several committees of the General Assembly, represent both in letter and in spirit, an adequate instrument, which can enable the General Assembly to carry out its functions effectively. Thus, the Special Committee's first conclusion is that the General Assembly's work might be considerably accelerated if the present rules of procedure were more faithfully observed, if all their potentialities were better known to the Chairmen and members, if some of the rules were clarified, if Chairmen performed their functions more boldly and if members offered them their full co-operation and goodwill in ensuring that the rules of procedure receive their normal application.

III. Recommendations Concerning the Establishment of the Agenda

9. In the light of the preceding considerations, the Special Committee recommends that the General Assembly should, on the proposal of the General Committee, fix at the beginning of each session the date by which it would endeavour to complete its work.

The Special Committee did not wish to go any further in this direction or to adopt proposals which would limit the duration of the session in a more rigid manner, although it was pointed out in the course of its debates that, to enable Governments to ensure adequate representation, sessions of the General Assembly should not exceed eight weeks.

The Special Committee thought that it would be undesirable to recommend too strict a rule. The probable duration of each session can only be determined, in present circumstances, on the basis of the number and nature of the questions submitted to the Assembly and of an estimate of the length of the debates which they may occasion. The Special Committee's proposal tends thus to render permanent and to strengthen the practice, which has developed during the last two sessions, of fixing a closing date which would represent a target for the Assembly.

*　　*　　*

10. The Special Committee considers that, in order to maintain the duration of sessions within normal limits, it is important that the provisional agenda of the General Assembly (provided for in rules 11 and 12), the supplementary list (rule 13) and requests for the inclusion of additional items (rule 14) should be scrutinized with greater care than in the past. The General Committee, in the first place, and the General Assembly itself, should examine all requests for inclusion in the agenda, not only with special attention to the importance of these questions in relation to the achievement of the purposes of the United Nations, but also in relation to the agenda as a whole and the time available for the session.

The Special Committee, therefore, deems it important to reaffirm the General Assembly's right to exclude certain questions from the agenda and also its right, under rule 14, to delete questions previously included. Such action by the General Assembly amounts, in fact, to postponement, since countries which have proposed an item for the Assembly's consideration have the right, in the event of their request being rejected, to propose its inclusion in the provisional agenda of the next session. Moreover, under rule 12, the General Assembly may itself decide to include in the provisional agenda of a future session any item that it has excluded or deleted from its agenda.

* * *

11. The Special Committee is of the opinion that the important and urgent character of additional items referred to in rule 14 should be determined with care. It believes that the inclusion of items proposed shortly before or during the session should constitute exceptions, not only because last-minute proposals may result in overloading the agenda, but also because delegations to the General Assembly find it very difficult to prepare for the examination of such proposals at short notice and to obtain adequate instructions from their Governments. The Special Committee proposes, therefore, that the inclusion of additional items in the agenda of a regular session should be decided by a two-thirds majority of the Members present and voting.

* * *

12. The Special Committee also wishes to draw the General Assembly's attention to its power to decide, at the beginning of or during the session, to refer certain items, without preliminary debate, to other organs of the United Nations, or to the author of a proposal for inclusion of an item, for further information or documentation. Such a decision would have the advantage of lightening the agenda

by avoiding the discussion of questions which are not very urgent and which could usefully be studied in detail by other organs, such as one of the existing subsidiary organs of the General Assembly, an *ad hoc* committee, one of the Councils, a specialized agency, or the Secretary-General. It was emphasized, in this connexion, that questions of an exclusively economic, social, or cultural nature should not as a rule be submitted to the General Assembly until they had been considered by the Economic and Social Council.

*   *   *

13. The Special Committee found that in the past some of the Main Committees of the General Assembly had devoted a particularly large number of meetings to the detailed consideration, article by article, of texts of international conventions. This was even the case where the text of a convention had been drawn up by an international conference on which all Member States had been represented. It was pointed out in this connexion that experience had shown that a Main Committee, by the very fact of its size, was not particularly fitted to draft conventions, and that when it was entrusted with the detailed study of conventions, it often did not have time to deal satisfactorily with the other questions for which it was responsible.

The Special Committee recognizes the importance of the sponsorship of conventions by the General Assembly. It believes that the authority of the General Assembly and the powerful influence its debates have on public opinion should, in many cases, be used for the benefit of international legislation by means of conventions. It therefore favours the retention by the General Assembly of the necessary freedom of action.

The Special Committee therefore confines itself to recommending that, when conventions have been negotiated by international conferences in which all the Members of the United Nations have been invited to take part, and on which they have been represented, not only by experts acting in a personal capacity but by representatives of Governments, and when these conventions are subsequently submitted to the General Assembly for consideration, the Assembly should not undertake a further detailed examination, but should limit itself to discussing them in a broad manner and to giving its general views on the instruments submitted to it. After such a debate, the General Assembly could, if desirable, adopt the conclusions reached by the conferences and recommend to Members the acceptance or ratification of such conventions.

This procedure might be applied in particular to conventions submitted to the General Assembly as a result of conferences of all

Member States convened by the Economic and Social Council under Article 62, paragraph 4 of the Charter.

14. Furthermore, when it is proposed that the General Assembly should consider conventions prepared by groups of experts not acting as governmental representatives, or by conferences in which all Members of the United Nations have not been invited to take part, it would be advisable for the General Committee and the General Assembly to determine whether one of the Main Committees, especially the Legal Committee, would have enough time during the session to examine these conventions in detail, or whether it would be possible to set up an *ad hoc* committee to undertake this study during the session.

If this is not possible, the Special Committee recommends that the General Assembly should decide, after or without a general debate on the fundamental principles of the proposed convention, that an *ad hoc* committee should be established to meet between sessions. Alternatively, the General Assembly might decide to convene a conference of plenipotentiaries between two of its own sessions, to study, negotiate, draft, and possibly sign, the convention. The conference of plenipotentiaries might be empowered by the General Assembly to transmit the instruments directly to Governments for acceptance or ratification. In this case too, the General Assembly might, at a subsequent session, express its general opinion on the convention resulting from the conference, and might recommend to Members its acceptance or ratification.

With regard to the drafting of legal texts, the Special Committee strongly recommends that small drafting committees should be resorted to whenever possible.

15. The Special Committee examined several proposals designed to relieve the General Committee of part of its present responsibilities by entrusting some of its functions to a special agenda committee meeting before the opening of the session. The main arguments in favour of the establishment of an agenda committee were that, at present, the General Committee performs its functions relating to the provisional agenda and the supplementary list during the first days of the session and the general debate in the plenary meetings and the work of the Committees is thereby delayed. In the opinion of the authors of the proposals, it would be advantageous to entrust the examination of the agenda to a committee which would be less pressed for time, thus making it easier for delegations to find grounds for agreement.

It was suggested that the agenda committee should consist of representatives of Members who were represented in the General

Committee of the preceding session or, alternatively, that it should be composed of representatives of fifteen Members elected annually by the General Assembly.

The meetings of the agenda committee would be held during the two- to three-weeks period preceding the opening of the session and its duties would cease, at the latest, when the members of the General Committee are elected. It was proposed that, in order to avoid repetitious debate, the agenda committee's recommendations on the agenda of the session should be submitted directly to the plenary meeting of the General Assembly for approval.

Some of the proposals provided that, apart from its work on the agenda of the session, the agenda committee might prepare, with the assistance of the Secretary-General, studies and recommendations on the organization of the session, on the possible priorities to be given to items on the agenda, and on the allocation of items to the Main Committees. It was also suggested that the agenda committee might estimate, with the help of the Secretariat, the time which would have to be devoted to the consideration of each item, in committee and in plenary meetings, and might thus facilitate the adoption by the General Assembly of a target date.

Several members of the Special Committee doubted whether the establishment of an agenda committee would actually result in a shortening of the General Assembly's sessions. They also had doubts concerning the degree of authority which the agenda committee would possess and the nature of its relationship with the General Committee. Other members were not ready to express a definite opinion on the proposals which had been submitted and thought that the matter should be further studied and re-examined at a later date.

The Special Committee decided, therefore, to bring the question to the attention of the General Assembly and to transmit to the Assembly the various written proposals which it has received. It also decided to request the Secretary-General to assist the General Assembly by preparing a study on proposals previously examined, to report on such technical, legal and financial aspects of the question as he may consider pertinent, and to submit to the Assembly his views on the composition and functions of an agenda committee.

16. The Special Committee also considered proposals to set up a committee for nominations of officers of committees or to entrust this task to the agenda committee. After studying these proposals carefully, the Special Committee decided not to make a recommendation in this respect to the General Assembly.

17. Having stressed the importance of a more careful study of

the agenda, the Special Committee deems it advisable to recommend that all requests for inclusion of an item in the agenda should be accompanied by a memorandum stating the reasons for the request and, if necessary, by the basic documents or by a draft resolution. Only the memorandum would be obligatory, and the advisability of annexing other documents, especially draft resolutions, would be left to the discretion of the authors of the request for inclusion. In the opinion of the Special Committee, however, this limited obligation would have not only the advantage of facilitating the task of the General Committee and the General Assembly, but also the additional advantage of enabling Member States to prepare themselves more thoroughly for the discussion of items submitted to the General Assembly for consideration.

The Special Committee wishes, however, to emphasize that the General Assembly could not refuse to include an item in the agenda on the sole grounds that the memorandum accompanying the request was inadequate.

*　　　*　　　*

IV. Recommendations Relating to the Organization of General Assembly Sessions

*　　　*　　　*

20. In order that more frequent meetings of the General Committee should not delay the work of plenary and committee meetings, the Special Committee wishes to mention that it would be desirable for the General Committee to be enabled to meet, whenever necessary, at the same time as the plenary or the Main Committees. (In such cases, one of the Vice-Presidents could take the chair at plenary meetings and the Vice-Chairman could replace the Chairman at Main Committee meetings.)

The Special Committee also considers that in order to save time at the beginning of the session, some of the Main Committees should not wait until the end of the general debate before starting their work.

*　　　*　　　*

22. In the past, some of the Main Committees have been allocated more items requiring prolonged consideration than have other committees. This has especially been the case with the First Committee. The Special Committee noted, however, that during the third session of the General Assembly, exception had been made to the principle laid down in rule 89, that 'items relating to the same category of subjects shall be referred to the committee or committees dealing with that category of subjects'.

The Special Committee feels that the allocation of items to committees might be effected in a less rigid manner and that questions which may be considered as falling within the competence of two or more committees, should preferably be referred to the committee with the lightest agenda.

23. Another means of lightening the task of any given Main Committee would be to consider directly in plenary meeting, without preliminary reference to committee, certain questions which fall within the terms of reference of the Main Committee. This procedure would moreover have the great advantage of reducing to a notable extent repetition of debate.

The consideration of questions in plenary meetings would have the benefit of the attendance of leaders of delegations and of greater solemnity and publicity. The slightly higher cost to the United Nations of plenary meetings, due in particular to the distribution of verbatim records of the meetings, would undoubtedly be compensated by the shorter duration of the session.

The General Committee would be responsible for suggesting to the General Assembly which items on the agenda might be dealt with in this manner. The Special Committee recommends that this method should be introduced on an experimental basis at future sessions.

The Special Committee is of the opinion that this procedure would be especially appropriate for certain questions the essential aspects of which are already familiar to Members, such as items which have been considered by the General Assembly at previous sessions and which do not require either the presence of representatives of non-member States or the hearing of testimony.

24. The problem of the repetition of debate on the same item during one session of the Assembly was the cause of particular concern to the Special Committee. It was recalled in this connexion that, in the past, the same item has sometimes been the subject of full discussion in the General Committee, in plenary meeting and in the Main Committee to which it was referred. It has then been debated in a sub-committee, referred back to the Main Committee and finally considered in plenary meeting.

The Special Committee considers that the General Assembly should make every effort to see that an item reaches as rapidly as possible the committee or sub-committee which has to consider its substance in detail, without detailed discussion of the same item in the General Committee and in plenary meeting.

Once the substance of the question has been considered by the competent committee, in which all Members have had full opportunity of stating their views, all repetition in the General Assembly of the various arguments or of considerations on the technical aspects of the problem should be avoided.

*　　　*　　　*

27. The plenary meeting which examines a Main Committee's report and adopts a resolution embodying the General Assembly's decision on a problem submitted to it, is of considerable importance. In many cases it is useful to allow a general debate concerning the principles on which the Committee's recommendations were based, or even to provide opportunity for improving the proposed draft resolution by the adoption of amendments. Nevertheless, in view of the identical composition of the plenary meeting and the Main Committees, it seems to the Special Committee that the re-discussion of questions should not be encouraged, except in cases where this may be useful for the work of the General Assembly and genuinely safeguards the legitimate rights of minorities.

*　　　*　　　*

V. Recommendations Relating to the Conduct of Debates in Plenary Meetings and in Committees

28. The Special Committee recalls that much time has been lost in the past by committees and by the General Assembly itself, owing to the fact that meetings have not begun at the scheduled time. Precise calculations on this subject prove that the accumulated delays undoubtedly cause a prolongation of the session.

The Special Committee is aware that the interval between the time fixed for the opening of the meeting and its actual opening is often profitably used by certain delegations in valuable informal conversations, which in many cases serve to facilitate debates. The Special Committee considers, however, that the General Assembly should insist on greater punctuality and should take the necessary measures to remedy the present situation.

*　　　*　　　*

30. The Special Committee had before it several proposals to limit the time to be allowed to speakers in plenary meetings and in committees. After studying the problem, the Special Committee expresses the view that a general time-limit for statements on the substance of a question is not desirable, and that, within the limits laid down in the rules of procedure, representatives should be entitled to give full expression to their points of view.

*　　　*　　　*

36. The Special Committee did not examine a proposal which had been submitted to it to introduce a new rule which would define the conditions upon which the application of the rules of procedure could be suspended. The representative of Canada, who submitted this proposal, did not, in view of the shortage of time, insist on its consideration by the Special Committee, but reserved the right of his delegation to raise the question during the debate on the report of the Special Committee by the General Assembly.

37. The Special Committee also feels it desirable to clarify the meaning and application of rules 64 and 102 relating to points of order. It is the opinion of the Special Committee that a valid point of order may relate to the manner in which the debate is conducted, to the maintenance of order, to the observance of the rules of procedure, or to the manner in which Chairmen exercise the powers conferred upon them by the rules. Thus, within the scope of the General Assembly's rules of procedure, representatives are enabled to direct the attention of the presiding officer to violations or mis-applications of the rules of procedure by other representatives or by the presiding officer himself. Points of order may also refer to legitimate requests for information, to material arrangements (temperature of the room, seating, interpretation system), to documents, translations and so on. On the other hand, no representative, when rising to a point of order, should be permitted to speak on the substance of the matter under discussion.

Under rules 64 and 102, presiding officers must give an immediate ruling on every point of order, and if the ruling is challenged, they must put it to the vote; no discussion may take place. Hence, there can be no question of seconding or debating a point of order. Moreover, as the presiding officer must immediately dispose of each point of order as it is raised, two or more points of order can never be before the Chair at the same time.

* * *

39. At this point the Special Committee desires to stress once more the importance of the role of the President of the General Assembly and of the Chairmen of committees. The satisfactory progress of the proceedings depends essentially on their competence, authority, tact and impartiality, their respect for the rights both of minorities as well as majorities, and their familiarity with the rules of procedure. The General Assembly, or the Committee, as the case may be, is the master of the conduct of its own proceedings. It is, however, the special task of the Chairmen to guide the proceedings of these bodies in the best interests of all the Members. The Special Committee considers that everything possible

should be done to help Chairmen in the discharge of these important functions. The President of the General Assembly and the General Committee should assist the Chairmen of committees with their advice. The Secretary-General should place his experience and all his authority at their disposal.*

The Special Committee is happy to note the Secretariat's valuable practice of holding daily meetings of the committee secretaries, under the chairmanship of the Executive Assistant to the Secretary-General, where the procedural questions arising from day to day in the General Assembly and committees are thoroughly examined. Furthermore, the Special Committee stresses the value of having, as in the past, a legal adviser from the Secretariat in attendance at meetings to give the Chairmen or the committee such advice as they may need for the conduct of their business and the interpretation of the rules of procedure.

VI. SECRETARY-GENERAL'S PROPOSAL FOR AN INTERVAL OF PRAYER OR MEDITATION IN MEETINGS OF THE GENERAL ASSEMBLY

40. The Special Committee has examined a proposal submitted by the Secretary-General, to the effect that in the first plenary meeting of the General Assembly on a given day, the President should invite the Members of the United Nations to observe one minute of silence dedicated to prayer or meditation. The Secretary-General, in introducing this proposal, explained to the Special Committee that many hundreds of letters from private individuals and organizations have urged that the General Assembly should devote a few moments of its time to prayer.

The Special Committee recognizes the lofty motives which have inspired the authors of these communications. It is, on the other hand, aware of the fact that the Members of the United Nations represent people belonging to nearly every religion, creed and philosophical outlook in the world, and that it would not be possible to introduce a public prayer which would satisfy all tenets and give offence to none. Some of the members also felt that too frequent repetition of an act of this nature might deprive it of some of its solemnity, and were generally inclined to favour a recommendation that one minute of silence should be observed at the opening and at the closing meeting of the General Assembly.

*   *   *

* A suggestion was made that the Secretary-General should prepare, from time to time, commentaries on the rules of procedure, which would be placed at the disposal of Chairmen and of representatives to the General Assembly.

APPENDIX 9

Extracts from the
Report of the Special Committee
on Measures to Limit the Duration
of Regular Sessions
of the General Assembly[367]

26 *June* 1953

I. INTRODUCTION

1. At its 380th plenary meeting, held on 16 October 1952, the General Assembly decided to include in the agenda of the seventh session the item 'Measures to limit the duration of regular sessions of the General Assembly'. The memorandum submitted on the subject by the Secretary-General for consideration by the governments of Member States was discussed at the 387th and 388th plenary meetings of the General Assembly, held on 23 and 24 October.

*   *   *

8. There is agreement among the members of the Special Committee that the best interests of the General Assembly, not the length of its sessions as such, must remain the overriding consideration in any study of measures designed to limit the duration of the regular sessions. It should be kept in mind that the Assembly has special characteristics which distinguish it from other more homogeneous parliamentary bodies; its processes are largely conditioned by the wide scope of its purposes and defined by the very nature of its composition. Furthermore, the question under review cannot be judged solely on technical grounds or on grounds of efficiency. The length of the regular sessions of the Assembly has been determined mainly by the complexity and number of the international problems which have been brought to its attention as the result of differences among the Members, and by the atmosphere of deep-seated international tension in which the Assembly's discussions have taken place.

9. It follows, therefore, that if the General Assembly of the United Nations is to fulfil the high responsibilities placed upon it by the Charter and if the peoples of the world are to look with increasing respect and confidence to that body as the highest forum of the international community, all questions relating to the manner in

which it functions must be considered primarily from the standpoint of their effect on the General Assembly as a whole. In the opinion of the majority of the members of the Special Committee, the unnecessary lengthening of the regular sessions would detract from the stature of the Assembly in the eyes of the world.

10. At the same time, it is the consensus of opinion that considerations of a practical nature must also be taken into account. The excessive length of regular sessions in itself has disadvantages for the Assembly as well as for the Organization as a whole. The past tendency to prolong the General Assembly each year has made it difficult for governments to maintain the same delegations throughout an entire session. Members of national governments and parliaments cannot be expected to be absent from their duties at home beyond a reasonable period of time. On the other hand, the work of the Assembly would benefit by the direct participation of leading statesmen, in so far as possible, at every stage of the deliberations. The majority of the members of the Special Committee believe that a greater continuity in the composition of delegations would have a favorable effect on the work of the General Assembly, and that continuity might be more easily attained if the duration of the regular sessions were more strictly limited.

11. The duration of the regular sessions has an important bearing also on questions of expense and efficiency. The necessity for every reasonable economy is the concern of all; unnecessary expenditures and unfruitful procedures must be avoided. An unduly long session is not only a burden on the United Nations budget, but it increases the expenditure incurred by the individual Members.

12. The total programme of all the organs of the United Nations cannot but be affected by the length of the regular sessions. It is essential that sufficient time should be allowed for the implementation of the Assembly's recommendations as well as for the Councils and subsidiary organs to carry out their work. Lengthy Assembly sessions shorten the period available for those purposes with possible detriment to the execution of programmes.

13. The Special Committee acknowledges that these and other difficulties related to the duration of the regular sessions should not be resolved at the expense either of the effectiveness of the General Assembly or of the right of any representative freely to explain his government's attitude on the problems before the Assembly. It is felt, however, that the Assembly, through the co-operation of its members, can initiate or strengthen certain practices so as to expedite and simplify the conduct of business.

*   *   *

III. AGENDA

* * *

16. The Special Committee believes that economy would result should the Assembly in future indicate clearly its intentions when drafting resolutions calling for the preparation of special or annual reports. Some previous resolutions have contained specific decisions that an item or the subject of a report should be placed on the provisional agenda of a subsequent session; others have called only for the submission of a report; yet others have requested that the question should be dealt with in a section of another report to be presented by an organ or by the Secretary-General.

17. It is evident that in some instances in the past, it was not the intention of the Assembly that the subject of a report should appear as an item in the agenda. In others, however, doubts existed on the point and an item covering such a report might have been included in the agenda when no action on the part of the Assembly was called for. The situation would be clarified if the practice were adopted of stating in the resolution whether it is intended that the report should be submitted to the General Assembly for consideration or to Members for their information. In the first case it would be included in the provisional agenda of the following session; in the second, it would not.

18. As regards, in particular, resolutions calling for the submission of annual reports, it is especially desirable to avoid any possible uncertainty as to whether or not the Secretary-General should include such reports each year in the provisional agenda.

19. Certain agenda items which recur from year to year do not necessarily require the attention of the Assembly at every session; during the seventh session, for example, with respect to at least three items it was decided that they should next appear on the agenda of the ninth session. This practice would no doubt help to relieve the agenda and it might result in an appreciable saving of time. In the view of the majority of the members of the Special Committee it would be desirable, therefore, for the Assembly to specify, whenever practicable, that an item of this character should appear only on the agenda of alternate sessions or at longer intervals.

* * *

21. The Special Committee further suggests that the work of the Assembly might progress more smoothly and the deliberations in the Main Committees might follow a more regular pace if the closing date of the sessions were taken into account by the Chairmen at the outset. Informal time-tables for the completion of the items

on a Committee's agenda, drawn up by the Chairman for his guidance early in the session, might be helpful in maintaining an even distribution of work throughout the entire period.

IV. REPORTS OF COUNCILS

22. The majority of the members of the Special Committee believe that consideration of the reports of the Economic and Social Council and the Trusteeship Council would be facilitated if the General Assembly were to encourage the Councils to continue the practice of indicating in their annual reports those matters on which they desire that the Assembly should take action. This trend, which should be strengthened, does not prejudice the right of the Assembly to debate any aspect of the reports, and it has the advantage of providing Members in advance with more precise information on what questions covered in the reports would be the subject of debate during a session of the General Assembly. It is, therefore, of particular interest that the reports of the Councils should be circulated to Members as much in advance of the opening of the sessions as the schedules of the Councils themselves permit.

*   *   *

V. SCOPE OF PROPOSALS MADE IN COMMITTEES

24. It is the view of the majority of the members of the Special Committee that the past tendency in Main Committees to interpret too liberally the scope of the items referred to them has, on occasions, caused the range of subjects dealt with during a session to extend beyond the limits set by the agenda items as adopted. There have been cases in which debates have taken place and draft resolutions have been proposed on matters only remotely or indirectly related to the items under discussion.

25. A reasonable interpretation of the limitations implied by the agenda of a Main Committee, as agreed upon by the Assembly, should not restrict the freedom of a Committee to give full consideration to its items; it should, however, provide a clear frame of reference for the debates, and the right and obligation of Chairmen to rule out of order extraneous remarks and proposals falling outside its bounds should be recognized.

VI. DEBATE IN COMMITTEES

26. The Special Committee discussed several suggestions submitted in connexion with the debates in Committees. Clearly, this is one of the most important areas in the proceedings of the General

Assembly and proposals touching on it should be viewed with caution. Certain practices, however, have developed over the years which, in the opinion of the Special Committee, could profitably be re-examined. The tendency has grown in the Main Committees automatically to observe independent and succeeding stages with respect to each item on the agenda—a general debate on the item, followed by debates on specific proposals, further debates on amendments and still others under the right of reply and the explanation of vote. This formal segmentation often provokes duplication of speeches and increases, as well, the risk of engaging in protracted procedural discussions.

27. The mechanics of a Main Committee cannot be simplified or altered beyond a certain point, it is true, but greater flexibility in the procedure for considering items is desirable. In general, the discussion on the broad aspects of a subject should be combined with the consideration of specific proposals. Time would be saved if Members were to introduce draft resolutions and amendments as soon as practicable in order that the Committees might direct their attention at the earliest opportunity to the examination of specific texts. The work in Committees would also be accelerated if the items proposed for inclusion in the agenda were more frequently accompanied by a draft resolution in accordance with the provisions of rule 20 of the rules of procedure.

*   *   *

29. The Special Committee also considered the suggestion that representatives should be entitled to submit written statements instead of making oral explanations of vote. In this connexion, it was pointed out that explanations of vote frequently touch on the substance of the question under discussion and that, consequently, if these statements were made after rather than before the voting takes place, they might tend to conform more strictly to the intent of rules 88 and 127; if, in addition, they were submitted in writing, time would be gained during the sessions. The Special Committee concluded, however, that serious problems would arise regarding such questions as, for example, the relevance of remarks which had been submitted in writing and the exercise of the right of reply with respect to them; it was further felt that this procedure would entail considerable difficulties in the preparation and distribution of the records of meetings. In view of these considerations and inasmuch as some members were opposed in principle to the suggestion, the Special Committee has not formulated recommendations to this effect.

30. On the other hand, the practice in plenary meetings of

imposing a limitation on the time allowed for explanations of vote has produced good results. The majority of the members of the Special Committee believe that the Main Committees could profitably follow the same procedure.

*   *   *

VIII. LIST OF SPEAKERS

38. The special Committee believes that the presiding officers of the General Assembly and of the Main Committees should urge the representatives to signify at their earliest convenience their desire to be placed on the list of speakers. Compliance with this request and readiness to speak in accordance with the order of the list would promote the orderly conduct of business in the Assembly and, particularly, in the Main Committees. This practice and the closure of the list as soon as is reasonably possible can lead to a measureable saving of time during the sessions.

IX. POINTS OF ORDER

*   *   *

41. A point of order is, basically, an intervention directed to the presiding officer requesting him to make use of some power inherent in his office, or specifically given him under the rules of procedure. It may, for example, relate to the material conditions under which the meeting is taking place. It may be a request that the presiding officer should accord the speaker some privilege which it is in the officer's power to grant. Under a point of order, a representative may request the presiding officer to apply a certain rule of procedure or he may refer to the manner in which the presiding officer should apply a given rule, or the rules of procedure as a whole.

*   *   *

XII. SCHEDULE OF MEETINGS

*   *   *

49. The Special Committee wishes to draw attention to the serious loss of time that results from the lack of punctuality in the opening of meetings and from adjournments before the appointed time. On the basis of two and one-half hours per meeting, during the sixth session, for example, the total apparent loss of time amounted to fourteen working days. Allowing that these figures are of only relative value inasmuch as they reflect a mechanical computation, it can be seen, nevertheless, that the duration of regular sessions could be effectively reduced if meetings were held more closely on schedule.

50. Early adjournment of meetings, and the late cancellation of others, frequently occur owing to a lack of speakers on the item which is being considered in a Main Committee. These situations could often be avoided by the inclusion of more than one item in the Committee's daily agenda; representatives would then be in a position, when necessary, to leave one item temporarily and pass to the discussion of another without interrupting the schedule of meetings.

*　　　*　　　*

APPENDIX 10

Extracts from the
Report of the *Ad Hoc* Committee on the
Improvement of the Methods of work of
the General Assembly[368]*

28 May 1963

I. INTRODUCTION

1. By resolution 1845 (XVII), adopted at its 1198th plenary meeting on 19 December 1962, the General Assembly decided to continue the *Ad Hoc* Committee on the Improvement of the Methods of Work of the General Assembly with the same membership and terms of reference as those decided on at the 1162nd plenary meeting, and requested the Committee to transmit to the Secretary-General by 31 May 1963 a report, with recommendations or suggestions, for circulation to Member States.

*   *   *

9. The Special Committee was gratified to note the great harmony which prevailed at its meetings. The members of the Committee endeavoured, above all, to approach the study of the methods of work of the General Assembly from a technical angle and to take into account what they believed to be the facts of the situation and the needs of the Assembly at the present stage of the development of the United Nations.

II. IMPROVEMENT OF THE METHODS OF WORK OF THE GENERAL ASSEMBLY

General observations

10. In his memorandum of 26 April 1962 on the work of the General Assembly Mr Mongi Slim, President of the sixteenth regular session, had stressed that the two factors which in his view called for a new study of the methods of work of the Assembly were, on the one hand, the substantial increase in the number of Member States in recent years and, on the other, the increase in the number

---

* The footnotes and a number of parenthetical references in the document have not been reproduced, with the exception of the footnote which appears on page 346.

and complexity of the problems regularly brought before the Assembly. Mr Slim was of the opinion that the organization of sessions and the procedures followed could be adapted to the requirements of the new situation, without entailing any major changes in the rules of procedure. He expressed his conviction that useful reforms could be introduced without 'restricting the opportunities for fruitful discussion likely to produce the thoroughly considered and agreed solutions which are required'.

11. In studying the methods of work of the General Assembly in accordance with its terms of reference the *Ad Hoc* Committee adopted the same approach. From the many suggestions received in writing by the Committee from Member States and from the oral statements heard by it, it was clear that the issue was not that of a revision of the rules of procedure. The present rules provide an adequate framework for the Assembly's work; they have stood the test of time; they have the great advantage that delegations are familiar with them; most of the other United Nations organs and many other international agencies have adapted them to their own needs; gaps in them have been filled by practice; and it does not seem necessary at this stage to correct the few flaws of drafting that may have survived the meticulous study made by the organs which preceded this Committee.

12. The *Ad Hoc* Committee noted, however, that in many cases sufficient use is not made of the opportunities which are offered by the present rules of procedure if they are applied correctly. In the recommendations that follow the Committee draws the attention of the General Assembly to some of the measures already provided for in the texts which might be resorted to more often with a view to the improvement and better organization of the proceedings at the sessions. Generally speaking, the Committee is of the opinion that the Assembly would gain in efficiency if the possibilities offered by its rules of procedure were better known by those responsible for their application—the presiding officers, the members of delegations and the Secretariat—and if these rules were applied regularly in their letter and in their spirit.

13. The Committee would like to point out that in the course of its work it refrained from recommending any measures which might have reduced the opportunities for action available to the General Assembly under the Charter. The development of the United Nations has made clear the role which can be played and the influence which must be exercised by the only principal organ of the United Nations having wide powers in which all Member States are represented on an equal footing. The work of the General

Assembly is accomplished through the public statements made on behalf of Members, through debates and through the multiple consultations which lead up to the submission of draft resolutions and culminate in their adoption. There should be no question of hampering this diplomatic process of negotiation and decision by imposing unduly rigid limitations. Full account must also be taken of the need to respect the freedom of expression of delegations which may find themselves in the minority on certain questions while, at the same time, safeguarding the right of majorities to obtain, in conformity with the Charter, the decisions they desire.

14. The Committee nevertheless believes that it is in the interests of both the United Nations and the Member States that the business of the General Assembly should be dispatched as expeditiously as these general considerations permit, that loss of time, from whatever cause it may arise, should be avoided and that, save in exceptional cases, when the international situation so requires, the sessions should not exceed the period of time which is now regarded as normal and which at the seventeenth session amount to thirteen weeks.

15. Accordingly, the Committee preferred not to accept the suggestions whereby the activities of the General Assembly would be spread over the whole year, or to propose the establishment of new subsidiary organs which might carry on the work of the General Assembly between the regular sessions. It favours the present system of intensive meetings during sessions of a limited duration which enable members of Government, members of Parliament and other authorized spokesmen for national public opinion, diplomats, experts and technicians to come together and exchange views both at meetings and outside the conference rooms.

A. Organization of Sessions

1. *The General Debate*

17. The *Ad Hoc* Committee carefully examined the manner in which what is known as the 'general debate' is conducted at the beginning of each regular session. The debate in fact consists of a series of statements made by most Chairmen of delegations on world problems and the role of the United Nations, in the light of the annual report of the Secretary-General on the work of the Organization and reports of other United Nations organs. With the increase in the number of Members, the length of the debate has appreciably increased, from thirteen meetings at the tenth session to twenty-nine

meetings at the seventeenth session. Because of its enhanced importance and the prominence of the speakers taking part in it, it has had the effect of delaying considerably the start of the work of the Main Committees and of somewhat slowing down that work.

18. The Committee recognizes the value of the general debate, which enables Governments to focus the attention of Member States on important international issues. It also realizes that, in view of the shortness of the time which Heads of Government or Ministers for Foreign Affairs can spend in New York, the general debate must be organized with considerably more flexibility than would otherwise be the case. It was observed that, if four statements could be made at each meeting and ten meetings could be held each week for the general debate at the opening of the session, it would be possible for the General Assembly to hear 120 statements in three weeks, a figure higher than the present membership of the Organization. The Committee does not recommend three weeks or any other specified period as the absolute limit for the completion of the general debate. It wishes, however, to stress the importance of ensuring that the debate proceeds as speedily as possible in an organized and regular manner and that as little time as possible remains unused during the meetings devoted to it.

19. The Committee noted with approval in that connexion the Secretary-General's practice of inquiring of delegations, by means of a circular letter sent before the opening of the session as to the dates on which they would like to speak. On the basis of delegations' replies, the Secretariat prepares a provisional list of speakers which is submitted to the President of the Assembly for that session soon after he is elected. In the Committee's view it would be desirable that delegations should abstain from reserving more than one date for their statements.

20. In the opinion of the *Ad Hoc* Committee, the President of the Assembly should ensure the successful completion of the general debate in the shortest possible time; thus, if it proves difficult to some delegations to take the floor at a date previously selected by them, the President should use the discretionary powers granted to him under the rules of procedure to determine in a final manner the order of speakers. The Committee recommends that, with the consent of the General Assembly, as provided in rule 75 of the rules of procedure, the President should close the list of speakers in the general debate earlier than is done at present, and as soon as he deems it feasible. It is for the President to approach delegations to ascertain whether they are prepared to make their statements earlier or later in order to prevent loss of time at meetings. As soon as the

list of speakers is closed, the delegations concerned could be notified of the dates fixed for their interventions, and they should ask the President to make changes only in exceptional circumstances or when they can themselves arrange to change places on the list with other delegations.

21. Delegations should give the President all possible co-operation. They might, for example, try to complete the preparation of their speeches one or two days before the days set for their interventions and thus enable the President to advance that date, with their consent, if there is a gap to be filled in the list of speakers.

2. Organization of work of the Main Committees

(a) Commencement of work of the Committees

22. The *Ad Hoc* Committee felt that if sessions were not to exceed the normal length of about thirteen weeks, and in order to prevent an accumulation of meetings in December, it was important to avoid, as much as possible, the loss of time early in the sessions. The Committee therefore considers that the Main Committees should begin their work promptly, as soon as the General Assembly has adopted its agenda and the items have been allocated to them for consideration. Thus all the Main Committees, except the First Committee, should begin work at the latest two working days after they have been notified of their agenda.

23. As regards the First Committee, the *Ad Hoc* Committee recognizes that, as a general rule, that Committee should not meet simultaneously with the plenary when the latter considers political questions. It is, however, important that the First Committee should meet as soon as possible, to organize its work, determine the order of discussion of the items allocated to it and start the systematic consideration of its agenda. At the beginning of the session, such meetings might be held when there is an interrruption in the general debate; later, meetings of the plenary might be held during one part of the day, the other part being allocated to the First Committee. The aim should be to enable the First Committee to proceed with its regular work as soon as possible after the opening of the session.

(b) Establishment of work schedules

24. The *Ad Hoc* Committee considers it useful to recommend that each Main Committee should, as soon as possible after the beginning of its discussions, prepare a work schedule which would indicate the approximate dates when the various items allocated to it would be discussed. Schedules of this kind, based on information supplied by the Secretariat, are now submitted to some committees.

They have the special advantage of informing delegations when the presence of experts on certain questions will be required in New York.

25. The Committee recommends that such schedules should be transmitted to the General Committee as soon as they have been approved by the Main Committees, in order to provide that Committee with an over-all view of the schedule of work for the session, and if necessary to enable it to make appropriate recommendations to the Committees through the plenary Assembly. The General Committee should also, when it seems appropriate, put forward for the approval of the General Assembly a closing date for the work of each Committee.

(c) *Grouping of related agenda items*

26. The Committee noted the practice in some cases of grouping together all provisional agenda items referring to a single problem. In the past, such groupings have been decided upon by the General Assembly on the recommendation of the General Committee following the adoption of a proposal initiated by the Secretary-General or one of its members; in other instances the Committee concerned took the initiative of regrouping items when adopting its schedule of work. The advantage of this procedure is that there is only one general debate on the question although several draft resolutions, relating to its different aspects, may be submitted. The Committee considered that the Secretary-General, in making his suggestions on the provisional agenda, the General Committee when it makes recommendations on it, and the individual committees when they adopt their work schedules, should bear this possibility in mind, it being understood that the authors of proposals aimed at grouping agenda items should whenever possible consult beforehand the delegations which have proposed those items for inclusion in the General Assembly's agenda, with a view to securing their agreement. The delegation of the Soviet Union pointed out that it considered that the agreement of the delegation or delegations which have proposed the relevant items for inclusion in the General Assembly's agenda should be required in every particular case before grouping agenda items and holding a single general debate on the question to which the items refer.

(d) *Concurrent consideration of more than one agenda item*

27. The Committee thought that in certain cases where time might be wasted, owing to lack of speakers or the absence of draft resolutions, Committees might well decide to suspend the consideration of an item and take up the next one. That could be done, for

instance, when the consideration of any item had to be interrupted to enable delegations to negotiate, or when some delegations were awaiting instructions from their Governments before taking a position.

28. On other occasions, where prolonged negotiations may be expected before agreement can be reached on a draft resolution, it should be possible so to organize the work of the Committee that one meeting a day would be devoted to the examination of one of the Committee's agenda items and another meeting to another item.

(e) *Greater use of sub-committees and working groups*

29. The increase in the number of Members of the United Nations has created a situation in which it frequently happens that more than one hundred delegations are present and most of them participate in the debates in the Main Committees. Although the presence of such a large number of delegations involves no practical difficulties when statements of the positions of Governments are being made, it makes it more difficult to discuss concrete points, to have a rapid exchange of views on subjects where ideas differ or to draft and modify texts. The Committee is of the opinion that in many cases the examination of agenda items by the committees would be greatly facilitated if, as soon as possible and especially when the main points of view have been expressed, the committee decided, on the initiative of its Chairman or of one or more of its members, to set up a sub-committee or working group, in conformity with rule 104 of the rules of procedure (98 in the case of the plenary Assembly). This procedure might be particularly helpful when there is general agreement on the question under discussion but disagreement on points of detail.

30. The *Ad Hoc* Committee would recall in this connexion that in the course of the first sessions of the General Assembly frequent use was made of sub-committees and working groups and that they were of great assistance to the General Assembly in the preparation of texts which to this day govern the structures of the United Nations in the formulation of important international instruments and in the solution of difficult political problems (one example is the sub-committee which dealt with the future status of the former Italian colonies). As far back as 1947, the report of the Committee on Procedures and Organization expressed itself on this subject as follows:

'The Main Committees should consider carefully at an early stage in their work how their programmes might be expedited by the establishment of sub-committees. It is, of course, impossible to adopt fixed rules on this matter. If the debate in full committee showed that there was general agreement on the question under discussion but disagreement on points of detail, it would clearly be desirable to set up a small drafting committee to prepare a resolution for submission to the Main Committee. Technical questions on which there is no substantial disagreement should be referred to sub-committees as quickly as possible. In some cases the work of sub-committees would be facilitated by working informally, and, on occasion, in private.'

31. The sub-committees or working groups could, in most cases, consist of representatives of the delegations with the closest interest in the agenda item, representatives who are specially competent to deal with the problem under discussion and others chosen in such a way as to ensure that the sub-committee or working group will be broadly representative, geographically and politically.

32. These bodies could meet either in public or in private, according to the circumstances, and could either follow formal procedures or discuss matters informally. Their function would be to make it possible for those primarily interested in an item to exchange views, thus facilitating subsequent agreement and compromise solutions; they could prepare draft resolutions or at least formulate alternative solutions; they could appoint rapporteurs to present their conclusions and to give the necessary explanations to the committee which established them. The committee itself would be entirely free to take final decisions but, since all aspects of the problem would have been given minute examination, it would undoubtedly find its own work greatly facilitated both as regards substance and as regards the time thus saved. It would, also, often be possible for the committee to consider other items on its agenda while the sub-committee or working group was carrying out its assignment.

(f) *Items peculiar to certain of the Main Committees*

(i) *Referral of items to the Economic and Social Council*

33. The Committee had before it proposals that economic and social items included in the agenda, which had not been examined previously by the Economic and Social Council, should be referred to the latter before being considered by the Second or Third Committee. It was suggested in that connexion that in urgent cases the Council could examine such items during its resumed second session which is customarily held in November or December.

34. The Committee did not feel that it ought to make any specific recommendation on this subject and confines itself to remarking that the Economic and Social Council might in many

cases, by decision of the General Assembly, usefully consider beforehand questions within its competence which are then to be allocated to the Second or Third Committee.

(ii) *Hearing of petitioners*

35. The Committee examined a table showing the amount of time spent by the Fourth Committee during the last three regular sessions in hearing persons who had made statements and replied to questions asked by members on conditions in the territories of concern to the Fourth Committee. Some of those persons had already been heard by subsidiary bodies of the Assembly before the session; some have addressed the Committee on more than one occasion.

36. The Committee was unwilling to accept suggestions which would have the effect of imposing restrictions on the Fourth Committee's freedom to make use of these sources of information. It considers, however, that time could be saved if the Secretariat notified persons invited by the Committee as early as possible of the dates on which they would be called upon to make their statements. That procedure would be facilitated if, as the Committee has proposed, the Fourth Committee could decide on its programme of work at the beginning of the session, including the dates on which the agenda items assigned to it would be examined.

3. *Role of the General Committee*

37. The *Ad Hoc* Committee considers that the General Committee of the Assembly should actively fulfil the important role assigned to it under the rules of procedure. In addition to the functions which it already exercises in connexion with the agenda of the session (rule 40) and those relating to the fixing of the closing date of the session (rule 41), the General Committee should try in particular to ensure better co-ordination of the proceedings of all committees of the General Assembly and of the work of the committees with that of the plenary Assembly (rules 41 and 42). As specified in rule 42, the General Committee should not hesitate to make practical recommendations with a view to furthering the progress of the work of the General Assembly and of its committees so that all appropriate action may be taken to complete the examination of agenda items by the date fixed for the closure of the session.

38. The *Ad Hoc* Committee considers that, for this purpose, the periodic meetings of the General Committee, provided for in rule 42 of the rules of procedure, should be spaced not more than three weeks apart in a normal period and should be held even more frequently at the beginning and towards the end of sessions.

B. CONDUCT OF THE DEBATES

1. *Role of the presiding officers*

39. The *Ad Hoc* Committee feels that it need hardly stress the importance of the role of the presiding officers and the authority which they should be able to exercise in discharging their functions under the rules of procedure. The smooth progress of the work of the organs over which they preside depends largely upon their skill, their familiarity with the Assembly's procedures and their impartiality. The President of the Assembly and the Chairmen of the Main Committees should be able to rely on the co-operation of all delegations and the full assistance of the Secretariat.

40. The Committee considers that, due regard being given to the principle of equitable geographical distribution and to the requirement under the rules of procedure that the General Committee should be so constituted as to ensure its representative character of the General Assembly as a whole, special importance should be attributed in the selection of presiding officers to such elements as the previous experience of candidates of the technique of chairmanship or familiarity with the work of the Assembly or of other United Nations bodies.

2. *Power of initiative of the presiding officers*

41. While not wishing to restrict the free course of debates in the General Assembly and its committees, the Committee considers that, under the rules of procedure, the presiding officers can, with skill, find in the provisions of the rules of procedure many ways of speeding up the work of the Assembly. Rules 35 and 108 confirm that they are responsible for directing the discussions and that their role is by no means a passive one or confined to calling upon speakers requesting the floor. Those provisions reaffirm, for example, that the presiding officers may propose the limitation of the time to be allowed to speakers and the limitation of the number of times each representative may speak on any question, the closure of the list of speakers or the closure of the debate. In the opinion of the Committee, the presiding officers, while maintaining the impartiality that their functions require of them, should not hesitate to exercise those prerogatives when they feel that this would contribute to the good progress of the Assembly's work.

3. *Beginning meetings at the scheduled time*

42. The Committee examined statistical information relating to the last two regular sessions of the General Assembly with respect

to the actual time of the opening and closing of meetings of the plenary Assembly and Main Committees. It was impressed by the considerable loss of time due to meetings beginning late or closing early.

43. With regard to the actual time when meetings start, the Committee noted the time gained by the President of the seventeenth session, who made it a practice to open the plenary meetings of the Assembly at the time scheduled in the *Journal of the United Nations*, or at most a few minutes later. Most delegations willingly submitted to that discipline and appreciated its advantages. The Committee therefore advises that in future the Presidents of the Assembly as well as the Chairmen of the committees should follow that precedent and begin the meetings at the scheduled time.

44. The presiding officers, assisted by the other officers and by the Secretariat, should keep in constant touch with delegations so that no valuable time is lost because no speakers are available. In order to avoid the adjournment of meetings before the normal hour, speakers who have expressed the wish to take the floor should hold themselves in readiness to make their statements when they are called upon to do so.

45. The Committee believes that this effort to make the fullest use of the time available for meetings might be encouraged if the Secretariat were to prepare a weekly chart of the delays incurred by each committee in starting meetings and the time lost by their premature closing. The chart might take the form of a document, to be submitted to the General Committee for consideration during its periodic meetings, and that Committee might make whatever recommendations or comments it considered appropriate.

4. *Time-limit on speeches*

46. With regard to a time-limit on speeches, the Committee had before it a number of proposals to limit, under the rules of procedure, the time allowed for statements made in the General Assembly or its committees during general debates, during the discussion of draft resolutions, in connexion with explanations of vote, or the right of reply, or when procedural motions are being discussed. In view of the complexity and variety of the situations which may arise in the General Assembly and the special importance of certain debates to some delegations, the Committee does not think it would be wise to make any general decisions which might have the effect of unduly limiting the right of representatives to express fully their views. It recalls, however, that not only are the presiding officers empowered under rules 35 and 108 to propose the limitation of the

time to be allowed to speakers but that under rules 74 and 115 any representative may make such proposals. Thus, depending on the circumstances, the General Assembly and its Committees can decide to limit under rules 74 and 115 of the rules of procedure the time allowed to speakers on certain questions or for certain types of statements. The General Committee of the Assembly, taking into account the progress made by the General Assembly in its work, may also make pertinent recommendations in accordance with rule 42 of the rules of procedure.

47. The Committee noted that the Assembly has almost never exercised its prerogative with regard to limiting the number of times representatives may speak. The Committee wishes to recall, however, the practice whereby representatives speak not only on behalf of their own delegations but also on behalf of other delegations sharing their views on the matter under discussion. The Committee notes that this practice has already helped the General Assembly to save time.

5. *List of speakers*

48. Apart from the above comments on making good use of meeting time and the reference to the power of presiding officers under rules 35 and 108 to propose the closure of the list of speakers, a power specifically provided for in rules 75 and 116, the Committee recommends that the name of a representative who is not prepared to speak when his turn comes should automatically be transferred to the bottom of the list of speakers unless, by agreement with the presiding officer, it can be arranged for that representative to speak earlier. However, it is the opinion of the Committee that the established practice whereby representatives are allowed to exchange places on the list of speakers should be maintained.

6. *Right of reply*

49. The Committee considered the circumstances in which representatives take the floor to 'exercise the right of reply'. It may be observed that a strict application of rules 75 and 116 would imply that the right of reply can only be exercised if the presiding officer feels that 'a speech delivered after the list of speakers has been closed makes this desirable'. The Committee is of the opinion that any delegation which has been attacked or criticized either by direct reference or by imputation is entitled, if it so desires, to exercise the 'right of reply'. The Committee also recognizes that there are other occasions when a representative may legitimately feel he should make a clarifying statement because of comments made with respect

to the attitude or policy of his country before the closing of the list of speakers.

50. It is solely within those limits however that the Committee feels that 'the right of reply' should be recognized by presiding officers. The Committee considers that the presiding officer is entitled under the rules of procedure to remind the representative who wishes to avail himself of the 'right of reply' of the limits to which the exercise of that right is subject.

7. *Explanations of vote*

51. In accordance with rules 90 and 129 of the rules of procedure, an explanation of vote may be permitted by the presiding officer either before or after the voting, except when the vote is taken by secret ballot; the presiding officer may limit the time to be allowed for such explanations. The Committee believes that it is the responsibility of the presiding officers to see to it that explanations of votes are used solely for their basic purpose, namely, to explain the reasons why a delegation wishes to cast an affirmative or negative vote or to abstain. The explanation of a vote should, therefore, not be an occasion for resuming discussions with other delegations.

8. *Points of order*

52. The Committee feels that it is useful to recall the correct procedure in connexion with points of order. The provisions of rules 73 and 114 of the rules of procedure are very clear in that respect. When a debate is interrupted by a representative's raising a point of order, the presiding officer, after the representative has been heard, must give a ruling immediately. He may not allow a discussion to be started on the subject. No other point of order should be discussed before the presiding officer has decided upon the previous one. The responsibility for deciding is his alone and the rules do not provide that he may request the Assembly or committee to make a ruling for him; a representative who is not satisfied with the presiding officer's decision is entirely free to appeal to the Assembly or the committee and such an appeal should be regarded as a simple difference of opinion concerning the application of the rules and not in any way as a reflection on the prestige of the Chair. The appeal 'shall be immediately put to the vote'; in other words no statement may be made except for the explanation by the representative making the appeal and that of the presiding officer concerning what he considers to be the correct application of the rules. The vote of the Assembly or committee on the appeal, as provided in rules 73 and 114, is final. Once the question is settled, the Assembly or com-

mittee reverts to the consideration of the agenda item. The delegation of the Soviet Union considered that an analysis of rules 73 and 114 of the rules of procedure, together with rules 36 and 109, would lead to the conclusion that in some complicated cases, when the presiding officer did not consider it possible to make a ruling, he might ask the Assembly or the committee to make a decision on the question to which the point of order referred.

53. The rules themselves are not very explicit as regards the type of intervention which the presiding officer can accept as a point of order, although rules 73 and 114 stipulate that 'a representative rising to a point of order may not speak on the substance of the matter under discussion'. In this connexion the Committee recalls that the committees which preceded it have already submitted to the General Assembly definitions or explanations of the matters which a point of order may cover. The 1949 Special Committee on Methods and Procedures of the General Assembly stated:

'It is the opinion of the Special Committee that a valid point of order may relate to the manner in which the debate is conducted, to the maintenance of order, to the observance of the rules of procedure, or to the manner in which the Chairmen exercise the powers conferred upon them by the rules. Thus, within the scope of the General Assembly's rules of procedure, representatives are enabled to direct the attention of the presiding officer to violations or misapplications of the rules of procedure by other representatives or by the presiding officer himself. Points of order may also refer to legitimate requests for information, to material arrangements (temperature of the room, seating, interpretation system), to documents, translations and so on. On the other hand, no representative, when rising to a point of order, should be permitted to speak on the substance of the matter under discussion.'

9. *Assistance to presiding officers*

54. As the Committee has already pointed out, every possible assistance should be given to the presiding officers in order to facilitate the exercise of their functions in accordance with the rules of procedure. In this connexion the Committee recalls that, in addition to the constant help they receive from the committee secretaries, presiding officers may seek the assistance from the Office of Legal Affairs whenever they need special advice with regard to the application of the rules of procedure or when difficult procedural questions are likely to arise. Advantages may also be derived from consultations between chairmen of main committees and the

President of the General Assembly and between chairmen of m[
committees on any complex procedural difficulties which may ari[
in their committees.

55. The Committee considers that it would be useful if th[
Secretariat were asked from now on to keep systematic note of the
various questions of procedure which arise in the General Assembly
and its committees and to assemble this information in a form
accessible to presiding officers and any representatives who might
wish to consult them. In this connexion, the Committee considers
that the summary records of meetings should contain fairly detailed
accounts of debates on procedural questions.

56. The Committee also discussed the usefulness of the preparation by the Secretariat of a repertory of past practice and of a
manual of procedure containing notes on the various rules and
examples of decisions illustrating their application. While considering the subject worthy of further study, the Committee does
not find itself in a position to make definite recommendations on the
matter.

C. Introduction of Mechanical Means of Voting

57. The Committee studied with care the question of advantages to be derived from the introduction in the General Assembly
of mechanical equipment which would facilitate the counting and the
recording of votes. Its members examined the working of such
equipment during a visit to the General Assembly of the State of
New Jersey. In addition to data annexed to the present report, i.e.
a description of the manner in which mechanical means of voting
could be used in the General Assembly, relevant financial implications and data as to the number of votes taken in the General Assembly during the last three sessions, the Committee wishes to report as
follows on the conclusions it has reached.

58. There was general agreement that an electric system for
registering votes would have the advantage of speed and its use
would result in a sizable saving of time which would, in turn, reduce
the expenses of the Organization and of Member States. The new
system would have the further advantage of being fully accurate,
especially in the procedure corresponding to a vote by show of hands
in connexion with which the Secretariat has met in recent years with
increasing difficulty. The system of electric voting would also have
the advantage of convenience since the results would be indicated
for sufficient length of time on mural panels, thus preventing confusion. It was acknowledged that the new system would not be
applicable to secret ballots. Some questions were raised as to the

financial implications of the installation of the electric system of voting and the effects on the budget of the Organization at a time when the Organization is facing financial difficulties. It was, however, the understanding of the Committee that the question would be considered by the Advisory Committee on Administrative and Budgetary Questions before the General Assembly reaches a final decision on the matter. Subject to further examination of the financial considerations involved, it was the view of the Committee that the Secretary-General should explore this possibility in order that the electric system of voting should be tried experimentally for one or two years in one or more conference rooms.*

D. Clarification of Certain Procedural Questions

59. In the course of its work, the *Ad Hoc* Committee examined certain questions which did not, strictly speaking, relate to the improvement of methods of work of the General Assembly but rather to certain procedural situations which might arise in the Assembly. The Committee wishes to draw the Assembly's attention to its views on two of these questions.

1. *Co-sponsors of draft resolutions or amendments*

60. The Committee considered a situation which has occurred in recent years where a large number of delegations wish to be designated as sponsors of certain draft resolutions or draft amendments submitted for the Assembly's approval. The Committee did not agree to suggestions that a limit should be placed on the number of delegations which might be so designated. It wishes, however, to make it clear that, in its view, it is for the authors of a proposal which has already been submitted to the Assembly or to a committee to decide whether other delegations should also become sponsors of it. Delegations wishing to become co-sponsors ought therefore to approach the original sponsors if they wish their names to be added to the list already published.

2. *Voting by secret ballot*

61. The Committee considered certain difficulties which may arise when one of the Main Committees proceeds to a vote by secret ballot, in accordance with rule 105 of the rules of procedure, and all

---

* The representative of the United States was of the opinion that, in view of the financial difficulties facing the United Nations, the equipment should be installed in a single conference room during the first year. The representatives of the USSR considered that no supplementary estimates should be involved and that the installation should be financed out of savings in the regular budget.

representatives are not in their places when the conference officer collects the ballot papers. The Committee recommends that in such cases committees should follow the practice of the General Assembly and that the balloting should be done by roll-call, representatives being allowed to vote up to the moment when the Chairman declares the voting closed.

E. Certain other Suggestions considered by the *Ad Hoc* Committee

1. *Establishment of an agenda committee*

62. The *Ad Hoc* Committee had before it a seggestion that an agenda committee should be established to consider the provisional agenda and the supplementary list of items proposed for inclusion in the agenda. This committee, which would carry out the work of the General Committee on the agenda before the opening of the regular session, would be automatically dissolved once the General Committee for the session was set up. The Committee did not consider it necessary to make a recommendation to the General Assembly on this matter.

2. *Designation of special rapporteurs*

63. The *Ad Hoc* Committee also considered the possibility of speeding up the work of the Main Committees by the designation, where appropriate, of special rapporteurs. It was said in this connexion that, in the case of questions already discussed by the General Assembly, the special rapporteurs might, for example, summarize the main issues on which there had already been discussion, prepare a brief and objective account of the history of the question and sometimes bring out the main points in dispute. If this procedure were to be followed, delegations taking the floor would not need to go over the same ground, and could confine themselves to stating the positions of their countries. The Committee decided not to make any proposal to the Assembly on this matter.

3. *Practice of 'extended remarks'*

64. The *Ad Hoc* Committee considered the possibility of introducing in the General Assembly the practice of certain national Parliaments which allow representatives to submit written statements to supplement or replace oral statements. The delegations which advocated this method pointed out that it would be particularly appropriate for explanations of votes, lengthy or technical statements and statements made in exercise of the right of reply. The majority of the Committee, however, did not support these

suggestions, the effect of which would be to alter the nature of the Assembly's debates considerably and to raise a certain number of practical problems which would be difficult to solve.

4. *Change in the opening date of the regular session*

65. The Committee also considered the suggestions made to it concerning a possible change in the opening date of the regular session of the General Assembly. Two suggestions in particular wer^ considered, one to bring the opening date of the session for- ι to the beginning of September, and the other to hold the lar session from March to June. These suggestions were mainly ᴍpted by a desire to avoid the holding of resumed sessions after end-of-year holidays, as has frequently happened in the past, ᴇn such sessions have proved long and costly.

66. The Committee did not accept the suggestion that the gular session of the General Assembly should be brought forward the beginning of September, considering, in particular, that the ʀst two weeks of September should be free for delegations to hold ʀivate consultations. Nor did the Committee accept the proposal hat the regular session of the General Assembly should be held in spring rather than autumn, as it wished to take into account the fact that many national Parliaments have busy sessions in that part of the year. The Committee noted with satisfaction that the Assembly had succeeded in ending its seventeenth regular session before the end-of-year holidays and it hopes that through the improvement of its methods of work it will be able in future in the normal way to end its sessions by the third week of December.

A NOTE ON
GENERAL ASSEMBLY DOCUMENTS

I once submitted an article to a scholarly quarterly published in a country which it is not necessary to mention here. The editor accepted the article, but asked me to 'insert a few footnotes'. I re-read the article several times, but for the life of me I was unable to see where footnotes were needed. I wrote to the editor asking if he would indicate where footnotes would improve the article. He replied that this was my responsibility, not his. The policy of the journal was to publish articles with footnotes, and he hoped I would cooperate by adapting my article to conform to editorial policy.

On the day I received this letter, I came across a reference in a book to the creation of the world. The author, as if to cite additional evidence that the world did in fact exist, had inserted as a footnote '*Genesis* 1:1'.

References can be pretentious and distracting, and I wish there were fewer in this book. I have, however, accepted the advice of those who know more about the matter than I do and given in the references that follow the symbols of United Nations documents quoted or referred to in the text.

A brief explanation is needed about the symbols used. Verbatim records are prepared for plenary meetings and meetings of the First Committee. Summary records, which give only a general picture of the discussion, are prepared for the other Main Committees and the General Committee. They are mimeographed in 'blue-provisional' form, and delegates are permitted to submit corrections of actual errors or omissions. The final records are printed and are referred to as G.A.O.R. (General Assembly Official Records), followed by the number of the session (whether a regular session, a special session, or an emergency special session); a note as to whether it was a plenary or committee meeting and, if a committee, its name or number; the number and date of the meeting; and the page or paragraph number.

Reports of principal organs and certain other reports are issued before or during the session in printed form as supplements to the official records. Other documents are first issued in mimeographed form with the symbol A/ followed by a number; most are printed after the session as Annexes to the Official Records, a different fascicle normally being issued for each item of the agenda. Documents of a technical or provisional nature whose immediate wide circulation is not necessary, and documents which for any other reason are of interest to only a limited circle, are issued in a 'limited' series, in which the serial number is preceded by the letter L. Documents whose content requires that they not be made public are issued in the 'restricted' series, in which the serial number is preceded by the letter R.

The resolutions of the General Assembly have been numbered consecutively and are cited as G.A. res., followed by the number of the resolution, the number of the session in parenthesis in roman numerals, and the date.

The *Journal* of the United Nations is issued daily in English and French and, during sessions of the Assembly, in Spanish also. It contains the programme of future meetings and agenda, a procedural summary of meetings held on the previous working day, and any announcements.

S.D.B.

REFERENCES

1. Sir Alfred Zimmern, *The League of Nations and the Rule of Law, 1918–1935*. London, Macmillan, 1936, p. 473.
2. Alexis de Tocqueville, *Democracy in America*. English translation edited by Phillips Bradley, New York, Knopf, 1954, vol. 1, p. 243; abridgment edited by Henry Steele Commager, London, Oxford University Press, 1946, pp. 160–1.
3. George Bernard Shaw in L. S. Woolf, *International Government*. New York, Brentano, 1916, pp. xi–xii.
4. G.A.O.R., 8th Session, Supplement No. 1 (1953), pp. xi–xii; 10th Session, Supplement No. 1 (1955), p. xii; 12th Session, Supplement No. 1 (1957), pp. 4–5.
5. Dean Acheson, *Power and Diplomacy*. Cambridge (Mass.), Harvard University Press (London, Oxford University Press; Toronto, Saunders), 1958, p. 126.
6. Lester B. Pearson, *Diplomacy in the Nuclear Age*. Cambridge (Mass.), Harvard University Press, 1959, p. 106.
7. G.A.O.R., 8th Session, 441st plenary meeting (23 Sept. 1953), paras. 16–18.
8. *The Messages and Papers of Woodrow Wilson*. New York, The Review of Reviews Corporation, 1924, Vol. II, pp. 985, 1118–19.
9. For a discussion of weighted voting, see Dag Hammarskjold, 'The Vital Role of the United Nations in a Diplomacy of Reconciliation', *United Nations Review*, Vol. IV (May 1958); John Foster Dulles, *War or Peace*. New York, Macmillan, 1957, pp. 191–4; *Strengthening the United Nations*, Report of the Commission to Study the Organization of Peace. New York, Harper, 1957, pp. 227–32.
10. Press conference, Note to Correspondents No. 1983 (30 April 1959).
11. Sir Harold Nicolson, *The Evolution of the Diplomatic Method*. New York, Macmillan (London, Constable), 1954, p. 84.
12. 'Parliamentary Diplomacy—Debate vs. Negotiation', *World Affairs Interpreter*, Vol. XXVI, No. 2 (Summer 1955), pp. 121–2. See also Philip C. Jessup, *Parliamentary Diplomacy*.

351

Leyden, A. W. Sijthoff, 1956, and Sydney D. Bailey, 'Parliamentary Diplomacy', *Parliamentary Affairs*, Vol. XVI, No. 3 (Summer 1963), pp. 308–314

13. Leon Trotsky, *The History of the Russian Revolution to Brest-Litovsk*. London, Allen and Unwin, 1919, p. 5; *From October to Brest-Litovsk*. Brooklyn (N.Y.), Socialist Publication Society, 1919, p. 84.

14. F. H. Soward and Edgar McInnis, with the assistance of William O'Hearn, *Canada and the United Nations*. New York, Manhattan Publishing, 1956, pp. 220–1.

15. G.A.O.R., 10th Session, Supplement No. 1 (1955), pp. xicxii; U.N. doc. SG/428 (25 June 1955); U.N. doc. SG/656 (3 Feb. 1958).

16. Francis P. Walters, *A History of the League of Nations*. London, Oxford University Press, 1952, Vol. I, p. 199. See also Pitman B. Potter, *Permanent Delegations to the League of Nations*. Geneva, League of Nations Association of the U.S., 1930.

17. Headquarters Agreement (1947), Art. V, Section 15.

18. Trusteeship Council Official Records, 24th Session, Supplement No. 5 (1959), para. 204.

19. Lord Hankey, *Diplomacy by Conference*. New York, Putnam (London, Benn), 1947, p. 35.

20. Articles 7, 97, 98, 100, and 101.

21. Article 99. See also Security Council Official Records, 16th Year, 964th meeting (28 July 1961), para. 86; and Michel Virally, 'Le rôle politique du Secrétaire-Général des Nations Unies,' *Annuaire Français de Droit International*. Paris, Centre National de la Recherche Scientifique, 1958, pp. 369–70.

22. Article 98.

23. Articles 24(1) and 27(3).

24. Articles 23, 61, 86, 17, 101, and 16.

25. Articles 4, 5, 6, 97, 108, 109, Statute Article 4.

26. Articles 10–15.

27. See Sydney D. Bailey, *The Secretariat of the United Nations*. Second edition, New York, Praeger, p. 58.

28. G.A.O.R., 14th Session, Supplement No. 1A (1959), p. 3.

29. Sydney D. Bailey, *The Secretariat of the United Nations*, pp. 55, 73, 76

30. G.A.O.R., 16th Session, 1046th plenary meeting (3 Nov. 1961), para. 30; 5th Committee, 894th meeting (4 Dec. 1961), para. 42; U.N. doc. SG/1102 (29 Dec. 1961).

31. Dean Rusk, 'Parliamentary Diplomacy—Debate vs. Negotiation, *World Affairs Interpreter*, Vol. XXVI, No. 2 (Summer 1955, pp. 129c30.

32. G.A.O.R., 18th Session, Annexes, Agenda item 60, A/5638 (3 Dec. 1963), Annex 1.

33. See, for example, the 'joint statement by the Latin American countries on the financing of UNEF, G.A.O.R., 11th Session, 5th Committee, 547th meeting (10 Dec. 1956), paras. 1–12; the statement in 1961 concerning the agreement of 'The Western European group to the distribution of seats on the Economic and Social Council, G.A.O.R., 15th Session, 987th plenary meeting (18 April 1961), para. 69; the representations of 'the Asian and African Member States' regarding Viet-Nam, G.A.O.R., 18th Session, Annexes, Agenda item 77, A/5542 (23 Sept. 1963); the statement on behalf of all Latin American States except Cuba, plus Jamaica and Trinidad and Tobago, on equitable representation on the Security Council and the Economic and Social Council, G.A.O.R., 18th Session, Special Political Committee, 422nd meeting (10 Dec. 1963), and the statements made at the end of the 18th session of the Assembly 'on behalf of the African group', 'on behalf of the Arab delegations', and 'on behalf of a certain number of delegations of socialist countries', G.A.O.R., 18th Session, 1285th plenary meeting (17 Dec. 1963).

34. See, for example, U.N. doc. A/AC.109/PV.119 (Feb. 26, 1963).

35. Thomas Hovet, Jr., *Bloc Politics in the United Nations*. Cambridge (Mass.), Harvard University Press (London, Oxford University Press). 1960, pp. 30–1.

36. G.A. res. 1192 (XII), 12 Dec. 1957, and 1990 (VXIII), 17 Dec. 1963.

37. Resolution XXX; text in the U.S. Department of State Bulletin, Vol. XII, No. 299 (18 March 1945), p. 450.

38. John A. Houston, *Latin America in the United Nations*. New York, Carnegie Endowment for International Peace, 1956, pp. 6–7.

39. G.A.O.R., 18th Session, Annexes, Agenda item 60, A/5638 (3 Dec. 1963), Annex 1.

40. Ibid.

41. See, for example, G.A.O.R., 14th Session, Special Political Committee, 138th meeting (28 Oct. 1959), para. 4 and 139th meeting (29 Oct. 1959), para. 3; 4th Committee, 932nd meeting (30 Oct. 1959), paras. 23–28.

42. G.A.O.R., 4th Session, 231st plenary meeting (20 Oct. 1949), p. 103, paras. 10–13.

43. G.A.O.R., 17th Session, Annexes, Agenda item 86, A/5123 (3 May 1962), para. 6.
44. G.A.O.R., 8th Session, Annexes, Agenda item 52, A/2620 (8 Dec. 1953), para. 8; A/2553 (9 Nov. 1953), para. 12.
45. G.A.O.R., 8th Session, Annexes, Agenda item 52, A/2436 (12 Aug. 1953), paras. 5 and 6.
46. G.A.O.R., 18th Session, Annexes, Agenda item 25, A/5423 (28 May 1963), para. 65.
47. G.A.O.R., 15th Session, Annexes, Agenda item 3, A/4743 (20 April 1961), paras. 3–5; G.A. res. 1618 (XV), 21 April 1961.
48. G.A.O.R., 18th Session, Annexes, Agenda item 3, A/5676 (14 Dec. 1963), paras. 4–5.
49. G.A. res. 1498 (XV), 22 Nov. 1960.
50. For a discussion of some of the legal aspects of the question, see the memorandum circulated by Secretary-General Lie, S.C.O.R., 5th Year, Supplement for January to May, S/1466 (9 March 1950), pp. 18–23; for a brief statement of the political arguments, see Sydney D. Dailey, *Short Political Guide to the United Nations*. New York, Praeger (London, Pall Mall), 1963, pp. 24–26.
51. G.A.O.R., 14th Session, Annexes, Agenda item 62, A/4182 (13 Aug. 1959).
52. G.A.O.R., 14th Session, Annexes, Agenda item 62, A/4340 (8 Dec. 1959), para. 12.
53. G.A.O.R., 14th Session, 852nd plenary meeting (10 Dec. 1959), paras. 90–120.
54. G.A. res. 1990 (XVIII), 17 Dec. 1963.
55. Trygve Lie, *In the Cause of Peace*. New York, Macmillan, 1954, pp. 4–5.
56. *Ibid*, p. 10.
57. G.A. res. 17 (I), 29 Jan. 1946; Rule 94.
58. G.A.O.R., 13th Session, 747th plenary meeting (16 Sept. 1958), paras. 19–20.
59. G.A.O.R., 16th Session, 1008th plenary meeting (20 Sept. 1961), paras. 4–12.
60. G.A.O.R., 4th Session, 231st plenary meeting (20 Oct. 1949), para. 22.
61. G.A. res. 1192 (XII), 12 Dec. 1957.
62. G.A. res. 1990 (XVIII), 17 Dec. 1963.
63. No document symbol appears on the Press Release.
64. G.A.O.R., 2nd Session, 6th Committee, Annex 4c (8 Nov. 1947), p. 268.

65. Report by the Executive Committee of the Preparatory Commission, PC/EX/113/Rev. 1 (12 Nov. 1945), pp. 19, 31, and 36.
66. G.A.O.R., 1st Session, Part 1, 18th plenary meeting (26 January 1946), pp. 282–3, 288.
67. G.A.O.R., 2nd Session, 6th Committee, Annex 4c (8 Nov. 1947), p. 270.
68. G.A.O.R., 2nd Session, 6th Committee, 57th meeting (12 Nov. 1947), pp. 140–2.
69. G.A.O.R., 4th Session, Supplement No. 12, A/937 (12 Aug. 1949), Annex 1, p. 18.
70. *Ibid.*, para. 16.
71. G.A.O.R., 18th Session, Annexes, Agenda item 25, A/5423 (28 May 1963), para. 17.
72. See, for example, the following documents circulated during the fifteenth session: A/4537 (13 Oct. 1960); A/4558 (3 Nov. 1960); A/4572 and A/4574 (14 Nov. 1960); A/4595, A/4596, and A/4597 (26 Nov. 1960); A/4631 (8 Dec. 1960).
73. G.A.O.R., 1st Session, Part II, General Committee, Annex 16, A/92 (24 Sept. 1946), para. 6(a), p. 97.
74. Sir Ernest Satow, *A Guide to Diplomatic Practice.* Second, edition, New York and London, Longmans, 1922, Vol. II, pp. 5–7.
75. G.A.O.R., 4th Session, Supplement No. 12, A/937 (12 Aug. 1949), para. 7; 8th Session, Annexes, Agenda item 54, A/2402 (26 June 1953), para. 8.
76. Article 10.
77. G.A.O.R., 1st Session, Part I, General Committee, Annex 3, A/BUR/3 (n.d.), pp. 49–50; U.N. doc. A/316 (8 July 1947); G.A. res. 1898 (XVIII), 11 Nov. 1963.
78. G.A.O.R., 4th Session, Supplement No. 12, A/937 (12 Aug. 1949), para. 10.
79. G.A.O.R., 8th Session, Annexes, Agenda item 54, A/2402 (26 June 1953), paras. 17–18.
80. Report by the Executive Committee of the Preparatory Commission, PC/EX/113/Rev. 1 (12 Nov. 1945), pp. 21, 31.
81. Report of the Preparatory Commission, PC/20 (23 Dec. 1945), p. 11.
82. G.A. res. 362 (IV), 22 Oct. 1949.
83. G.A. res. 791 (VIII), 23 Oct. 1953.
84. G.A. res. 1104 (XI), 18 Dec. 1956.
85. G.A. res. 1192 (XII), 12 Dec. 1957.
86. G.A. res. 1990 (XVIII), 17 Dec. 1963.
87. G.A.O.R., 16th Session, 1107th plenary meeting (7 June

1962), paras. 39–42; General Committee, 146th meeting (8 June 1962), para. 1.

88. G.A.O.R., 1st Session, Part I, 3rd plenary meeting (11 Jan. 1946), p. 69.

89. G.A. res. 17 (I), 29 Jan. 1946.

90. G.A. res. 173 (II), 17 Nov. 1947. The Rule is now numbered 43.

91. League of Nations Assembly Official Journal, 13th Ordinary Session, 1st Committee, Annexes, Special Supplement No. 105, p. 44.

92. Ibid., pp. 11, 12.

93. G.A.O.R., 1st Special Session, General Committee, 29th–31st meetings (29–30 April 1947), pp. 12–87.

94. G.A.O.R., 3rd Session, Part I, General Committee, 43rd meeting (22 Sept. 1948), pp. 11–12.

95. G.A.O.R., 3rd Session, Part II, General Committee, 60th meeting (8 April 1949), p. 43.

96. G.A.O.R., 10th Session, General Committee, 104th meeting (29 Sept. 1955), paras. 2–4.

97. G.A.O.R., 17th Session, General Committee, 148th meeting (19 Sept. 1962), paras. 5–21, 32–35.

98. G.A.O.R., 18th Session, General Committee, 153rd meeting (18 Sept. 1963).

99. Report of the Preparatory Commission, PC/20 (23 Dec. 1945), pp. 11. 12, 123, 124.

100. G.A.O.R., 1st Session, Part I, 6th Committee, 3rd meeting (21 Jan. 1946), pp. 7–8; 18th plenary meeting (26 Jan. 1946), pp. 271–4.

101. G.A.O.R., 1st Session, Part II, General Committee, Annex 16, A/92, para. 6(d).

102. G.A.O.R., 4th Session, Supplement No. 12, A/937 (12 Aug. 1949), para. 25. (This provision is now the last sentence of Rule 40).

103. Ibid.

104. Ibid., para. 12; See also G.A.O.R., 18th Session, Annexes, Agenda item 25, A/5423 (28 May 1963), paras. 33–34.

105. G.A.O.R., 1st Session, Part I, General Committee, 9th meeting (2 Feb. 1946), Annex 8, pp. 17, 21, 54.

106. G.A.O.R., 1st Session, Part II, General Committee, 24th meeting (5 Nov. 1946), p. 80.

107. G.A.O.R., 1st Session, Part II, General Committee, 25th meeting (6 Nov. 1946), p. 88.

108. G.A.O.R., 4th Session, 6th Committee, 146th meeting (29 Sept.

1949), paras. 28–43; 148th meeting (1 Oct. 1949), paras. 95–105.

109. Herbert V. Evatt, President of the third session, referred in the General Committee to informal meetings between presiding officers and the Secretary-General; G.A.O.R., 3rd Session, Part II, General Committee, 57th meeting (5 April 1949), p. 1.
110. G.A. res. 1898 (XVIII), 11 Nov. 1963.
111. G.A.O.R., 13th Session, General Committee, 118th meeting (19 Sept. 1958), para. 25.
112. *Ibid.*, para. 22.
113. G.A.O.R., 13th Session, 752nd plenary meeting (22 Sept. 1958), para. 33.
114. G.A.O.R., 12th Session, General Committee, 114th meeting (4 Oct. 1957), para. 17.
115. G.A.O.R., 1st Session, Part II, General Committee, 19th meeting (24 Oct. 1946), p. 70.
116. G.A.O.R., 8th Session, General Committee, 88th meeting (22 Sept. 1953), paras. 51–52.
117. G.A.O.R., 11th Session, General Committee, 110th meeting (14 Feb. 1957), para. 19.
118. G.A.O.R., 14th Session, 798th plenary meeting (17 Sept. 1959), paras. 14–15.
119. G.A.O.R., 3rd Session, Part II, 190th plenary meeting (12 April 1949), p. 22.
120. G.A.O.R., 10th Session, General Committee, 103rd meeting (22 Sept. 1955), para. 17.
121. G.A.O.R., 8th Session, 435th plenary meeting (17 Sept. 1953), para. 52.
122. G.A.O.R., 10th Session, General Committee, 102nd meeting (21 Sept. 1955), para. 44.
123. G.A.O.R., 7th Session, 381st plenary meeting (17 Oct. 1952), paras. 141, 143.
124. G.A.O.R., 8th Session, General Committee, 87th meeting (16 Sept. 1953), para. 11.
125. G.A.O.R., 8th Session, *Ad Hoc* Political Committee, 34th meeting (25 Nov. 1953), para. 55.
126. P.C.I.J., Series B, No. 4, pp. 23–24.
127. See, for example, Waldo Chamberlin, *Memorandum concerning the Conduct of the Business of the General Assembly*. New York, Carnegie Endowment for International Peace, 1949, para. 42, p. 23; Eric Stein, *Some Implications of expanding United Nations Membership*. New York, Carnegie Endowment for International Peace, 1956, p. 42.

128. G.A. res. 111 (II), 13 Nov. 1947.
129. G.A.O.R., 4th Session, Supplement No. 12, A/937 (12 Aug. 1949), Annex 1, p. 15.
130. *Ibid.*, para. 2(g), p. 15.
131. *Ibid.*, p. 20.
132. *Ibid.*, para. 15, p. 6.
133. *Ibid.*
134. G.A.O.R., 4th Session, 6th Committee, Annexes, A/997 (24 Sept. 1949), paras. 36–39.
135. G.A.O.R., 4th Session, 6th Committee, 156th meeting (8 Oct. 1949), paras. 1–43.
136. G.A.O.R., 7th Session, 387th plenary meeting (23 Oct. 1952), paras. 25, 81.
137. G.A.O.R., 18th Session, Annexes, Agenda item 25, A/5423 (28 May 1963), para. 62.
138. Waldo Chamberlin, *Memorandum concerning the Conduct of the Business of General Assembly*, para. 27, p. 17.
139. Eric Stein, *Some Implications of expanding United Nations Membership*, p. 41.
140. G.A.O.R., 4th Session, Supplement No. 12, A/937 (12 Aug. 1949), Annex 1, p. 17.
141. *Ibid.*, para. 11.
142. G.A.O.R., 4th Session, 6th Committee, 143rd meeting (27 Sept. 1949), paras. 58, 61, 68, 70.
143. *Ibid.*, paras. 65, 71, 80.
144. See, for example, Thucydides, *The History of the Peloponnesian War*.
145. G.A.O.R., 4th Session, Supplement No. 12, A/937 (12 Aug. 1949), para. 23; Rules of Procedure, Annex 1.
146. G.A.O.R., 2nd Session, plenary meetings, Annex 4, A/388 (23 Sept. 1947), para. 24.
147. G.A.O.R., 4th Session, Supplmeent No. 12, A/937 (12 Aug. 1949), para. 12.
148. G.A. res. 1898 (XVIII), 11 Nov. 1963.
149. *Ibid.*
150. G.A.O.R., 18th Session, Special Political Committee, 399th meeting (5 Nov. 1963).
151. G.A.O.R., 18th Session, General Committee, 154th meeting (18 Sept. 1963), paras.
152. G.A.O.R., 6th Session, 6th Committee, 259th meeting (29 Nov 1951), para. 15.
153. G.A.O.R., 14th Session, 6th Committee, 646th meeting (4 Dec. 1959), para. 21.

154. G.A.O.R., 15th Session, Annexes, Agenda item 65, A/4605 (1 Dec. 1960), para. 35 *et seq.*
155. U.N. doc. A/C.2/222 (Nov. 22, 1963); G.A.O.R., 18th Session, Second Committee, 946th and 947th meetings (5 Dec. 1963); U.N. doc. A/5651 (9 Dec. 1963).
156. G.A.O.R., 8th Session, Annexes, Agenda item 54, A/2402 (26 June 1953), paras. 26–27.
157. G.A.O.R., 4th Session, Supplement No. 12, A/937 (12 Aug. 1949), para. 39.
158. G.A.O.R., 2nd Session, plenary meetings, Annex 4, A/388 (23 Sept. 1947), para. 14; 4th Session, Supplement No. 12, A/937 (12 Aug. 1949), para. 17; 8th Session, Annexes, Agenda item 54, A/2402 (26 June 1953), para. 22.
159. Note No. 2798 (12 Sept. 1963), pp. 22–25; *Journal* No. 3241 (28 Sept. 1963).
160. G.A.O.R., 1st Special Session, General Committee, 32nd meeting (2 May 1947), p. 92.
161. G.A.O.R., 4th Session, Supplement No. 12, A/937 (12 Aug. 1949), para. 39; Rules of Procedure, Annex 1.
162. G.A.O.R., 4th Session, Supplement No. 12, A/937 (12 Aug. 1949), para. 38; See also 18th Session, Annexes, Agenda item 25, A/5423 (28 May 1963), para. 41.
163. G.A.O.R., 1st Special Session, General Committee, 33rd meeting (2 May 1947), p. 125.
164. G.A.O.R., 8th Session, Annexes, Agenda item 54, A/2402 (26 June 1953), para. 28.
165. U.N. doc. A/C.1/PV.1025 (8 Oct. 1959), pp. 17–21.
166. U.N. doc. A/316 (8 July 1947).
167. G.A.O.R., 2nd Session, plenary meetings, Annex 4, A/388 (23 Sept. 1947), para. 19; 4th Session, Supplement No. 12, A/937 (12 Aug. 1949), para. 28; 8th Session, Annexes, Agenda item 54, A/2402 (26 June 1953), para. 49; 18th Session, Annexes, Agenda item 25, A/5423 (28 May 1963), paras. 42–45; see also G.A. res. 1898 (XVIII), 11 Nov. 1963.
168. G.A.O.R., 7th Session, 388th plenary meeting (24 Oct. 1952), para. 3.
169. G.A.O.R., 7th Session, 387th plenary meeting (23 Oct. 1952), para. 78.
170. G.A.O.R., 8th Session, Annexes, Agenda item 54, A/2402 (26 June 1953), para. 49.
171. G.A.O.R., 4th Session, Supplement No. 12, A/937 (12 Aug. 1949), para. 36, and Annex 1, pp. 18–19.

172. G.A.O.R., 4th Session, Supplement No. 12, A/937 (12 Aug. 1949), Annex 1, p. 16.

173. G.A.O.R., 15th Session, 881st plenary meeting (1 Oct. 1960), paras. 108–9

174. G.A.O.R., 16th Session, 1033rd plenary meeting (11 Oct. 1961), paras, 52–188; 1034th plenary meeting (11 Oct. 1961), paras. 1–90.

175. G.A.O.R., 7th Session, 6th Committee, 352nd meeting (16 Dec. 1952), para. 2.

176. *Sir Thomas Erskine May's Treatise on the Law, Privileges, Proceedings and Usages of Parliament*, edited by Sir Edward Fellowes and T. G. B. Cocks. Sixteenth edition, London, Butterworth, 1957, p. 470

177. G.A.O.R., 7th Session, 388th plenary meeting (24 Oct. 1952), para. 73.

178. G.A.O.R., 8th Session, Annexes, Agenda item 54, A/2402 (26 June 1953), para. 41; 4th Session, Supplement No. 12, A/937 (12 Aug. 1949), para. 37.

179. See 72 *supra*.

180. G.A.O.R., 4th Session, Supplement No. 12, A/937 (12 Aug. 1949), Annex 1, p. 16.

181. G.A.O.R., 7th Session, 387th plenary meeting (23 Oct. 1952), paras. 84–85.

182. G.A.O.R., 7th Session, 6th Committee, 349th meeting (13 Dec. 1952), paras. 41–43.

183. G.A.O.R., 7th Session, 388th plenary meeting (24 Oct. 1952), para. 73.

184. Repertory of United Nations Practice, Vol. I (1955), Article 21, para. 81.

185. G.A.O.R., 2nd Session, plenary meetings, Annex 4, A/388 (23 Sept. 1947), para. 20; 4th Session, Supplement No. 12, A/937 (12 Aug. 1949), para. 30; 8th Session, Annexes, Agenda item 54, A/2402 (26 June 1953), para. 31; 18th Session, Annexes, Agenda item 25, A/5423 (28 May 1963), paras. 46–47.

186. G.A.O.R., 7th Session, 6th Committee, 349th meeting (13 Dec. 1952), paras. 40–41.

187. G.A.O.R., 6th Session, *Ad Hoc* Political Committee, 26th meeting (19 Dec. 1951), paras. 9–48.

188. G.A.O.R., 4th Session, Supplement No. 12, A/937 (12 Aug. 1949), Annex 1, p. 18.

189. Waldo Chamberlin, *Memorandum concerning the Conduct of the Business of the General Assembly*, para. 73, p. 40.

190. G.A.O.R., 8th Session, Annexes, Agenda item 54, A/2402 (26 June 1953), para. 29.
191. G.A.O.R., 18th Session, Annexes, Agenda item 25, A/5423 (28 May 1963), para. 64.
192. G.A.O.R., 1st Session, Part I, 30th plenary meeting (12 Feb. 1946), pp. 440–2; 3rd Session, Part II, 195th plenary meeting (14 April 1949), pp. 130–40; U.N. doc. E/CN.14/19 (31 Jan. 1959), pp. 86–87.
193. Alexis de Tocqueville, *Democracy in America*, Chapter XV.
194. G.A.O.R., 5th Session, Annexes, Agenda item 49, A/1356, para. 22.
195. G.A. res. 1810 (XVII), Dec. 17, 1962.
196. G.A.O.R., 4th Session *Ad Hoc* Political Committee, 56th meeting (3 Dec. 1949), paras. 116, 118, p. 339.
197. G.A.O.R., 8th Session, *Ad Hoc* Political Committee, 33rd meeting (24 Nov. 1953), para. 49.
198. James Rives Childs, *American Foreign Service*. New York, Holt (Toronto, Oxford University Press), 1948, p. 64.
199. G.A.O.R., 15th Session, Third Committee, 1056th meeting (17 Dec. 1960), paras. 44–60.
200. U.N. doc. A/AC.18/68 (29 June 1948), para. 19n.
201. *Ibid.*, para. 20.
202. Julius Stone, *Legal Controls of International Conflict*. New York, Rinehart (London, Stevens; Sydney, Maitland Publications), 1954, p. 172.
203. G.A.O.R., 3rd Session, Supplement No. 10, A/605 (13 Aug. 1948), para. 47, p. 29.
204. *Ibid.*, Annexes 11, 111, pp. 34–35.
205. G.A.O.R., 3rd Session, Part I, *Ad Hoc* Political Committee, 28th meeting (9 Dec. 1948), p. 327.
206. G.A.O.R., 18th Session, Annexes, Agenda item 25, A/5423 (28 May 1963), para. 63.
207. Economic and Social Council, Rules of Procedure, Rule 66.
208. G.A.O.R., 13th Session, Special Political Committee, 100th meeting (5 Nov. 1958).
209. G.A.O.R., 12th Session, Annexes, Agenda item 69, A/3699 (16 Oct. 1957); General Committee, 116th meeting (18 Oct. 1957); 708th, 710th–714th plenary meetings (22 Oct. –25Nov. 1, 1957).
210. G.A.O.R., 13th Session, Annexes, Agenda item 41, A/4073 (12 Dec. 1959), paras. 13–14.
211. G.A.O.R., 14th Session, Annexes, Agenda item 40, A/4350 (11 Dec. 1959), para. 6.

212. G.A. res. 812 (IX), 17 Dec. 1954.
213. G.A. res. 814 (IX), 17 Dec. 1954.
214. G.A. res. 909 (X), 25 Nov. 1955.
215. G.A. res. 1190 (XII), 12 Dec. 1957.
216. G.A. res. 1617 (XV), 21 April 1961.
217. G.A. res. 1719 (XVI), 19 Dec. 1961.
218. G.A. res. 1840 (XVII), 19 Dec. 1962.
219. G.A.O.R., 18th Session, Annexes, Agenda item 84, A/5668 (12 Dec. 1963).
220. Articles 4, 25, 49, 94, and 103.
221. H. Field Haviland Jr., *The Political Role of the General Assembly*. New York, Carnegie Endowment for International Peace, 1951, p. 93.
222. Dean Acheson, *Power and Diplomacy*, p. 80.
223. For the procedure when the Security Council is electing Judges of the International Court and more than the required number of candidates receive a majority, see p. 186; also U.N. docs. S/5445 (24 Oct. 1963), S/5449 (31 Oct. 1963), and S/5461 (21 Nov. 1963).
224. G.A.O.R., 4th Session, Supplement No. 12, A/937 (12 Aug. 1949), Annex 11; 10th Session, Annexes, Agenda item 51, A/2977 (30 Sept. 1955), paras. 55–70.
225. G.A.O.R., 18th Session, Annexes, Agenda item 25, A/5423 (28 May 1963), paras. 57–58 and Annex VIII; G.A. res. 1957 (XVIII), 12 Dec. 1963.
226. G.A.O.R., 18th Session, Annexes, Agenda item 25, A/5442 (18 July 1963), paras. 2–3.
227. G.A.O.R., 4th Session, Supplement No. 12, A/937 (12 Aug. 1949), Annex II; 18th Session, Annexes, Agenda item 25, A/5423 (28 May 1963), Annex VIII.
228. G.A.O.R., 18th Session, Fifth Committee, 1043rd meeting (18 Nov. 1963) and 1044th meeting (19 Nov. 1963); 1278th plenary meeting (12 Dec. 1963).
229. G.A.O.R., 2nd Session, plenary meetings, Annex 4, A/388 (23 Sept. 1947), paras. 28–29.
230. G.A.O.R., 18th Session, 1255th plenary meeting (6 Nov. 1963).
231. Articles 7, 9, 23, 61, 86, 97, and 101 of the Charter; Articles 2–15 of the Statute of the Court.
232. Article 23(1).
233. Ruth B. Russell, assisted by Jeanette E. Muther, *A History of the United Nations Charter*. Washington, Brookings (London, Faber), 1958, p. 444.
234. *Ibid.*, pp. 648–9.

235. G.A.O.R., 1st Session, Part I, 4th and 5th plenary meetings (12 Jan. 1946).
236. G.A.O.R., 8th Session, 450th plenary meeting (5 Oct. 1953), para. 19.
237. G.A.O.R., 2nd Session, 109th plenary meeting (13 Nov. 1947), p. 750.
238. G.A.O.R., 10th Session, 551st plenary meeting (6 Dec. 1955), para. 64.
239. G.A.O.R., 10th Session, 559th plenary meeting (16 Dec. 1955), paras. 197–201.
240. *Ibid.*, paras. 271, 301–2.
241. G.A.O.R., 11th Session, Annexes, Agenda item 68, A/3332 (10 Nov. 1956).
242. G.A.O.R., 11th Session, 612th plenary meeting (7 Dec. 1956), paras. 18–22.
244. G.A.O.R., 14th Session, 857th plenary meeting (12 Dec. 1959), paras. 301–6.
245. *Ibid.*, paras. 307–31.
246. See, for example, G.A.O.R., 18th Session, Annexes, Agenda item 21, A/5487 (4 Sept. 1963), para. 6; Agenda items 81, 82 and 12, A/5686 (31 Dec. 1963), para 24; U.N. doc. A/SPC/96 (10 Dec. 1963).
247. G.A.O.R., 14th Session, 862nd plenary meeting (12 Oct. 1959), para. 22.
248. G.A.O.R., 15th Session, 987th plenary meeting (18 April 1961), para. 69.
249. Economic and Social Council Official Records, 28th Session, 1069th meeting (6 July 1959), paras. 39–47; 1074th meeting (10 July 1959), paras. 13–17, 47–52; see also press conference by the Secretary-General, Note No. 2015 (23 July 1959).
250. G.A.O.R., 14th Session, Supplement No. 1A, A/4132/Add. 1 (20 Aug. 1959), p. 3.
251. G.A. res. 1923 (XVIII), 5 Dec. 1963; 1945 (XVIII), 11 Dec. 1963; 1958 (XVIII), 12 Dec. 1963; 1992 (XVIII), 17 Dec. 1963.
252. Documents of the United Nations Conference on International Organization. New York and London, U.N. Information Org., 1945, Vol. III, p. 600.
253. *Ibid.*, p. 619.
254. U.N. doc. PC/EX/TC/4, para. 5.
255. U.N. doc. PC/EX/TC/6, 8, and 9.
256. G.A.O.R., 13th Session, 775th plenary meeting (8 Oct. 1958), paras. 13–20.

257. G.A.O.R., 16th Session, Fifth Committee, 893rd meeting (1 Dec. 1961), para. 1.
258. G.A.O.R., 14th Session, 857th plenary meeting (12 Dec. 1959), para. 160.
259. G.A.O.R., 14th Session, Annexes, Agenda item 8, A/4150 (17 July 1959).
260. *Ibid.*, A/4214 (17 Sept. 1959), para. 13.
261. G.A.O.R., 14th Session, 857th plenary meeting (12 Dec. 1959), paras. 225–226.
262. G.A.O.R., 14th Session, Annexes, Agenda item 17, A/L.277 (12 Dec. 1959).
263. *Ibid.*, A/L.275/Rev. 1 (12 Dec. 1959).
264. *Ibid.*, 857th plenary meeting (12 Dec. 1959), paras. 135–77, 210–17.
265. U.N. doc. A/4448 (21 Aug. 1960).
266. G.A.O.R., 15th Session, 979th plenary meeting (7 April 1961), paras. 1–2.
267. Articles 2 and 9 of the Statute of the International Court of Justice.
268. Articles 4(1) and (2), 5, and 6 of the Statute.
269. Clyde Eagleton, 'Choice of Judges for the International Court of Justice', *The American Journal of International Law*, Vol. 47, No. 3 (July 1953), pp. 462–3.
270. The procedure of election is based on Articles 2 to 4 and 8 to 12 of the Statute of the Court, Rules 40 and 61 of the Provisional Rules of Procedure of the Security Council, Rules 151 and 152 of the Rules of Procedure of the General Assembly, and to some extent on precedents established during the first session of the Assembly (23rd to 26th plenary meetings) and the 9th meeting of the Security Council.
271. Article 4 (3) of the Statute and G.A. res. 91 (I), 11 Dec. 1946; 264 (III), 8 Oct. 1948; 363 (IV), 1 Dec. 1949; 806 (VIII), 9 Dec. 1953.
272. G.A.O.R., 15th Session, 915th plenary meeting (16 Nov. 1960), paras. 18–46.
273. Security Council Official Records, 6th year, 567th meeting (6 Dec. 1951), paras. 26–114; 9th year, 681st meeting (7 Oct. 1954), paras. 18–34; 12th year, 793rd meeting (1 Oct. 1957), para. 6; 18th year, 1071st meeting (21 Oct. 1963).
274. U.N. docs. S/5445 (24 Oct. 1963), S/5449 (31 Oct. 1963), and S/5461 (21 Nov. 1963).
275. G.A. res. 11 (I), 24 Jan. 1946.
276. *Ibid.*

277. G.A.O.R., 18th Session, Annexes, Agenda item 25, A/5423 (28 May 1963), paras. 29–32; G.A. res. 1898 (XVIII), 11 Nov. 1963.
278. Harold Nicolson, *Peacemaking*. Boston, Mass., Houghton Mifflin (London, Constable), 1933, p. 261.
279. Standing Order No. 66.
280. Alexander Loveday, *Reflexions on International Administration*. Oxford, Clarendon Press, 1956, p. 185.
281. Article 17.
282. 158 of the Rules of Procedure, and Financial Regulations 3.6 and 3.9. The Financial Regulations were adopted by G.A. res. 456 (V), 16 Nov. 1950, amended by res. 950 (X), 3 Nov. 1955, and res. 973B (X), 15 Dec. 1955. They are issued under the symbol ST/SGB/Financial Rules/1.
283. Financial Regulations, 3.8 and 3.9, and Financial Rules 103.6, 103.11 to 103.13.
285. 156 and 157 of the Rules of Procedure.
286. G.A.O.R., 7th Session, Annexes, Agenda item 69, A/2214 (7 Oct. 1952), paras. 39–40; G.A.O.R., 7th Session, 5th Committee, 371st meeting (9 Dec. 1952), paras. 31–34; G.A. res. 681B (VII), 21 Dec. 1952; G.A.O.R., 8th Session, Annexes, Agenda item 49, A/2429 (3 Aug. 1953), paras. 5–6.
287. *Source*: G.A.O.R., 17th Session, Annexes, Agenda item 62, A/C.5/953 (5 Dec. 1962).
288. Financial Regulation 13.1
289. 154 of the Rules of Procedure.
290. Financial Regulation 13.2.
291. G.A.O.R., 15th Session, Annexes, Agenda item 50, A/4715 (22 March 1961).
292. Based on information in G.A.O.R., 15th Session, Annexes, Agenda item 50, A/4715 (22 March 1961), Annex 111; 16th Session, Annexes, Agenda item 53, A/4870 (16 Sept. 1961); 17th Session, Annexes, Agenda item 61, A/5223 (24 Sept. 1962); 18th Session, Annexes, Agenda item 57, A/5525 (18 Sept. 1962).
293. G.A.O.R., 14th Session, 5th Committee, 715th meeting (7 Oct. 1959), paras. 9–16; 718th meeting (13 Oct. 1959), paras. 13–16; 720th meeting (15 Oct. 1959), paras. 1–6.
294. G.A.O.R., 14th Session, 4th Committee, 914th meeting (19 Oct. 1959), paras. 5, 7, and 8.
295. Financial Regulation 3.7; Article 18(2) of the Charter.
296. Article 17(2).
297. G.A. res. 14A(1), 13 Feb. 1946.

298. 159 and 160 of the Rules of Procedure.
299. G.A.O.R., 6th Session, 5th Committee, 319th meeting (18 Dec. 1951), para. 80; 348th meeting (2 Feb. 1952), paras. 52–54.
300. See, for example, G.A.O.R., 18th Session, Supplement No. 10 (1963), para. 2.
301. Report of the Preparatory Commission, PC/20 (23 Dec. 1945), p. 108.
302. *Ibid.*, G.A. res. 14A(1), 13 Feb. 1946; G.A. res. 69(1), 14 Dec. 1946; G.A. res. 238(111), 18 Nov. 1948); G.A.O.R., 7th Session, Supplement No. 10 (1952), paras. 11–12; G.A. res. 1137 (XII), 14 Oct. 1957.
303. G.A.O.R., 16th Session, Supplement No. 10 (1961), para. 19.
305. G.A. res. 1927 (XVVIII), 11 Dec. 1963.
306. Financial Regulation 5.5; G.A.O.R., 17th Session, Annexes, Agenda item 67, A/5392 (19 Dec. 1962), para. 16.
304. G.A.O.R., 17th Session, Supplement No. 10 (1962), para. 7.
307. G.A. res. 250 (III), 11 Dec. 1948.
308. Financial Regulation 5.3.
309. Issued under symbol ST/ADM/SER.B/—.
310. Article 19; 161 of the Rules of Procedure.
311. Financial Regulation 5.4.
312. G.A.O.R., 13th Session, Supplement No. 10 (1958), para. 25; U.N. docs. A/C.5/759 (10 Oct. 1958), and A/AC.113/1 (21 Jan. 1963), para. 64.
313. U.N. doc. A/C.5/824 (26 Sept. 1960), para. 2.
314. Note No. 2768 (21 May 1963); U.N. doc. A/5431 (11 June 1963).
315. Financial Regulations 5.1 and 6.2.
316. G.A.O.R., 17th Session, Annexes, Agenda item 62, A/C.5/951 (15 Nov. 1962), para. 5.
317. G.A.O.R., 17th Session, Supplement No. 5, para. 11.
318. G.A.O.R., 17th Session, Annexes, Agenda item 62, A/5331 (4 Dec. 1962); G.A. res. 1863 (XVII), 20 Dec. 1962; 18th Session, Annexes, Agenda item 58, A/5635 (3 Dec. 1963); G.A. res. 1986 (XVIII), 17 Dec. 1963.
319. G.A. res. 1739 (XVI), 20 Dec. 1961.
320. G.A. res. 74 (I), 7 Dec. 1946.
321. Financial Regulations 10.4, 11.4, and Annex.
322. Article 17 (3)
323. G.A. res. 14A(1), 13 Feb. 1946.
324. Financial Regulations 6.6 and 6.7.
325. G.A.O.R., 16th Session, Annexes, Agenda item 60, A/5031 (13 Dec. 1961), para. 22; G.A. res. 1729 (XVI), 20 Dec. 1961.

326. G.A.O.R., 1st Emergency Special Session, Annexes, Agenda item 5, A/3302 (6 Nov. 1956), para. 15; 11th Session, Annexes, Agenda item 66, A/3383 (21 Nov. 1956), para. 6; 5th Committee, 541st, meeting (3 Dec. 1956), paras. 78–79.

327. G.A. res. 1089 (XI), 21 Dec. 1956; 1090 (XI), 27 Feb. 1957.

328. G.A. res. 1151 (XII), 22 Nov. 1957; 1337 (XIII), 13 Dec. 1958.

329. G.A. res. 1441 (XIV), 5 Dec. 1959; 1575 (XV), 20 Dec. 1960; 1733 (XVI), 20 Dec. 1961.

330. G.A.O.R., 11th Session, 5th Committee, 547th meeting (10 Dec. 1956), para. 8.

331. G.A. res. 1583 (XV), 20 Dec. 1960.

332. G.A. res. 1619 (XV), 21 April 1961; 1732 (XVI), 20 Dec. 1961.

333. G.A. res. 1620 (XV), 21 April 1961.

334. G.A.O.R., 16th Session, Annexes, Agenda item 62, A/4971 (15 Nov. 1961).

335 G.A. res. 1731 (XVI), 20 Dec. 1961.

336. G.A. res. 1739 (XVI), 20 Dec. 1961; see also res. 1989 (XVIII), 17 Dec. 1963.

337. I.C.J. Reports 1962, p. 151.

338. G.A. res. 1854 (XVII), 19 Dec. 1962.

339. G.A. res. 1854 (XVII), 19 Dec. 1962; 1865 (XVII) and 1866 (XVII), 20 Dec. 1962.

340. G.A.O.R., 4th Special Session, Annexes, Agenda item 7, A/5407 (29 March 1963).

341. G.A.O.R., 4th Special Session, 5th Committee, 986th meeting (22 May 1963).

342. G.A. res. 1874–1880 (S-IV), 27 June 1963.

343. G.A. res. 1989 (XVIII), 17 Dec. 1963.

344. G.A.O.R., 18th Session, 5th Committee, 1050th meeting (2 Dec. 1963).

345. G.A. res. 1885 (XVIII), 18 Oct. 1963; 1986 (XVIII), 17 Dec. 1963.

346. Press conference, Note to Correspondents No. 2108 (4 Feb. 1960).

347. See Consultative Assembly of the Council of Europe, doc. 1420 (9 May 1962).

348. Neville Chamberlain, *In Search of Peace*. New York, Putnam, 1939, p. 174.

349. G.A.O.R., 14th Session, Supplement No. 1A A/4132/Add. 1 (20 Aug. 1959), p. 3.

350. G.A.O.R., 18th Session, Annexes, Agenda items 81, 82, and 12,

A/5686 (31 Dec. 1963), para. 32; see also my article 'Peking and the UN Charter Amendment', The World Today, Vol. 20, No. 5 pp. 208–215.

351. *The Rule of Law in a Free Society*. Geneva, International Commission of Jurists, 1959, p. 195.

352. See *Report of the Committee on Ministers' Powers* (Cmd. 4060). London, H.M. Stationery Office, 1932, p. 73.

353. G.A.O.R., 17th Session, Supplement No. 1A, A/5201/Add. 1 (24 Aug. 1962), p. 5.

354. See *supra*.

355. G.A.O.R., 18th Session, Annexes, Agenda item 25, A/5423 (28 May 1963), paras. 29–32; G.A. res. 1898 (XVIII), 11 Nov. 1963.

356. See, for example, G.A.O.R., 18th Session, 4th Committee, meetings 1507 (9 Dec. 1963) and 1508 (10 Dec. 1963); Annexes, Agenda item 23, A/5629/Add. 1 (13 Dec. 1963), para. 4.

357. G.A.O.R., 11th Session, Annexes, Agenda item 8, A/BUR/142 (8 Nov. 1956), para. 13; see also 8th Session, Annexes, Agenda item 54, A/2402 (26 June 1953), para. 19.

358. U.N. doc. A/C.2/222 (22 Nov. 1963).

359. G.A.O.R., 17th Session, Annexes, Agenda item 27, A/5181 27 Sept. 1962), para 4; item 25, Addendum, A/5238 (8 Oct. 1962), para. 112 (a).

360. G.A.O.R., 17th Session, Supplement No. 1A, A/5201/Add. 1 (24 Aug. 1962), pp. 4–5.

361. U.N. doc. A/C.4/630 (4 Dec. 1963).

362. U.N. doc. A/520/Rev.

363. G.A. res. 844 (IX), 11 Oct. 1954.

364. U.N. doc. A/316 (8 July 1947).

365. G.A.O.R., 2nd Session, plenary meetings, Annex 4, A/388 (23 Sept. 1947).

366. G.A.O.R., 4th Session, Supplement No. 12, A/ 937 (12 Aug. 1949), pp. 2–12.

367. G.A.O.R., 8th Session, Annexes, Agenda item 54, A/2402 (26 June 1953), pp. 2–7.

368. G.A.O.R., 18th Session, Annexes, Agenda item 25, A/5423 (28 May 1963).

INDEX

DATE DUE